The Presidency of
JOHN F.
KENNEDY

AMERICAN PRESIDENCY SERIES

Donald R. McCoy, Clifford S. Griffin, Homer E. Socolofsky
General Editors

George Washington, Forrest McDonald
John Adams, Ralph Adams Brown
Thomas Jefferson, Forrest McDonald
James Madison, Robert Allen Rutland
James Monroe, Noble E. Cunningham, Jr.
John Quincy Adams, Mary W. M. Hargreaves
Andrew Jackson, Donald B. Cole
Martin Van Buren, Major L. Wilson
William Henry Harrison & John Tyler, Norma Lois Peterson
James K. Polk, Paul H. Bergeron
Zachary Taylor & Millard Fillmore, Elbert B. Smith
Franklin Pierce, Larry Gara
James Buchanan, Elbert B. Smith
Abraham Lincoln, Phillip Shaw Paludan
Andrew Johnson, Albert Castel
Rutherford B. Hayes, Ari Hoogenboom
James A. Garfield & Chester A. Arthur, Justus D. Doenecke
Grover Cleveland, Richard E. Welch, Jr.
Benjamin Harrison, Homer B. Socolofsky & Allan B. Spetter
William McKinley, Lewis L. Gould
Theodore Roosevelt, Lewis L. Gould
William Howard Taft, Paolo E. Coletta
Woodrow Wilson, Kendrick A. Clements
Warren G. Harding, Eugene P. Trani & David L. Wilson
Herbert C. Hoover, Martin L. Fausold
Harry S. Truman, Donald R. McCoy
Dwight D. Eisenhower, Chester J. Pach, Jr., & Elmo Richardson
John F. Kennedy, James N. Giglio
Lyndon B. Johnson, Vaughn Davis Bornet
Gerald R. Ford, John Robert Greene
James Earl Carter, Jr., Burton I. Kaufman

The Presidency of
JOHN F.
KENNEDY

James N. Giglio

UNIVERSITY PRESS OF KANSAS

To the many students and faculty

at Southwest Missouri State University

who have had a positive

impact on my life and work

Published by the University Press of Kansas (Lawrence, Kansas 66049),
which was organized by the Kansas Board of Regents
and is operated and funded by Emporia State University, Fort Hays State
University, Kansas State University, Pittsburg State
University, the University of Kansas, and Wichita State University

Library of Congress Cataloging-in-Publication Data

Giglio, James N., 1939–
The presidency of John F. Kennedy / James N. Giglio.
p.   cm. — (American presidency series)
Includes bibliographical references (p.   ) and index.
ISBN 0–7006–0515–0 (alk. paper)
ISBN 0–7006–0520–7 (pbk. : alk. paper)
1. United States—Politics and government—1961–1963.
2. Kennedy, John F. (John Fitzgerald), 1917–1963.
I. Title. II. Series.
E841.G54   1992
973.922′092—dc20   91–16841

Printed in the United States of America

10 9 8 7 6 5 4

The paper used in this publication meets the minimum requirements
of the American National Standard for Permanence of Paper
for Printed Library Materials Z39.48–1984.

CONTENTS

FOREWORD

The aim of the American Presidency Series is to present historians and the general reading public with interesting, scholarly assessments of the various presidential administrations. These interpretive surveys are intended to cover the broad ground between biographies, specialized monographs, and journalistic accounts. As such, each will be a comprehensive, synthetic work which will draw upon the best in pertinent secondary literature, yet leave room for the author's own analysis and interpretation.

Volumes in the series will present the data essential to understanding the administration under consideration. Particularly, each book will treat the then current problems facing the United States and its people and how the president and his associates felt about, thought about, and worked to cope with these problems. Attention will be given to how the office developed and operated during the president's tenure. Equally important will be consideration of the vital relationships between the president, his staff, the executive officers, Congress, foreign representatives, the judiciary, state officials, the public, political parties, the press, and influential private citizens. The series will also be concerned with how this unique American institution—the presidency—was viewed by the presidents, and with what results.

All this will be set, insofar as possible, in the context not only of contemporary politics but also of economics, international relations, law, morals, public administration, religion, and thought. Such a broad approach is necessary to understanding, for a presidential administration is more than the elected and appointed officers composing it, since its work so often reflects the major problems, anxieties, and glories of the nation. In short, the authors in the series will strive to recount and evaluate the record of each administration and to identify its distinctiveness and relationships to the past, its own time, and the future.

The General Editors

ACKNOWLEDGMENTS

One of the enjoyable aspects of writing a book is being able to thank the many people and institutions who assisted in the labor. First of all, my gratitude to the archivists and librarians who graciously helped, especially Megan Desnoyers, Suzanne Forbes, William Johnson, and Ronald Whealan of the John F. Kennedy Library; Helen Near and Peggy Bolando of the Federal Bureau of Investigation; Nancy Bressler of the Seeley G. Mudd Manuscript Library, Princeton University; and Willa Garrett, Frances Rottman, and Lynn Cline of the Duane Meyer Library, Southwest Missouri State University. I also appreciate the Kennedy-era participants and scholars who willingly visited with me or answered mail or telephone inquiries: David Brinkley, James MacGregor Burns, Willard Cochrane, Robert Donovan, Myer Feldman, Orville Freeman, John Kenneth Galbraith, George E. Herman, Mary McGrory, Mike Mansfield, Clark Mollenhoff, Herbert S. Parmet, Robert Pierpoint, Arthur Schlesinger, Jr., Charles Spalding, Theodore C. Sorensen, and Lee White.

It is a particular pleasure to thank an old friend, Dominic J. Capeci, Jr., of Southwest Missouri State University, who read and commented on most of the manuscript, and Bert Park, M.D., of the Papers of Woodrow Wilson Advisory Committee, Frank Mazzella and Clifford Whipple of Southwest Missouri State University, and Donald Zelman of Tarleton State University, who critically perused selected portions of the study. I especially want to acknowledge the perceptive comments of the American Presidency Series editors, Clifford Griffin of the University of Kansas, Homer E. Socolofsky of Kansas State University, and most of all, Donald

R. McCoy of the University of Kansas, a mentor and friend for the past fifteen years.

A special thanks to the National Endowment for the Humanities for a summer research fellowship and a Travel to Collections stipend, to the John F. Kennedy Library Foundation for a research grant, and to Southwest Missouri State University for two travel grants and for awarding me a sabbatical leave and a teaching-load reduction. My appreciation to *Agricultural History* for extending permission to reprint material verbatim from my article, "New Frontier Agricultural Policy: The Commodity Side, 1961–1963" in volume 61 (Summer 1987).

Last, but not least, my heartfelt thanks to my wife, Fran, who remains an inspiration, and to my sons, Peter and Tony, for their companionship and affection.

1

★ ★ ★ ★ ★

THE ROAD
TO THE WHITE HOUSE

November 22, 1963, will forever be a day of national mourning. At approximately 1:00 P.M., John Fitzgerald Kennedy, 47 years old, 6 feet tall, 165 pounds, handsome, vibrant, maturing significantly as the thirty-fifth president, died of gunshot wounds in Dallas. He had visited Texas to mend a political squabble that had weakened the state Democratic party for the coming election year. Kennedy remains the only twentieth-century president to be assassinated since McKinley. In many respects how Kennedy died is as important as how he lived.

His tragic death has colored our perception of Kennedy and his presidency. To many Americans he is a martyred, gallant Sir Lancelot who enabled us briefly to embrace the legend of Camelot. All manner of good would have occurred had he lived. To others scorning such hagiography, he has become a cold warrior who created unnecessary crises and enmeshed us in Vietnam. These critics remind us of his faint-hearted response to the civil rights movement and of his inability to push New Frontier programs through Congress. They have also exposed him as a playboy willing to risk national security for sexual pleasure.

Further complicating the assessment is the enormous impact of the Kennedy style. No president in the twentieth century combined his rhetoric, wit, charm, youth, and Hollywood appearance. He inspired young Americans to choose politics and government service as honored professions; he motivated them to serve as Peace Corps volunteers in Africa and as Green Beret advisers in South Vietnam. He also affected us in lesser ways: His refusal to wear hats inadvertently influenced males

1

to discard theirs, just as his longer hair style made crew cuts unfashionable.

Moreover, Kennedy's presidency has challenged historians because he served a mere thousand days in office. While some of his key legislative proposals such as civil rights and the tax cut showed promise of success by fall 1963, would an almost certain second term have resulted in the passage of medicare and other promised programs? At the time of his death, Kennedy had also negotiated the Nuclear Test Ban Treaty and fashioned a détente with the Soviet Union. Could he have avoided the debacle in Vietnam? In short, to evaluate Kennedy after less than three years in office is like assessing Truman's presidency before the successes of the Marshall Plan and the Truman Doctrine. Yet much can still be written about the Kennedy presidency and its legacy.

John F. Kennedy was the first president born in the twentieth century, on 29 May 1917, in the Boston suburb of Brookline. He was the second of nine children of Joseph P. and Rose E. Kennedy. His father, a third-generation Irish Catholic, had graduated from the prestigious Boston Latin School and Harvard after excelling in athletics and campus politics. In marrying the attractive and courtly daughter of John F. ("Honey Fitz") Fitzgerald, mayor of Boston, he had further elevated himself.

By 1917 Joe Kennedy was already on the way to becoming an entrepreneurial wizard. Through hard work, adroitness, and brashness, his millions multiplied from Wall Street, movie-producing, and liquor-importing activities. In 1929, three years after moving the family to New York partly to escape the snubbing of Boston Brahmins, he began a trust fund for his children to ensure their financial independence. His wealth and power proved to be important in the successes of his sons. Just as significantly, he molded them into fierce competitors and piqued their interest in public issues. Even though he was away for weeks at a time, he viewed his children as extensions of himself and relished their achievements and well-being.

Nevertheless, the father's dominance frustrated a young Jack Kennedy. Unable to compete with an older brother, Joseph, Jr., who reminded people of his father, Jack first sought identity through historical novels and biography. As a boy he was closer to his mother, who nursed him through a sickly childhood. Even that relationship was not altogether satisfactory, since he had to share his mother with eight brothers and sisters. Her greatest concern was Rosemary, a retarded younger child, whose struggle, Rose recalled, sensitized her children to the unfortunate and underprivileged. As Jack grew older, friction developed between him and his mother because her disciplinarian and overly tidy ways conflicted with his dilatory and sloppy habits. Perhaps, as Doris Kearns Goodwin explains, his irresponsibility represented an effort to express his individuality amid tremendous family pressures.

Problems with his physical health proved much more serious. Born with an unstable back, probably because the left side of his body was smaller than the right, he contracted scarlet fever before his third birthday, weakening his overall physical condition.[1] He nearly died of diphtheria and suffered from asthma and allergies. During adolescence he frequented the Mayo Clinic for a mysterious "blood condition" described as jaundice, and he complained of an irritable gastrointestinal tract, which resulted in a duodenal ulcer and chronic colitis by his twenties. Whether emotional disturbances might have aggravated his physical problems cannot be determined, but young Jack was certainly sick much of the time. His brother Robert later wrote that "when we were growing up together we used to laugh about the great risk a mosquito took in biting Jack Kennedy—with some of his blood the mosquito was almost sure to die."[2]

It is significant that he learned to put aside his disabilities; a Kennedy could do no less. He went on for years, his mother later wrote, "thinking to himself—or at least trying to make others think—that he was a strong, robust, quite healthy person who just happened to be sick a good deal of the time."[3] The competitiveness, absolute commitment, and zest for life stemmed from his father, but the curiosity, the stoic, shy, and gentle nature, and the remarkable courage came more from his mother.

His wit, self-centeredness, and charm, slowly emerging in adolescence, reflected a mixture of his father and his grandfather, Honey Fitz, whose effervescence was legendary. Likewise, Honey Fitz and P.J., the paternal grandfather, who once served in the state senate, provided the family's political tradition. But it was Jack's father who developed his son's interest in international issues, particularly after Joseph became ambassador to Great Britain during the Roosevelt administration of the late 1930s.

At his mother's insistence, Jack's education had begun at parochial schools, but he and his brothers soon transferred to private sectarian institutions, where his father felt they could best compete with children of the establishment. Consequently, in the midst of the depression, Jack attended Choate, a conservative preparatory school in Connecticut. Known as a dilatory student even though an avid reader, he also had only marginal success in athletics as his assorted illnesses and frail frame continued to inhibit his development. He did much better socially; his fun-loving spirit and prankish ways delighting all but a stodgy headmaster. At Harvard afterward, he reached his maximum height of six feet.

Still frail at 149 pounds, he continued to apply more effort to athletics and extracurricular activities than he did to academics, despite aggravating his back condition while playing football and tennis. He remained aloof from social causes and political groups such as the Young Democrats; the depression had no impact upon him, nor did the New Deal spark his interest.

Kennedy's major academic achievement occurred in 1940. His senior thesis not only earned him graduation honors but it was also published. *Why England Slept* reflected a young Kennedy's growing interest in contemporary relations following an extended European sojourn during his father's ambassadorship. The book's main premise, that a democracy is inherently handicapped in mobilizing society against a totalitarian menace, was related to a concern that the United States must avoid Britain's recent experience, culminating in the appeasement of Hitler at Munich in 1938. The Nazi invasion of Western Europe in spring 1940 made Kennedy's study especially poignant.

Even though the book did not always express Joe Kennedy's viewpoints, it profited from his considerable assistance. After providing Jack with research materials and ideas, the father ensured its publication by asking *New York Times* journalist Arthur Krock to rewrite the pedestrian text. He also induced *Time-Life* publisher Henry Luce to compose a foreword. Krock's literary agent finally secured a publisher. After favorable reviews and appreciable sales, Joe Kennedy wrote his son: "You would be surprised how a book that really makes the grade with high-class people stands you in good stead for years to come."[4] The making of John F. Kennedy had begun.

The war continued that development. After his father pulled strings to get him sea duty despite his unstable back, Kennedy found himself in the South Pacific as a PT boat commander. It represented his first opportunity for leadership, and he soon learned how to interact with people from various socioeconomic backgrounds. Indeed an engaging and daring personality made him popular with his crew. What transformed Kennedy into a war hero, with all its future political implications, was the destruction of PT-109 on 2 August 1943. A Japanese destroyer rammed his fragile boat in the Solomon Islands, forcing Kennedy and other shipmates to rescue drowning crewmen. Kennedy's coolness under fire, a trademark of his presidency, and his courage were clearly evident; the press furthermore embellished Kennedy's efforts while ignoring the contributions of others. Kennedy never encouraged this, but a former ambassador's son naturally drew the attention of friendly journalists. John Hersey's 1944 account, published in the *New Yorker*, said nothing, either, of the circumstances leading to the PT-109 ramming, probably the only time a Japanese destroyer got that close to a PT boat. Joe Kennedy ensured that Hersey's essay had mass distribution by using his influence to secure a *Reader's Digest* reprint. In the years ahead, in the tradition of William Henry Harrison and Theodore Roosevelt, Joe Kennedy continually invoked the legend of the PT-109 whenever his son's political fortunes were on the line.

Ironically, Jack Kennedy's heroics probably encouraged Joe, Jr., a navy pilot stationed in England, to volunteer for a dangerous mission on a radio-controlled plane loaded with explosives targeted for German-occupied France. On 13 August 1944 the plane exploded before he could bail out. Hank Searls in *The Lost Prince* writes of Joe, Jr.'s frustration in the wake of Jack's successes and of his failure to win recognition. Their father never completely recovered from the loss. Of all his sons, none more consciously absorbed his personality and beliefs than Joe, and none could have embraced more a father's ambition that he become the first Catholic president of the United States. To what extent Jack unconsciously felt guilty for the loss is impossible to say. He did realize, however, that he had little choice but to follow in his brother's footsteps. As early as Christmas 1944, after his discharge from the navy, he told his service friend, Paul (Red) Fay: "I can feel Pappy's eyes on the back of my neck."[5] In 1957 the former ambassador reinforced that impression. "I got Jack into politics. I was the one. I told him Joe was dead and that it was therefore his responsibility to run for Congress. He didn't want to. He felt he didn't have the ability and he still feels that way. But I told him he had to."[6] The myth that Jack had always wanted to be in politics developed after his drive for the presidency had begun. It would not have done to portray him as a puppet of his father.

Despite Jack's reluctance to enter politics, he did have appreciable advantages. He could lean on his father's resources, his own service record, and the influence and knowledge of others like Honey Fitz. Although shy and somewhat uncertain, the brown-haired, green-eyed Kennedy had an almost indefinable quality that attracted people to him. His natural good looks, boyish charm, and frailty combined with his coolness under fire, his ability to make light of difficult situations, his congeniality, and his earthiness inspired allegiance. Moreover, he possessed an interest in statesmanship and government, which he had hoped to express in teaching or writing.

Still, his disadvantages were formidable. Many Democrats despised his father. Questions of integrity aside, they disliked Joe's isolationism, his growing contempt for Roosevelt and New Deal liberals, and his friendship with Joseph McCarthy, the intensely anti-Communist Republican senator from Wisconsin. Jack Kennedy's greatest handicap, however, remained his health, which deteriorated further after the war. While traveling abroad in 1947 he became so severely ill that he was given last rites. The diagnosis, which became a poorly kept secret for almost thirty years, was Addison's disease, a life-threatening failure of the adrenal glands to produce hormones to fight infections and regulate body metabolism. Jack probably developed an early stage of the disease during childhood, as his mysterious jaundice during adolescence suggests. The after effects of wartime stresses might have contributed to the health crisis of 1947. Understanding the danger, he confided to journalist Joseph Alsop that "he expected to die in his early forties."[7] That realization had a profound effect upon how he viewed life and reinforced his fatalism, detachment, and playboy ways. Cortisone saved Kennedy's life, however. Available in oral form by 1951, it could not cure Addison's disease, but it enabled Kennedy to lead a more normal existence.

The politically minded Kennedy family explained Jack's yellowish coloration and wan appearance as a recurrence of wartime malaria. It was not so easy to dismiss his back problems, which the Kennedys attributed to injuries sustained during the PT-109 sinking. Jack had undergone unsuccessful back surgery in 1944, and by the mid-1950s the discomfort had become so acute that he walked with crutches. He underwent a "double-fusion" operation in 1954, despite the enormous risk of another Addisonian crisis. Near death, he once again received extreme unction. After a lengthy convalescence he had surgery in 1955 to remove a silver plate that had been placed in the spine. Even afterward pain constantly afflicted him. His brother Robert later wrote, "At least one half of the days that he spent on this earth were days of intense physical pain."[8] Remarkably, Jack Kennedy faced each crisis with grace and courage, contributing considerably to his own recovery.

Kennedy's Catholicism, a decided advantage in Massachusetts, also became a liability in presidential politics. Bigots and libertarians opposed Kennedy on religious grounds; so too did liberals, fearing that the religious issue could politically ruin the Democratic party. No one dreaded that more than state and local Catholic officeholders, who believed that a Catholic-led ticket would provoke a backlash and cause their own defeat. The Catholic hierarchy, including Francis Cardinal Spellman, also opposed Kennedy because of his resistance to federal aid to parochial schools by the late 1950s. In some respects religion became Kennedy's greatest obstacle because of the long-standing public sentiment against Catholic presidential aspirants.

John Kennedy's political success, then, resulted from his capitalizing on advantages and strengths while overcoming handicaps or weaknesses. This speaks well of the people who guided and advised Kennedy, including his father, who stayed in the background as he sold him "like soap flakes." Only the greatest cynic, however, would ignore the transformation of Kennedy into a major political candidate as a result of his own hard work, dedication, and sacrifice, which reflected a deeper ambition and drive than early observers thought existed.

The political journey began in 1946 when a twenty-eight-year-old Kennedy filed for the Eleventh Massachusetts Congressional District seat. He did so after incumbent James Michael Curley once again sought the mayoralty of Boston. Since the Kennedys now resided in Hyannis Port on Cape Cod and in Palm Beach, Florida, Jack quickly moved into Boston's Bellevue Hotel to establish residency.

Predominantly Democratic, the Eleventh District spanned the northern tier of the Boston area from Cambridge and Somerville in the west to the North End and then to East Boston. Although containing a well-heeled intellectual and business constituency, the Eleventh served primarily ethnics—Italian and Irish Catholics mainly—who worked on the docks and in the shipyards, markets, and factories, living mostly in crowded tenements and three-deckers. Kennedy ran away with the primary and faced only token opposition in the general election. Much of the credit belongs to the political and financial resources of Joe Kennedy, who deftly promoted his "war hero" son as a leader of the new generation. To a lesser extent, Jack's tireless effort, even more characteristic of subsequent campaigns, also contributed as he drew, among others, on former school chums Torby Macdonald and Kenneth O'Donnell, navy buddies Paul Fay and Jim Reed, and recent acquaintance David Powers, who introduced him to the Irish communities of Charlestown and East Boston. Many of these people remained close to Kennedy until his death.

Kennedy projected an indescribable grace in this—and subsequent—campaigns. "There was a basic dignity in Jack Kennedy," Powers contended, "a pride in being that appealed to every Irishman who was beginning to feel a little embarrassed about the sentimental, corny style of the typical Irish politician as the Irish themselves were becoming more middle class."[9] He successfully combined a Harvard intellectualism and an Irish cultural heritage, making him perhaps the first Irish Brahmin in American politics.

Kennedy served three terms in the United States Congress and managed to reconcile his conservative beliefs to the needs of his district. Influenced by his father, he feared the oppressive hand of government on the "free enterprise system" and the rights of individuals. Moreover, he believed that deficit spending was fundamentally wrong. In 1949 he joined the economy bloc's efforts in the House to slash total appropriations by $600 million. During the Korean War he strongly advocated a balanced budget, thinking it could be achieved through tax increases. He also voted to cut appropriations for the Tennessee Valley Authority, and he often favored reducing funds for the Agriculture and Interior departments.

Nonetheless, Jack responded to the needs of his urban-class district as pragmatically as his father had accommodated the New Deal. James MacGregor Burns rightly labeled him a bread-and-butter liberal. Kennedy supported low-income housing, raising the minimum wage, extending Social Security benefits, liberalizing immigration laws, and subsidizing Catholic education. He opposed reducing appropriations for school lunches and weakening rent control. He voted against the Taft-Hartley Act of 1947, even though he believed organized labor to be selfish and undemocratic. On this and similar issues, Kennedy was more conservative than his public position; eschewing labels, he especially took umbrage at being called a liberal.

He was even more of an independent on matters of foreign policy. He did, however, support the administration's early containment policies such as the Truman Doctrine and the Marshall Plan, which assisted non-Communist Europe militarily and economically. Kennedy had learned the lessons of America's earlier experiences with noninterventionism. Thus he was a proponent of the North Atlantic Treaty Organization (NATO) and favored American forces in Europe to deter Communist expansion. He was much more critical of Truman's Asian policy, however. On the House floor in 1949 he blamed Roosevelt, Truman, and George C. Marshall for the fall of China to communism. He sounded more like a Republican in attacking Roosevelt's Far Eastern concessions at the Yalta Conference in 1945, and he faulted the Truman administration for not providing enough for national defense. Kennedy echoed many of his father's criticisms in this period, but unlike his father, he was not a neo-isolationist. Instead his antiadministration expressions mirrored a strongly anti-Communist viewpoint while representing a district sympathetic to Joe McCarthy's anti-Communist crusade. Kennedy's independent posture also might have reflected an unconscious reaction to the control his father had over his life; revealingly, he refused to defer to the House and party leadership.

Kennedy showed his independence and detachment in other ways. He was frequently absent from the Congress and often appeared in khaki pants and sneakers. According to Supreme Court Justice William O. Douglas, a family friend, Kennedy found time "heavy on his hands." He "was sort of drifting. And when he started drifting, then I think [he] became more of a playboy."[10] Nothing bored him more than housekeeping chores related to his district. When the paperwork mounted, he told his personal secretary, Mary Davis, "You'll just have to work a little harder."[11] Only a dedicated staff saved him from possible embarrassment.

Being ill much of the time further contributed to Kennedy's indifference. He often seemed preoccupied with death. Not only had his brother died during the war but he had also lost a sister, Kathleen, in an airplane crash in 1948. He had been especially close to the effervescent "Kick." Moreover, he took little satisfaction in an institution too unwieldy for decisive action. He also undoubtedly felt pressure to move upward. Prompted by his father, he decided in 1952 to challenge the formidable Senator Henry Cabot Lodge, Jr., a Boston Brahmin and key Republican leader. Kennedy did so despite an undistinguished congressional career in which he had sponsored no significant legislation or provided any leadership.

Kennedy's defeat of Lodge in 1952 was, of course, an enormous surprise and turned Kennedy into a nationally known figure and a dominant Democrat in his state. He won in part because of his family's tremendous expenditure of effort and money. A behind-the-scenes Joe Kennedy again had proved invaluable as an organizer and facilitator; he had persuaded the Boston Post to switch its support to Kennedy by promising the owner a five hundred thousand dollar loan. James Landis of Joe's New York office was an effective strategist and speech writer. According to one intimate, Joe dominated everything; he even told everyone where to sit at meetings. Jack Kennedy also relied on the veterans of the 1946 campaign, including O'Donnell, Macdonald, and Powers. His mother and sisters hosted teas, which were immensely popular, particularly when the dashing candidate arrived to dazzle the ladies.

The 1952 contest involved Kennedy's future brother-in-law, R. Sargent Shriver, Jr.; the sagacious and reliable Lawrence F. O'Brien; and the twenty-seven-year-old Robert Kennedy, who ran the statewide effort. Robert's organizational talents and drive made him an extraordinary asset. The more experienced O'Brien, meanwhile, contributed to the establishment of a network of three hundred campaign directors who operated independently of the local party chairman and the state organization. As for Kennedy, he exhibited the very dedication and commitment that he had lacked in Congress, traversing the back roads of the Bay State, often in pain.

Kennedy also won because his organization took advantage of Lodge's initial inattention to the campaign. Even though few ideological differences existed between the two candidates, Kennedy effectively criticized Lodge for having failed to arrest the economic decline of New England as industries moved South where cheaper labor existed. Ironically Lodge came under attack for supporting the Democratic party's "appeasement" policy in Asia. Kennedy's political independence thus proved to be an asset as he divorced himself from an unpopular Truman administration and the policies of the past.

Within a year of his senatorial victory, America's "most eligible bachelor" married Jacqueline Bouvier in Newport, Rhode Island, in high society's wedding of the year. Intentionally or not, the marriage made him more politically respectable. Jacqueline's dark-haired beauty seemed to complement Jack, and she exposed him to poetry, ballet, and classical music while he introduced her to touch football and politics, with mixed results for both individuals. His frequent absences on Senate-related business and his continual attraction to other women made the marriage something less than picture book.

Kennedy's philandering became another poorly concealed secret. Religious scruples had no impact since he took pride in his conquests. Although cortisone may have intensified his sexual appetite, Jack's behavior seemed more influenced by his father's sexual promiscuity and by his relationship with his mother. Joe Kennedy had taught his sons that sexual adventurism was acceptable, even laudatory. Rose's stoical acquiescence, excessive religiosity, overly disciplinarian manner, and apparent inattention during Jack's formative years had left Jack with a veiled antagonism—if not anger. He emerged from that upbringing with a cynical view of women and marriage. At the same time he managed to maintain the appearance of a devoted husband and father.

Meanwhile, the hiring of a new administrative assistant in 1953 furthered his image as an intellect. Bespectacled, lean, reticent, intense, and completely devoted, Theodore C. Sorensen, a recent graduate of the University of Nebraska Law School, soon became indispensable to Kennedy's political fortunes as a brilliant research writer in the progressive tradition of Senator George Norris of Nebraska. Sorensen generated essay after essay under Kennedy's byline for the *Atlantic Monthly*, the *New Republic*, and other contemporary magazines. His well-crafted speeches artfully expressed Kennedy's ideas and thoughts, enhancing an eventually polished delivery.

Yet Kennedy impressed few national leaders during his first term. Pledged to revitalizing the New England economy, he made little headway, yet he courageously championed the St. Lawrence Seaway project at the supposed expense of Boston and other northeastern ports. Much more at issue was his failure to oppose Joe McCarthy, whose reckless disregard for Senate rules and procedures led to a resolution of censure in 1954. Kennedy faced a dilemma. Even though he was a Republican, the Irish-Catholic McCarthy remained close to Joe Kennedy, who thought him a dedicated public servant. While Jack Kennedy often rejected his father's legislative advice, this was a different matter. McCarthy had given Robert Kennedy a job on his investigating committee, had dated Kennedy's younger sister, Patricia, and had been a houseguest in Hyannis Port. Besides, Kennedy liked the jovial McCarthy and was initially sympathetic to his anti-Communist crusade. Moreover, strong public sentiment existed for McCarthy in Massachusetts, particularly in Catholic South Boston.

Consequently, Kennedy sought to strike a balance between liberals, who were angered about McCarthy's violation of civil liberties, and conservatives, who were concerned about defending national security. When the resolution of condemnation finally came out of committee in 1954, Kennedy was recovering from back surgery. Unable to participate, he was the only Democrat who failed to vote or pair against McCarthy. He later explained that he had relinquished the right to pair his vote by absenting himself from the discussions. Liberal critics like Eleanor Roosevelt, recognizing his deeper predicament, remained suspicious of Joe Kennedy's son into the next decade.

Ironically, while still convalescing, Kennedy turned to the study of Americans who had exhibited political courage during trying times, focusing upon those willing to view the national interest above conflicting sectional concerns. This preoccupation with courage from one who admired it enormously derived in part from his recent failure to show it when it counted politically. Whether *Profiles in Courage* (1956) represents a form of expiation is conjectural, but its success cannot be denied. Sales zoomed followed by favorable reviews, testimonials, and finally the coveted Pulitzer Prize for biography. *Profiles* received the award despite its not being ranked among the judges' eight recommendations. Herbert Parmet, Kennedy's definitive biographer, suggests that Joe Kennedy's friend, Arthur Krock, might have exhibited undue influence. Much more at issue was whether Kennedy had even written the book. Columnist Drew Pearson, among others, suspected that it was ghostwritten, and only after Kennedy's vehement denial did such criticism subside. Years later Parmet confirmed Pearson's worst suspicions when an exhaustive inquiry revealed that although an ailing Kennedy had sponsored and shaped the work, the research and drafts had been done by several people, particularly Professor Jules Davids of Georgetown University and Ted Sorensen. The clear, crisp prose of the final draft bore the distinct mark of Sorensen.[12] The whole affair suggests the tremendous resources at Kennedy's disposal and his willingness to shade the truth for political advancement.

Profiles in Courage indeed made Jack Kennedy a national political celebrity at a time when the Democratic party cried out for new leadership to combat the popular Eisenhower presidency. Not only had Kennedy written a prize-winning book, he had defeated the seemingly invincible Lodge. As a Catholic and an independent he could attract Democrats who had left the party in 1952, and his handsome appearance and charming style could win even more votes. After three years of rather undistinguished service in the Senate, Kennedy sought to capitalize on his new notability by pursuing the vice-presidential nomination. He ignored his father's appraisal that former governor Adlai Stevenson of Illinois, the 1952 nominee, would surely lose again to Eisenhower in November. Moreover, if Kennedy were on the ticket, his Catholicism would be blamed for that defeat, thus weakening a future presidential bid. Showing more independence and believing that he could win, Kennedy instructed Sorensen to submit material to news magazines, outlining the advantages of Stevenson's choosing a Catholic running mate while focusing on Kennedy's overall availability. Although disliking intraparty fights immensely, Kennedy, aided by O'Brien and O'Donnell, gained control of the state Democratic Central Committee that spring and delivered the Massachusetts delegation to Stevenson at the Democratic National Convention in August.

Stevenson, seeking to exploit Kennedy's popularity, had asked him to place his name in nomination. Following Kennedy's electrifying address and Stevenson's nomination, the latter decided to leave the choice of running mate to the delegates. A night of furious activity followed, with Kennedy hustling for delegate support only to fall to Sen. Estes Kefauver of Tennessee after coming within 166 1/2 votes of victory. Kennedy had shown surprising strength, particularly in the South, where pro–civil rights Kefauver was most disliked. Although bitterly disappointed, Kennedy remained gracious. By losing in heroic fashion he emerged as the real winner of 1956, following the collapse of the Democratic ticket that fall.

Kennedy's quest for the presidency in 1960 began in the crucible of the 1956 convention. He knew that as an outsider, however, he would have to seek the nomination aggressively, and he began early. Starting in 1957, he traversed the countryside, fulfilling speaking engagements. During one period in 1958 he received 437 invitations. He often risked his life, visiting remote places in small planes, facing impossible weather conditions. Recognizing that Democratic liberals like Hubert Humphrey could not win without southern support, he also realized that southerners like Lyndon Baines Johnson of Texas were handicapped in the liberal North. He sought to broaden his liberalism without offending the South. Pragmatically, he became more of a welfare-state advocate and more attuned to civil liberties. In explaining his gradual drift leftward Kennedy later suggested that "some people have their liberalism 'made' by the time they reach their late twenties. I didn't. I was caught in the crosscurrents and eddies. It was only later that I got into the stream of thought."[13]

In a thoughtful and influential biography on Kennedy in 1959, political scientist James MacGregor Burns contended that Kennedy's liberalism lacked emotional commitment and his detachment was a clue to understanding him. Burns explained Kennedy's detachment in terms of the family's having abandoned its Irish moorings without having been accepted by the upper class. Jack's earlier brushes with death may have further contributed to his coolness or indifference. Whatever the cause, it reinforced his political moderation and placed him safely in the mainstream of the party. On the one hand he embraced the liberal agenda of recent Democratic presidents; on the other hand he remained a financial conservative. He also continued to reject ideological self-labeling. When pressed he usually called himself a "realist" or "an idealist without illusions."[14]

His political moderation faced a major test in 1957. For the first time since Reconstruction, the Senate—under Lyndon Baines Johnson's leadership—deliberated over a civil rights bill that evoked considerable conflict. Kennedy sided with southern Democrats in placing the bill before the unfriendly Judiciary Committee, chaired by segregationist Senator James Eastland (D.-Miss). Southerners praised him for becoming the "living antithesis of Earl Warren." Yet Kennedy then joined with liberals to vote for Title III of the bill, which would have given the attorney general injunctive power over civil rights violators and school desegregation. After its anticipated defeat Kennedy returned to a prosouthern posture by voting for an amendment granting jury trials to violators of black voting rights. The amendment brought Kennedy considerable praise in the South and equal condemnation in civil rights circles. Unquestionably, political considerations influenced Kennedy's voting pattern, causing one colleague to ask, "Why not show a little less profile and a little more courage?"[15]

As a moderate, Kennedy fared better the next year, following the Senate Rackets Committee's investigation of corruption in the Teamsters Union's hierarchy. Robert Kennedy, the committee's chief counsel, induced him to join the investigation against their father's wishes. Through their efforts Teamster president David Beck faced criminal prosecution. This investigation reinforced the prejudices of conservatives that all union leaders were crooks. Kennedy's problem then became one of retaining organized labor's support while eliminating its abuses.

As chairman of the subcommittee on labor he skillfully fashioned a bill that addressed both labor racketeering and reforms beneficial to organized labor, thus managing to win over George Meany and Walter Reuther, the key labor leaders. Through two years of legislative struggle, during which Kennedy received little cooperation from the Republican opposition, he saw the Kennedy-Ives bill so stripped of its prolabor provisions that he withdrew sponsorship in 1959 when it passed Congress as the Landrum-Griffin Act. Nevertheless, Kennedy had impressed colleagues and others with his command of labor law and his debating ability. More significantly, for the first time he had made a sustained commitment on a major legislative issue. In the process he received national attention from the media.

Kennedy also made the headlines following a Senate speech in 1957 on France and Algeria. By then a member of the Senate Foreign Relations Committee, his greatest interest remained foreign affairs, where he was outspoken, independent, and original. Along with most Democrats he opposed President Eisenhower's reduction of the military budget and reliance on nuclear deterrence. Like most senators he believed in the domino theory and viewed communism as a monolith. Yet he differed with the Democratic leadership in his opposition to European colonialism. His anticolonialism undoubtedly stemmed partly from his Irish heritage and his father's strong isolationist antipathy to empire. He had become particularly outspoken after visiting Asia in 1951. He strongly criticized French control in Indochina, which he believed created Communists out of nationalists. He argued that the United States should stop extending military assistance to French Indochina, where France must provide self-rule. Otherwise Indochina—and soon all of Southeast Asia—would be lost. During France's trying days in Vietnam in 1954 he advocated Vietnamese independence within the French Union as a way to counteract the popularity of Ho Chi Minh and the Communist movement. After the 1954 Geneva Accords he opposed free elections uniting the two Vietnams, believing naively in a democratic revolution in the South as a viable alternative to a united Communist Vietnam.

His Algerian speech in 1957 represented an extension of his anticolonialism. French suppression of rebels in that North African colony, according to Kennedy, became an American problem since it affected France's commitment to NATO. Particularly disturbing was France's use of American military equipment in Algeria, which turned Algerians against the United States. Moreover, Kennedy recognized that Western imperialism weakened criticism of Soviet domination in Eastern Europe. It could also lead to Communist governments in the emerging nations unless the West understood the nationalistic aspirations of the oppressed. The Third World hung in the balance, Kennedy believed.

Kennedy's speech invited considerable criticism from the leadership of both political parties. Even Adlai Stevenson felt that the United States should not antagonize a NATO ally. Dean Acheson argued as well that France's departure would lead to chaos in Algeria. Still, Kennedy's much publicized address won him the plaudits of Third World nationalists and Frenchmen opposing government policy. It also added to his many invitations to speak and write on matters of foreign policy. The prestigious *Foreign Affairs* published a major essay under his byline that Sorensen and the staff had composed. "A Democrat Looks at Foreign Policy" spelled out more fully Kennedy's awareness of the nationalistic forces at work throughout the world and the necessity of extending economic support. That neglect, he believed, represented one of the Eisenhower administration's greatest shortcomings. Kennedy favored economic assistance even to Communist countries such as Poland as a way to encourage anticommunism and tie America more closely to nationalistic movements elsewhere. By 1958 Kennedy was becoming a leading spokesman of a new Democratic foreign policy. Nevertheless, he remained as anti-Communist as Richard Nixon but recognized that new cold war approaches must be adopted.

A major publicity blitz accompanied Kennedy's heightened Senate activity. Joe Kennedy generated much of it, quietly using journalistic friends such as Luce and Krock. Led by Sorensen, Kennedy's staff contributed by publishing an enormous amount of material under the Kennedy signature. Articles appeared in popular magazines—*Look, Life*, and *McCalls*—and in serious journals like the *Georgetown Law Review*. By 1960 the Kennedy staff had also prepared a compilation of Kennedy's major foreign policy statements, *The Strategy of Peace*, which attracted enormous attention. Various magazines leaped at the opportunity to initiate feature stories; *Time* did a cover story and *Redbook* focused on Jackie. ABC's *Navy Log* meanwhile revived "PT-109." Campaign biographies soon appeared, including Burns's exceptional *John Kennedy: A Political Profile*.

Kennedy's emerging national popularity contributed to his reelection victory in 1958 when he defeated an understaffed Vincent Celeste by a record 875,000 majority. Edward Kennedy, the youngest brother, managed the characteristically smooth operation. Also making his debut was brother-in-law Steve Smith, the "comptroller of the currency." But Joe Kennedy's $1.5 million outlay and his other contributions remained significant, along with the organizational abilities of O'Brien, O'Donnell, and several others.

As the new decade began, Kennedy stood out as the most popular Democrat; the Gallup Polls showed him leading runner-up Stevenson by twelve points. Contemporary political writer William V. Shannon, commenting on Kennedy's celebrity status, wondered "what has all this to do with statesmanship?" Manufactured imagery had indeed overshadowed his modest successes in leadership. Getting much attention was Kennedy the war hero, the Pulitzer Prize-winning intellectual, the youthful, robust leader who vowed in the wake of the somnolent Eisenhower era to get America "moving again." Too, Kennedy's charm, natural good looks, and attractive family continued to draw considerable media attention. During a time when television courted a consuming nation, Kennedy used the medium to his advantage.

Kennedy announced his presidential candidacy on 2 January 1960 in the Senate caucus room before a crowded press conference. At the National Press Club two weeks later he proposed the theme for the coming campaign: "We will need in the sixties a President who is willing and able to summon his national constituency to its finest hour—to alert the people to our dangers and our opportunities—to demand of them the sacrifices that will be necessary."[16] Two months later he won the uncontested New Hampshire primary. Afterward his main challenger, Senator Humphrey of Minnesota, lost Wisconsin and West Virginia, despite strong anti-Catholic sentiment. In West Virginia the Humphrey organization had even adopted "Give Me That Old-Time Religion" as a theme song to exploit prejudices. Kennedy won because of a superior organization, enormous energy and money, and the prevailing Kennedy image. He had also successfully tackled the religious issue: "Nobody asked me if I was a Catholic when I joined the United States Navy. Nobody asked my brother if he was a Catholic or Protestant before he climbed into an American bomber plane to fly his last mission." He pointed out that in the presidential oath, one swears "to support the separation of church and state; he puts one hand on the bible and raises the other hand to God as he takes the oath. And if he breaks his oath, he is not only committing a crime against the Constitution, for which the Congress can impeach him—and should impeach him—but he is committing a sin against God."[17] Kennedy won the remaining primaries and through the efforts of his father and others made strong headway in such nonprimary states as Pennsylvania, New York, New Jersey, Illinois, and California.

At the Democratic National Convention in Los Angeles in July, Kennedy managed to overturn the challenge of old party warhorses—Stevenson and Johnson—in winning a first-ballot victory. In his acceptance speech he again urged Americans to make sacrifices in facing the challenge of the sixties: "The New Frontier is here whether we seek it or not—in uncharted areas of science and space, unsolved problems of peace and war, unconquered pockets of ignorance and prejudice, unanswered questions of poverty and surplus."[18] Soon afterward he confided that Johnson was his choice for the vice-presidency, which angered liberals and labor, causing the Kennedy brothers to reassess that decision. But important considerations dictated the choice. Johnson was more likely to overcome the growing opposition to Kennedy in the South, where his religion was now more known; at the least Johnson could win Texas. Too, given his experience as Senate majority leader, he could persuade senators to vote for the administration programs. If he remained majority leader, however, his political and personal differences with Kennedy might only grow. Moreover, Joe Kennedy urged his son to retain Johnson. For whatever reasons, Kennedy's selection represented a brilliant political stroke that revealed both his pragmatism and his moderation.

Kennedy's campaign against Richard Nixon, Eisenhower's vice-president, involved little fundamental differences in ideology. Both accepted the welfare state and containment policy. Yet while Nixon was obligated to defend the Eisenhower record, Kennedy, buttressed by a liberal Democratic platform, exploited its shortcomings, including the president's failure to keep pace with the Soviet Union in education, technology, and intercontinental ballistic missiles (ICBMs). He referred to America's declining prestige in the world—particularly with the newly emerging nations of Africa and Asia. He also pointed to the loss of Cuba to the Communists and the failure of the summit conference that spring after the disastrous U-2 affair.

Domestically he focused on the slow rate of economic growth and the neglect of the aged, the poor ("seventeen million Americans go to bed hungry at night") and the farmer ("our number one domestic problem"). Despite the risk of losing southern backing he finally identified himself more with black America by calling Coretta Scott King, wife of the imprisoned civil rights leader, Martin Luther King, Jr., to express his concern. Always he emphasized the importance of the presidency in getting the "country moving again," a phrase he often employed in his all-purpose speech. Americans, the majority of them Democrats, seemed to respond more enthusiastically to Kennedy's challenge than to Nixon's defense of the status quo. More and more, Kennedy's charisma stirred Americans as he polished the cadence in his speeches, delivered with a crisp Boston accent and a finger repeatedly thrust forward to emphasize a point.

Kennedy sought to capitalize on his personal and party strengths while reducing his sizable obstacles, none more formidable than his Catholicism. He continued to stress his strong belief in the separation of church and state and the injustice of disenfranchising Americans from the presidency because of religion. Never was he more eloquent and courageous than when he spoke before the hostile Houston Ministerial Association in September. In a well-publicized address, he responded patiently to the concerns of Protestant America. While religious bigotry persisted for the remainder of the campaign, at least he destroyed it as an intellectually respectable issue.

Even more effectively did he deal with the issue of his youth and inexperience, first raised by Harry Truman, who urged Democrats on the eve of the Democratic National Convention to select a more mature and experienced candidate. Kennedy demolished that argument on national television by suggesting that if "fourteen years in major elective office is insufficient experience, that rules out . . . all but a handful of American Presidents, and every President of the twentieth century."[19] Early in the campaign, however, it was Nixon whom pundits perceived as more mature and able to withstand the Soviets and govern the country. Kennedy's TV debates with Nixon, more than anything else, showed the impact that television would have on the sixties and exhibited Kennedy's effectiveness in that medium. Kennedy came across as knowledgeable and competent—the equal of the vice-president. The first debate decidedly strengthened Kennedy's campaign; he not only put Republicans on the defensive over recent Communist successes but he also appeared poised and self-confident. In perhaps his worst campaign performance, Nixon perspired profusely, looked haggard, and seemed too agreeable. He had in fact erred in debating Kennedy. What made matters worse, Nixon's makeup people had let him down; in a campaign based so much on imagery, Nixon lost the key first debate largely because of his appearance. One survey suggested that four million people made up their minds on the basis of the debates, with Kennedy gaining a three-to-one margin.

Yet Kennedy received less than a 120,000 plurality out of over 68 million votes cast, the narrowest presidential victory ever, even though he did better in terms of the electoral vote, with 303 to 219. More than anything else, the religious issue cut into Kennedy's plurality, costing him an estimated 17 percent of the normally Democratic vote in the South. Protestant defectors were also high in the Midwest. Yet enough Catholics crossed over in the industrial Northeast to enable him to capture key states there. Allen Matusow rightly concludes that religion hurt Kennedy in the popular vote but aided him in the electoral calculation.[20] Anti-Catholicism aside, Kennedy attributed the thin margin also to a prevailing—and false—sense of prosperity and peace. He felt disappointed in the results, made even more embarrassing by charges, later confirmed, that he won Illinois through the election-rigging of Boss Richard J. Daley of Chicago. Kennedy had little mandate to change America, as he well knew. The 1960 vote would remain an enduring obstacle in the days ahead.

Before his inauguration Kennedy had only seventy-two days to organize a government, but much of the work had begun during the campaign. Seven task forces emerged, later increased to twenty-nine, focusing on such concerns as Latin America, Africa, and agricultural policy. Kennedy invited the leading talent of the country to participate, many of whom later graced his administration. Their reports became the basis for many of Kennedy's new policies and programs. Aware of the terrible transition between the Truman and Eisenhower administrations, Kennedy tapped two former Truman appointees to assist with the interregnum: Clark Clifford, a Washington, D.C., lawyer, and Richard Neustadt, a professor of political science at Columbia University and author of the highly-acclaimed *Presidential Power*. When Neustadt asked about his relationship with Clifford, Kennedy responded: "I don't want you to relate to Clifford. I can't afford to confine myself to one set of advisors. If I did that, I would be on their leading strings."[21] Clifford cooperated with the Brookings Institution, studying presidential transitions, and became Kennedy's chief liaison with the Eisenhower administration. Both he and Neustadt provided Kennedy with worthwhile suggestions, making the Eisenhower-Kennedy transition one of the smoothest ever.

Staffing the new administration occupied most of the president-elect's time. He worked closely with Sargent Shriver, whose committee instituted a nationwide talent hunt. Many others were involved, including Robert Kennedy and establishment figures such as Robert Lovett, Truman's undersecretary of state, and journalist Joseph Alsop. The committee sought prospects who showed judgment, integrity, ability to work with others, industry, devotion to Kennedy programs, and toughness—an indication of the style of the new administration. Kennedy also preferred associates who were not too ideological, emotional, talkative, moralistic, or dull.

His first action involved the reappointment of Allen Dulles as director of the Central Intelligence Agency and J. Edgar Hoover as chief of the Federal Bureau of Investigation. Liberals were rightly upset. At the time Kennedy's actions appeared to be reassurances to conservatives. Yet given Dulles's involvement in the secret plan to overthrow Castro and Hoover's damaging evidence on Kennedy's early sexual escapades, the president-elect seemed to have little choice. Of utmost concern, the FBI held tapes of Kennedy's assignations in 1942 with Inga Arvad, an attractive Dane who had supposed connections with Adolf Hitler during a period when Kennedy served as a naval intelligence officer on the East

Coast.[22] Kennedy also appointed as secretary of defense the highly rec-ommended Robert S. McNamara, a young, brilliant, independent-minded Republican whose bespectacled gaze and slickly combed hair belied his aggressiveness. At the time president of Ford Motor Company, McNamara received the appointment after he had turned down the Trea-sury post. His precise and efficient mind immediately impressed Ken-nedy, who permitted him free rein over department-related appoint-ments.

More troublesome was the Department of the Treasury, given the gold drain and balance-of-payment problems. Robert Lovett had turned down the appointment following McNamara's refusal. Kennedy then rejected the advice of his father, brother, and liberals by favoring Eisenhower's undersecretary of state, Douglas Dillon. Dillon's financial conservatism, critics thought, would only reinforce Kennedy's. A con-cern also existed that Dillon might someday publicly oppose Kennedy's economic policies. Kennedy made the appointment after Dillon's reas-surances of fair play and support of economic growth. Kennedy obvi-ously liked and trusted Dillon, a nonideological Republican much like McNamara. Dillon's appointment ensured some cooperation with Repub-licans on economic policy and guaranteed that sweeping changes in economic growth would be virtually nil. To balance Dillon Kennedy selected liberal Democrats David Bell and Walter Heller as budget director and chair of the Council of Economic Advisers, respectively. A former Truman special assistant, Bell was a Harvard economics professor; Hel-ler, a Humphrey Democrat, taught economics at the University of Min-nesota.

Finding a secretary of state proved even more frustrating. Senator J. William Fulbright of Arkansas, the cerebral chair of the Senate Foreign Relations Committee, most impressed Kennedy. But Robert Kennedy, Fulbright's strongest critic, argued that his anti–civil rights reputation created problems, particularly with newly emerging African nations. Meanwhile the president-elect faced strong liberal pressure to appoint Adlai Stevenson, whom he thought indecisive and politically inept. Moreover, Stevenson had refused to back Kennedy's nomination in Los Angeles. Kennedy, wanting to be his own secretary, also desired some-one with less of a constituency, and Stevenson reluctantly accepted the ambassadorship to the United Nations. Kennedy thereupon appointed Dean Rusk as secretary of state after rejecting the dovish Chester Bowles, who became undersecretary of state, and David Bruce, who accepted the ambassadorship to England. The balding and soft-spoken Dean Rusk, whom critics called Buddha as much for his personality as for his appear-ance, had strong recommendations from Lovett and Dean Acheson. Rusk had been a Rhodes Scholar, assistant secretary of state for Far Eastern affairs in the Truman administration, and head of the Rockefeller Foundation. Kennedy found him self-effacing but competent and lucid during the interview.

Kennedy's initial choices for attorney general were Abraham Ribicoff, governor of Connecticut, and Adlai Stevenson, neither of whom desired the post. Fatherly pressure to appoint the thirty-four-year-old Robert increased, despite his lack of legal experience, his reputation for being "ruthless," and his being the president-elect's brother. Aware of the impending criticism and anxious to strike out on his own, Robert opposed the appointment. Jack Kennedy too had "very serious reservations," but his father remained adamant. Eventually, Kennedy persuaded Robert that he needed a confidant in the cabinet. Always adept at using humor to overcome conflict, Kennedy suggested that he would make the announcement by opening "the front door of [my] Georgetown house early some morning . . . look up and down the street, and, if there's no one there, I'll whisper, 'It's Bobby.' "[23] In fact he made the announcement at midday after telling his brother to brush his hair. Despite the swirling criticism, he knew that in Robert Kennedy he had his most trusted associate on board.

Kennedy rounded out his cabinet by appointing former Minnesota governor Orville Freeman as secretary of agriculture. A World War II hero and former Humphrey man, the populistic Freeman had nominated Kennedy at Los Angeles. Also selected was Ribicoff for secretary of health, education, and welfare. A liberal, Ribicoff was an early Kennedy supporter, as was Cong. Stewart Udall of Arizona, an angular, energetic Mormon known for his defense of natural resources, who became secretary of interior. The brilliant Arthur Goldberg of Illinois was named secretary of labor; he had gained the Kennedys' trust and respect during the fights over labor legislation of the late 1950s. For secretary of commerce, Kennedy appointed Governor Luther Hodges of North Carolina, who provided southern and business ties and at sixty-two was the oldest cabinet appointee. Finally, Edward Day, a California businessman and former Illinois insurance commissioner, received the postmaster generalship after the aging black Cong. William Dawson, by prearrangement, had turned it down.

Like most cabinets, Kennedy's represented a balancing of interests and sections. Given his close election, he felt a greater need to assure the opposition. Ideologically, three of his selections could have sat with Eisenhower; two were Republicans. Yet liberals like Freeman and Udall provided a counterweight. Few were ideologues—most were confident managers who emphasized efficiency, order, and, above all, results. The

National Review called it "an opportunistic patchwork." Perhaps, but it contained very competent people, some with impressive achievements. It was also a young cabinet—forty-seven was the average age, contrasted to Eisenhower's fifty-seven. In another dissimilarity, fewer members came from business backgrounds (four to Eisenhower's seven). Few cabinets comprised more former public officials: seven had served as congressmen, governors, or top-level national administrators. Yet the three top posts were filled with technocrats. In general, the cabinet reflected Kennedy's cautious pragmatism more than any commitment to "get the country moving again." In this regard it was not much different from Franklin Roosevelt's first executives.

Appointments to the White House staff included the alter ego Sorensen as chief counsel in charge of legislative programs, domestic policies, and speeches. Kennedy chose McGeorge Bundy as special assistant for national security affairs. A former Harvard dean, young, bright, self-assured, the Republican Bundy soon rivaled Sorensen as major adviser. Meanwhile, former speech writer Richard Goodwin would continue to write speeches and eventually concentrate on Latin American affairs. Harris Wofford, recently on the faculty at Notre Dame Law School, served as civil rights aide, and Rooseveltian scholar Arthur Schlesinger, Jr., became the unofficial court historian and coddler of disgruntled liberals. The so-called Irish Mafia also occupied staff positions, O'Donnell as appointments secretary and O'Brien as assistant to the president for congressional relations and personnel. The ebullient Pierre Salinger became press secretary. It was an assemblage of fine minds, recalled Wofford, who felt uneasy because they seemed "too much like Kennedy—cool, skeptical, pragmatic."[24]

Kennedy announced all of his cabinet selections and most of the staff personnel by mid-December. Earlier that month he had also met with President Eisenhower at the White House, where they had discussed Berlin, the Far East, and Cuba. Unlike Ike's meeting with President Truman in 1952, this one, Kennedy ensured, was cordial. He had impressed Eisenhower with his desire to learn from the previous administration. Afterward he and Jackie alternated between Georgetown and Palm Beach for the holidays. Conferences and meetings still abounded as the New Frontiersmen prepared for the January twentieth inauguration.

2

★ ★ ★ ★ ★

ASSUMING COMMAND

As president, John F. Kennedy inherited a nation in transition. Although the United States remained the world's most prosperous country, Japan and West Germany had begun to challenge that preeminence; and the United States barely held on as the world's greatest power in the face of Soviet technological advances. Strains between the U.S. and its allies began to weaken the Western alliance, too, as stresses threatened Soviet control of the Communist bloc. By the early 1960s a multipolar world was gradually replacing a bipolar one, and much a part of it was the growing number of newly emerging nations in Africa and Asia. The two superpowers vied for their allegiance as the cold war moved deeper into the Third World arena. At home the postwar civil rights movement made advances, a prelude to what was about to come. At the same time, postwar economic growth continued, despite occasional lapses. It would reach even higher levels by the late 1960s during the Vietnam War.

The postwar baby boom continued to accelerate population growth. In 1960 there were 180.6 million Americans, representing an increase of 15 million from 1955.[1] By 1965 there would be an additional 14 million, with black population increases keeping pace in this period. There were nearly 19 million blacks in 1960 compared to 15 million in 1950, representing a 22 percent rise; white America showed 2 percent less growth over the same period. The foreign-born population decreased from 11.3 million to 9.7 million, however, indicating that the generation of the great migration of the early 1900s was rapidly expiring. Meanwhile, quotas kept current immigration figures low; only 265,398 immigrants entered the country in 1960. That year the overall population contained 63.6 million Protestants, 42.1 million Roman Catholics, and 5.3 million Jews.

The 1960 census indicated that Americans continued to move westward and southward, a trend that carried over into the 1970s. The West had the greatest regional increase with 8 million people, reflecting a 39 percent boost. California set the pace with an addition of 5 million. The black population in the West almost doubled from 1950 to 1960. It was only fitting that the Brooklyn Dodgers moved to Los Angeles and that the New York Giants left the Polo Grounds for San Francisco in 1958. During the next decade the Pacific states came to include three other major league franchises. Among the southern states Texas and Florida underwent the largest population expansion, gaining about 2 million each between 1950 and 1960. Overall, the South had an increase of 5.5 million as more Americans followed corporations into nonunion states even though blacks continued to leave the South during the 1950s for northern and western communities. By 1960 Americans moved more readily than their parents had. Seventy percent lived in the state of their birth that year compared to 77 percent in 1940.

Americans continued to migrate into urban areas (towns of twenty-five hundred or more). According to the 1960 census, 125.2 million lived in urban communities and 54 million resided in rural ones, compared to 96 million and 54.2 million, respectively, in 1950. Most of the urban increase went to the suburbs. During the ten-year period the number of suburbanites increased from 36.8 to 54.4 million, a gain of 48 percent. They lived in subdivisions on the city's outskirts. By 1960 suburbia represented a white middle-class neighborhood of ranch houses with two-car garages, two baths, three bedrooms, and spacious lawns. Of all the housing in America in 1960, one-fourth had been erected during the 1950s; for the first time in this century, more Americans owned their own houses than lived in rental units.

The quality of life had also improved for most Americans. Better medical care contributed to the higher life expectancy rate of 69.7 years in 1960 in contrast to 68.2 in 1950 and to the lower infant mortality rate of 26 per 1,000 in 1960 compared to 29.2 a decade earlier. Educational opportunities also improved as the number of college graduates increased from 352,881 in 1955 to 476,704 in 1960, reaching 768,871 seven years later. More Americans availed themselves of television sets and automobiles, which rose from 3 million to 45.7 million and 40 million to 61.6 million, respectively, in the decade of the 1950s. In 1960, 75 percent of American households owned at least one car, 87 percent a TV, and 86 percent a refrigerator. Higher incomes enabled people to better their circumstances.

In 1960 the average employee earned $4,743, an increase of $1,750 since 1950.

These figures reveal the record-level prosperity that had begun in the postwar era, spawned by the cold war and the consumer culture. The swollen military budgets of the Korean War in particular provided a major impetus. The postwar baby boom guaranteed markets for products from disposable diapers and baby foods to entertainment items of every sort. Greater demand for a larger variety of consumer goods characterized the decade and afterward. Reflecting this new economic growth, the gross national product index (1958=100) jumped from 59.7 in 1945 to 103.3 in 1960. National income rose from $241.1 billion in 1950 to $414.5 billion in 1960, while the consumer price index (1967=100) went from 72.1 to 88.7 during the same period.

Corporate profits increased dramatically from $19 billion in 1945 to $50 billion in 1960. Moreover, the share of business assets controlled by the nation's two hundred largest companies rose from 48.9 percent to 55 percent in the years 1950–1962. In 1962 the one hundred largest manufacturing corporations drew 57.6 percent of the net profits. General Motors remained the world's largest corporation, with a payroll of nearly seven hundred thousand. Other corporations, especially in the automobile, electrical, and chemical industries, also performed extremely well.

Despite the prevailing prosperity, millions of people still remained impoverished. Economist John Kenneth Galbraith's influential *Affluent Society* (1958) unwittingly misled Americans into thinking that poverty and gross inequalities had been eradicated. In fact, in 1960 the top 5 percent continued to receive 20 percent of the national income. Twenty-five percent of Americans lived in poverty, even though many of them owned automobiles and TVs. They lacked the wherewithal to secure adequate housing, medical care, and other essentials of life, let alone the means to provide for retirement. As Michael Harrington suggested in *The Other America* (1962), poverty became more hidden, disguised by inexpensive clothing and concealed by beltways and interstate highways that no longer required driving through decaying inner cities and blighted rural areas. The poor included the aged everywhere, Puerto Ricans in New York, Hispanics of the Southwest, blacks residing in ghettos, Indians languishing on reservations, and many rural Americans. One-fourth of the poor were sixty-five years or older and one-fourth worked on farms.

During the 1950s farmers often suffered, whether their incomes fell to poverty levels or not. Agricultural income overall was down almost $1 billion in 1960 from the $17.6 billion in 1950. In contrast, manufacturing

25

income rose from $76.2 billion to $125.8 billion over the same period. And though farmers continued to decline from 15.3 percent of the total population in 1950 to 8.7 percent a decade later, their man-hour productivity (1958=100) skyrocketed from 61.9 in 1950 to 106.5 in 1960 and to 128.7 in 1963, an indication of the improving technology in cultivation.

Changing occupational trends since World War II also dictated a greater demand for white-collar workers, who jumped in number from 21.2 million in 1950 to 27.2 million in 1960. Manual and service workers rose only from 30.4 million to 33.2 million over the same decade. Union membership showed an estimated 2 million increase over the same period. Women continued to move into the job market, a trend first encouraged by the wartime needs of the 1940s. In 1940 14.1 million women held jobs, compared to 18.4 million in 1950 and 22.2 million in 1960. The increase in women employees reflected a larger percentage of married women who sought to supplement family incomes. Even though grossly underpaid, some 40 percent of all women had jobs in 1960; even more significantly, about the same proportion of mothers of school-aged children went to work.

No change brought on greater controversy and turmoil than civil rights. Sensitive Americans of the World War II generation had understood the hypocrisy of fighting racism abroad while permitting it to exist at home. They realized too that they could not condemn Soviet human rights violations if such abuse persisted here. Despite some advances in the forties and fifties, primarily on legislative and judicial fronts, results fell well short of equality. By 1960 most southern blacks remained unable to vote and faced segregated facilities, both private and public. But the black plight was not restricted to the South; blacks languished in northern ghettos, while whites moved into suburban areas. Poverty alone did not explain the predicament: Blacks were victims of racial discrimination because most banks, realtors, and property owners deliberately excluded them from better housing. Fifty-seven percent of all non-white housing was substandard, according to a Civil Rights Commission report of 1960.

Moreover, sizable income differentials existed between whites and blacks at all educational levels. For example, in 1959 the median income of a black family headed by a college graduate was $5,654, compared to $7,373 for a comparable white family. In 1960 black life expectancy was seven years less than that for whites; the black infant mortality rate was nearly twice that for whites; and the black maternal mortality rate was almost four times higher than that for whites.

By 1960 such injustices spurred civil rights activity. It was led, among others, by the Reverend Martin Luther King, Jr., the nonviolent leader of the Montgomery bus boycott of 1955; Roy Wilkins, the executive secretary of the National Association for the Advancement of Colored People; and James Farmer of the Congress of Racial Equality. Impetus also came from more unlikely sources. On 1 February 1960 four black freshmen at North Carolina Agricultural and Technical State University sat at the lunch counter of the Woolworth store in downtown Greensboro to protest a "whites only" policy. They inspired similar sit-in demonstrations across the South, awakening a generation of young activists, black and white, numbering in the tens of thousands.

While America seemed a less satisfied, materialistic, and conformist society by the time of Kennedy's inauguration, Americans appeared unready for the sweeping changes of the 1960s. Few thought that race relations constituted a major problem, nor did they approve of sit-in demonstrations in the South. Most were gradualists, willing to wait for a resolution of racial issues. A majority of Americans thought of themselves as conservatives, especially on welfare-related issues; conservatives in fact outnumbered liberals in the public opinion polls until late 1963. Thus more Americans wished that Kennedy would move more to the right in his proposed domestic programs, suggesting that even if Americans were not wedded to the status quo, they were unwilling to travel much beyond it. By far their greatest concern related to matters of war and peace. To them the cold war was very much a reality, and they looked to Kennedy primarily for leadership in foreign policy.[2]

John F. Kennedy assumed the presidency on a sunny, frigid, snow-covered January twentieth. Attended by thousands of shivering guests, the inauguration program began at 12:21 P.M. in the Capitol Plaza. The glaring sun prevented the eighty-five-year-old poet Robert Frost from reading a poem he had written for the occasion; unable to proclaim "the glory of the next Augustan age," he recited a piece he had committed to memory. Afterward Chief Justice Earl Warren swore in a hatless and coatless Kennedy, whose hand was on the family Bible, the Roman Catholic Douay Version, as he repeated the oath of office.

Kennedy's inaugural address made the occasion memorable. One of the briefest of such speeches, it was also one of the most eloquent, made more so by the increasingly polished Kennedy delivery. The writing was unmistakably Theodore Sorensen's, although the ideas and some of the phraseology came from Kennedy. Uplifting and optimistic in tone, it reflected the nationalism, spirit of sacrifice, and sense of mission that Kennedy had injected into the presidential campaign: "My fellow Americans, ask not what your country can do for you, ask what you can do for your country. My fellow citizens of the world, ask not what America will do for you, but what together we can do for the freedom of man."

Scholars of a later generation have been struck by its militancy and globalism.[3] Perhaps no passage from it has been more quoted than "let every nation know, whether it wishes us well or ill, that we shall pay any price, bear any burden, meet any hardship, support any friend, oppose any foe to assure the survival and the success of liberty. This much we pledge— and more." But in fact a dual theme ran through the address— and presidency—in which Kennedy raised "the arrows and the olive branch" simultaneously, to employ Sorensen's terminology.[4] Even though promoting military strength and global commitment, Kennedy also sought peace through negotiation, cooperation, and arms limitation. "Civility is not a sign of weakness," he stressed. He proposed a new beginning in United States–Soviet relations, which he knew concerned Americans greatly.

This dual approach partly reflected political realities. Kennedy strove to accommodate hardliners in his own party as well as Republicans who accused Democrats of softness on communism. At the same time he pragmatically sought the approbation of Democratic liberals who favored defusing cold war issues. The address also reinforced his continual identification with an emerging global nationalism and his acceptance that nations could be neutral in the cold war. He made no mention of domestic goals because of their divisive nature.

Kennedy's address won the approval of both liberals and conservatives. The *New Republic* focused on its fresh, conciliatory, and optimistic perspective, essential for better relations with the Soviets. The *National Review*, meanwhile, applauded its strong defense of the containment policy and its lack of reference to "welfarism." The *New York Times* thought it "superb," praising its efforts to find common ground with the Communists. The *Washington Post* and the *Chicago Tribune* also responded favorably, as did Nikita Khrushchev of the USSR, Prime Minister Harold Macmillan of Great Britain, President Charles de Gaulle of France, and Senators Everett Dirksen (R.-Ill.), Barry Goldwater (R.-Ariz.), and Hubert Humphrey (D.-Minn.).

Following the address Kennedy spent most of the afternoon at the reviewing stand, in twenty-degree weather, watching the parade as some forty-one floats and seventy-two bands passed by. That evening he and Jacqueline attended inaugural balls and parties. On several occasions he abandoned her to attend other galas, including Frank Sinatra's, where he mingled with Angie Dickinson, Kim Novak, and other Hollywood celebrities; afterward he stopped by the Georgetown home of Joseph Alsop for a postinaugural party. By the time he returned to the White House, it was 3:30 A.M; Jackie had retired several hours earlier. Anyone still doubting the stamina and vigor of the new president could rapidly put that concern aside. No one had enjoyed himself more that day.

The next day Kennedy was on the job before 9:00 A.M., the designated time for the staff swearing-in ceremony. Also that morning the president acquainted himself with the Oval Office, which was bare except for a dilapidated desk and rug. The cork floor contained small holes thought to be caused by termites, until close inspection revealed that Eisenhower's golf shoes had created the problem; apparently he had walked back and forth between the putting green outside and the Oval Office without changing shoes. By the next week Kennedy had had the office repainted from a "nauseous" green to an off-white. He brought in pictures of Jackie and their children, Caroline and John, and a watercolor painting by Jackie. His refinished desk, constructed from the timbers of the British HMS *Resolute*, was a nineteenth-century creation found in the White House basement. It soon contained personal mementos, such as pieces of scrimshaw—bits of whale teeth etched with sailing ship designs—and various reminders of the PT-109 episode. Naval paintings, ship models, and flags would also adorn the office.

JFK, as the press frequently called him, came to the Oval Office with an exalted view of the presidency. He sought to be a strong, active president in the Democratic tradition of Woodrow Wilson, Franklin Roosevelt, and Harry Truman. He adopted the conventional wisdom that great presidents were powerful instruments who advanced social justice at home and American interests abroad. He had said as much at the National Press Club on 14 January 1960: "We will need in the sixties a President who is willing and able to summon his national constituency to its finest hour— and to alert the people to our dangers and opportunities—to demand of them the sacrifices that will be necessary."[5] That September he also suggested that "if this nation is to reassert the initiative in foreign affairs, it must be presidential initiative. If we are to rebuild our prestige in the eyes of the world, it must be presidential prestige. And if we are to regain progressive leadership on our domestic problems, it must be presidential leadership. If the President does not move, if his party is opposed to progress then the Nation does not move—and there is no progress."[6]

He often contrasted himself to Eisenhower, who had supposedly weakened the nation by a failure to lead, creating a vacuum that the legislative branch was ill-equipped to fill. Whether Kennedy was aware of Ike's "hidden-hand" leadership is irrelevant. Eisenhower had conveyed the image of a tired, aging leader of an outmoded party, an image that Kennedy exploited in 1960. Moreover, Kennedy accepted the premise of Arthur Schlesinger, Jr., that America stood cyclically "on the threshold of a new political era, and that vigorous public leadership would be the essence of the next phase."[7] He had based his campaign on that assumption, believing perhaps that he could accelerate change. The negative

29

effects of such an extended presidential commitment were something that Kennedy—and the American people—failed to consider.

Kennedy's conception of presidential leadership meant more than moral and legislative leadership: He wished to unleash the president from the office of the presidency. He believed that Eisenhower had so institutionalized the presidency that he was no longer free to act. Kennedy specifically objected to the extent to which Eisenhower had shared power with the cabinet (which met weekly); the chief of staff, Sherman Adams; and the National Security Council (NSC), created in 1947 to advise the president on foreign and defense policy. The NSC especially became a formidable body under Eisenhower, with its newly created planning board that defined issues placed before it; the Operations Coordinating Board, which ensured that decisions were carried out; and the special assistant for National Security Affairs, the White House liaison. To this Ike proposed to add a first secretary of the government to oversee all foreign affairs agencies. In short Kennedy saw a ponderous bureaucratic system, resulting in group or corporate decisions.

As president, Kennedy proved less willing to delegate executive power outside the Oval Office. His staff, far smaller than Eisenhower's or Johnson's, consisted for the most part of loyalists from the Senate or his campaign staff, many of them still in their thirties. They remained completely devoted to Kennedy and knew exactly what he wanted. In delegating considerable responsibility to them, Kennedy felt certain that they represented his interests and will; he called them a ''band of brothers,'' fictionalizing a harmony and fraternal spirit that he knew never existed. Only their loyalty to him masked occasional jealousies and rivalries. Many staff members were actually less self-assured than myth would have it. If they sometimes appeared brash, it concealed insecurities, particularly during the first year.[8] Never did they meet with Kennedy collectively; he thought formal, regular meetings a waste of time. His relationship with some staffers was so close that they communicated effectively with a minimum of conversation. They also knew, despite his levity and casualness, that he disliked small talk.

Unlike his predecessor, Kennedy eschewed a chief of staff to coordinate staff activities and insulate him from administration officials or congressmen. He relied instead on several senior staff members, including his appointments secretary, the taciturn and abrasive Kenneth O'Donnell, who handled arrangements and served as political adviser. O'Donnell jealously guarded entry into the Oval Office, making it potentially difficult even for staffers to see the president. Kennedy consequently relied on his personal secretary, Evelyn Lincoln, to act as a safety valve to enable staffers and others to enter from her office. Staff members had open access to the president, knowing that if the Oval Office door were ajar they were free to enter. Those whom Kennedy had less reason to see had to face O'Donnell.

Few senior staffers saw the president more than special counsel Sorensen, whom Kennedy called his "intellectual blood bank." Operating out of the White House west wing, he assisted Kennedy in developing domestic policies and programs and in expressing them in messages to Congress and in speeches. His greatest influence remained as speech writer, where he could incorporate ideas into drafts that committed JFK to positions or policies consistent with Kennedy's political philosophy. Only someone sensitive to the president's nuances and to the times could have served in this way. By 1961 Sorensen more and more mirrored Kennedy's caution and pragmatism on most domestic issues.

Sorensen drove himself relentlessly in the early months, working around the clock to draft presidential messages to Congress for a legislative program that included education, health, defense, natural resources, and agriculture. Assisting him were aides—Myer (Mike) Feldman, Lee White, and Richard Goodwin. Sorensen assigned White to housing, natural resources, education, and eventually to civil rights matters. Feldman handled most of the other domestic areas, including agriculture. Next to Sorensen, he wrote most of the presidential messages to Congress. Goodwin remained a speech writer until Kennedy named him deputy assistant secretary of state for inter-American affairs late in 1961. Sorensen oversaw staff assignments and most of the paper work conducted in the president's name. He monitored the activities of special assistant to the president Harris Wofford, who reported to the president on civil rights and the Peace Corps.

Kennedy sometimes assigned work to staffers, often on the basis of who happened to be in the Oval Office at the time. Assuming that staffers were generalists, he on occasion asked Feldman to handle a foreign policy matter because he was handy. Schlesinger, an assistant on domestic affairs, became the adviser for Latin American affairs and the United Nations partly because he had been in the president's office when those subjects needed attention. Kennedy also tended to assign tasks on the basis of a staffer's previous experience. Thus he put Feldman in charge of all executive orders after he had struggled through the administration's first effort.[9]

Like other senior staffers, Pierre Salinger frequented the Oval Office. Gregarious and cherubic, "Plucky" was as talkative and good-natured as Sorensen and O'Donnell were silent and serious; he brought humor and brashness to press briefings. Following Kennedy's 1960 election victory and obviously in his cups, he elatedly told reporters that if "the

31

Eisenhower administration was noted for its golf, the Kennedy administration would be known for its f——ing."[10] He became a comic fall guy
for the president, who liked a good laugh. One staffer remembered,
"after the President had had a hard day, Pierre would wander into the
office, and Kennedy would stick his cigar in his mouth and lower his voice
and snarl at him, 'Dammit, Salinger, you've fouled us up again.' It didn't
mean anything; it just helped him unwind."[11] Salinger's plump appearance and good humor belied a hard-working and shrewd nature. He had
come from a journalistic background before joining Robert Kennedy as an
investigator on the Senate Rackets Committee in 1957; after that he had
successfully handled press relations during the campaign.

As press secretary, however, Salinger paled next to his Republican
predecessor, the efficient and knowledgeable James Hagerty. Salinger's
preparation and information left something to be desired, but this was
often beyond Salinger's control, for the president preferred to deal directly with the press on major issues, doing so with considerable skill and
charm. Salinger's job was to work closely with him on press releases and
briefings, before employing a blusterous humor and quick wit to make up
for deficiencies in news. Reporters genuinely liked Salinger and found it
difficult to remain angry with him.

Salinger's great influence as an innovative image builder was revealed when, despite the opposition of Sorensen and others, he persuaded the president to hold press conferences before live television to
provide "more direct communications with the people." Kennedy, a success on TV in the past, ignored the potential risks, which had deterred
previous presidents from performing live. As it turned out Kennedy's
televised press conferences proved to be a smashing success. Salinger
also engineered Kennedy's magnificent live interview with three leading
correspondents on national, prime-time television—George E. Herman,
William H. Lawrence, and Sander Vanocur—on 17 December 1962. This
sort of focus partly influenced two of the major networks to expand their
news coverage from a fifteen minute to a half-hour evening format, enabling anchormen Walter Cronkite and Chet Huntley to devote more time
to the Kennedy presidency. Because of Salinger, Kennedy became the
first American president to be interviewed by a Russian journalist. That
antiwar interview, published in Izvestia, circulated throughout Russia for
months, resulting in favorable world reaction. Salinger's friendship with
Khrushchev's son-in-law and editor of Izvestia—Aleksei Adzhubei—and
with other Soviet officials also improved relations with the Soviet Union.

On matters of foreign policy, Kennedy relied mostly on McGeorge
Bundy, special assistant for national security affairs, who quickly carried
out Kennedy's instructions to streamline the NSC. He abolished the

NSC-related boards and some fifty interdepartmental committees and cut the national security staff from about seventy-five to fifty people. Bundy's job was to present Kennedy with clear alternatives on problems of foreign policy and to oversee the bureaucracy. To assist him Bundy had a ten- to fifteen- member staff, including experts in European affairs, economics, intelligence, and communications. Kennedy meanwhile relied little on the NSC, as meetings were reduced to monthly affairs to brief members or to rubber-stamp already agreed-upon decisions.

Bundy's office became more significant following Kennedy's growing disenchantment with the State Department for its lack of fresh approaches and its dilatoriness, which caused Kennedy to remark, "Damn it, Bundy and I get more done in one day . . . than they do in six months in the State Department."[12] In the aftermath of the Bay of Pigs, Bundy moved his office from the Executive Office Building to the west-wing basement, where a communications center was established, containing teletype machines to receive messages from military, diplomatic, and intelligence centers around the world. That same information went to State, Defense, and the CIA. In essence Bundy's operation began to duplicate the work of the State Department as it gathered material on the Common Market, NATO troop levels, Cuba, and Vietnam.

Bundy became the first of the powerful national security advisers. He saw the president as often as four times a day compared to the four-times-a-week visits of his counterpart in the Eisenhower presidency. Bundy supplanted Secretary of State Rusk as the primary foreign policy adviser even though Kennedy continued to listen to Rusk, McNamara, and others. After the Bay of Pigs debacle Kennedy also turned to Sorensen and Robert Kennedy, gravitating to the best minds of his administration. In the end he relied on his own judgment in making key decisions. No president kept a tighter rein on foreign policy, yet few presidents learned to listen to as many divergent viewpoints.

Kennedy, however, depended much less on the cabinet than had his Republican predecessor. Always the outsider, he favored White House staffers—people he had long known and trusted—over the permanent government of which cabinet members were a part. He found cabinet meetings particularly useless, once asking, "Why should the Postmaster General sit there and listen to a discussion of the problem of Laos?"[13] Cabinet meetings also lent themselves to vague discussions, self-interested presentations, and lobbying efforts, all inviting Kennedy's displeasure. Consequently, he kept meetings to a minimum—one a month, some of which he canceled—and he worked closely with Frederick Dutton, special assistant to the president, to set the agenda. Dutton's counterpart in the Eisenhower administration had held the inflated title of secretary of the cabinet, an indication of the significant and formal role the cabinet played in Ike's presidency.

Kennedy used cabinet meetings mostly for briefings or matters of general concern, such as budgetary considerations, but he never employed them as an instrument for decision making. Policy evolved out of small, ad hoc meetings of staffers, cabinet members, and others in the Oval Office. There Kennedy listened intently in his rocking chair before asking pointed questions and coming to a decision. Staffers had the authority to make decisions without Kennedy's presence. Yet not even Sorensen, Feldman later claimed, had the right to make final judgments as Sherman Adams could do in the Eisenhower administration. Staffers cleared all significant decisions orally with Kennedy.

Kennedy's reluctance to meet regularly with the cabinet did not sit well with cabinet members. Some felt cut off or left out; others sincerely believed that Kennedy would have benefited from free-wheeling and frank discussions. Secretary of Agriculture Orville Freeman especially regretted that Kennedy neglected to discuss fiscal policies with the cabinet. Stewart Udall, secretary of the interior, also felt that the president failed to utilize a politically sagacious group who represented the "eyes and ears of the country."[14] Such responses suggest that Kennedy's under-utilization of the cabinet not only deprived him of open exchanges that might have assisted policy but also created morale problems that led to resignations.

Kennedy preferred to communicate in less direct ways. It was standard operating procedure that each cabinet member submit a weekly synopsis of his most significant activities. Such summaries became so lengthy that Kennedy had Dutton reduce them to five or six pages. The president read them religiously, often scrawling in the margin such cryptic comments as "I want more information . . . on this."[15] Sometimes he phoned a cabinet member for clarification.

Kennedy also communicated with cabinet members through the White House staff. Particularly on policy or budgetary matters cabinet personnel were expected to work through Sorensen's office. For example, Postmaster General Day, Hodges of the Commerce Department, Dillon of Treasury, and Freeman ordinarily went to Feldman; Abraham Ribicoff of HEW generally saw Sorensen; White handled issues related to civil rights. Staff members had the authority to speak for Kennedy on most matters, and they also reviewed reports and memoranda and asked penetrating questions. Sorensen in particular sometimes came across as "very abrupt and highly critical."[16] If differences occurred between a staffer and a cabinet member or if an issue were especially significant, Kennedy became directly involved. Otherwise he stayed away from most departmental activities to concentrate on foreign affairs; consequently the White House staff discouraged most cabinet personnel from bothering the president. Some resented that approach, particularly Ribicoff, who felt that he had become a "lackey" for the president's assistants. By 1962 he had returned to Connecticut to run for the United States Senate. Hodges showed his displeasure by including an item in the June 1961 cabinet agenda, "a candid discussion with the President on relationships with the White House staff," a point Kennedy ignored.[17]

Yet Kennedy frequently met with certain cabinet members. No one was closer to him than his brother, whose devotion and affection were unlimited. Their relationship uniquely enabled Robert to challenge him when he thought him wrong; no one was more persistent and candid in giving advice. The president respected him especially for his frankness, his organizational skills, his compassion, and his high moral standards. He came to rely on him as a lightning rod for untested ideas and as a personal adviser. Not since Roger Taney of the Andrew Jackson administration did an attorney general have as much access to a president. Yet Kennedy never hesitated to reject his advice, nor did he always consult him on important matters. Bobby was particularly sensitive about the president's failure to use cabinet members more effectively. He expressed the frustrations of Freeman and others, as well as his own, in a confidential memorandum written less than eight months before Kennedy's death:

> The best minds in Government should be utilized in finding solutions to . . . major problems. They should be available in times other than deep deep crisis and emergencies as is now the case. You talk to McNamara but mostly on Defense matters, you talk to Dillon but primarily on financial questions. . . . These men should be sitting down and thinking of some of the problems facing us in a broader text. I think you could get a good deal more out of what is available in Government than you are at the present time.[18]

Next to his brother, Kennedy summoned Rusk, McNamara, and Dillon to the Oval Office the most because of their links to international affairs and national defense. Rusk sometimes saw the president two or three times a day during crises and at least two times a week otherwise. However, he rarely met with Kennedy alone. A quiet, gentle, unassuming, and cautious man, Rusk never dominated these meetings, nor did he eagerly express foreign policy recommendations while others were around. He sought to moderate, not to influence, foreign policy debate. As secretary of state he felt that he should present recommendations to the president privately, a procedure Kennedy found amusing. He quipped that when they were alone "Rusk would whisper that there was still one too many persons present."[19] Rusk never became personally close to Kennedy; he was the only cabinet member whom the president did not address by his first name. Kennedy drew closer to the frank, incisive, and bold McNamara and Dillon, who eventually rivaled senior staffers and Robert Kennedy as trusted advisers. No cabinet member used Evelyn Lincoln's Oval Office entrance more than Dillon. Rusk meanwhile seemed content to work through Bundy in dealing with the White House, lacking the forcefulness to penetrate the palace guard.

No cabinet official found it more difficult to see the president than Postmaster General Day. He came to the Oval Office only five or six times a year, partly because of Kennedy's belief that the Post Office Department ought to be an administrative agency rather than a cabinet office. After 1961 Kennedy saw Freeman nearly as infrequently, for nothing bored him more than agricultural policy, particularly after legislative failures occurred. Also, Freeman was not aggressive—or conservative—enough to win Kennedy over on other issues. For similar reasons, Kennedy saw little of Interior Secretary Udall, known as a poor administrator. He also gave Commerce Secretary Hodges little encouragement because he was perceived as dull and taking too long "to say hello."[20]

Nevertheless, Kennedy did meet with individual cabinet members between Christmas and New Year's at the family winter home in Palm Beach, Florida. The trip was labeled a working holiday, and Kennedy spent time relaxing by the pool when he was not meeting with Sorensen, Budget Director David Bell, and other administrative officials. Their task was to formulate the legislative program and the proposed budget for the coming year. Cabinet members came and went to review departmental recommendations. In the weeks and months ahead, departmental heads worked closely with the White House staff to finish various legislative proposals.

The White House coordinated the lobbying efforts, once bills were introduced. The person in charge was Kennedy-intimate Larry O'Brien, special assistant to the president for congressional relations, who reported directly to the president; this put him on the same level with O'Donnell, Sorensen, and Bundy. Outgoing, diplomatic, and bright, O'Brien had served briefly as a congressional assistant prior to his involvement with the Kennedy campaigns. His small staff included Mike Manatos of Wyoming, a one-time Senate aide, to lobby the Senate and Henry Hall Wilson, a youthful North Carolina lawyer and politician, assigned to the House of Representatives. Wilson's southern roots made him more acceptable to southern and border-state Democrats, a group crucial to administration successes. Assisting Wilson, Richard K. Donahue and Charles U. Daly were to "hand hold" neglected liberal Democrats from urban and industrial areas. Overall, O'Brien's staff represented youth, congressional inexperience, and a pro-Kennedy leaning in past party politics.

O'Brien's goal was to build "an invisible bridge down Pennsylvania Avenue" from the White House to the Capitol. In order to do this he took control of some forty congressional liaison officers from the federal departments and agencies who had previously bargained directly with friends in Congress, regardless of the president's legislative priorities. O'Brien required them to attend weekly meetings and to file reports on their relations with Congress. His approach reflected the characteristic Kennedy viewpoint that the permanent government must follow the White House lead. O'Brien's influence extended even to private lobbies such as the AFL-CIO.

Never before was such an energetic lobbying operation orchestrated from the White House. Initially lobbying had been an ad hoc activity; the Eisenhower administration had established a White House office of congressional relations, leading to a systematic, permanent, and continuous effort. The office lacked presidential backing, however, and concentrated on opposing Democratic initiatives rather than on pushing administrative programs. Too, the Eisenhower people, influenced by Ike's strong sensitivity to separation of powers, stayed away from the Capitol, conducting most of their business over the phone. Of course, all of this changed during the Kennedy era; O'Brien sought personal contact on Capitol Hill to sell the Kennedy programs.

Kennedy knew that it would not be easy. The 1960 election had added twenty-one Republicans to the House and two to the Senate. The Democrats still controlled the House, 263 to 174, and the Senate, 64 to 36; but a conservative coalition of Republicans and southern Democrats had frustrated progressive legislation since the close of Roosevelt's second term. In the House that coalition controlled 285 of the 437 members; in the Senate, 59 out of 96. Southern Democrats headed twelve of twenty House committees, including Armed Services, Rules, and Ways and Means; and they chaired ten of the sixteen Senate committees, including Armed Services, Finance, Foreign Relations, and Judiciary.

The securing of southern Democratic votes became the White House's top priority even though it also hoped to attract some liberal and moderate Republican support. O'Brien received the immediate cooperation of the Senate Democratic leadership, including Mike Mansfield (Mont.), the Senate majority leader. The support of House Speaker Sam Rayburn (Tex.) came a bit more slowly, but Rayburn and other Democrats soon worked closely with administration lobbyists. The tactful O'Brien charmed politicos at get-acquainted cocktail parties and in the Capitol corridors and offices, coming across as knowledgeable, likeable, and a man of his word. He proceeded slowly and carefully with southern Democrats. "We tried to . . . make them just a little bit more liberal than they were. Many of them were anxious to help us out, and we had this going for us."[21]

O'Brien began with persuasion and education. He and his lieutenants apprised legislators of impending measures and suggested ways in which that legislation would benefit their home districts or states. O'Brien had the authority to alter a bill to accommodate the opposition. If still unsuccessful, he could resort to patronage. Even though the official responsibility for job patronage fell to John Bailey, chairman of the Democratic National Committee, O'Brien's office managed it on a day-to-day basis, adopting the maxim that good news came from the White House and bad news came from the Democratic National Committee in notifying congressmen about patronage decisions relating to postmasterships, judgeships, and other government appointments. In rarer instances, O'Brien secured federal grants and contracts for various congressional districts, particularly Democratic ones. Of course in return for their support the district congressionals became the political beneficiaries of such assistance.

If these approaches failed, O'Brien then turned to the power and authority of the president. Kennedy made little impact upon the legislative process despite his Tuesday morning leadership breakfasts, frequent private conversations with legislative leaders, and coffee hours for the rank and file. The limitations were glaring in the light of his desire to be a strong president and have become even more so, given the legislative achievements of his successor, Lyndon Baines Johnson.

Kennedy's reputation as an outsider contributed to his ineffectiveness. Despite fourteen years in the Congress he had made few close friends there. Detached, independent, and harboring presidential aspirations, he had never penetrated the inner circle; Senator Richard Russell (D.-Ga.), Rayburn, and Johnson had had only nominal contact with him. If anything Kennedy impressed them as being overly ambitious, inexperienced, and overrated. Nor would his narrow presidential victory obligate the congressional leadership to his liberal legislative agenda, particularly since he had surrounded himself with advisers who were even younger—and much more inexperienced—than he was.

Kennedy's style also affected his legislative performance. Part of the problem was a formality and privacy that too often intruded upon his wit and charm. Senator Claiborne Pell (D.-R.I.) remembered that Kennedy did not like putting his arm around other men; Senator Edmund Muskie

(D.-Maine) referred to a "submissive desire on the part of senators and congressmen to have a personal relationship . . . and a feeling of frustration that it wasn't there."[22] Others likewise mentioned that same lack of intimacy—that incapacity for expressing warmth or admiration—for those whom he did not respect. Congressmen liked Kennedy, but they did not feel close—or personally obligated—to him.

Other critics focused more on his unwillingness to fight or work harder for his programs. According to Republican Senator Leverett Saltonstall (Mass.), Kennedy relied too much on his staff and the congressional leadership. O'Brien concurred that he "rarely asked a member for his vote. . . . That was not his style. If there were arms to be twisted, that was our job."[23] Instead of cajoling or bargaining with Congress, according to Senator Pell, Kennedy resorted to reason; if that failed, he surmised that the time was not ripe. He was sensitive about pushing Congress too hard, not wanting to jeopardize other administrative proposals. "Great innovations," Kennedy quoted Jefferson, "should not be forced on slender majorities." He preferred to delay until the climate or the numbers changed. At least one staffer, Charles Daly, attributed Kennedy's inaction to an unwillingness to cut into the more pleasurable activities of his office. Even Schlesinger conceded that working with Congress "was [not] the part of the Presidency which gave him the greatest pleasure or satisfaction." His predilection for compromising too soon on programs compounded the problem. Congressmen, according to administrative assistant Wilbur Cohen, consequently looked upon Kennedy as a "nice boy who could [not] get what he wanted." Senator Allen Ellender (D.-La.) knew no president "less aggressive," and House Ways and Means Chairman Wilbur Mills (D.-Ark.) referred to his "timid approach."[24] Whatever the reasons, Kennedy was not a strong president in dealing with Congress.

Kennedy might have made better use of Vice-President Lyndon Johnson, the once-powerful Senate majority leader, but that proved difficult. Johnson accepted the vice-presidential nomination partly because of a belief that "power is where power goes." He thought that he could transform that office into an imposing instrument by becoming chairman of the Democratic conference, which would enable him to preside at formal meetings of the Senate's Democratic members. Seventeen Democrats opposed the move, supposedly because it violated the separation of powers; in reality several senators resented the possibility of his remaining their leader. Johnson, correctly interpreting the rebuff as a personal rejection, never attended another caucus and retreated into a shell. Others confirm that his heart was no longer in the legislative process.

Furthermore, several Kennedy advisers disliked the coarse Texan.

The president's brother, who had strongly opposed Johnson's selection in 1960, remained hostile, or so Johnson thought. His feelings toward Robert Kennedy were reciprocal as he confided to an intimate, "I don't like that little son-of-a-bitch and I never will."[25] Friction between the two continued; so too did slights from staffers. Johnson especially resented their calling him Lyndon rather than Mr. Vice-President. Lee White later admitted neglecting to inform Johnson properly—if at all—about meetings on civil rights, an area of involvement for Johnson. On one occasion White failed to produce enough copies of a memo, forcing the vice-president to look over White's shoulder to read it.[26]

Outwardly, relations between the president and Johnson remained cordial. Kennedy had come to the presidency with respect and affection for Johnson; at the same time, Johnson's crude, comic, and aggressive ways had amused Kennedy. He laughingly—and admiringly—referred to him as "that god-damned river boat gambler."[27] As president, Kennedy sought ways to involve Johnson in meaningful activity. Johnson chaired the President's Committee on Equal Employment Opportunity and the Space Council. Kennedy invited him to attend cabinet meetings, many of the ad hoc sessions in the Oval Office, and various briefings, seeking his counsel on many matters. Johnson also represented the president in functions at home and abroad. Even so, Kennedy failed to consult him about the Bay of Pigs, the steel crisis of 1962, and more surprisingly, the forced integration of James Meredith into the student body at the University of Mississippi that same year.

Apparently neither could overcome completely the natural, inevitable antagonism that exists between a president and a vice-president, particularly if the latter is politically senior to the former. It seemed as if Kennedy could never do enough to satisfy Johnson's enormous ego and energies. At the outset Johnson had unprecedentedly requested an office next to the president's. Kennedy confided that he had "never heard of such a thing" and gave him an office in the Executive Office Building across the street.[28] Immediately following the inauguration, Johnson sent an executive order for Kennedy's signature that in its audacity rivaled Secretary of State William Seward's April 1861 memorandum to President Lincoln, a fact not lost to senior staffers. Just as Seward had sought extraordinary powers on the eve of the Civil War, Johnson too requested "general supervision" over a wide range of issues. He also required that all departments and agencies supply him with reports, policy plans, and information that generally went to the president.[29] Kennedy followed Lincoln's lead in burying the memo, further frustrating the vice-president. It also bothered Johnson that his advice was frequently ignored at Oval Office meetings. "Bobby is first in and last out," he told journalist Jack Bell. "And Bobby is the boy he listens to."[30] Johnson reacted by frequently descending on Kennedy with complaints about the attorney general and others in the White House, a matter that Kennedy handled with courtesy and patience.

"There were times," according to Benjamin Bradlee of *Newsweek*, "when LBJ's simple presence [seemed] to bug" Kennedy.[31] This transcended considerations of personality. The vice-president's primary duty, Kennedy understood, was to await the president's death, inviting an inevitable antagonism. Johnson sensed the dilemma: "Everytime I came into John Kennedy's presence, I felt like a goddam raven hovering over his shoulder."[32] Ultimately, Johnson failed to transform the office of the vice-presidency, nor could Kennedy use him effectively in dealing with Congress.

Kennedy had greater opportunity to influence the Supreme Court, for two Court resignations occurred during his presidency. In spring 1962 Justice Charles E. Whittaker quit because of poor health, and later that year the seventy-nine-year-old Justice Felix Frankfurter retired. Both were identified with the Court's majority conservative bloc, which favored judicial restraint. They often voted to uphold lower-court criminal actions, congressional and state enactments, and federal and state administrative decisions. Meanwhile, the Court's activist liberal wing, led by Chief Justice Earl Warren, pressed for a more literal observance of the Bill of Rights, especially regarding First Amendment guarantees of speech, press, religion, and association. The activists often sought to reverse decisions and actions coming from lower courts and administrative and legislative bodies. With the Court almost evenly divided, Kennedy's appointments would likely affect future cases of civil rights and personal liberties.

In March 1962 Kennedy appointed Byron "Whizzer" White to replace Whittaker. An all-American halfback at the University of Colorado, a Rhodes Scholar, and a naval veteran, the balding and bespectacled White had become an avid Kennedy backer in 1960 and had served as assistant attorney general, managing the day-to-day operations of the Justice Department. No Kennedy adviser had recommended White for the court. Robert Kennedy had first suggested William H. Hastie, a hard-working black Harvard Law School graduate and circuit court judge; the attorney general believed that "it would mean so much overseas that we had a Negro on the Supreme Court." He consulted Chief Justice Warren, who balked because "he's not a liberal and he'll be opposed to all measures we are interested in, and he would be completely unsatisfactory."[33] Justice William Douglas concurred. Sorensen also opposed Hastie because Kennedy was considering another black, Robert C. Weaver, for a cabinet

41

post, inviting the charge of reverse racism. Sorensen, who studiously considered the options, argued that "the first appointment should be one hailed by all for his judicial mien."[34] He recommended Harvard law professor Paul Freund. Kennedy objected, supposedly because of Freund's Harvard pedigree, too many of which already graced the administration. He ended up appointing White, whom he had known and admired in college and now especially respected. To Kennedy, Byron White combined physical and mental excellence; he was tough, cool, and non-ideological, everything a New Frontiersman should be. Yet White not only lacked judicial experience, he remained at best a moderate. He failed to bring to the Court a deep commitment to civil liberties and racial justice, and he soon sided with the conservative bloc, particularly on decisions involving personal liberties and race.

Kennedy's nomination of Arthur J. Goldberg in September 1962 proved to be his most significant Court appointment. Goldberg was so well respected as labor secretary that the president felt he was losing "his right arm." Moreover, Sorensen, at the time of Whittaker's resignation, had advised Kennedy to save Goldberg as a possible Chief Justice. Frankfurter's retirement politically required Kennedy to replace him with another Jew; consequently, Goldberg's liberal beliefs seemed not as significant as his religion and proven ability. Yet Goldberg enabled the Court's liberal wing to obtain a slim edge, leading to a series of five-to-four decisions on cases of personal liberty. Furthermore, few defended civil rights as emphatically as Goldberg. Without Goldberg's leadership, the Warren Court would not have reached the preeminence it had by the mid-1960s.

Below the Supreme Court level, Kennedy generally played little part in judicial appointments. Neither did the attorney general, who delegated most of the responsibility of selection to subordinates. Yet few administrations had appointed more federal judges to the circuit and district courts. The Omnibus bill of spring 1961, increasing the number of judges, enabled the administration to make 130 appointments in less than three years, which compares favorably with Eisenhower's record-setting 201 selections for an eight-year period. In early 1961 Kennedy outlined the standard for nomination when he suggested that those selected must be "men and women of unquestioned ability."

At the same time the administration customarily sought candidates from the party faithful. Of concern was whether they were hostile to Kennedy, but another consideration related to a candidate's endorsement by the American Bar Association. The Kennedy administration proved more willing to ignore an ABA recommendation than Eisenhower's had been because of a reluctance to give that group a veto power and because of differences over criteria for appointments. (The Kennedy people, for example, favored qualities of mind and character over "an easy familiarity with the courtroom.") More difficult to ignore was the influence of administration senators who made judicial appointments "with the advice and consent of the president." Kennedy consequently was expected to defer to segregationist senators who chaired key committees. Since none was more powerful than Senator James Eastland (D.-Miss.), chairman of the Senate Judiciary Committee, the president and attorney general soon became involved in some decisions over judicial nominations.

How successful was the administration in selecting "men and women of unquestioned ability?" Even Victor Navasky's critical *Kennedy Justice* concedes that the Kennedys named "more decent judges than dishonest, incompetent or racist ones."[35] More than 91 percent of the appointments were Democrats, which differed little from the Roosevelt and Truman percentages (Ike had appointed 92.5 percent Republicans). Ten of Kennedy's appointments in the North were blacks, including Thurgood Marshall of the Second Circuit Court of Appeals. The administration gave less attention to women, although Sarah T. Hughes, who later swore in Johnson as president of the United States, received a judgeship.

Yet even Schlesinger refers to the Kennedy judicial appointments in the South as "disastrous."[36] There the administration had failed to meet its objectives of selecting "people who would uphold the law of the land." Five out of twenty appointments in the Fifth Circuit (six states of the Deep South) were segregationists, including the notorious William Harold Cox of Mississippi. Cox, who had been a college roommate of Eastland, had his enthusiastic endorsement. Without appointing Cox, Kennedy probably would not have had the Judiciary Committee's approval of Marshall or its support on other appointments and issues. Besides, Cox had obtained the ABA's rating of Extremely Well Qualified and had promised the attorney general that holding up the Constitution "would never be a problem." Nevertheless, Roy Wilkins, executive secretary of the NAACP, prophetically warned that "for 986,000 Negro Mississippians, Judge Cox will be another strand in their barbed-wire fence, another cross on their weary shoulders and another rock in the road up which their young people must struggle."[37] Significantly, the Eisenhower administration in 1955 had rejected Cox. William Rogers, deputy attorney general, literally laughed at Eastland's recommendation. In any case, within weeks after Cox's appointment, he referred to Negro litigants as "niggers" and unlawfully obstructed black voting registration drives and other civil rights activities in Mississippi.

Carl Brauer provides the most sympathetic assessment of the administration's difficulties. Besides having to deal with powerful southern senators who favored their own judicial candidates, the Kennedy administration had to accept the fact that civil rights sympathizers in the Deep South were ostracized. Consequently their judicial or legal careers were not prominent enough to qualify them for federal judicial appointment, nor did they have the necessary political connections.[38] Still, the southern judges appointed under Eisenhower had at least as good a record in civil rights, despite Kennedy's pledge to do more for black America. Even more a contradiction was Kennedy's decision to forgo civil rights legislation and executive action for litigation while appointing southern judges to frustrate that effort.

In organizing his administration, however, Kennedy believed that issues related to foreign policy would make or break it and predictably gave his greatest attention to that area. Just as predictably, the administration's initial problems came in the arena of foreign policy.

3

★ ★ ★ ★ ★

YEAR OF CRISES AND CONFLICT

The Kennedy foreign policy belonged to a new generation of leadership—to former junior officers of World War II who had become impatient with the supposedly stagnant national leadership of the 1950s. Like many of his middle-aged counterparts, John Kennedy understood the folly of appeasement and the necessity of strength and sacrifice for the national interest. His presidential campaign against the Eisenhower administration had been a crusade to "get America moving again." He had chided Republicans for having permitted the rise of communism in Cuba and in other Third World countries. He had made much of a "missile gap," signifying the United States' supposed loss of nuclear superiority. That notion had come from studies by the Eisenhower administration, made public by Secretary of Defense Neil McElroy, who had predicted in 1959 a three-to-one advantage for the Soviet Union in intercontinental ballistic missiles by the early 1960s. Kennedy advocated the acceleration of missile programs and the expansion of conventional forces so that the United States could negotiate with the Soviet Union, quoting Churchill that "you arm to parley."

Yet Kennedy became a victim of his own rhetoric. Having promised to act tougher and do more, he limited his options in foreign policy. Furthermore he negated his open-mindedness about communism and his belief that nuclear-arms agreements were possible. Kennedy's foreign policy becomes more understandable when one considers the Democratic party's vulnerability to the charge of being soft on communism, originating in the 1950s.

Khrushchev's national liberation speech, delivered two weeks before Kennedy's inauguration, further hardened the president. The Soviet chairman had proclaimed the ultimate triumph of communism. It would come, he said, not through nuclear or conventional war but through "national liberation wars in the Third World." He called Asia, Africa, and Latin America "the most important centers of revolutionary struggle against imperialism," and he pledged Soviet support to those areas. "Communists are revolutionaries," he asserted, "and it would be a bad thing if they did not take advantage of new opportunities."[1] An alarmed Kennedy made the NSC and key military personnel read the speech although he viewed it as a calculated personal test as much as an expression of Soviet policy. Because of the cold war environment of the 1960s it was virtually impossible to understand that Khrushchev's harangue was more a message to Communist China than a challenge to the United States. Amid a growing Soviet-China conflict Khrushchev sought to persuade the world Communist movement that peaceful coexistence and revolutionary militancy were compatible, a belief that a more militant China opposed.

Thus the militant aspects of Kennedy's inaugural address two weeks later reflected his concern with Khrushchev's remarks. Kennedy became further convinced that he needed to shift and strengthen military priorities. A critic of Eisenhower's doctrine of massive retaliation, he believed even more that the United States needed to bolster its conventional forces. Retired Gen. Maxwell Taylor's *Uncertain Trumpet* (1960) reinforced that belief, as did Secretary of Defense Robert McNamara's report that only fourteen American combat divisions existed, of which only eleven were combat ready. According to McNamara only three were deployed in the United States, meaning that the nation had little strategic reserve with which to respond to emergencies elsewhere. Moreover, there was a shortage of ammunition, armored personnel carriers, recoilless rifles, and other materiel. A weak airlift capacity, resulting primarily from obsolescent planes, compounded the problem. The tactical air force was no better: Of the sixteen wings of fighter bombers, more than three-quarters of the planes had no all-weather capability, and they lacked the necessary non-nuclear ordnance, including sufficient Sidewinder missiles and modern air-to-ground missiles.

Kennedy quickly increased the defense budget by 15 percent, doubled the number of combat-ready divisions in the army's strategic reserve, and expanded combat units in the navy and marines. He also created a new containment dimension—counterinsurgency—in response to Communist guerrilla activities in Third World countries, contending that guerrilla-like tactics were necessary to deal with guerrilla-like warfare. In the 1950s that approach had proved successful in Malaya, the Philippines, and Greece. In early 1961 Kennedy instructed the Special Warfare Center at Ft. Bragg, North Carolina, to include the study of new methods of combating guerrilla warfare. The special-forces personnel at Ft. Bragg increased from fewer than 1,000 to 12,000 in his administration. Kennedy designated the green beret as the symbol of the new force, and it soon became a fixture on his desk. Also, special-forces centers emerged in Panama, Okinawa, Vietnam, and West Germany. By June 1963 some 114,000 American and 7,000 foreign military officers had undergone counterinsurgency training, as did foreign service officers before embarking on Third World assignments.

In January 1962 Kennedy also created a fifteen-member ad hoc Special Group (Counterinsurgency), chaired by Gen. Maxwell Taylor and embraced by Attorney General Robert Kennedy, a key member. It coordinated American counterinsurgency activities on behalf of foreign governments threatened by Communist insurrection. It focused much of its attention on Latin America and Southeast Asia. Like Kennedy, the group saw counterinsurgency not only in terms of cloak-and-dagger operations but also as a progressive political and social force that would assist local governments in winning the hearts and minds of the people. The latter task was not so easily accomplished because of uncooperative, despotic governments and insensitive United States officials, who often clashed with American ideals.

Kennedy likewise increased the United States nuclear capability even though new intelligence information caused McNamara and the CIA to doubt a missile gap. Pressured by the military and motivated by a desire to gain greater supremacy, Kennedy soon committed the United States to one thousand intercontinental ballistic missiles, his justification being that "we dare not tempt [the Soviets] with weakness. For only when our arms are sufficient beyond doubt can we be certain beyond doubt that they will never be employed."[2]

The buildup sent Moscow the wrong message and consequently ended any possibility of putting a cap on nuclear weaponry. Instead it made Khrushchev aware of his own missile gap, leading to the continual escalation of nuclear weaponry on both sides, a lesson that Kennedy would not learn until late in his presidency if at all. The increase of non-nuclear forces also had mixed results. Though sometimes serving as a deterrent, they added to an escalating military budget, which reached an unprecedented $50 billion by the end of 1963 and contributed to America's growing involvement in Vietnam.

In his first week in office Kennedy privately referred to that country as a major area of crisis along with Laos, the Congo, and Cuba. Yet none tormented Kennedy more in his first months—if not his entire presidency—than Cuba. Because of his imprudent action relating to the Bay of Pigs in April, the promise of the Kennedy presidency was nearly dashed in its first one hundred days. As it turned out, Cuba would always remain a vexation to him.

Cuba had become a trouble spot during the Eisenhower era after Castro overthrew the corrupt dictatorship of Fulgencio Batista in January 1959. Fidel Castro at first personified the democratic hero, seeking land reform, profit-sharing for sugar workers, the confiscation of illegal land-holdings, and the implementation of the 1940 liberal constitution. Most Americans initially applauded Castro, but his belief that political reform was meaningless without economic reconstruction soon conflicted with powerful American interests dominating the Cuban economy. His anti-American rhetoric also created suspicions as did a budding Marxist ideology that eventually converted Cuba into a Communist dictatorship. Whether the United States pushed Castro into the Communist camp still generates scholarly controversy, but one thing is certain: Americans abhorred Castro's seizure of American utilities, mining, oil, and other holdings. By early 1960 the Eisenhower administration threatened legal action and embargoed arms shipments to Cuba. When the Soviets contracted to purchase 1.7 million tons of Cuban sugar, the rift between the United States and Cuba widened. In June Castro seized American oil refineries after United States oil companies refused to refine crude oil coming from the Soviet Union. Eisenhower then suspended the Cuban sugar quota for the remainder of the year, resulting in Castro's seizure of the remaining American sugar mills and Cuba's closer ties to the Soviet Union. Soviet arms and military advisers soon entered Cuba.

These actions caused the Eisenhower administration to judge Castro as a dangerous menace who threatened United States interests throughout Latin America, a view that the Organization of American States did not share. Consequently, the administration determined to topple Castro. When economic and diplomatic action proved ineffectual, covert means followed. Under the directorship of the aging Allen Dulles and under the effective control of no one, the CIA even consorted with Mafia bosses in an attempt to assassinate the Cuban dictator. In March 1960 the CIA received Eisenhower's permission to train Cuban exiles in Guatemala for possible military action against Castro. The original plan called for a few hundred anti-Castro guerrillas infiltrating Cuba to join with Castro resisters operating out of sanctuaries in the Escambray Mountains. By fall 1960 a collapsing resistance movement caused the CIA to focus on a larger amphibious invasion force supported by a Cuban anti-Castro tactical air force. Marine officers soon joined CIA operatives and four hundred Cubans in Guatemala as training for the impending invasion began.

The Cuban operation remained a carefully guarded secret during the Kennedy-Nixon presidential campaign. At that time Kennedy had assaulted the Eisenhower administration for permitting a Communist dictatorship ninety miles from United States shores, but his position had changed markedly from the time the Cuban had come to power. Initially Kennedy had said virtually nothing, at least until the publication of *The Strategy of Peace* in January 1960. At that point, he was courting liberal intellectual support for his presidential nomination as well as expressing a sensitivity to nationalistic uprisings. Consequently, in the book's introductory remarks on Latin America he characterized Castro as "part of the legacy of [Simon] Bolivar."[3] He proposed the restudy of Bolivar in order to understand the "new contagion for liberty and reform now spreading south of our borders." Not until well into the fall campaign, after Republicans had attacked his early appraisal of Castro, did an embarrassed Kennedy indicate that he had supposedly failed to read the ghostwritten effort of staffer Harris Wofford.

The fact is that Kennedy had changed his assessment of Castro. The Cuban's growing pro-Soviet and totalitarian stance undoubtedly caused Kennedy to believe that the original revolution had been subverted. His political antenna—as well as his anti-communism—persuaded him to focus on Cuba in speech after speech, emphasizing Republican lack of firmness. Arthur Schlesinger remembers Kennedy wondering in this period how he would have handled Castro if he had had the power: "Then [Kennedy] paused, looked out the window and said, 'what the hell, they never told us how they would have saved China.' "[4] His strongest statements came on 20 October when he accused Nixon of supporting a policy of "blunder, inaction, retreat, and failure" toward Cuba. He then provocatively recommended that the non-Batista democratic forces should be strengthened. "Thus far," he claimed, "these fighters for freedom have had virtually no support from our Government."[5] Reaction was immediate, but not any got more attention than Richard Nixon's angry retort during the fourth debate that intervention would violate the Bogotá Treaty of 1948 and the UN charter, both of which prohibited intrusion in the internal affairs of another nation. Thus, an American-sponsored Cuban invasion would cause the United States to lose "all of our friends in Latin America," and lead to condemnation by the UN and probable military failure.[6] Nixon was never more prophetic or more insincere, for privately he had been the strongest supporter of the CIA scheme to overthrow Castro.

Whether Kennedy knew of the plan at this time remains a question. An angered Nixon believed that he did, claiming in *My Six Crises* (1962) that Dulles had inappropriately briefed Kennedy on CIA plans and preparations and charging that in speaking out, Kennedy had endangered "the security of a United States foreign policy operation."[7] Kennedy denied prior knowledge, and Dulles later publicly asserted that he had provided no information on plans and policies in the briefing. Others, like Dulles's CIA replacement John McCone, later claimed, however, that Dulles had fully informed Kennedy. Even Richard Goodwin, who allegedly wrote the "freedom fighter" statement, later said little to refute McCone.

Kennedy's first briefing after the election came on 18 November with Dulles and Richard Bissell, CIA deputy for planning, at the Kennedy family Palm Beach residence. Kennedy had already announced the reappointment of Dulles, which CIA planners surely considered a ringing endorsement of the Cuban invasion. Dulles had moved in the same social circles as Joe Kennedy, and a mutual respect existed between the two families. Bissell, an Ivy Leaguer holding a Yale doctorate in economics, had worked on the Marshall Plan and had taught at MIT before joining the CIA in 1954. Among his students were Walter Rostow and McGeorge and William Bundy—all future Kennedy administration members. At the CIA he had engineered the U-2 spy operation, the overthrow of the Arbenz government in Guatemala, and the scheme to assassinate Castro. Bissell was known for his brilliance, daring, and articulateness. Overlooked were his failings, including the aborted CIA-directed coup in Indonesia in 1958. By 1961 he had impressed Kennedy so much that he viewed Bissell as Dulles's eventual successor.

On 29 November, in another CIA briefing, Dulles provided Kennedy with more information about the military training in Guatemala. Kennedy told Dulles to continue the work. Operating under the nominal supervision of the Special Group of the National Security Council, the CIA concentrated on Trinidad on the south coast of Cuba as the proposed landing site, where a port existed with a friendly population close to the Escambray Mountains. The planned operation floundered in Eisenhower's closing days, however. The Special Group had doubts about its feasibility, and the CIA failed to establish a provisional Cuban government in exile, which strengthened Eisenhower's resolve to put a lid on the operation. As Trumbull Higgins has written, Ike was a "master at providing caveats enabling him not to intervene . . . where people expected him" to do so.[8] Yet Ike characteristically told Kennedy on 19 January that he must assume responsibility for the overthrow of Castro and his dangerous government, recommending the acceleration of the proposed invasion. Of course Eisenhower was in an enviable position of claiming credit if it succeeded and having Kennedy accept responsibility if it failed.

President Kennedy probably knew nothing of Eisenhower's apprehensions. More significantly, he soon abolished or weakened the various institutional checks connected with the NSC, including the Special Group, detaching the CIA from any institutional control. Secretary of the Treasury Douglas Dillon later blamed the Bay of Pigs debacle on the loss of the checks and balances incorporated into the NSC procedures of the previous administrations.

Another problem arose when the Joint Chiefs of Staff (JCS) became involved in the evaluation of the CIA plan in late January. They felt handicapped because the excessively secret nature of the operation prevented them from doing the necessary staff studies. Furthermore, Dulles and Bissell neglected to work with the CIA deputy director for intelligence, Robert Amory, Jr., or with the State Department Cuban desk or its Bureau of Intelligence and Research. Consequently, the absence of accurate intelligence information relating to the internal conditions in Cuba and the topography of the proposed landing areas proved to be a major weakness of the plan. Finally, the joint chiefs stressed that success depended on a "substantial popular uprising or substantial follow-on forces," giving the plan a "fair chance" of attainment without overt United States intervention.[9] Gen. David Shoup, commandant of the Marine Corps, privately expressed stronger criticism.

The inexperienced Kennedy administration, barely thirty days in office, ignored the pitfalls and warning signals lurking about it. The president and his staff remained in awe of experts, causing the administration to accept too readily the joint chiefs' tepid endorsement and the CIA's excessive enthusiasm. Dulles and Bissell had in fact completely lost objectivity, so anxious were they to see the invasion succeed. To a great extent Defense Secretary McNamara and National Security adviser Bundy also failed to be critical and endorsed the CIA's proposed invasion. Secretary of State Rusk, whom Kennedy particularly depended upon, provided little leadership.

Rusk had grave reservations about using military forces against Castro. He feared the disastrous political ramifications of United States involvement and also questioned CIA estimates that Cubans would rebel against Castro. For these reasons he preferred an economic boycott. Yet never did he speak out against an invasion at the various ad hoc meetings where his influence would have mattered. He elected to express his concerns to Kennedy privately, seeking in meetings only to reduce the United States role in the operation. Harriman later claimed that Rusk might have stopped it had he spoken out forcibly against it.[10] However, that would have been uncharacteristic of him. Once he sensed the president's will, he became the good soldier and constitutionalist, preferring that the president lead. Rusk had disappointed Kennedy for his lack of leadership and courage; but he also became a convenient scapegoat for administration officials, who thought him a second-class intellect and out of place in the stylish environment of the New Frontier. Still, Rusk did nothing more than play the role Kennedy had carved out for him, that of an obedient technocrat who had the establishment's blessing.

In the administration only Schlesinger expressed immediate disapproval of the proposed invasion. Hearing about it in early February, he sent the president a memorandum, arguing that "this would be your first dramatic foreign policy initiative. At one stroke you would dissipate all the extraordinary good will . . . toward the new Administration throughout the world. It would fix a malevolent image of the new Administration in the minds of millions."[11] Schlesinger's concerns drew little attention in the weeks ahead, for CIA officials persuaded the president that the United States must move quickly against Castro. As Bissell repeatedly suggested, "you can't Mañana this thing."[12]

The CIA warned that the approaching rainy season would rapidly shut down guerrilla training in Guatemala, adding to the restiveness of a growing force that represented virtually every political position in Cuban life, including the *Batistianos*, a source of continual conflict. Cuban exiles in Miami, Florida, also grew impatient. Moreover, the CIA cautioned that the Cuban dictator would soon receive jet airplanes from the Soviet Union; the longer the United States waited, the more difficult it would be to topple Castro. As it turned out it was already too late.

March brought key changes in the CIA plan. A liaison committee responsible to the joint chiefs raised questions about Trinidad as an invasion site. Because of the unlikelihood of achieving surprise at that popular port, the odds for a successful invasion were estimated at well below 50 percent, particularly since Kennedy insisted that the United States would not intervene overtly or participate in any rescue bailout. The president himself desired a less conspicuous landing, preferably at night, making a Cuban internal uprising even less likely. As much as Kennedy wanted the operation to succeed, he remained wary of possible direct U.S. involvement. Rusk and others reinforced those feelings as they scaled down United States commitments in the weeks ahead. They naively thought that other countries would overlook American covert activity, despite increasing leaks about the CIA encampment in Guatemala. Ironically, the more the United States reduced its role, the more the chances increased for military failure.

By mid-March the CIA proposed the Bay of Pigs as an alternative site. Located about forty miles west of Trinidad along the Zapata peninsula, the bay was a remote area with nearly eighty miles of swamp separating it from the Escambrays. CIA planners, trying to put the best face on the change, suggested that a landing force would encounter little opposition there, reducing the need for much air cover. Moreover, a dilapidated airstrip nearby could receive the rebel B-26 bombers landing from Nicaragua, which the United States could claim were Castro defectors. The JCS, again handicapped by secrecy and time constraints, accepted—but did not approve—the site as a suitable alternative to Trinidad. Kennedy probably remained unaware of the chiefs' persistent pessimism. The Bay of Pigs area particularly troubled them because it was closer than Trinidad to Castro's main forces in the Havana region. Adm. Arleigh Burke, for one, conceded that the new plan (Operation Zapata) had less than a 50 percent chance of success. The CIA meanwhile led Kennedy to believe that the invaders could steal away into the mountains to fight as guerrillas if the invasion failed. This proved to be impossible, however, because of the intervening swamps, causing an angry Robert Kennedy to write later that his brother would have withdrawn approval if he had been aware of that problem.

Not only did Kennedy neglect to examine closely the plan's weak areas in the weeks ahead, he also ignored the skepticism and opposition of several knowledgeable people, including Senator J. William Fulbright, chairman of the Senate Foreign Relations Committee, who argued in late March that a Cuban invasion would violate the OAS charter, hemispheric treaties, and United States legislation and it would be denounced throughout Latin America and the United Nations. Fulbright most eloquently expressed his views before a 4 April ad hoc meeting of Kennedy, Rusk, and CIA officials. He called the operation "wildly out of proportion to the threat," warning that "it would compromise our moral position in the world and make it impossible for us to protect treaty violations by the Communists."[13]

The invasion plan also shocked Undersecretary of State Chester Bowles, who opposed it largely on moral and political grounds. Bowles's written response went to Rusk, who probably did not forward it to Kennedy, but the president heard directly from another liberal voice, Ambassador John Kenneth Galbraith, whom Bowles had alerted. Galbraith warned Kennedy about "adventurism," which failed to "count the larger costs either of success or failure" and resulted in such disasters as MacArthur's march to the Yalu or the U-2 incident of 1960. "We Democrats," he reminded, "with our reputation for belligerence and our basically hostile press have far less margin for mistakes than had the Republicans."[14] He urged Kennedy to pursue restraint. Schlesinger, in two separate memoranda to the president in early April, also questioned two premises: that because the equipment and personnel of the invasion force were Cuban, the United States would not be held accountable and that the invasion would touch off a mass insurrection, leading to the overthrow of Castro. Schlesinger feared a protracted stalemate, resulting in political pressure for American armed forces to sustain the rebellion. This, of course, would destroy the "reawakening world faith in America." Yet Schlesinger remained silent during the crucial meetings at the White House because of a reluctance to challenge openly the conventional wisdom. His efforts to work through Robert Kennedy also failed. Robert, whom the president brought into the operation belatedly, told Schlesinger that he "thought that [Schlesinger] was performing a disservice" in raising questions at such a late date.[15]

Dean Acheson, one of the few outsiders Kennedy consulted, did not mince words, however. The reputed cold warrior must have surprised the president when he responded that he did "not think it was necessary to call in Price, Waterhouse [public accountants] to discover that 1,500 Cubans weren't as good as 25,000 Cubans." It seemed to him that "this was a disastrous idea."[16] How many others might have expressed strong reservations may never be known. Some never had the opportunity. Adlai Stevenson, head of the United States delegation to the UN, surely would have responded negatively if he had been consulted fully. He had written Kennedy on 31 January that he had heard that Castro's popularity was much stronger than the administration thought. The politically sensitive Theodore Sorensen of the White House staff knew nothing until invasion day.

Of even more concern were the increasing newspaper leaks as D-day drew near, making any effort to maintain secrecy a cruel joke. On 7 April, the *New York Times* reported that between five thousand and six thousand men had been training in the United States and Guatemala for the purpose of liberating Cuba. A livid Kennedy publicly disclaimed the possibility of a large invasion and denied the planned use of American troops. At the same time the administration successfully pressured the media not to publish stories that threatened the national security. Ironically, weeks afterward Kennedy told Turner Catledge, the *Times'* managing editor, that if that newspaper had ignored the administration's requests, "you would have saved us from a colossal mistake."[17]

What led Kennedy to make the most regrettable decision of his public career? Unquestionably, the CIA exerted the greatest influence. Kennedy, an admirer of Ian Fleming's James Bond thrillers, had an overly exalted view of that agency. Dulles's assertion in late March that he felt more confident about the Bay of Pigs success than he had about the CIA over-throw of the leftist Arbenz Guatemalan government in 1954 bolstered Kennedy. Kennedy did not know, however, how misleading Dulles's analogy was, as the latter had had misgivings about the Guatemalan operation. In any case, Guatemala had contributed to the CIA's aura of invincibility, overshadowing the agency's failure to sack the Sukarno government in Indonesia in 1958.

Kennedy also mistakenly thought the JCS were confident of the invasion's success, undoubtedly because that is what he wanted to believe. Yet for some reason the chiefs suppressed their misgivings. Kennedy later recalled asking Adm. Arleigh Burke prior to the invasion, "Will this thing work?" Burke had indicated that "the plan is good." "Hell, I'd been reading about 'Thirty Knot' Burke for a long time," Kennedy commented. "I thought he was tremendous."[18] This was the same Burke who had privately labeled the CIA plan as "weak" and "sloppy."

Still, Burke represented only one aspect of an "assumed consensus" that apparently characterized the key meetings. Social psychologists call it group-think, a term describing the herd instinct that occasionally takes hold, stifling independent thought. That phenomenon ripened partly because of the great prestige of Dulles and Bissell. Dulles—according to Roswell Gilpatric, the deputy secretary of defense—provided the ambience; Bissell became the convincing advocate who could take on a McNamara intellectually. Dulles and Bissell aside, the participants' lack of familiarity with Kennedy and with each other also contributed to the circumscribed responses, creating a hesitancy to raise questions or to express doubts or concerns. Above all, the enormous shadow of Eisenhower seemed to cover the room. No one wished to challenge "the greatest military man in America," least of all an inexperienced president who had criticized Ike for not confronting Castro. Peter Wyden refers to a "smell of hierarchy" that permeated the cabinet room because of the newness, inexperience, and unfamiliarity in the Kennedy administration. Schlesinger confirms that impression in alluding to his own reluctance to speak out.

Perhaps the problem goes deeper. Kennedy's penchant for informality and reduced institutional checks created a situation where insufficient bureaucratic safeguards existed, and the excessive security only compounded the problem. At the very least he might have discussed the plan in the cabinet, where more frank give-and-take would have transpired. Afterward Labor Secretary Arthur Goldberg chided Kennedy for ignoring that body: "There are two people in the Cabinet you should have consulted on this one . . . men who know some things and who are loyal to you and your interests." Kennedy asked who they were. "Orville

Freeman and me," Goldberg responded.[19] Freeman, a former marine who had made amphibious landings, understood how tough they could be under the best of circumstances; Goldberg explained that his own World War II intelligence background also would have been of use.

Other considerations drove Kennedy forward, however. In mid-April he had sent marine colonel Jack Hawkins to Central America as an outside evaluator whose briefing, according to Robert Kennedy, was the "most instrumental paper in convincing the president to go ahead." Hawkins, a decorated veteran of Tarawa, claimed that "he had never seen such an effective military force" and recommended forcefully that they go ahead with the landing.[20] No advice needed more qualification. The high spirits of the troops could not erase the facts that they lacked sufficient preparation (only about 135 out of 1,400 were soldiers and some had never fired a rifle) and that they differed vehemently over political objectives. The Cuban brigade also posed a potential problem in the event of the invasion's cancellation: Guatemala did not want the Cubans. It would not do to bring them to the United States, where they could criticize the president for his lack of courage or resolve. Kennedy explained to Schlesinger that if the government had to get rid of the brigade, it was "much better to dump them in Cuba than in the United States."[21]

Moreover, Kennedy sincerely believed that Castro had subverted a democratic and nationalistic revolution. In order to curb communism in Cuba, the original purposes of the revolution had to be restored. Schlesinger, who had acquiesced in the decision to invade, provided the rationale in a State Department White Paper that sought to identify the United States with social and economic reform within the hemisphere. The logic and facts were self-serving enough that one historian later labeled the paper "an unfortunate example of how history was mis-construed to serve political ends."[22]

In the end Kennedy consented because his prior actions, statements, and beliefs had put him into a position where he had no other practical choice. Even Sorensen later acknowledged that a "disapproval of the plan would be a show of weakness inconsistent with his general stance."[23] If Kennedy had occasional apprehensions and doubts, as his supporters suggest, those emotions had nothing to do with the morality or rightness of the operation. Kennedy wanted it to succeed badly; ultimately he thought it would. He was banking on the phenomenal luck he had had since 1956. Associates, wrote Schlesinger, thought he had the "Midas touch."

In retrospect the Bay of Pigs invasion had no chance of success. Scholars have rightly called it "the perfect failure." Several monumen-tally fallacious assumptions characterized the operation from the very beginning. Kennedy and his immediate advisers erroneously believed that Cuban rebels could become guerrillas in the Escambrays. Dulles and Bissell matched that misconception by assuming that Kennedy would not permit the invasion to fail, even if it meant using U.S. military forces. Only afterward did Dulles understand that Cuba was an "orphan child JFK had adopted—he had no real love and affection for it [and] proceeded uncertainly towards defeat . . . only half sold on the vital necessity of what he was doing."[24] Despite knowing better both Kennedy and Dulles had hoped for a popular insurrection against Castro, which never materialized. Furthermore, the CIA grossly underestimated the leadership of Castro and the military proficiency of his army and air force, which were more than a match for the Cuban brigade.

The operation broke down tactically even before the invasion force left Guatemala. The first air strike (D-2) on 15 April—eight old B-26 bombers from Nicaragua—had managed to destroy about 50 percent of Castro's air force. A second rebel strike, proposed for the next day in the original plan, might have completed the destruction. As it turned out the first assault caused Castro to disperse his aircraft, institute a military alert, and round up thousands from the underground. Whatever element of surprise the Bay of Pigs incursion might have had was now lost. Kennedy, advised by Rusk and Bundy, also rejected an air strike scheduled for the morning of the invasion on the seventeenth, largely because the U.S. cover had been blown away. One rebel Cuban plane from the 15 April strike, as a result of engine problems, had landed in Key West, Florida, instead of returning to Nicaragua. Chief UN delegate Adlai Stevenson innocently parroted the CIA story that the aircraft was a defection from Cuba, only to find out otherwise. Even more galling, the embarrassed Stevenson had to listen to the harangue of the Cuban foreign minister at the UN that "this act of imperialistic piracy" was "the prelude to a large scale invasion attempt . . . by the United States."[25] Kennedy's decision to prohibit the additional air strike probably kept Stevenson from resigning. Kennedy's action, however, frustrated Bissell, whose B-26s could now be used only for air cover over the beachhead on D-day.

Despite the inadequacy of that cover Kennedy ignored the urgings of the CIA and the vice-president to employ United States fighter cover as the invasion proceeded. Meanwhile, the Cuban brigade faced immediate detection. Much sooner than expected Castro had ordered his regulars and militia to the area. His remaining aircraft also attacked the invaders' outmoded landing craft, many of which were damaged from the unexpected reefs; some men had to swim to shore without weapons. Additionally, Castro's T-33 jet trainers shot down four B-26s, and a Sea Fury fighter plane sank a ship containing the ammunition reserve and most of the communication equipment. Everything that could go wrong did; lack of coordination, proper planning, and effective leadership had made this a disaster in every respect.

By the second day, Tuesday, 18 April, it seemed clear that the operation would fail. The day before Kennedy had returned from Glen-Ora, the family Virginia home, where he could exercise plausible denial. Outwardly he seemed calm and cool; the remarkable self-control that had carried him through earlier personal crises remained with him. On the eighteenth he attended a scheduled cabinet meeting and talked for about twenty-five minutes, covering every aspect of the operation, including his understanding of why it had failed. According to Fred Dutton he never asked the cabinet members to rally around or to avoid criticism, nor did he "give them a public line they were to take."[26] Afterward he walked out on the grass, where his brother met him; inwardly he was hurting. Robert Kennedy later commented that he noticed that the president "kept shaking his head, rubbing his hands over his eyes. We'd been through a lot . . . together, and he was more upset this time than he was any other."[27] Both Bissell and Dulles were visibly shaken. The former, who had a habit of twisting his hands, was, according to Robert, "twisting them even more by the time this was over." Dulles, while visiting Nixon's home on the nineteenth, was asked if he wanted a drink; he responded, "I certainly would—I really need one. This is the worst day of my life!"[28] Talking to Nixon, he blamed the invasion's failure on Kennedy's last-minute cancellation of the rebel air strikes.

In retrospect, what doomed the invasion was not that at all; both Bissell and Bundy eventually admitted as much. The problem went beyond the weakness of the rebel air power. Castro had a vastly superior ground force, including tanks, which eventually would have prevailed even if his air force had been destroyed. Only American military intervention would have saved the operation, and this was exactly what Nixon, whom Kennedy obligatorily consulted on 20 April, recommended. Nixon advised him to "find a proper legal cover . . . and go in." He then provided the justification, including "protecting American citizens living in Cuba and defending our base at Guantánamo. . . . I believe that the most important thing at this point is that we do whatever is necessary to get Castro and communism out of Cuba."[29]

Kennedy argued that American action in Cuba would cause Khrushchev to "probe and prod" in Berlin and elsewhere, but Nixon quickly pooh-poohed that appraisal. The extent to which Kennedy understood the irony of this exchange in the light of the 1960 campaign may never be known. Nevertheless, later that week the president also visited with Eisenhower at Camp David amid Maryland's Cactoctin Mountains, where he explained to Eisenhower his perception of what had happened. He did not ask Ike for advice; what he needed was his support, which he received, when Eisenhower told the press that he was "all in favor of the United States supporting the man who has to carry the responsibility for our foreign affairs." Privately Eisenhower characterized Kennedy's leadership as a "Profile in Timidity and Indecision."[30]

Kennedy satisfied least the Democratic Left and the Republican Right in his handling of the Bay of Pigs invasion. The former remained convinced that the United States had erred morally and politically and had lost trust and prestige throughout Latin America because of its actions. Rightists believed that the United States should have done everything necessary to win in Cuba; otherwise, the United States would appear weak to Castro and the Soviet Union. Both Dulles and Nixon clearly reflected that viewpoint, and at least one Latin American leader expressed similar beliefs. According to Robert Campos, Brazilian ambassador to the United States, although President Quadros of Brazil opposed the Cuban invasion, he felt that "it should have been carried through and this sort of indecisiveness . . . gave him . . . an impression of weakness on Kennedy's part." Quadros claimed "there are two ways of being respected—one is by wisdom and the other by might"—and in the Cuban experiment he felt that "none of those had been achieved."[31]

Yet Kennedy had acted characteristically. Always a nationalist and a moderate, he felt that the Cubans themselves must restore the democratic principles of their revolution and topple those who had betrayed the cause. The United States could provide some of the means by which this could be done, but under no circumstances could this country become directly involved in the military operations. However, his distinction between indirect and direct support seemed meaningless to most critics of the Bay of Pigs fiasco. Nor did other nations comprehend such distinctions—least of all the Soviet Union.

Convinced of the rightness of his course, Kennedy learned to live with that criticism. Philosophically, he understood that "victory has a hundred fathers and defeat is an orphan." He publicly accepted full responsibility for the failure, knowing that to admit the error was the proper thing to do. Even Kennedy expressed disbelief, however, that his approval rating in the Gallup poll jumped to 83 percent.

What most concerned him was the plight of the Cuban rebels. About twelve hundred of the some fourteen hundred brigade members had been captured; the remainder had been killed in combat. Kennedy felt personally responsible for the loss. For more than a year and a half, working through his brother and others, he sought their release from

Cuban prisons. Through an exchange of drugs and food, Castro finally released them, and Kennedy himself welcomed the rebels at the Orange Bowl in Miami in December 1962.

Kennedy also felt an obligation to the Cuban Revolutionary Council, the diverse anti-Castro element, which theoretically had sponsored the invasion. Housed in Miami, where it had awaited embarkation to Havana after Castro's proposed ouster, it instead suffered despair and disillusionment, following the defeat of the Cuban brigade. It was left to Schlesinger and Latin American affairs adviser Adolf Berle to fly to Miami and meet with embittered council members, who indicted the CIA for detaining them and for botching the overthrow of Castro. Negative feelings toward Kennedy rose because of his irresolution.

The president met with the council on the nineteenth in the Oval Office. He spoke "slowly and thoughtfully," expressing his sorrow for what had happened. He explained why he could not intervene militarily, even though he remained committed to the freedom of Cuba. As the meeting drew to a close, Kennedy told the Cubans that "I want you all to understand that, as soon as you leave the White House, you are all free men—free to go whenever you want, free to say anything you want, free to talk to anyone you want."[32] Kennedy's response moved them, despite their concealed anger.

Khrushchev also required Kennedy's attention. On the eighteenth, the Soviet leader had rebuked the American president: "It is not a secret to anyone that the armed bands which invaded [Cuba] have been trained, equipped and armed in the United States. . . . We shall render [the] Cuban government all necessary assistance in beating back the armed attack on Cuba."[33] Kennedy blamed the Cuban problem on the loss of liberty and freedom, which led to the rebel invasion. He again denied any intention of intervening militarily, and he responded to Khrushchev's veiled warning that events in Cuba might affect peace elsewhere by suggesting that the Soviets must not use this as a pretext to "inflame other areas of the world."[34] Four days later Khrushchev contended that the "whole world" knew that the United States had played a direct military role in the Cuban invasion, asserting that the United States hypocritically opposed Castro because he failed to "meet [the] tastes of [the] ruling circles." Khrushchev denied that the Soviet Union sought advantages, privileges, or military bases in Cuba; only "simpletons" could believe this, he concluded.[35]

The Bay of Pigs affair spawned over two years of correspondence between the two leaders. For the most part, they communicated outside of government channels, sometimes even about personal or family matters, which gradually led to greater empathy between them. They soon learned that they shared a mistrust of and disappointment with bureaucratic government and came to respect each other very much. The first Cuban crisis, however, only worsened Soviet-American relations and heightened suspicions, particularly on the Soviets' part. Moreover, Khrushchev concluded that the inexperienced Kennedy lacked backbone and could be pressed. Kennedy's earlier suspicions of Khrushchev were also reinforced, leading him to believe that he must act cautiously but resolutely.

More immediately Kennedy sought an investigation of the failed Cuban invasion and asked retired Gen. Maxwell Taylor to chair a study group. Kennedy had met the former army chief of staff in 1948. Despite having had virtually no contact with Taylor throughout the 1950s, he respected the views and intellect of the still vigorous fifty-nine-year-old former paratrooper commander. Kennedy also placed Dulles, Robert Kennedy, and Admiral Burke on the Cuban study group; Robert's inclusion ensured the safeguarding of his brother's interests, and Dulles and Burke guaranteed that the CIA and military would be fairly treated. None of the four had reason to question the government's actions against Castro—yet another reason why they were selected. Kennedy did not want anyone raising embarrassing moral questions; consequently, their investigation would focus completely on the tactical aspects of the operation. During the twenty-one meetings, in which some fifty witnesses were interviewed, Taylor drew closer to Robert Kennedy, admiring his ability to interrogate witnesses and his protectiveness of his older brother. Robert meanwhile was impressed with Taylor's intellectual ability, judgment, and ideas, and they soon became close friends. Undoubtedly Robert had some impact on Taylor's perceptions of what had gone wrong.

After six weeks of meetings the study group turned in a final report to Kennedy on 13 June, confirming the confusion, lack of coordination, and inadequate planning that had plagued the operation and also concluding that the invasion had lacked sufficient air cover. The report focused much of its attention on the CIA and joint chiefs. It faulted the CIA for misleading the president into thinking that the Cuban brigade could "dissolve" into the countryside as guerrillas and that a popular uprising was in the cards; it rebuked the joint chiefs for failing to make clear their reservations about the enterprise; and it regretted civilian interference without adequate consultation even though conceding that Kennedy's canceled air strike had no bearing on the ultimate result.

The group thought that the operation could have succeeded only with direct American involvement and only under the jurisdiction of the Department of Defense. Moreover, it criticized the administration for the lack of permanent government machinery to coordinate cold war policies and operations. "Top level direction [instead] was given through ad hoc meetings of senior officials without consideration of operational plans in writing and with no arrangement for recording conclusions and decisions reached."[36] The report failed to analyze the possible motives of Dulles, Bissell, or other major participants, the intended objectives of the operation, or the alternative approaches opened to Kennedy. In his 1972 memoirs, Taylor, however, did systematically discuss the president's possible alternatives and concluded that United States air and naval power probably would not have assured the brigade's success. In retrospect Taylor thought that the operation should have been canceled. While Kennedy, of course, had not done this, he at least had prevented the United States from risking more of its resources and prestige in such a questionable endeavor.

But what lessons did the president learn from the Bay of Pigs? Court historians such as Schlesinger and Sorensen concluded that the failed invasion had a substantial impact, leading to changes in personnel, policy, and procedures. Kennedy afterward relied less on the so-called experts and more on those he knew best. Robert Kennedy and Sorensen, neither of whom had participated in the key meetings on Cuba, quickly assumed central advisory roles on all major issues. Bundy's expanded NSC staff, now meeting daily, took on greater authority over security matters. Furthermore, officials who had once reported directly to Kennedy on foreign policy now went to Bundy first to effect greater coordination. General Taylor also became Kennedy's personal adviser on military affairs until his appointment as chief of staff. Robert Kennedy later claimed that the president cleared every foreign policy decision through Taylor. Overall, the White House played a stronger role in national security matters. Rusk and the State Department became the real losers; their lack of leadership prompted Kennedy to revamp personnel at State during summer 1961.

Kennedy soon dismissed Dulles and Bissell, as part of the CIA censure. He told the latter that if a parliamentary system had existed, the president would have had to resign rather than Bissell. Partly for political reasons, he replaced Dulles with another Republican—John McCone, Eisenhower's former chairman of the Atomic Energy Commission and a noted cold warrior. Richard Helms, an intelligence veteran and Bissell antagonist, became Bissell's replacement.

The Bay of Pigs also reinforced Kennedy's inclinations not to send forces into Laos; he could hardly do so after having refused to commit troops against communism some ninety miles from U.S. shores. Kennedy's decision to challenge the Soviets to a race to the moon might have been linked to the Bay of Pigs failure as much as to Yuri Gagarin's orbital space flight four days before Operation Zapata. Eisenhower privately charged that Kennedy's efforts to regain U.S. prestige had led to a financially costly, unwise effort, weakening a carefully planned space program involving communication, meteorology, and reconnaissance.

Yet no major institutional changes occurred after the Bay of Pigs. Taylor, in the Cuban report, had suggested an elaborate, interdepartmental strategic-resources group to effect cold war planning and coordination across departmental lines. With such an agency, Taylor reasoned, the Bay of Pigs invasion would not have happened. Yet Kennedy rejected Taylor's recommendation, perhaps because it resembled the cumbersome agencies of the Eisenhower era and because of Rusk's insistence that it would impinge on the traditional responsibilities of the State Department. Nor did the CIA undergo significant reform, despite the shifting of paramilitary operations to the Defense Department and the adoption of feeble mechanisms to supervise it.

The CIA would in fact play a key role in the covert activities of the Special Group (Augmented), an agency recommended by Taylor with a permanent membership and staff, including Taylor, Robert Kennedy, McCone, and chairman of the JCS Gen. Lyman Lemnitzer. The Special Group sought Castro's removal, a growing obsession of the Kennedys. Richard Helms later conceded that the group became "a circuit breaker so that . . . things did not explode in the President's face . . . [and so] that he was not held responsible for them."[37] This included the attempted assassination of Castro, an effort that had begun in the Eisenhower presidency. Operation Mongoose also involved the Special Group and the CIA in covert sabotage operations in Cuba. Kennedy strongly supported this, indicating how little he had learned from the Bay of Pigs. Whether the president knew of efforts to kill Castro is uncertain. Senatorial friend George Smathers (D.-Fla.) later testified, as did others, that Kennedy had discussed the question. The Senate Intelligence Committee's investigation in 1975 consequently raised the possibility that authority had come from Kennedy. There is no doubt that Robert Kennedy knew—and enthusiastically supported it. He objected only after finding out in May 1962 that the CIA was employing Mafia elements to kill Castro. He was "mad as hell" after hearing that the two Mafia members involved—Sam Giancana and John Roselli— faced Justice Department investigations. Thus the administration's activities concerning Castro after the Bay of Pigs go a long way toward explaining the Cuban missile crisis of fall 1962.

The crisis in Southeast Asia had also commanded the president's attention from the very outset. After looking at the Vietnam material on 28 January, Kennedy remarked to Deputy National Security adviser Walter Rostow, "This is the worst [problem] we've got, isn't it?"[38] Yet Laos seemed an even more immediately urgent situation, as attacking Communist Pathet Lao forces threatened to overrun the countryside. On the day preceding the inauguration Kennedy had sought President Eisenhower's advice. Eisenhower, appearing "fit, pink cheeked, and unharassed," described Laos as the "cork in the bottle. If Laos fell, then Thailand, the Philippines, and of course Chiang Kai-shek would go," he explained.[39] Eisenhower opposed the inclusion of Communists in any coalition government; the result, he suggested, would be a Communist government. Christian Herter, Eisenhower's secretary of state, informed Kennedy that France and Great Britain opposed military intervention even if it would keep Communist China, the Soviet Union, or North Vietnam out of Laos. Yet Eisenhower would favor unilateral intervention "as a last desperate hope" to save Laos.[40] In reality he had been much more cautious in his own administration, but of course he could more easily raise that option now that he was leaving office. He even might have relished putting the ball in the court of a successor who had accused him of not doing enough to prevent the spread of communism.

The problem of Laos had its origins in the Geneva Accords of 1954, which divided French Indochina into Vietnam and the independent interior kingdoms of Laos and Cambodia. Occupying the coastal area, Vietnam was to be temporarily severed at the seventeenth parallel until unifying elections were held in 1956. In 1955 the United States replaced the French in South Vietnam and encouraged Ngo Dinh Diem, its leader, to oppose the elections. The oppressive Diem soon faced an insurgency in the south with the United States supplying Diem against the Communist rebels (Vietcong), who eventually relied on assistance from Hanoi.

Laos is a hammer-shaped, land-locked nation west of North Vietnam, bordered by China on the north, Thailand on the west, Cambodia on the south, and South Vietnam on the southeast. A major north-south route traversed Laos into Cambodia and South Vietnam, which China supposedly sought and North Vietnam would use in supplying the Vietcong, making Laos strategically important.

Following the accords, the courtly, genial, well-educated Souvanna Phouma became Laos' prime minister. Of all the leaders, Prince Souvanna came the closest to commanding popular support among a diverse population, which included the Meo people of the mountain villages and the more tranquil Lao of the Mekong lowlands. In the 1950s and 1960s, Souvanna sought a truly neutral government that would comprise the Communist Pathet Lao, nominally led by Souvanna's half-brother. This policy made Souvanna unacceptable to the Eisenhower administration, which took a dim view of truly neutral regimes. Consequently, the United

States became a major contributor to the instability in Laos, where American instigation often caused innumerable changes in the governments.

After Souvanna's ouster in 1958 the Eisenhower administration supported the pro-Western neutrality of Phoui Sananikone, who excluded the Pathet Lao and began a purge of their cadres in the northern provinces, causing an insurgency in the countryside. The emerging conflict revealed the inability of the Laotian army to fight and rocked the stability of the government. The American-assisted army, besieged by corruption and untrained in guerrilla warfare, was no match for Pathet Lao teams trained in North Vietnam, China, and the Soviet Union. The wavering Phoui government meanwhile fell in December 1959 before a CIA-encouraged coup, which brought to the forefront an extreme anti-Communist and pro-American general, Phoumi Nosavan.

The Eisenhower administration counted on the ambitious but unprincipled Phoumi to stop the Communist takeover in Laos, but he never could gain political control. After a coup in 1960 by Kong Le, a junior officer favoring neutrality, Phoumi expediently joined a coalition government involving Souvanna Phouma but excluding the Pathet Lao. Phoumi's forces soon attacked Kong Le's troops in the capital of Vientiane, forcing Kong Le northward, where he joined with the Pathet Lao. Phoumi then turned on Souvanna, who in desperation accepted a Soviet airlift of military equipment from Hanoi. The Soviets probably had become involved to prevent Souvanna's and the Pathet Lao's dependence on rival Communist China. Phoumi thereupon established a new government with Prince Boun Oum as prime minister, a regime the United States and the Western powers recognized, while the Communist countries backed Souvanna. Shortly after Phoumi's unsuccessful military efforts against Kong Le and the Pathet Lao, Kennedy assumed the presidency.

Kennedy had long understood that outmoded American policies contributed to the rise of communism in Third World areas and also felt that popular neutral governments could curb Communist insurgency. Yet he exaggerated the threat of communism and Soviet activity in Laos. By accepting the challenge, he thought that he could send a message to Moscow that he intended to protect newly emerging nations from outside Communist influence. To do any less would resurrect the Republican charge that Democrats were soft on communism. There were compelling reasons, then, why Kennedy sought to prevent a Communist takeover in Laos. Consequently he never seriously questioned whether United States security interests were involved, despite Schlesinger's observation that "Laos was not a dagger pointed at the heart of Kansas."[41] Indeed

Kennedy devoted more time to the problems in Laos than to any other issue during his first one hundred days.

The president first brought the issue of Laos before the American people during a television news conference on 23 March 1961. Behind him were three maps of Laos on easels, showing the progression of Pathet Lao control since August 1960. By the spring of 1961, according to Kennedy, the Communists had extended their influence over the mountainous eastern half of the country. He outlined the increased outside support to the Pathet Lao, including the Soviet airlift and weapon and cadre assistance from North Vietnam. In "Lá os" (as he pronounced it), he sought "a truly neutral government, not a cold war pawn; a settlement concluded at the conference table, and not on the battlefield." But "the armed attacks by externally supported Communists" had to end. Otherwise, he implied, United States military intervention would result.[42]

Support existed in the Kennedy administration for military action. It was recommended by a task-force study of Laos, commissioned by the president and written by State Department, CIA, and White House staff personnel. Despite differences the JCS also favored intervention, provided that nuclear weaponry could be used as a last resort. In March Kennedy did send five hundred marines to Thailand to facilitate a helicopter base in an area near Laos, yet he resisted pressure to commit large-scale forces that could have led to Chinese intervention. Robert Kennedy recalled that "we would have sent . . . a large number of American troops into Laos if it hadn't been for [the Bay of Pigs failure] because everybody was in favor of it."[43]

It would have been difficult for Kennedy to make a substantial military commitment to Laos even without the Bay of Pigs, however. He soon realized with "stunned amazement" that if he ordered only ten thousand troops to Southeast Asia, he would seriously deplete the strategic reserve. Inadequate airlift capabilities also would have prevented him from moving additional forces in quickly to counteract any large-scale response from China. Besides, there was little congressional support for intervention even though he knew the Republican leadership would accuse him of appeasement if Laos fell. Democratic Senate Majority Leader Mike Mansfield warned him that intervention in land-locked Laos "would be worse than Korea, would cost a great deal more and [would] very likely bring us into conflict with the Communist Chinese."[44] Even Douglas MacArthur told Kennedy at the general's Waldorf-Astoria suite in April that "it would be a mistake to fight in Laos," where China would have every advantage.[45] Great Britain and France had already informed the administration that they wanted a diplomatic settlement. One month prior to the Cuban invasion, Kennedy realized the futility of a military solution when he told the French Ambassador Hervé Alphand that "he didn't want to see the United States involved in a war in the jungles of Laos."[46]

The Bay of Pigs outcome strengthened Kennedy's resolve to seek a diplomatic solution in Laos. His confidence in the JCS had reached rock bottom; their advice reflected considerable disagreement, and as he examined their contingency plans for military intervention, he found them poorly thought out. Not only did some chiefs now recommend 140,000 men as an initial intervention force, they also continued to insist on the authority to employ nuclear weapons. JCS chairman General Lemnitzer volunteered, "If we are given the right to use nuclear weapons, we can guarantee victory."[47]

Kennedy's response was much more measured. He retained the appearance of a military presence by instructing U.S. military advisers in Laos to wear uniforms to bolster pro-U.S. Laotians and to serve as a signal to Moscow. He also approved covert operations against the North Vietnamese operating in Laos, on 11 May permitting the infiltration of agents into North Vietnam for sabotage and harassment. Kennedy understood that the military situation in Laos must not deteriorate further, prior to the resumption of negotiations to explore a peaceful settlement.

This meant more military supplies to Phoumi. Unlike the Eisenhower administration, however, he had no faith in the Laotian general. To Ben Bradlee of the *Washington Post*, he called Phoumi a "total shit."[48] Like his predecessor, Kennedy at first seemed unwilling to include the Pathet Lao in any reorganized Laotian government, nor did he see the necessity of bringing in Souvanna. In his 15 March 1961 press conference, he continued to speak in general terms of a "genuinely independent and neutral Laos." If Kennedy had had his choice he would have retained the pro-Western government of Boun Oum, with the inclusion of more neutralists.

Prospects for settlement began by 1 April when the Soviets responded favorably to a British note appealing for a cease-fire and the convening of an international conference. Khrushchev apparently viewed Laos as a stumbling block to the resolution of more important issues. He appealed to the other Communist participants to accept a conference and the reinstitution of the International Control Commission to ensure the neutrality and independence of Laos. Kennedy had already met with Khrushchev's foreign minister, Andrei Gromyko, on 27 March in the White House Rose Garden, where he expressed hope for a settlement and reaffirmed his determination to prevent a Communist takeover.

In the weeks ahead the president dropped some of his preconditions for a conference, such as the cessation of the Soviet airlift. After the Bay of

Pigs, he became more amenable to a neutral government that included Souvanna and the Pathet Lao; peace seemed to be the only alternative in Laos. No one had greater influence on Kennedy in this period than Averell Harriman, a former diplomat and cabinet member of the Roosevelt-Truman era. Supposedly too old at sixty-nine for a major policy post, Harriman became Kennedy's "roving ambassador," bringing to the administration a freshness, decisiveness, and wisdom that heretofore had been lacking. In March Harriman had met Souvanna in New Delhi, where the Laotian made a favorable impression. Undersecretary of State Chester Bowles, ambassador to India John Kenneth Galbraith, and ambassador to Laos Winthrop Brown also favored Souvanna even though the preponderance of officialdom in the CIA, the Pentagon, and the State Department continued to view him as a dangerous Communist.

The Geneva Conference, co-chaired by the British and the Soviets, convened on 16 May after the International Control Commission verified the cease fire. Secretary of State Rusk headed the American delegation, but Harriman soon replaced him. The sessions began slowly, as South Vietnam, Thailand, and the Boun Oum regime protested the Pathet Lao and neutralist candidates. The president had cabled Harriman to do what was necessary to fashion a settlement. He reported directly to Kennedy, treating the State Department as a service organization instead of as a policy-making body. Harriman ruffled some feathers by pruning the unwieldy American delegation and removing a hardline cold war strategist in favor of a promising young foreign-service officer who shared his own viewpoints.

Harriman struggled at first, as the cease-fire unraveled, as various factions in Laos continued to oppose one another, and as American policymakers remained divided. Kennedy contributed to the problem of policy, military planners charged, by dismantling Eisenhower's NSC system, making it more difficult for American officials to determine the administration's position. Thus the JCS felt free to continue the existing policies, including the backing of Phoumi for other than tactical reasons. Harriman also soon learned that the Soviets had little control over the North Vietnamese, the Pathet Lao, and the Chinese Communists, dispelling a myth that communism represented a monolithic force. In the ensuing weeks Harriman had his work cut out for him; ultimately, he would play a key role in the neutralization of Laos in summer 1962. He had little interference from Kennedy, who was occupied by other crises in foreign policy in 1961—the most important of which involved Khrushchev and Berlin.

4

★ ★ ★ ★ ★

MORE CONFLICT AND CRISES

Of the problem areas in foreign policy that Kennedy inherited, none seemed more potentially dangerous than Berlin. Unlike Laos and the Congo, Berlin directly involved United States national security. Unlike Cuba, it also affected Soviet security. That divided German city, one hundred miles inside Communist East Germany, made 1961 a difficult year for the young president, especially since it also revealed serious institutional differences over matters of foreign policy. At stake were the West's World War II occupation rights to West Berlin and the issue of access routes into that city. The fate of West Germany and the Western alliance seemed to hang in the balance.

The division of Germany and Berlin had emerged from the ashes of World War II, the result of the failure of the United States, the Soviet Union, and Great Britain to agree on whether Germany should be dismembered or remain whole. At the Yalta Conference in February 1945 the three powers provisionally settled on four military occupation zones in Germany and four-power custody of Berlin (to include France), with the Soviets occupying the eastern parts of the nation and the city. An Allied Control Commission, composed of the four zone commanders, would effect coordination. In 1946 economic unity among the zones virtually disintegrated, primarily because of Soviet and French opposition, and it became clear that a reunified Germany on Western terms would not be an immediate reality. Consequently, the United States took the lead in creating a separate West German state, causing the Soviets to follow suit in the Eastern zone. Western involvement in Berlin meanwhile continued, despite Soviet protests that the West had forfeited its rights there because of the breakdown in the four-power administration of Germany.

The Soviets had challenged the Western presence in West Berlin in 1948 with a blockade and again in late 1958 when Khrushchev had threatened to sign a separate peace treaty with East Germany unless the Western powers relinquished West Berlin. In both instances the Soviet Union had reacted to what it regarded as menacing changes in the status quo—first the planned creation of a separate West Germany and then West German rearmament, resulting in the deployment of nuclear missiles with American control of the warheads. Khrushchev, prone to medical metaphors, called West Berlin a bone in his throat because of its political, economic, and military threat. Most disconcerting to him, East German refugees fled into West Berlin by the thousands monthly, and Western espionage agents out of Berlin easily operated in East Germany. Moreover, Khrushchev understood that if he extracted concessions over West Berlin, NATO could be appreciably weakened. These reasons explain Khrushchev's ultimatum to make West Berlin a "free city." Though the Eisenhower administration wavered in the face of crisis, it did not break. Following the U-2 affair, an angry Khrushchev postponed the Berlin problem until the arrival of the new administration.

Although often reiterating United States commitments to West Berlin, Kennedy favored a modus vivendi with the Soviets to resolve the German question. This seemed a realistic alternative to the reunification of the two Germanies—a goal he and the West publicly favored. Recognizing the importance of East Germany to the Soviets, he understood the need to increase the status of that government without recognizing it diplomatically. In a 1959 interview he also suggested a reduction of Allied forces and the termination of propaganda activities in West Berlin in return for an agreement reaffirming Allied access to the city. Both sides, he maintained, needed to achieve a "precarious balance." To concede too much, he felt, would neutralize West Germany and Western Europe and weaken the American position elsewhere. He made it clear that he would favor war, if necessary, to defend West Berlin.

Kennedy and Khrushchev had first met in 1959 on the occasion of the latter's visit with the Senate Foreign Relations Committee. Unlike Nixon's kitchen debate later that year, this was an amiable meeting. In fact, Khrushchev's hope for a Kennedy victory in 1960 concerned Averell Harriman enough that he admonished the Soviet leader to be equally tough on both contenders to avoid helping the Republicans. After the election Khrushchev sent Kennedy a congratulatory telegram and wired Harriman that the slate was wiped clean after the bitterness of the Eisenhower era. To show good faith, Khrushchev soon released the two surviving members of a United States Air Force RB-47 aircraft who had been detained since 1 July 1960, following an overflight into Soviet air space.

Despite his strong suspicions of the Soviet state Kennedy remained determined to reduce tensions, but he consulted with several old Soviet hands before deciding on an appropriate response. On 11 February he met with Charles Bohlen, George Kennan, Harriman, and Llewellyn Thompson (who had replaced Bohlen as ambassador to the Soviet Union.) They reinforced his inclination to meet with Khrushchev as soon as possible, although Bohlen shared Kennedy's belief that summits were not proper places for decision making. A personal meeting, however, would enable Kennedy to have a greater understanding of what he was up against. Aware of how European monarchs had miscalculatingly stumbled into World War I, he most feared the possibility of a nuclear holocaust resulting from human error, a feeling that intensified after he attended a briefing by Pentagon experts on the disastrous effects of such an exchange. The projected wholesale loss of human life staggered a visibly shaken Kennedy.

Hardliners also influenced the president's early approach to Khrushchev and Berlin. None had more opportunity to do so than Dean Acheson who, like Harriman, represented the foreign policy establishment of the Truman era. Once again the best and the brightest of the "new generation" served rather inconspicuously in the early administration. In March Kennedy asked Acheson to conduct studies on NATO and the German problem, which had long commanded the former secretary of state's interest. Schlesinger claimed that Kennedy went to Acheson to elicit a worst-case scenario of Soviet intentions. His selection reflects his preeminence in shaping Democratic positions on foreign policy as chairman of the Advisory Committee for Foreign Relations during the late 1950s. Throughout that period Acheson, an early victim of Republican soft-on-communism charges, had sought vindication in positioning himself to the right of Eisenhower's foreign policy. Few remained as critical of the Soviet Union. To Kennedy that became an important consideration since he perceived the strong anti-Communist feeling in the country, a sentiment which he had sought to exploit in 1960. Kennan recalled that Kennedy wanted to ease differences with the Russians without being "attacked at home for being soft on Communism."[1]

Acheson reported on Berlin with his customary aplomb during British Prime Minister Harold Macmillan's White House visit in early April. In the process he resurrected the certainties of the Truman era: First, the Soviets would attempt to force the Berlin issue soon. Second, negotiations would settle neither this issue nor the larger German problem because there was nothing to negotiate. Finally, only a show of force mattered whenever the Soviets sought to cut off the approach routes. At that point he suggested moving a division down the Autobahn to provide a clear indication of Western intention. A Soviet military response, which Acheson thought unlikely, would, of course, lead to war, requiring Western rearmament. Acheson's chilling scenario shocked Macmillan and his foreign secretary, Lord Home, who both saw room for negotiation. Home responded that after all these years Western occupation in Berlin was "wearing thin"; Acheson suggested that perhaps Western power was "wearing thin."

Kennedy gave no indication where he stood in response to Acheson's assumptions. The day afterward, however, Schlesinger reported that Acheson's remarks had deeply dismayed Harriman and UN Ambassador Adlai Stevenson because he was committing the United States to "dangerous positions in advance of full exploration of alternatives. Harriman, Stevenson, and Acheson are our three elder statesmen in the field of foreign affairs," Schlesinger continued. "All have served the republic brilliantly, and all are honorable and towering figures. As a rule of thumb, I would vote with any two of them against the third." Stevenson reiterated that Acheson's Soviet "position should be the conclusion of a process of investigation, not the beginning." Harriman's response was much more pointed: "How long is our policy to be dominated by that frustrated and rigid man? He is leading us down the road to war."[2] The administration's debate over Berlin widened and intensified after Kennedy's June meeting with Khrushchev in Vienna. That this meeting came about, however, suggested that Acheson did not have Kennedy's complete attention.

Kennedy prepared thoroughly for Vienna. He blocked out time daily to read Khrushchev's major speeches and Soviet history; he questioned journalists such as Walter Lippmann and James Reston of the *New York Times*; he asked Senator Hubert Humphrey, who had had an eight-hour conversation with Khrushchev in 1959, for a personality sketch; and he quizzed Bohlen, Acheson, Harvard professor Henry Kissinger, an expert on international relations, and many others. He also requested transcripts of conversations between U.S. statesmen and Khrushchev. At this point he had yet to appreciate the value of the sagacious Harriman, thinking him a dull old man with a hearing problem. Not until Kennedy reached Paris did Harriman have an opportunity to advise the president on Khrushchev. At a formal dinner party, he only had a few minutes to whisper

Don't be too serious, have some fun, get to know Khrushchev a little, don't let him rattle you, he'll try to rattle you and frighten you, but don't pay any attention to that. Turn him aside, gently. . . . His style will be to attack and then see if he can get away with it. Laugh about it, don't get into a fight. Rise above it. Have some fun.[3]

Harriman's advice conflicted with those who argued that Kennedy must be tough to overcome his youth and his irresolution during the Bay of Pigs.

The Kennedys left for Europe on 30 May, arriving in Paris the next day. Remarkably, the president concealed a stabbing back pain caused by shoveling dirt at a mid-May tree planting ceremony in Ottawa. To all appearances, the Paris visit with Gen. Charles de Gaulle, the French president, was an overwhelming success, with favorable media attention, huge, cheering crowds, elaborate state luncheons and dinners, and considerable attention given to Jacqueline Kennedy's grace, beauty, and gowns. So much did she captivate de Gaulle and Parisians that Kennedy introduced himself at a news conference as "the man who accompanied Jacqueline Kennedy to Paris, and I have enjoyed it."

Kennedy's talks with the haughty, aging French nationalist were cordial and frank. De Gaulle concurred with him that the West must defend its rights in West Berlin; calling Khrushchev a bluffer, de Gaulle doubted that he wanted war over Berlin. At the same time he expressed reservations about negotiations with the Soviets. On the Laotian problem, even though opposing a military solution, he agreed to withhold public criticism in the event of U.S. intervention. More significantly, he recommended a neutral coalition headed by Souvanna Phouma, which Kennedy would soon accept.

Beneath the Paris cordiality emerging differences threatened American relations with France and other NATO nations. De Gaulle insisted that France—and other Western European countries—must play a more important role in the defense of the Continent, particularly since the United States refused to furnish NATO allies with atomic warheads. Furthermore, Kennedy's emphasis on strengthening conventional weapons only convinced de Gaulle that the United States would not use nuclear weaponry to defend Western Europe. De Gaulle also thought the United States had become vulnerable to Soviet nuclear retaliation, which meant France must become less dependent on America.

De Gaulle favored France's obtaining its own nuclear force and operating outside the constraints of the NATO military superstructure in conjunction with other continental nations. He envisioned a third force (under his leadership)—a developing superpower of European nations—to moderate the two "barbarian" powers—the United States and the Soviet Union. He was not dissuaded by Kennedy's assurance that the United States would use its nuclear weaponry to defend Western Europe in the event of a conventional Soviet invasion. After all, de Gaulle contended, nations could not be expected to commit their nuclear arsenal in defense of other states. Nor could Kennedy mollify him by proposing an instrument whereby NATO nations could place their fingers on the nuclear trigger; such control would be nominal, de Gaulle argued, for it would still be American control. Ultimately de Gaulle would develop his own *force de frappe*.

De Gaulle proved indifferent when it came to the inclusion of Great Britain in the Common Market, which Kennedy felt would further elevate Western Europe politically and economically. Moreover, that country could serve as a voice for the United States. Britain's traditional economic ties to the Commonwealth, however, caused de Gaulle to insist that the British must choose between that arrangement and continental alignment. Britain's reluctance to abandon Empire preference soon led de Gaulle and German Chancellor Konrad Adenauer to doubt that Britain wanted unconditional membership.

Despite developing differences, the three-day stay in Paris had represented a public-relations success for Kennedy. The next morning Air Force One touched down at the Vienna airport amid a light rain and an enthusiastic crowd. Khrushchev had arrived a day earlier; in contrast, he had been greeted by strong silence as he drove through the streets of Vienna.

The Vienna conference took place on 3 and 4 June and included Rusk, Thompson, Bohlen, and Foy Kohler, the assistant secretary for European affairs. Foreign Minister Andrei Gromyko, Mikhail Menshikov, Soviet ambassador to the United States, and Anatoly Dobrynin, chief of the American bureau in the Soviet foreign ministry, accompanied Khrushchev. The respective staffs played little part in the discussions. Kennedy, in light of the Bay of Pigs, seemed especially eager to show himself in control and on top of things. It would not do for him to consult frequently with his secretary of state before responding, as Eisenhower had done; nor could he make concessions weakening the Western position in Berlin, where the Allies and public opinion expected him to remain strong. The Soviet premier meanwhile viewed Kennedy "as a youngster who had a great deal to learn and not much to offer."[4] Kennedy's conduct during the Bay of Pigs had encouraged Khrushchev to believe that he would fold under pressure. Still, Khrushchev had his own problems. His political position at home had weakened following the growing Soviet-Sino rift, the U-2 incident, and the collapse of the Paris summit meeting. Besides, presidium hardliners such as Frol Kozlov, East German party boss Walter Ulbricht, and the Soviet military command in East Germany remained anxious to challenge Western rights in Berlin. Khrushchev needed a diplomatic victory at Vienna.

Vienna represented perhaps the most frank discourse between the two superpowers since 1945. The meeting revealed fundamental ideological differences, suspicions, and antagonisms that had mounted since the early period of the cold war. Nothing seemed to change as a result of the meeting, at least not immediately, but their experiences in Vienna in time enabled the two leaders to appreciate and better understand each other. Kennedy eventually learned to discount Khrushchev's menacing rhetorical flourishes, and Khrushchev came to realize that Kennedy, although youthful and low key, was determined and sincere.

Their first meeting took place in the music room at the American embassy. Both men—one impulsive, mercurial, and old enough to be the other's father—explored such issues as East-West relations, Berlin, Laos, a nuclear test ban, and space-flight cooperation. Beginning with the first session Kennedy and Khrushchev drifted into an ideological debate, which Soviet experts had advised Kennedy to avoid. It began after Kennedy stressed that both sides must understand each other's views, respect each other's national interests, and do nothing significantly to affect the balance of power. "My ambition," he said, "is to secure peace."[5] The greatest danger to peace, he reiterated, remained miscalculation, which could spark a nuclear exchange. Both parties, he emphasized, must ensure that they conduct themselves responsibly. He acknowledged that the United States had regrettably miscalculated in the past—he himself had done so in Cuba.

Kennedy faulted the Soviets for their denial of self-determination whenever Communist minorities foisted themselves upon the popular will, as they sought to do in Laos and the Congo. Khrushchev denied that his country had ever thwarted public feeling; he contended that Kennedy's desire for the status quo represented nothing more than the attempted obstruction of historical inevitability, as communism continued to replace capitalism, a long-time successor of feudalism. Khrushchev labeled wars of national liberation as "sacred" and pledged to support them against reactionary forces everywhere. At the same time, he berated the United States for rejecting its past by supporting colonial regimes. When Kennedy reminded him that the United States supported UN action against Belgian interests in the Congo, Khrushchev responded that America's voice was timid.

Neither side shared much sympathy for the other's position. Khrushchev's occasional belligerence further disrupted serious discussion, and he reacted strongly against Kennedy's use of "miscalculation," which he viewed as patronizing. After one ideological exchange, Kennedy finally replied, "Look, Mr. Chairman, you aren't going to make a Communist out of me and I don't expect to make a capitalist out of you, so let's get down to business."[6] On another occasion O'Donnell saw the two walking in the garden after lunch, with Khrushchev "circling around Kennedy and snapping at him like a terrier and shaking his finger."[7]

Khrushchev showed a more charming side during the luncheon and state dinner at the Schönbrunn Palace, where he matched de Gaulle in his attentiveness toward Jackie. Kennedy's wit also emerged. At the luncheon Kennedy asked Khrushchev the nature of the medals on his chest. When the Soviet identified them as Lenin Peace Medals, Kennedy responded, "I hope you keep them." After Khrushchev offered to purchase a new tractor model being manufactured in the United States, a smiling Kennedy suggested, "I won't sell you one, Mr. Chairman, but I will think seriously about selling you 1,000."[8]

Eventually they focused on Laos, a matter much on Kennedy's mind but one in which Khrushchev had little interest. The president mentioned American commitments there, inviting Khrushchev's anger: "What business did the U.S. have claiming special rights in Laos?"[9] Khrushchev thought United States policy emanated from delusions of grandeur. When Kennedy proposed a cease-fire to permit a neutral and independent Laos, Khrushchev agreed to use his influence; this represented Kennedy's one concrete achievement at Vienna.

Kennedy also sought to exploit the developing Sino-Soviet rift, hoping to create with Khrushchev a "stable viable world order," dominated by the two superpowers, to prevent China from becoming a nuclear power.[10] The Soviet Union's fear of a China with nuclear power had little effect on Khrushchev at Vienna, however. He also defended China's right to Taiwan and to membership in the United Nations. When Kennedy proposed that Khrushchev get to know the Chinese better, the Soviet said that "he already knew them very well." Given the political climate in the Communist world, Khrushchev undoubtedly realized that he must maintain a hardline position in order to curb China's increasing influence. Other Communist countries had already viewed China more favorably because of Khrushchev's alleged softness toward the West. Like Kennedy, Khrushchev constantly had to prove his toughness.

The two leaders spent more time exploring the possibilities of a nuclear test ban, increasingly a high priority for Kennedy. Not only would this reduce the threat of a nuclear holocaust by preventing other nations from developing nuclear weaponry, it would also lessen atmospheric contamination. The latter concern assumed a poignancy after Kennedy's conversation with Jerome Wiesner, the White House science adviser, during a rainy afternoon later in his presidency. Kennedy asked Wiesner how the fallout returned to the earth after a nuclear test; Wiesner told him it came down in the rain. Looking out the window into the Rose Garden, the president wondered whether radioactive substance was falling as a result of a recent American nuclear test. "Possibly," Wiesner replied. Afterward, Kennedy continued to stare at the rain in the garden, not saying a word. "I never saw him more depressed," O'Donnell wrote.[11]

Yet at Vienna a wide gulf remained between the United States and the Soviet Union over a nuclear test ban. Khrushchev, the Americans contended, opposed adequate enforcement. To the Soviet chairman, any more than three on-site inspections per year would constitute espionage; to the United States, three were not enough. Additionally, Khrushchev wished to tie a test-ban agreement with general disarmament, which Kennedy felt should follow an accord on testing. Most important, Khrushchev no longer retained any faith in the UN, following its alleged lack of neutrality during the Congo crisis. He favored a commission equally representing Western, neutral, and Communist nations, which Kennedy opposed because of a built-in veto to nullify any meaningful system of inspection. Kennedy himself hindered a breakthrough with his repeated boosting of armaments, causing Khrushchev to threaten to follow suit. By July the Soviet boss in fact would announce a one-third increase in military spending. Kennedy's arm-to-parley approach even caused Adlai Stevenson to question whether Kennedy viewed disarmament primarily for its "propaganda value," an expression Kennedy himself employed.[12]

The German problem proved to be more exasperating. An animated Khrushchev called it intolerable; after alluding to sixteen years of indecision by the big powers, he demanded a German peace treaty to ease tensions. With an official ending of World War II in Europe, Khrushchev reasoned, the commitments resulting from Germany's surrender would become invalid, including Western access to and involvement in Berlin. Moreover, a treaty would guarantee the boundaries of East Germany, Poland, and Czechoslovakia. But Kennedy adamantly rejected any surrender of Western contractual rights in West Berlin and he reiterated considerations of national security, which required the United States to honor its obligations. The Soviet leader then threatened to sign a separate agreement with East Germany at the end of 1961 if the West remained in Berlin. If the Americans wanted war, he warned, the Soviet Union could do nothing about it. Kennedy, looking Khrushchev in the eye, responded, "It will be a cold winter."[13]

Khrushchev had a profound impact on John Kennedy at Vienna. Despite de Gaulle's and Harriman's advice to dismiss the Soviet's threats, Khrushchev seemed to have stunned him. At times Kennedy had reacted in a stiff, defensive manner; more often he characteristically chose to listen, causing insiders such as Kennan to assert that Kennedy became "strangely tongue-tied."[14] The inexperienced young president seemed psychologically unprepared for Khrushchev's ultimatum, perhaps because the State Department had inexplicably predicted that Khrushchev would probably show flexibility in regard to Berlin.

Kennedy left Vienna disturbed and upset, believing that Khrushchev meant to cause trouble over Berlin. He remained convinced that the United States was ill-prepared to meet that challenge. Reston of the *New York Times*, who interviewed Kennedy at the American embassy following the conference, later described him as "shaken and angry" because Khrushchev "had bullied and browbeaten" him.[15] Afterward Kennedy departed for England to inform Macmillan about the discussions at Vienna and confided that Khrushchev was "much more a barbarian" than he had anticipated.[16] On national television on 6 June, more circumspectly, he described the "informal exchange" at Vienna as frank but "very sober" and "somber." Without referring to an ultimatum, he conceded that

> Mr. Khrushchev did not talk in terms of war. He believes the world will move his way without resort to force. He spoke of his nation's achievements in space. He stressed his intention to outdo us, to prove to the world the superiority of his system over ours. Most of all, he predicted the triumph of communism in the new and less developed countries.

Kennedy implied that the United States must do more to prepare itself.

For the remainder of the summer the administration concentrated on Berlin, and Kennedy concerned himself about little else. He approved of a Berlin task force headed by Kohler, assistant secretary for European affairs, and his deputy, Martin Hillenbrand, both career diplomats who had dealt with Berlin since 1958. Their tasks included composing a reply to Khrushchev's aide-mémoire of 4 June that comprised the Soviet position on Berlin. The president also put his brother on the NSC, partly to generate debate. In fact, Jack Kennedy became so directly involved with the Berlin task force, either personally or through Bundy, that one State Department official called him the Berlin desk officer. Bundy meanwhile initiated a study in consultation with an interdepartmental group.

Bolstered by Khrushchev's strident behavior at Vienna, Acheson took charge by late June with his own study, which the president had commissioned, doing so at a time when no other report existed and when the State Department seemed to be floundering. He asserted the existing state of affairs to Felix Frankfurter, who wished to know who was at "the helm of the Ship of State." "Often no one," Acheson wrote, even though "Adlai had a control wheel in New York," and "there are several around the White House which are not locked up at night so that Caroline and some of the other children . . . often play with them. . . . Then of course Dean Rusk has one in the State Department, but he hasn't learned how to work it very well."[17]

His report, vintage Acheson, argued that Berlin represented a test of wills. He saw no reality in the conflict over the right of West Berlin to exist as it was. The issue had become a Soviet pretext, Acheson argued, not to rectify an intolerable situation but to test United States resistance. He labeled it as the greatest challenge since the Communist attack on South Korea and thus he opposed further negotiations. Instead he recommended a prompt military buildup of conventional and nuclear forces and the declaring of a state of national emergency. In the event of interruption of American access into West Berlin, he favored an airlift and then a general probe too large for East Germany to stop alone. If the crisis intensified, Acheson left room for both nuclear war and for negotiations only to ensure Western rights to Berlin.

Acheson's recommendations inspired an administration debate that was lacking during the Cuban crisis. Those who accepted Acheson's world view (with variations) included Kohler of the State Department, Paul Nitze of Defense, and Rostow and probably Bundy of the White House staff. Eventually moderate voices challenged Acheson's "declaration of war," including Abram Chayes, State Department legal adviser, Sorensen, Schlesinger, Harriman, and Ambassador Thompson. They viewed Acheson's proposals as "dangerous." Moreover, they also understood Khrushchev's frustration over Berlin and thought he was merely seeking to consolidate his position in Eastern Europe. They favored continued discussions with the Soviet Union. Rusk disappointed this group because of his failure to take a strong position. On the one hand he thought Acheson's report too provocative, but at the same time he placed little faith in negotiations. Schlesinger later wrote that "no one quite knew where he stood."[18] Rusk aroused even greater enmity when the State Department took six weeks to provide Kennedy with a reply to Khrushchev's memorandum on Berlin. The president and White House staffers labeled the department's dilatory performance as bureaucratic foot-dragging. Chayes called the State Department document a "scissors and paste job out of documents used in the [earlier] Berlin crisis," describing the style as "turgid" and the tone as "more Stalinist than the Soviets."[19] At any rate, the draft memorandum failed to provide the United States with a viable position for negotiation. Embarrassed by the delay, Kennedy had no choice but to send it to Khrushchev, but he and

Sorensen wrote a covering piece to soften the impact. The president's confidence in the State Department had reached rock bottom.

Rusk insisted, however, that no "good clear negotiation position" existed since there was nothing significant that the United States could give away. Furthermore, the Soviets would perceive any change in American policy as a sign of weakness that would further escalate the crisis. Any American response to the Soviets also had to take into consideration the position of the NATO Allies, particularly the West Germans, who enjoyed a customary veto over United States policy on Berlin. Both the West Germans and the French either opposed or feared negotiations with the Soviets, while the British wished to explore all alternatives to possible war over Berlin. In the interest of Allied unity, others needed to be consulted, and this required time.

Despite these obstacles, Hillenbrand of State later claimed that the department had submitted a draft memorandum to the White House within a "week or so." But staff procedures "were so sloppy" that it ended up in the safe of presidential assistant Ralph Dungan, who went on a two-week vacation. Indeed no one knew the whereabouts of the draft when State inquired about it. A returning Dungan accepted full responsibility for the confusion. According to Hillenbrand, "staffers neglected to inform the president what had happened and the State Department took the blame."[20]

By mid-July Kennedy had decided on a Berlin policy; during the previous weeks he had thought of little else. "He's imprisoned by Berlin," exclaimed Interior Secretary Stewart Udall, who found him difficult to reach.[21] Ultimately, moderates such as Thompson, Sorensen, Taylor, and Robert Kennedy reinforced the president's own inclinations. His message to the American people on 25 July spelled out the administration's approach. Following Acheson, it somberly outlined the Soviet threat to West Berlin, but it also recognized the Soviet Union's historical concern about its security in Central and Eastern Europe. Kennedy made it clear that "we" intended to defend Western rights in West Berlin, despite a lack of consensus among the Allies. He responded to the concern that West Berlin was militarily untenable by suggesting that so were Bastogne and Stalingrad during World War II. Yet in focusing on Western rights to West Berlin, he curiously ignored rights in East Berlin, including Western access and the quadripartite status, both affirmed at the Potsdam Conference of July 1945. Thus his approach made it less difficult for the Soviets to construct the Berlin Wall one month later.

Without proclaiming a national emergency, Kennedy asked Americans to endure sacrifices to preserve the status quo in West Berlin. These included a massive military buildup in addition to the March and May

80

expansions. Specifically, he requested from Congress $3.24 billion more for the armed forces, which represented a $6 billion increase in the defense budget since January. He proposed that the army's authorized strength jump from 875,000 to 1 million men; draft calls doubled and tripled in the months ahead. Even more significant were the call-up of reserve units and the extension of tours of duty. In the ensuing weeks U.S. military forces in West Germany came to full strength; the intention was to present the Soviets with a credible scenario whereby tactical and strategic nuclear responses would follow if conventional units failed to do the job. Berlin, journalist Richard Rovere perceptively wrote at the time, enabled Kennedy to establish a viable, flexible military response that otherwise would have proved too financially costly.

Nevertheless, Kennedy recommended no immediate tax increase, despite his brother's argument that Americans could more readily identify with a sacrificial call by paying higher taxes. Walter Heller, chairman of the Council of Economic Advisers, talked Kennedy out of a more drastic approach by arguing that budget increases contributed much less to inflation than "possible psychological reactions," which a tax rise and a declaration of national emergency might incite.

Kennedy nonetheless announced in his 25 July speech a proposed civil defense program to include fallout shelters in existing structures, which were to be stocked with food, water, and other necessities for survival. In proposing this, Kennedy raised the specter of nuclear war, labeling shelters a form of insurance. Coming on the heels of the Berlin crisis, the idea brought about an overreaction that occasionally reached hysterical levels. The Defense Department contributed to the problem by preparing a pamphlet suggesting that families construct individual shelters, which, of course, remained financially prohibitive for most Americans. According to Adam Yarmolinsky, McNamara thought that the American people ought to have enough self-reliance to deal with the problem and recommended sending a letter to every homeowner explaining how to provide greater security for the family. Misleading information soon followed from nongovernmental sources to embarrass the administration. *Life* magazine published an article, which suggested improbably that American families had "97 chances out of 100" to survive a nuclear attack, provided that they had a fallout shelter. Its emphasis on individual—rather than on community and public—shelters ran counter to Kennedy's approach, as did the argument that shelters contributed to the nation's total deterrent. That a Kennedy cover letter accompanied the *Life* article especially concerned administration officials.[22]

The controversy over fallout shelters became more embarrassing when get-rich-quick shelter manufacturers fed on the national panic that the administration had provoked. Greed accompanied by hysteria sometimes reached bizarre levels. In a widely quoted article, Father L. C. McHugh, a Jesuit priest and former professor of ethics at Georgetown University, argued that shelter owners had the moral right to kill panicky neighbors seeking protection. Some parents even admonished their children to conceal the location of their shelters.

The reaction caused Kennedy to regret focusing on fallout shelters without providing a comprehensive shelter program or a clear-cut policy. He said little more about it for the remainder of the year, as the Defense Department rewrote its informational pamphlet in an effort to reduce hysteria and to refocus on community shelters. It quietly located sixty million shelter spaces, but the administration's long-range program of providing federal incentives for the construction of community shelters in hospitals, libraries, and schools failed to obtain congressional support in 1962 and 1963.

Kennedy's 25 July speech emphasized more than national preparedness; once again he stressed the need for negotiations consistent with the maintenance of freedom and liberty in West Berlin. Even though he clearly preferred to defuse the German problem, this part of his speech received little public attention because of its generalities and brevity. To hardliners such as Acheson, Kennedy's response seemed weak, but only Vice-President Johnson had supported Acheson's proposed declaration of national emergency in the NSC meetings. In exasperation Acheson confided to Harry Truman of "a weakness in decision at the top" and of the administration's preoccupation with "image." He felt that Kennedy had failed to convince Khrushchev that "we are deadly in earnest about Berlin."[23] Besides finding Acheson too hawkish, Kennedy became increasingly irritated after Acheson told a group of retired foreign service officers that observing Kennedy at Vienna "was like watching a gifted young performer with a boomerang knock himself out."[24]

Acheson's perception of the 25 July address differed markedly from Khrushchev's; he called it a preliminary declaration of war. If war came, Khrushchev warned, it would be won by the biggest rockets. He boasted that his country had the rocket capacity to deliver a hundred-megaton "superbomb," which Soviet scientists were eager to test. But Khrushchev soon tempered his outburst by suggesting that he believed in the president's good sense. He wondered why the two countries could not negotiate their differences.

Khrushchev remained under enormous pressure to deal successfully with Berlin. What moved Ulbricht of East Germany were the more than four thousand people leaving his country weekly for West Berlin. "East Germany is hemorrhaging to death," Kennedy told Rostow in late July.

He recognized that Khrushchev faced an unbearable situation that threatened the Eastern bloc and he knew that the Soviet leader had few realistic alternatives. Given the administration's strong military stand on West Berlin, he doubted that Khrushchev would try to force the United States out. Yet Kennedy had pointedly ignored Western rights in East Berlin in his speeches and had also shown moderation by raising the possibility of negotiations. That left one plausible solution.

On Sunday 13 August the Soviets began to build a wall separating the two Berlins to stem Western influence and to keep East Germans from "voting with their feet," as Rusk described it. During the first week the wall consisted of nothing more than barbed wire and street barricades, which failed to prohibit movement into West Berlin. In fact, thousands at first assembled on both sides of the barrier; by 16 August three hundred thousand West Berliners had joined Mayor Willy Brandt in an emotional protest. Concrete blocks and watch towers soon followed, slowly isolating East Berlin from the West.

The Soviet action had inexplicably caught U.S. officials in West Berlin off guard, causing a seven-hour delay in their reporting to Washington. Kennedy received word at Hyannis Port later that Sunday; the story broke in the press nationwide the following day. Initially, most Americans favored immediate action. O'Donnell spoke for many when he privately clamored for American soldiers to apply pliers to the barbed wire. Eisenhower reportedly urged Kennedy to use bulldozers, and retired general Lucius Clay, the crusty hero of the 1948 Berlin blockade, also recommended removal. The American press responded more cautiously. Even the antiadministration *Chicago Tribune* focused its enmity on Khrushchev and the Western Allies. The conservative *National Review*, rather than concentrating on immediate action, criticized the national government for fifteen years of "containment-coexistence-appeasement." Clearly, few journalists wished to risk war over East Berlin. Neither did Republican leaders, who withheld public criticism until the crisis passed. A July Gallup Poll had already revealed that only 58 percent of the public favored defending East Berlin although 78 percent supported retaining troops in West Berlin to "give hope" to Eastern Europe. Kennedy's immediate actions reflected public sentiment—one that he helped to shape.

Most likely Khrushchev had not surprised Kennedy. Rostow maintained that "JFK had thought through the Wall and decided on his policy before the event." Senate Foreign Relations chairman J. William Fulbright, reflecting the administration's viewpoint, had stated in a TV interview on 30 July that "I don't understand why the East Germans don't close their borders."[25] Not only did Kennedy anticipate the wall, he seemed to have encouraged and welcomed it. It solved the East German problem, which might have invited a stronger Communist response, perhaps leading to a popular uprising and subsequent West German intervention. Once the wall went up, Kennan, Bohlen, and others reinforced Kennedy's apparent belief that Khrushchev, by stopping the flow of refugees and sealing off East Berlin, sought to head off confrontation. Kennedy had no intention of challenging the Soviet Union in its sphere of influence. He privately contended that the East Germans probably had the legal right to seal the border, even though that action was inhumane. Surely, he argued, none of this was worth a war.

Nonetheless, he knew a response must follow; West Berlin Mayor Brandt wanted action. Kennedy ended up sending General Clay to West Berlin as his personal ambassador, along with Charles Bohlen to prevent Clay from overreacting. Vice-President Johnson also went to reaffirm Kennedy's commitment to Berlin. Sending a battle group of fifteen hundred men through East Germany to West Berlin was designed to do the same thing. For one day the administration remained anxious, as the troops proceeded along the Autobahn to the Berlin Gate to be greeted by Johnson and Clay. At the Berlin House of Representatives later in the day, Johnson intoned, "This is the time for confidence, for poise, and for faith— for faith in ourselves. It is also a time for faith in your allies, everywhere throughout the world. This island does not stand alone."[26]

Yet the construction of the wall did reveal limitations in the West's commitment to Berlin. It suggested that, unlike Bonn's traditional goal of German reunification, the Kennedy administration would accept a de facto policy acknowledging two Germanies. Could a de jure policy that designated West Berlin a free city be that far away? Unquestionably hardliners encouraged Khrushchev to continue the pressure in the weeks ahead, even though the Soviet leader sensed Kennedy's intentions to honor his obligations to West Berlin. The wall, then, marked only the most intense phase of the Berlin crisis, which continued unabated well into 1962.

Khrushchev's decision to resume nuclear testing on 30 August, following Kennedy's military buildup, did little to improve superpower relations. Soviet hardliners probably pushed Khrushchev to do so because of their profound beliefs in close Soviet-Chinese collaboration and in a tough approach toward the United States. In July Khrushchev had told John L. McCloy, Kennedy's special assistant on disarmament, that he faced heavy pressure to begin testing. The Soviets soon embarked on atmospheric tests in which at least thirty major explosions occurred between September and November. Kennedy, under pressure to follow suit, eventually announced that military security dictated the United States' resumption of nuclear testing, which would occur underground.

Yet Kennedy also sought ways to resume negotiations with the Soviet Union. Beginning in August, Soviet and East German military personnel had interfered with air access into West Berlin, dropping chaff to upset American radar and projecting blinding search lights from the ground on incoming planes. In early September Kennedy settled on a negotiating position in which he proposed the internationalization, under UN control, of the Autobahn to Berlin; a UN plebiscite in Berlin; the submission of the legal conflict to the World Court; and a nonaggression pact between NATO and Warsaw Pact powers. The invitation to the Soviets went through Ambassador Thompson. The president asked Rusk to take charge of the talks, cautioning him to be flexible and reasonable. Above all, Kennedy continued, "make the framework of our proposals as fresh as possible—they should *not* look like warmed over stuff from 1959."[27]

By September Khrushchev turned to a "back-channel" personal correspondence with Kennedy to bypass his own hardliners. Kennedy's military buildup, the world reaction to Soviet atmospheric testing, and the unresolved crisis in Berlin undoubtedly concerned him. He, too, wished for the resumption of negotiations. His confidential letters generally went to Kennedy's press secretary Pierre Salinger or to Robert Kennedy, surreptitiously delivered by Khrushchev loyalists Georgi Bolshakov, editor and spy, and Mikhail Kharlamov, press spokesman for Andrei Gromyko. Kharlamov prefaced the delivery of the first letter with the comment, "The storm in Berlin is over." A pajama-clad Kennedy, in a New York hotel prior to his UN speech, read the letter proposing rapprochement. After repeatedly reviewing it with Salinger, Kennedy finally remarked, "If Khrushchev is ready to listen to our views on Germany, he's not going to recognize the Ulbricht regime—not this year, at least—and that's good news."[28] Indeed by 17 October Khrushchev, in a speech before the Twenty-second Congress of the Communist party, terminated the deadline for the German peace treaty.

Kennedy's response to Khrushchev's initiatives took several forms. He wrote that before there could be an early summit on Berlin, there must be good faith in Laos. According to Salinger, Khrushchev promised this in a subsequent missive, which rambled for twenty-six pages, adding, in effect, that "you and I, Mr. President, are . . . reasonable men, we agree that war between us is unthinkable. We have no choice but to put our heads together and find ways to live in peace."[29] Kennedy also delivered probably his best speech since the inaugural before the General Assembly of the United Nations on 25 September. Kennedy sent Khrushchev a message, crafted largely by Sorensen, and exploited the anti-Soviet reaction following the Berlin Wall and the resumption of atmospheric testing. He again emphasized the finality of war—"mankind must put an end to war—or war will put an end to mankind." To Kennedy the dangers of war coming about by accident or miscalculation remained obvious. He challenged the Soviet Union "not to an arms race, but to a peace race." He publicly came out for "general and complete disarmament under effective international control," which could be secured through the UN. The way to begin was by agreeing to a nuclear test ban. If inspection or controls continued to be a problem, he proposed beginning with a ban on atmospheric testing, which required no verification procedure. The United States and Great Britain had already presented these proposals to the Soviets at Geneva, where test ban talks had been occurring since 1958.

Kennedy's UN address also represented an effort to boost the United Nations following the tragic death of Secretary General Dag Hammarskjöld on 18 September. No world leader seemed more supportive of that organization than Kennedy. "Were we to let it die, to enfeeble its vigor, to cripple its powers, we would condemn our future," Kennedy warned. The key to its successful continuance depended on the selection of a strong individual to replace Hammarskjöld. Kennedy discredited Khrushchev's recommendation that the Secretary General's position be represented by three people, contending that "even the three horses of the Troika did not have three drivers, all going in different directions." Thanks largely to Kennedy, the United States won out with the selection of U Thant of Thailand. Though the Kennedy period marked the continuation of America's enormous influence in the UN, that was to change in the years to come.

Kennedy also addressed the matter of Laos in his UN speech. Ignoring the unpopularity of the regime in power, backed by the United States, he argued that the situation in Laos could not be labeled a war of national liberation because Laos lived under its own government. He opposed colonialism, but he also abhorred Communist violations of self-determination, which threatened Third World nations like Laos. He reaffirmed his commitment to a "truly neutral and independent Laos" in reminding Khrushchev of his own pledge at Vienna as Laotian negotiations at Geneva reached a critical stage. Both Kennedy and Khrushchev privately expressed the sentiment that an agreement would have an important effect on Germany. In his UN address Kennedy in fact called Southeast Asia and Berlin the two threats to world peace. Until spring 1962, however, Laos remained an unsolvable mess, which went well beyond the Soviets' influence to resolve. Harriman, too, had all that he could do to keep Phoumi and State Department officials from sabotaging any proposed neutral coalition involving Souvanna.

Meanwhile, Kennedy instructed Rusk to begin discussions with Gromyko in New York City; both were there for the fall session of the UN. Rusk retained serious doubts about negotiations: To negotiate in the shadow of the Berlin Wall suggested weakness or even submission, and unlike Kennedy, he remained pessimistic about the ultimate outcome of such talks. He recommended that instead discussions take the form of "exploratory talks" to determine whether a basis for negotiations existed. Thus he was able to succeed in selling the talks to de Gaulle and Adenauer, who gave reluctant approval, their major concern being the United States' compromising on basic rights over Berlin.

The Rusk-Gromyko discussions continued through September and October. Rusk presented Kennedy's proposals, but neither side agreed on any significant concessions, endlessly repeating their own positions. Rusk accepted that approach since he viewed negotiations as a way to defuse crises. If U.S. proposals were accepted, however, they might arouse the antagonism of de Gaulle and Adenauer, who remained suspicious of Kennedy's intentions. As for Khrushchev, he could argue that the West now better understood the Soviet position and thus could seek a mutually acceptable solution to Berlin. He used that justification to overcome his own hardliners and announced the cancellation of the Berlin ultimatum in mid-October.

Kennedy had greater appreciation for Rusk during this period. Even though no settlement had resulted, the crisis eased and the United States had held firm. Furthermore, Rusk and Gromyko came to respect each other and managed to engage in some levity as they tried to make the best of a bad situation. In time, discussions were scaled down to the ambassadorial level, prior to the resumption of the Rusk-Gromyko meetings in March 1962. Still, occasional incidents occurred around Berlin that escalated East-West tensions. On one menacing occasion a sizable number of Soviet and American tanks faced each other across the Berlin border before Khrushchev apparently ordered the Soviets to withdraw. The Soviets from time to time continued to harass the Allied aircraft using the air corridors to West Berlin by flying Soviet MIGs along their path, thus causing the United States to adopt contingency plans for fighter escorts into the city. Such actions persuaded the administration that the Soviets would continue to test Western resolve over West Berlin as talks moved on aimlessly. With characteristic bluster Khrushchev called Berlin a "bunion on [the American] toes, and that any time he had trouble with us, he would just step on our toes and twist his heel . . . and then take off his hat and say 'Thank you very much.' "[30]

Unlike the ignoble Bay of Pigs adventure, Kennedy had credibly confronted the Berlin crisis of 1961. He had relied on both the instruments of power and of negotiations, as outlined in his inaugural. By quickly strengthening U.S. conventional military forces and adhering consistently to certain basic beliefs, he convinced Khrushchev that the West would defend its rights in West Berlin. His characteristic moderation caused him to reject Acheson's declaration of national emergency, which might have painted Khrushchev into a corner. Not only did Kennedy favor negotiation but he also sought fresh approaches to enable both sides to live with the problem. At the very least he persuaded Khrushchev of his own reasonability, even though they both understood the pressures each faced from hardliners in their own governments. Kennedy also displayed more maturity in assessing the recommendations of subordinates and learned to encourage frank dialogue from a broader element.

In referring to Kennedy as a "cold war monger" over Berlin, revisionist historians have surely overstated the case. Kennedy had not instigated the conflict, nor could he have ignored the Khrushchev ultimatum at Vienna. A tour de force was necessary. Yet it is also fair to say that Kennedy overreacted to Khrushchev's rhetorical outbursts in June; his speech on 25 July needlessly panicked Americans over civil defense. The president's preoccupation with Berlin also detracted from his attention to other problems, particularly domestic ones. One can even question the extent of Kennedy's arms buildup in 1961, given the resulting expansion of Soviet armaments and the limited nature of Khrushchev's ultimatum, which wore the earmarks of a bluff.

Kennedy understandably felt compelled to respond to domestic political considerations. The Gallup Polls suggested that Americans expected him to defend Western rights in Berlin. When Kennedy took six days to protest the Berlin Wall and did nothing significantly to challenge that intrusion, he eventually came under criticism. Others have faulted him for making it too evident that he preferred negotiations over mobilization. The debate continues whether the Soviet decision to ease the pressure resulted from Kennedy's willingness to negotiate or from his marshaling of forces.

Bowles, Kennedy's undersecretary of state, later expressed the administration's problems in more fundamental terms, contending that no new broad policies emerged to tackle world issues and that instead the administration spent its time reacting to emergencies. He especially faulted the State Department, which he called a "fire brigade" rather than a "creative agency."[31] Bowles, by summer 1961, found himself embroiled in a major controversy with the foreign policy establishment, which led to his dismissal in November. The most puzzling question of why such a respected liberal should have been fired remains. As one probes the matter one learns more about Kennedy and his style of leadership and the nature of the institutional conflicts over foreign policy in 1961. The findings go a long way in explaining the difficulties the administration experienced in that area.

Kennedy had contributed to the problem in 1960 by appointing Bowles undersecretary of state for political affairs before he selected Rusk, choosing Bowles largely out of political considerations. Bowles had been the first significant liberal to work for Kennedy prior to the national convention. He had epitomized the eastern establishment that had embraced Roosevelt during the 1930s and 1940s. After serving capably as Roosevelt's price-control director during World War II, Bowles became governor of Connecticut and later a United States Congressman. A throwback to Henry Wallace, Eleanor Roosevelt, and other "one worlders" and "world New Dealers," Bowles had aligned himself with Adlai Stevenson in the 1950s in thinking that world poverty, not Soviet aggrandizement, represented the greatest danger. He advocated the reduction of military aid and extensive economic assistance to the Third World without political strings. No one opposed colonialism more, in recognizing that European intrusion contributed to Communist successes. He articulated the need for a sweeping reevaluation of American foreign policy. He strongly favored a two-China policy in which the United States would recognize both Communist China and Taiwan. Probably the first American to predict the Soviet-Chinese rift, Bowles, more than anyone, understood its significance.

The traditionalist Rusk, meanwhile, conformed to the Acheson wing, which focused on Third World issues from a NATO perspective. Rusk viewed the Soviet Union as a near carbon copy of the Stalinist model and felt the same about China. He remained wedded to the conservatives, who had permeated the East Asian section of the State Department since the Korean War. The reticent Rusk and the gregarious Bowles shared an incompatibility of style, approach, and worldview.

A misunderstanding over how Bowles would function as undersecretary compounded their differences. Rusk wanted Bowles to manage the creaky bureaucracy and to serve as his alter ego in policy. Bowles failed to understand that Rusk did not want him to make major changes. Rusk had an enormous respect for departmental careerists who worked at the country desks. He willingly delegated responsibility to them, knowing that they would respond professionally and predictably. As an insider and a traditionalist, he accepted the necessity of policy continuity, particularly in relation to the Soviet Union and Germany. Conversely, Bowles viewed the State Department as an archaic institution badly in need of revitalization from the lingering doctrines of Acheson and Dulles and from the impact of McCarthyism, which especially had weakened the East Asian department. More often than not, he saw State engaged in crisis management instead of involved in long-range planning to shape the nationalistic forces of the Third World and to resolve problems elsewhere.

As undersecretary Bowles gave much attention to planning and policy review. He worked closely with G. Mennen Williams, assistant secretary for African affairs, in adjusting policy to the realities of African nationalism. He also toyed with schemes to neutralize Southeast Asia. Bowles made his greatest impact in selecting ambassadors who embodied the spirit of the New Frontier. This particularly rang true with Africa, where he ensured that appointees would respond sympathetically to the newly created nations. He often bypassed senior Foreign Service officers for journalists, scholars, and liberal Democrats whose backgrounds somehow qualified them for the position. Edwin Reischauer, the leading American scholar of Japanese history, perhaps became Bowles's most notable appointment. Reischauer owed much of his success in Japan to a deep understanding of Japanese culture, a Japanese wife, and the ability to speak the language.

Bowles less successfully infused the State Department with innovative people; Rusk refused to permit him the authority to revamp personnel and policies. He in fact blamed Bowles for many of its problems, labeling him an "administrative bottleneck."[32] Papers accumulated on his desk, Rusk insisted, because Bowles ignored the department's day-to-day operations as a result of a preoccupation with long-range planning. Conversely, the undersecretary believed that his desire to effect change rather than a supposed administrative laxness created the conflict.

By spring 1961 Rusk felt that Bowles had to go. By that time the department had come under fire for failing to meet the demands of the White House, which considered State's approaches on Cuba, Berlin, and Laos either dated, unimaginative, or irrelevant. Its reports seemed to take forever to reach the Oval Office. The department's advice on a Middle East matter created a reaction "so sour [that Kennedy] wanted to know whose idea it was." On that same day Kennedy described a departmental draft letter to Chiang Kai-shek as "hopeless" and therefore wrote his own response.[33] According to Robert Kennedy, most State Department letters—particularly to Khrushchev or de Gaulle—also underwent extensive White House revision.

Kennedy as a result began to question Rusk's leadership. Robert, one of Rusk's greatest critics, even faulted Rusk for being "tremendously influenced by what the president wanted to do."[34] He later claimed that his brother talked about replacing him, but no evidence exists that Kennedy intended to do so in 1961. That spring Bundy in fact told friends at a dinner party that "something has to be changed at State and you can't fire the Secretary of State"—at least not a few months into the administration.[35] Bowles consequently became the scapegoat.

Kennedy had ambivalent feelings about Bowles, despite sharing a belief in the necessity to reshape foreign policy. That commitment had been a distinctive Kennedy trademark during his candidacy. Yet an exceedingly close election and Khrushchev's belligerent stance dictated prudence. While Kennedy continued to seek imaginative and fresh ideas, he did so with the stricture that they politically serve his foreign policy, something that Bowles failed to always appreciate. Bowles moreover fell short of the president's litmus test—that New Frontiersmen must be tough, amoral, nonideological, and reticent. Regarding the latter, Robert Kennedy reflected his brother's viewpoint that Bowles had "a great tendency of never getting to the point" and of "talking around the subject . . . [with] all the long sentences and big words."[36] More significantly, he sometimes talked too candidly with outsiders.

Bowles's reaction to the Bay of Pigs invasion added to White House reservations. A James Reston story in the *New York Times* publicized his objections to the operation, spurring other press stories that Bowles was releasing information to protect his reputation. Salinger soon stopped staffer Harris Wofford in a White House hallway and said, "That yellow-bellied friend of yours, Chester Bowles, is leaking all over town that he was against it. We're going to get him."[37] Robert Kennedy also accosted Bowles. "It was depressing enough as it was," Kennedy remembered; "we didn't need somebody coming in and making sure everybody understood that [he wasn't] in favor of this in the first place. Everybody rather resented it."[38]

Bowles's subsequent departmental proposal on Cuba, presented at the NSC, particularly infuriated the attorney general. He called it "worthless" and a "disgrace," probably because it failed to propose forceful action. He reacted even more angrily in May following the United States-supported assassination of Rafael Trujillo, the tyrannical Dominican Republic dictator. As did others at an NSC meeting, Robert Kennedy favored American military intervention to protect American lives and to prevent a possible Communist takeover. Bowles, sitting in Rusk's absence as acting secretary of state, resisted even limited American military involvement on the same moral and legal basis that he had opposed the Bay of Pigs. According to one account Robert "unleashed a cascade of epithets on Bowles," causing others in the room to "wince in sympathy for him."[39] Bowles had to call Kennedy in Paris to restrain the attorney general.

By that summer Bowles had become the target of a massive attack. Rusk pushed for his removal as did career foreign service and departmental officers, who resented his ambassadorial appointments and his efforts to reshape foreign policy; traditionalists elsewhere detested Bowles primarily for ideological reasons. Acheson called him a "misfit," and Lyndon Johnson went beyond ideology in ridiculing Bowles. "He's losing us friends all over the world with his goddamned halitosis. I got a whiff of it the other day and if it had been Khrushchev instead of me, there'd likely be a war on now."[40] Meanwhile, long-time Kennedyites such as O'Donnell had disliked Bowles ever since he had refused to campaign for Kennedy in the crucial Wisconsin primary because of a prior pledge to Humphrey. Hawkish columnists, including Joseph Alsop, continued to view him with scorn and suspicion.

Sorensen, an avowed liberal who rarely questioned Kennedy's motivations, claimed that ideology and Bowles's alleged disloyalty had nothing to do with the dismissal: "The president liked Bowles, liked most of his ideas and liked most of his personal recommendations. But the State Department team needs a manager."[41] This explanation squares with Kennedy's intent to retain Rusk at least until after the 1964 election, necessitating a more harmonious and effective departmental leadership. Robert Kennedy, however, later admitted the president's and his own personal displeasure with Bowles. "Bowles," according to the attorney general, "always seemed to have some dam up the Nikon River [in Africa]—he always had some plan, a particular point that he was getting across. . . ." Moreover, "when he disagreed with the President, he talked to the press." Kennedy called Bowles a weeper and a self-promoter, and his own disdain for Bowles undoubtedly influenced the president.[42] Even Schlesinger conceded that John Kennedy became particularly "aggrieved" and "disturbed" over Bowles after the Bay of Pigs for dodging "responsibility after the fact." Others such as Benjamin Bradlee of *Newsweek* similarly expressed the president's feelings.[43] Ideology and personal displeasure indeed played a part in Bowles's removal.

Most revealing was the way the administration managed his departure. On 6 July Rusk asked Bowles to accept a roving ambassadorship to the newly developing Third World countries. When Bowles objected press stories based on "White House sources" soon emerged, alluding to Bowles's administrative deficiencies as undersecretary. Columnist Charles Bartlett, a close friend of Kennedy's, also referred to Bowles's difficulties with departmental career officers and to his organizational inexperience. Soon Joseph Alsop and others joined in the attack, suggesting that the White House—most likely Kennedy—was involved.

Bowles, mounting a counteroffensive, visited the president on 12 July to argue his case. Kennedy sought to deflate the controversy smoothly by offering Bowles other alternatives, including an ambassadorship to Brazil or Chile. He professed that perhaps he should have appointed Bowles secretary of state; nonetheless, the department had failed to produce the desired foreign policy initiatives under the existing arrangement. Since it was not feasible to remove Rusk, Bowles regrettably must leave, Kennedy concluded. The meeting ended with Bowles requesting more time to make a decision.

In the ensuing weeks an avalanche of liberal support poured into the White House on Bowles's behalf. Stevenson, Williams, Walter Reuther of the United Auto Workers, and Orville Freeman, among others, came to his defense. Wofford, in a lengthy memorandum to Kennedy, expressed most clearly the reasons for Bowles's retention: First, "It would be a setback to the United States in the world." Bowles's dismissal after opposing the Bay of Pigs invasion would send the wrong message to nations in Africa, Asia, and Latin America. Second, "It would be a setback politically at home." Bowles's firing would be another indication to the Stevenson and Humphrey element that Kennedy was rejecting their world view. Third, "It would be a setback to the State Department itself." Bowles's departure would eliminate the one person who had sought new ideas, imaginative subordinates, and much needed reforms. Fourth, "It would be a setback in your efforts to devise a new foreign policy." The recent crisis indicated more than ever the need for policy planning and reevaluation. "You need someone," Wofford continued, "who from the time he wakes up . . . knows that the Cuban invasion was wrong."[44] Pro-Bowles articles in the *New Republic*, the *Washington Post*, and the *New York Times* soon followed, and Bowles rapidly became a symbolic test of Kennedy's liberalism. Under these circumstances he found it exceedingly difficult to remove Bowles. Revealingly, he also rejected proposals from Schlesinger and others to place someone immediately beneath Bowles to manage the department on a day-to-day basis while Bowles focused on policy planning and personnel. Instead at a press conference on 19 July, Kennedy expressed his "complete" confidence in Bowles and indicated that for the present he would remain as undersecretary, although the president reserved the right to make personnel changes later. At a press briefing, Salinger commented obliquely that Bowles's resignation was "not currently expected." To trusted Hugh Sidey of *Time* magazine, the president casually said that "Bowles will go."[45]

Bowles's reprieve ended after the controversy had abated. Without prior warning, Rusk, over the weekend in late November, called Bowles to his office and handed him a press release, indicating that George Ball would replace him, Harriman would become assistant secretary for Far

Eastern Affairs, George McGhee would serve as junior undersecretary, and Rostow would replace McGhee as head of the Policy Planning Council. Sorensen came over to the State Department to persuade an angered Bowles to accept an alternate position. The sometimes animated conversation carried into the evening, Sorensen later wrote, with neither reaching for the light switch. Bowles reluctantly accepted the post of president's special representative and adviser on Asian, African, and Latin American affairs, receiving ambassadorial status, a salary increase, a White House office, a car, and other "status symbols of officialdom." He also had Kennedy's assurance that he would contribute directly to policy formation, a never-fulfilled promise. As Sorensen later admitted, "it was not a real post."[46] After a year of travel, writing reports, and making recommendations that no one took seriously, Bowles resigned in December 1962. Afterward Kennedy persuaded him to return to India as ambassador, a position he had held during the Truman administration.

Meanwhile, the situation at the State Department seemed little improved despite the blood transfusion from the White House and the closer working relationship between Rusk and Ball. According to Schlesinger, "The department remained a puzzle to the President. No one ran it"—neither Rusk, Ball, nor Harriman, all of whom remained a few steps ahead of crises.[47] After Bowles's departure Robert Kennedy soon blamed the department's problems on Ball, "not a good administrator," and on McGhee, "a real zero."[48] Of course, the dissatisfaction with Rusk remained.

The White House problem with Foggy Bottom clearly went beyond the Rusk-Bowles turmoil, partly reflecting a natural bias of the Kennedys against the State Department, probably engendered by old Joe Kennedy. Often the Oval Office contributed to the department's difficulties by creating task forces, which bypassed State on various crises. The department, of course, had played no part in the preparation for the Bay of Pigs. Moreover, White House troubleshooters such as Schlesinger and Goodwin frequently interfered in foreign policy matters, much to Rusk's chagrin. Kennedy himself impatiently employed back-channel communications, surprising desk officers by telephoning for information. The attorney general had his own lines into State and involved himself in both personnel and policy matters. The White House's activism and aversion to formal procedures complicated the decision-making process, weakened Rusk's authority, and played havoc with departmental morale. Bundy's beefed-up operation in the White House basement, enabling Kennedy to bypass State more, was the most serious blow. Even though Rusk still had Kennedy's ear, the president heard many voices by fall 1961.

Harriman clearly moved into range after making substantial progress in securing the neutralization of Laos. By late September he had fashioned a tentative agreement providing for a coalition government under Souvanna. The United States accepted the inclusion of the Pathet Lao in the cabinet but not in the key positions of defense and interior. The proposed accords stipulated that North Vietnam would not use Laos as a corridor for infiltrating men and equipment. Moreover, an understanding emerged between the Soviet Union and Great Britain, the International Control Commission co-chairmen, that the former would ensure the compliance of China and North Vietnam and the latter, the United States.

Yet nearly nine months transpired before a final agreement occurred. American officials in State, Defense, and the CIA contributed to the problems by seeking to abort the neutralization of Laos. Almost as frustrating to Harriman, Marshal Thanarat Sarit of Thailand opposed the accords because a neutral Laos was more vulnerable to communism and because General Phoumi was his cousin. In October Phoumi posed the greatest obstacle by attacking the Pathet Lao near the Chinese border around Nam Tha. Encouraged by CIA operatives, Phoumi pointed to alleged North Vietnam violations of the cease-fire to justify his own violations. Harriman convinced the Kennedy administration to cut off financial assistance to the Boun Oum government, and at a meeting in Laos in March 1962, he "shook his finger" at Phoumi, angrily accusing him of destroying his country. He also told an unhappy Sarit that he must accept the coalition.[49]

Although the Sarit government soon relented, Phoumi continued to oppose Souvanna as the proposed prime minister, intensifying military activities in the North. Even so, Nam Tha fell to the Pathet Lao without resistance on 6 May, once again revealing the gross inadequacies of the Laotian military. Thailand more than ever felt threatened with a possible Communist takeover in Laos. The pressure mounted on Kennedy to take more decisive action. McNamara, Eisenhower, and even Harriman, favored sending troops to Laos as a show of force. After considering this, Kennedy in May decided on only a token force of about three thousand men to be deployed in the Mekong Delta area. He did this to appease Eisenhower, whom he carefully cultivated, and to allay Thailand's fears rather than to assist Phoumi.

By June Phoumi's position had weakened appreciably. He soon grudgingly agreed to a settlement in which he and Souphanouvong of the Pathet Lao would be deputy premiers and Souvanna would be prime minister and minister of defense. Overall, Souvanna's people would hold seven cabinet seats, the Pathet Lao would obtain four, and the remaining four seats would go elsewhere. The nineteen nations who signed the

Geneva Protocol on 23 July, including China, agreed to respect Laos' territorial integrity and sovereignty, and the United States gradually withdrew its forces from Thailand over the next four months.

The Geneva agreement ended the crisis in Laos and made Harriman a hero in Kennedy circles. His supposed deafness now became the subject of several amusing anecdotes. Bundy, among others, called him "the crocodile" because "the old man" had an uncanny knack of responding quickly—with "mouth open, and I bite"—whenever presidents surveyed the room for "a split second" to determine who agreed and who disagreed with a proposed decision. Stories soon followed about his tough negotiating style at Geneva. Robert Kennedy consequently gave Harriman a gold crocodile tooth, and Harriman's staff presented him with a silver one "from your victims."

Harriman himself described the Laotian agreement as "a good bad deal," knowing the accords would be tough to enforce.[50] In fact the Pathet Lao soon violated the understandings, arousing the opposition of Souvanna. North Vietnamese troops remained in northeastern Laos, where they sought to preserve their corridors into South Vietnam. As this situation heated up in the south, North Vietnamese activity intensified in Laos. The Soviet Union apparently lacked the influence or the willingness to control Ho Chi Minh, nor did Kennedy pressure the Soviets to do so, causing Rostow later to write that this represented "the greatest single error in American policy of the 1960s."[51] Yet the Geneva settlement had brought the immediate crisis to an end. Conditions in Laos were much improved from the early days of the Kennedy presidency.

By summer 1962 the foreign crises and conflicts had temporarily abated. Following the dreadful disaster of the Bay of Pigs and the unfulfilling meeting at Vienna, Kennedy could now take pride in arresting the imposing threats of Berlin and Laos. He must have breathed a sigh of relief. Still, he faced increasing challenges and frustrations at home, not the least of which involved his proposed New Frontier program.

5

★ ★ ★ ★ ★

LAUNCHING
THE NEW FRONTIER

The New Frontier embraced the past as much as it did the present, for it embodied the reform objectives of Franklin Roosevelt, Harry Truman, and other previous liberal party leaders. Most of Kennedy's legislative proposals had evolved from Roosevelt's Economic Bill of Rights address of 11 January 1944. Subsequent party platforms and policy papers had honed Roosevelt's ideas, becoming linked to Kennedy through his senate sponsorship, the 1960 party platform, and his campaign promise to get America moving again. Kennedy merely reflected the latest Democratic effort to promote the Roosevelt legacy. In many ways his liberalism was terribly traditional; it sought to consolidate and extend the great Democratic gains of the past.

Kennedy began his presidency by focusing on what he called five "must" bills: federal assistance to public schools, hospital insurance for the aged, legislation for housing, aid to depressed areas, and increased minimum wages. In a meeting at the family's Palm Beach residence in December 1960, he and party leaders had fashioned the legislative agenda. Kennedy also characteristically relied on task forces to put the final touches on the five bills and on the other legislative proposals that soon followed.

Despite his desire to be a strong executive, Kennedy knew that dealing with Congress would be difficult. The congressional graveyard was full of failed domestic proposals, going back to Roosevelt. Moreover, not only had Kennedy barely carried the popular vote in 1960 but public opinion polls also had reflected the lack of fervor for reform in the country. Even after Kennedy's popularity rose in spring 1961, indications were that he was more liked than his programs. Congress mirrored the relative conservatism of the times: Twenty-one liberal Democrats had lost House seats in 1960. Even though the Democratic party still had a commanding legislative majority, the conservative South contributed 108 Democrats to the House and 21 to the Senate. On social issues they often joined with Republicans to defeat progressive legislation. The tradition, begun during Roosevelt's 1937 court-packing fight, was an imposing force during the Kennedy years.

Adding to the difficulties, Lyndon Baines Johnson no longer wielded power in the Senate. No individual dominated, as authority reverted to several "feudal lords" who chaired key standing committees. Once again the Senate had returned to its pre-Johnson, disorganized, often unmanageable, and independent state. The taciturn, genial Mike Mansfield (Mont.), respected by both friends and foes alike, proved too mild-mannered as majority leader to be effective. In the House the aging Speaker Sam Rayburn (Tex.) had lost his grip. By fall he was dead, succeeded by the vacuous-looking John McCormack (Mass.), no match for even a dying Rayburn. McCormack cared little for Kennedy, primarily because of intraparty animosities in Massachusetts, which worsened during the presidency. On the opposition side partisanship intensified after the "stolen" presidential election. The vitriolic Charles Halleck (Ind.), who had replaced congenial Joseph W. Martin (Mass.) as Republican House leader in 1959, became virtually an insurmountable obstacle.

Moreover, Kennedy hurt himself by failing to exhibit the skills and persistency that would make his successor Lyndon Johnson so successful. The early foreign policy crises contributed to the legislative problems, causing Kennedy to count too much on Larry O'Brien's office of congressional relations. Despite O'Brien's brightness and determination, he knew few legislators on Capitol Hill in early 1961. He also sometimes antagonized key people such as Thomas "Tip" O'Neill, a Democratic congressman from Kennedy's old district, and Robert Baker, the secretary of Senate Democrats. Baker contended that O'Brien had "no appreciation for the complexities of Capitol Hill."[1] He and O'Neill questioned whether Kennedy even had an effective congressional liaison team. Others resented that some of O'Brien's people indelicately pressured wavering congressmen. Orren Beaty, a former administrator in Kennedy's Interior Department, later admitted that O'Brien's staffers sometimes "trampled on Congressional feelings." On one occasion, according to Beaty, Richard Donahue bumped into a ranking Republican following a close House vote and crowed, "I guess we rubbed you guys' noses in it."[2]

The House Rules Committee fight of early 1961 had an important effect on administration-congressional relations. It pitted Rayburn against reactionary Howard W. Smith (Va.), the stooped and courtly seventy-nine-year-old Democratic chairman of the House Committee on Rules. Smith's committee had enormous power to prevent bills from going to the floor for a vote. Indeed it had played a key role in chloroforming several Democratic proposals—including housing—in the closing days of the Eisenhower administration. It now threatened to turn Kennedy into a "do-nothing" president from the outset. The twelve-member committee included eight Democrats and four Republicans, which generally created a crippling tie vote because two southern Democrats often sided with the Republicans. Kennedy and Rayburn had considered several solutions, including removing a southern Democrat, before deciding to enlarge the committee by three—two Democrats and one Republican—ensuring an eight-to-seven vote on most bills.

The administration could ill afford to lose the Rules Committee scrap. Consequently it put aside a time-honored deference to congressional independence after it became evident that the House remained divided on the issue despite Rayburn's grueling efforts. Kennedy became more concerned when Rayburn failed to produce a precise head count on who opposed committee expansion. The president found this incomprehensible in light of his own attention to numbers during the 1960 campaign. Not only did O'Brien now become involved in lobbying congressmen, so too did Robert Kennedy and Interior Secretary Udall, a former House member, after O'Brien's initial inquiries indicated that Rayburn would lose by seven or eight votes. Kennedy himself also made several calls.

On 31 January 1961 the administration managed a 217-to-212-vote victory. Twenty-two Republicans voted for enlargement to offset the sixty-four southern Democrats who turned against the New Frontier. Roughly one-eighth of the Republicans and one-third of the southern Democrats voted for the change; rarely again would Kennedy have as much House Republican support. Afterward Rayburn and administration officials professed elation, but the narrow vote portended what was to come. The fight also exposed weaknesses in Rayburn's leadership and aroused animosity on Capitol Hill over White House interference in internal matters. The honeymoon had ended before it had ever begun.

Kennedy nevertheless presented much of his legislative program in the first weeks of his presidency with little hesitation. An exception was civil rights, which party leaders thought too controversial for immediate submission. Viewing every proposal as a "child of the Kremlin," Halleck claimed that Kennedy overwhelmed everybody with a "message a day," without taking into consideration the cost of the programs. Sen. Everett Dirksen, Republican minority leader from Illinois, expressed similar sentiments, arguing that the New Frontier program "is the New Deal taken out of a warming oven."[3] Such responses undoubtedly heightened Kennedy's own concerns about expenditures and deficits; yet aside from a political obligation, he also believed that his legislative proposals would serve to stimulate a stagnant economy.

Kennedy submitted the minimum-wage bill in February, proposing to raise the hourly wage to $1.25 and to extend coverage to 4.3 million additional workers (e.g., laundry workers and intrastate bus and truck drivers). Kennedy had stated in Buffalo during the campaign that "as long as the average wage for laundry women . . . is 65 cents an hour for a 48 hour week . . . there is a need for our party."[4] Under the direction of Democrat Adam Clayton Powell (N.Y.), the bill moved swiftly through the Education and Labor and the Rules committees to the floor of the House, where it met immediate opposition from Republicans and southern Democrats, who thought $1.25 too high and deplored an extension of the minimum wage to previously uncovered workers. Special interest groups, particularly large laundry operators from the non-union South, lobbied for exemptions.

Administration officials soon entertained compromise proposals, the most important coming from Democrat Carl Vinson (Ga.), an irascible congressional veteran who explained, amid considerable laughter, that his amendment "washes laundries clean out of the picture."[5] The removal of 150,000 laundry workers, mostly black women, would supposedly gain an additional ten to twelve House votes. Yet the Kennedy bill failed by 186–185. When O'Brien called the White House with the news, Kennedy, in frustration, plunged a letter-opener into the top of his desk. All too obviously, the House leadership and O'Brien's office had mismanaged the floor fight. The administration had shown itself too willing to compromise too early, playing into the opposition's hands. Particularly irksome, several potential supporters had missed the roll call, and as a result the House narrowly approved a vastly inferior nonadministration bill that excluded workers not employed in interstate enterprises.

In the Senate, where the Democratic majority was stronger, an amended administration bill passed; and following a House-Senate conference the House ultimately accepted most of the Senate version. Kennedy finally won a nominal victory, but it came at the expense of laundry workers and another 350,000 workers who were denied coverage so that those who most needed assistance failed to receive it. Whether laundry workers would have lost more jobs to automation if employers had had to pay higher wages, as critics contended, misses the point. Kennedy had rightly believed that exceedingly low wages represented a form of exploitation that had no place in a modern society.

Kennedy's proposed measures to improve education faced even greater obstacles. Whether to exclude parochial schools from federal assistance remained a devisive issue. No matter what its posture, the administration would lose support. The greatest potential loss came from northern Catholic Democrats who generally voted for progressive legislation, but any education bill would have difficult sledding, given the greater number of Republicans in the House since 1960 and a Catholic president to heighten emotion.

The school-assistance bill, submitted in February, requested federal assistance to the states of $2.3 billion over a three-year period for the construction, operation, and maintenance of public schools or for teachers' salaries or both. The amount of grant money each state received would be based on its per capita income. The bill followed assumptions growing out of the 1940s that many states and local governments remained financially unable to ensure an adequate education because of crowded classrooms, underpaid teachers, and the absence of special programs. It also provided for college scholarship grants and for loans to construct academic facilities.

The administration bill called for only public-school assistance. Kennedy adhered to the narrow constitutional grounds of separation of church and state, his 1960 campaign position. A Catholic president, he believed, could do no less, a conclusion that others did not share. Health, Education, and Welfare Secretary Abraham Ribicoff advised that there must be "something for Catholics" to ensure passage. Indeed, the education bill would invite a rash of Catholic criticism. Francis Cardinal Spellman called the president's program "not fair and equitable."[6] The National Catholic Welfare Conference favored the bill's defeat unless it included loans to nonpublic schools. Opposition also came from Republicans, who focused on the program's cost. Southern Democrats questioned federal intrusion, partly because federal funds might be withheld from racially segregated schools. Kennedy equivocated on the loan issue to win Catholic support and accepted the inclusion of special-purpose loans for parochial schools to be used for the construction of college classrooms or the purchase of science equipment. The National Defense Education Act of 1958 had provided for such loans to private schools. That special-purpose loan feature, Kennedy insisted, could be included in supplemental legislation.

Even though the Senate passed the education bill, it ran into trouble in the House of Representatives. Ironically, it faced its first defeat in the

Rules committee by an eight-to-seven vote, as five Republicans and three Democrats (two came from the South) comprised the majority. Democrat James J. Delaney (N.Y.), representing a Catholic district in Queens, cast the key vote, adamantly labeling the bill discriminatory despite considerable pressure from the administration. He knew that an NDEA bill providing special-purpose loans for parochial schools had no chance of surviving a Rules committee vote.

Administration leaders then adopted a parliamentary maneuver on a watered-down bill to circumvent the Rules committee. The procedure resulted in a 170–242 floor vote against consideration. Only six Republicans voted affirmatively, while eighty-two Democrats, mostly from the South, voted against it. Sorensen called the defeat of the education legislation the administration's biggest domestic disappointment in 1961. The religious issue proved significant, but it alone failed to explain the outcome. A split in the House leadership contributed, with McCormack favoring private-school aid and Rayburn opposed to any teachers' salary assistance. Kennedy might have worsened matters when he adopted a well-publicized anti–private school posture, only to give ground under pressure. A more conciliatory position initially might have prevented the strong opposition from the Catholic hierarchy. Even if the religious issue had been better handled, however, Kennedy probably would have still lost in the House because of the conservative coalition.

Medical insurance for the aged also ran into trouble in 1961. Introduced in February, the Kennedy proposal would have levied an additional 0.25 percent increase in Social Security payroll taxes to pay hospital and nursing bills of persons eligible for Social Security old-age benefits. Opinion polls suggested that most Americans favored it because the elderly and their families found it exceedingly difficult to meet rising health-care costs. Kennedy explained on 9 February that this was "not a program of socialized medicine" because "every person will choose his own doctor and hospital." Nonetheless, American Medical Association spokesmen, the bill's greatest critics, argued that it would introduce "compulsion, regulation and control into a system of freely practiced medicine." Furthermore the taxpayers' cost would be prohibitive.

On 24 July the House Ways and Means Committee finally began hearings on the bill. Chairman Wilbur Mills (D.-Ark.), a long-time opponent of health benefits tied to Social Security, joined with other southern Democrats and Republicans to curb action. Kennedy refused to pressure Mills unduly so as not to jeopardize other pending legislation. The administration decided instead to introduce in the Senate a medicare amendment to the House-passed Public Welfare bill. To encourage bipartisan support twenty-one Democrats and five Republicans sponsored the compromise amendment. To dramatize and increase public pressure, Kennedy addressed a Madison Square Garden throng of senior citizens—before a national TV audience—in one of thirty-three meetings held to promote medical assistance for the aged. He spoke passionately of the need for such assistance and condemned the AMA for its opposition, but to no avail.

The Senate tabled the amendment by a vote of fifty-two to forty-eight. No Republican voted for it aside from its five sponsors, and twenty-seven Democrats, mostly from the South, also turned their backs on the administration. The key vote came from Democratic Senator Jennings Randolph (W. Va.), who voted against medicare after sitting on the fence for most of the deliberations. The impact of Senator Robert Kerr (D.-Okla.) as a power broker apparently exceeded that of Kennedy and administration spokesmen. Kerr had campaigned for Randolph in 1960 and had promised to amend the welfare bill to eradicate West Virginia's indebtedness. Had Randolph voted favorably, Kennedy would have held Senator Carl Hayden (D.-Ariz.), despite in-state opposition, and Vice-President Johnson would have then cast the tie-breaking vote. Even if the bill had passed the Senate, however, it would have faced major problems in the House. The education and medicare bills, more than any others, came to symbolize Kennedy's domestic frustration in 1961, regardless of his other legislative successes. He eventually abandoned medicare for the aged, later writing to new HEW Secretary Anthony Celebrezze that "events will not permit legislative action in 1963" but that "we should proceed on the assumption that we are attempting to secure it."[7]

Kerr's continued opposition to medicare became an important consideration. The president had wooed the powerful Kerr early and had his backing on tax, trade, and other legislation—something that Kennedy did not wish to jeopardize. Kerr had extracted a steep price, including administration consideration on the Arkansas River Navigation Project and other costly local projects and the chairmanship of the Senate Space Committee, which brought even more federal money into Kerr's home state. Kennedy even trekked to Kerr's northeastern Oklahoma bailiwick in 1961 to solidify the relationship. To the inquisitive Sooner governor, J. Howard Edmondson, Kennedy had wryly explained, "Why, Howard, I'm going to Oklahoma to kiss Bob Kerr's ass."[8] Medicare notwithstanding, Kerr's sudden death on New Year's Day, 1963, became another obstacle in Kennedy's path, in light of Kerr's countervailing influence on reactionary Harry Byrd (D.-Va.), chairman of the Senate Finance Committee.

Despite the failure of legislation for education and medicare Kennedy fared better on two other 1961 proposals. Congress passed his "depressed areas" bill in April, providing for a four-year, $394 million redevelopment program for areas plagued by chronic unemployment. The act funded commercial and industrial development, technical assistance in community planning, and the retraining of unemployed workers and created the Area Redevelopment Administration, under the auspices of the Commerce Department. The bill received the support of southern Democrats after administration spokesmen promised that federal money would be channeled into depressed areas of the South. Kennedy had first committed himself to the program in 1960, after viewing firsthand the poverty of West Virginia. In Charleston, West Virginia, that September he pledged that within sixty days of his election he would submit a program to bring new jobs and industry to the neglected areas of the country. The Area Redevelopment program had some initial success. By late 1962, 662 areas participated, twenty-six thousand jobs were created, and training programs emerged for nearly fifteen thousand people. But it suffered a major setback in 1963 when the House failed to provide Area Redevelopment with $455.5 million in new funds. By 1965 the operation ended, having spread itself too thin.

Kennedy's housing legislation in June 1961 also passed, despite considerable Republican opposition. Kennedy called the Housing Act of 1961 "the most important and far-reaching" housing legislation since 1949.[9] It broadened and extended existing programs such as urban renewal, public housing, and housing for the elderly and college students. It established the first middle-income housing program, authorizing low-interest, thirty-five-year loans, with a required 3 percent downpayment, on new construction for those whose income was too high to qualify for public housing. It also provided funds for the development of mass-transportation facilities and for open-space land in the cities. Overall, Congress appropriated $4.88 billion to fund the omnibus housing venture, partly because of the 1960–1961 recession.

Kennedy found it much more difficult to obtain a Department of Urban Affairs. He had promised in 1960 to launch a comprehensive program for the cities to be administered by a new department with cabinet-level status. He earmarked Robert Weaver, the recently appointed administrator of the Housing and Home Finance Agency and potentially the first black cabinet appointee, for department secretary. He planned to follow these moves with a controversial open-housing order, another campaign promise. The Urban Affairs bill failed to make it out of committee in 1961, however, the resistance mostly centering around the proposed appointment of Weaver. Aside from Weaver's color, southerners also resented his strong support of racially integrated housing. Senator James Eastland (D.-Miss.) even charged him with having "a pro-Communist background."[10] Rural congressmen saw nothing in the bill for them, and

Republicans opposed the expansion of the federal bureaucracy. In January 1962 the bill met its first defeat in the Rules committee by a vote of six to nine. Two southern Democrats, James W. Trimble (Ark.) and William M. Colmer (Miss.), who usually voted for the administration, broke ranks, largely on the basis of race during an election year.

Kennedy countered by submitting to the House a reorganization plan to create the Urban Affairs Department. (The Rules Committee did not act on matters of reorganization.) The bill also went to the Senate, where it had greater likelihood of success. Its passage there, even if it subsequently failed in the House, would at least give Democrats a stronger campaign issue that fall, but the Republican House leadership surprised the Democrats by proposing a quick vote against the plan. At that point the Senate bill sat in the Government Operations Committee, where Chairman John L. McClellan (Ark.) tepidly opposed it. White House staffer Lee White advised Kennedy to postpone action until the following year if McClellan remained "set against it."

Senator Mansfield, acting on Kennedy's apparent approval, instead forced the bill out of the committee prematurely on a discharge motion prior to House action. This only hardened the opposition of McClellan and others. McClellan called the motion an "unwarranted and wanton attack upon the committee system of the Congress."[11] On 20 February the Senate voted fifty-eight to forty-two against it, in effect killing the bill. Only four Republicans voted for discharge and thirty-six Democrats (eighteen southern) went against it. On the following day the House disapproved the plan for reorganization, 264–150. The vast majority of southern Democrats abandoned the administration, as did 153 out of 176 Republicans; the extent of the defeat was staggering and humiliating. The two principals on the administration side both accepted the blame. Kennedy acknowledged that he "played it too cute," while Mansfield accepted responsibility for "jumping the gun" in the Senate, thereby incurring McClellan's understandable opposition. Democratic Senator Joseph S. Clark (Pa.) also believed the bill had been handled badly, faulting Larry O'Brien the most.[12] Certainly enough blame existed to go around, but even if the administration had moved faultlessly, the House would have undoubtedly still balked. Weaver's race remained an obstacle, as did the House's rural orientation. Because of such failures, by 1962 Kennedy had lost luster, particularly with liberals. The Americans for Democratic Action, in its October newsletter, complained about the "failure of leadership" on the "executive level."[13]

Still, the administration claimed other legislative successes. In 1961 it had achieved an increase in minimum social security benefits, doubled federal grant monies for sewage-treatment programs, established recreational facilities, such as the national seashore preserve on Cape Cod, and financially committed the federal government to the fight against juvenile delinquency. The following year the legislative achievements included the significant Trade Expansion Act—the first major trade bill since Roosevelt's Trade Agreements Act of 1934. The 1962 bill gave the president a five-year authority to cut tariff duties by 50 percent, to eliminate tariffs altogether on certain goods, and to take retaliatory action against "unreasonable" trade policies. The legislation would enable Americans to sell on more equal terms with the European Common Market, as both sides sought to negotiate lower tariffs. Increased trade with Europe would improve the unfavorable balance of trade, of major concern to Kennedy. The bill also provided economic incentives to Common Market countries to approve Great Britain's entry, an objective Kennedy pursued mostly for political reasons. Even though Britain's rejection slowed down the move toward Western unity, the Common Market tariff wall was gradually lowered in 1963, and United States exports appreciably increased.

Also in 1962 Kennedy secured the Manpower Development and Training Act, which he labeled "perhaps the most significant legislation in the area of employment since the historic Employment Act of 1946."[14] The law established programs to retrain workers who had inadequate or obsolete skills. By the end of 1962 the administration claimed 351 approved projects for 12,600 trainees in forty states. Later studies reveal, however, that the training was for low-level jobs. Yet even critic Allen Matusow concedes that manpower-program graduates had an "advantage over other disadvantaged workers competing for the same jobs," and they earned a higher wage.[15] Congress in 1962 also extended consumer protection to prescription drugs. The new law required drug manufacturers to register with the government and to open their plants to inspection; it also demanded that new drugs be proven effective and safe before being sold commercially. Congress moreover continued Kennedy's commitment to the environment by approving legislation for the Padre Island National Seashore and the Point Reyes National Seashore.

The following year Congress responded favorably to Kennedy's proposals on mental health and retardation by authorizing $329 million in grants for the construction of facilities for research and treatment of the mentally ill and retarded and by approving funds for the training of teachers of mentally retarded, deaf, and handicapped children. Nearly $300 million went to the states and communities for the prevention and treatment of mental retardation. Few legislative matters concerned Kennedy more because of his sister Rosemary's retardation. Congress also acted on his omnibus education bill of 1963 by appropriating construction funds and student loans to medical, dental, and related professional schools. Another bill extended assistance to existing and proposed vocational programs. A third bill authorized nearly $1.2 billion in grants and loans for construction or improvement of public and private facilities for higher education. At least on the college level and in a limited way, assistance to private schools was worked out, leading to its further resolution during Johnson's presidency. Kennedy's partial victory, historian Hugh Graham wrote, reflected "a political determination to meet the expectations of the Democratic coalition that would be needed to re-elect him, and a resentment at the political embarrassment of repeated legislative defeats."[16]

The same can be said about Kennedy's farm program, which sought to address the long-standing problems of overproduction, sagging commodity prices, low farm income, and increased federal expenditures. Historians have unaccountably ignored that program even though Kennedy was concerned enough about agricultural decline to have called it the "number 1 domestic problem" during the 1960 campaign. The difficulties had worsened in the Eisenhower period, as Democrats blamed Agriculture Secretary Ezra Taft Benson for the record 3 million persons who left the farms, the 636 percent increase in stored surpluses, the 35 percent drop in net farm income, and the $4.2 billion annual increase in farm-program costs from 1953 to 1960. Democrats faulted Benson for inadequate or nonexistent marketing and production controls and for lowering the Democratic fixed-price-support of 90 percent parity. Benson, they contended, had erroneously assumed that less federal price assistance would encourage farmers to reduce production.

Kennedy had expressed no interest in agricultural issues during the 1950s. He told Harvard economist John Kenneth Galbraith that "I don't want to hear about agricultural policy from anyone except you and I don't want to hear about it from you."[17] Coming from a state with few commercial farmers, Kennedy pragmatically supported Benson's reduced, flexible price supports, a position that hurt him nationally, beginning with his vice-presidential bid of 1956. By the late 1950s, however, he became one of Benson's greatest critics in positioning himself for the presidential nomination. In 1960 he promised beleaguered farmers a new program based on concepts of supply management in which they would receive full parity of income with nonfarmer producers if they accepted mandatory production or marketing controls. He suggested that American agricultural abundance could be used more imaginatively in domestic and foreign policies. Specifically, he proposed the elevation of net farm income, the reduction of surpluses, and the cutting of United States Department of Agriculture (USDA) expenditures.

Mandatory controls became the crucial aspect of Kennedy's farm program. In terms of permanency and stringency, the approach went beyond Roosevelt's efforts. It also reflected Kennedy's urban, fiscally conservative nature, which demanded that farmers heed the sacrificial call of the New Frontier in return for a guaranteed parity of income with non-farmers on their invested capital, labor, and management. With resulting reduced commodities, the federal government's expenditures in the area of crop storage would also be likely to lessen substantially. Under the direction of Secretary of Agriculture Orville Freeman, a bright, vigorous, and adept administrator, the administration submitted a comprehensive farm bill to Congress in April 1961, which included mandatory acreage and marketing restrictions. Because the bill required Congress to surrender some of its legislative powers to the executive branch, the control feature never made it out of committee.

Not until spring 1962 did the administration again seriously propose permanent controls for feed grains (corn, barley, oats), wheat, and dairy products. The Food and Agriculture Act recommended a mandatory acreage allotment along with diversion payments for producers of feed grains. Wheat restrictions combined mandatory acreage and marketing allotments whereby farmers would receive certificates on their reduced acreage, limiting the bushels they could market. In return they would receive diversion payments for removing land from production and a price-support level between 75 and 90 percent of parity on the domestic allotment and up to 90 percent on the export allotment. In determining national allotments for wheat and feed grains the administration took into account the amount of surplus stocks it wished to drop into the market.

The administration recommended controls on dairy products because recent fears of cholesterol and strontium-90 had reduced demand significantly. Freeman had begun a massive campaign "in the spirit of the New Frontier to walk or run and drink a glass of milk."[18] The news media noted the number of glasses he and the Kennedy family consumed daily; being allergic to milk, the president could not have consumed very much. Still, dairy income continued to fall, costing the federal government about $500 million in price supports in 1962. As a consequence the 1962 bill proposed that milk producers be assigned a mandatory marketing allotment based on a percentage of their production in 1961. In return, dairy farmers would receive higher incomes, as support prices would be elevated to 90 percent of parity. Overproduction would result in fines for both grains and dairy products.

For nine months opposing interests fought ferociously in Congress over the Food and Agriculture bill. The conservative American Farm

Bureau, the largest and most powerful farm organization, led the opposition in blaming the farmers' woes on the continued interference of the federal government since the 1930s. The administration quickly lost out on dairy controls; the feed-grain control provision also fell in the Senate Agricultural Committee by a nine-to-eight vote. Along with some emergency voluntary control measures, only the mandatory wheat-control provision survived in modified form, slated for 1964 adoption provided that farmers voted favorably. If the referendum rejected controls, price supports would revert to 50 percent of parity, rather than to zero parity which the administration proposed.

The voting alignment for the Food and Agriculture bill typified most agricultural—if not most domestic—legislation of the period. In the House, of the 202 in favor, only 2 were Republicans, both "lame ducks." One hundred sixty House Republicans voted against the bill along with thirty-seven Democrats. In the Senate, in a vote of fifty-two to forty-one, not one Republican voted affirmatively; thirty-four voted against it as did seven Democrats. On farm-related issues Republicans responded even more negatively, no doubt because of the Democratic attack against Benson in the 1950s.

Ideology also played a part. Historically, Republicans have had more aversion to government involvement which, they believed, vitiated individual freedom, and the American Farm Bureau effectively exploited that sentiment. On farm-related issues, southern Democrats, representing rural constituencies, were less inclined to cast negative votes. Nevertheless, the clash over mandatory controls made summer 1962 extremely difficult for Freeman, and along with O'Brien's people he spent much of his time on Capitol Hill. The administration's strategy to focus on recalcitrant southern and urban Democrats saved the mandatory wheat provision. Freeman, as usual, found Kennedy receptive to contacting congressmen whose support was deemed necessary.[19] At the same time Freeman hinted that Kennedy had appeared too willing to accept existing political realities, too reluctant to push hard. Senator Allen Ellender (D-La.) of the Senate Agriculture Committee also faulted him for being too detached and unaggressive in his dealings with Congress and much preferred the legislative style of Johnson.[20]

The arm-twisting instead came from overaggressive and inexperienced White House lobbyists, who had not learned that "Congress is an equal partner of the Executive branch of Government." Moreover, Kennedy's programs, congressmen contended, were out of tune with the times: One Democrat suggested that "much of it is old stuff, right off the New Deal table." Congressmen also disapproved of the administration's efforts to extend the authority of the federal government; charges persisted that Kennedy was creating a "police state" and a "regimented economy."[21]

The results of the wheat referendum on 21 May 1963 further reflected an antistatism. Wheat farmers voted overwhelmingly against the administration's program providing for support prices up to 90 percent in return for strict controls on acreage allotment. Never before had wheat farmers rejected by referendum a governmental program. In essence they accepted 50 percent parity for no mandatory controls, giving them $1.25 rather than $2.00 per bushel of wheat. A strong campaign had preceded the election, in which the Farm Bureau, the Republican party, and the far Right waged an ideological war over "who will run the farms of America . . . farmers or political bureaucrats?" The Farm Bureau expressed it as "Freedman v. Freeman."[22] During the campaign the opposition also assured farmers that the administration would undoubtedly propose a better wheat bill minus mandatory restrictions if the referendum failed.

Reaction against governmental interference would have been considerably less, perhaps, if farmers had received greater economic incentives to vote for the referendum. Willard Cochrane, Freeman's key adviser, admitted as much twenty-three years afterward: "We offered the wheat farmers nothing better than they were already receiving [in the existing program], but told them we would lower price supports if they rejected mandatory controls. The farmers bet that we were fooling. . . ."[23] In short they were in no mood to sacrifice, especially after the anti-Kennedy forces argued that the administration would surely come up with a better wheat bill.

The wheat referendum ended the administration's efforts to introduce mandatory controls, putting a momentary lid on legislation to assist wheat farmers. By the time of Kennedy's assassination in November, Cochrane was advising Freeman to consider a new voluntary wheat program with economic incentives to farmers who agreed to limit production. Cochrane understood, however, that such programs could not pass an urban-based Congress without a reduction in farm-program costs. Moreover, with voluntary controls, nonparticipating farmers could always increase production enough to frustrate efforts to reduce surpluses. The wheat program ultimately remained a voluntary one.

Nevertheless, the Kennedy administration had some success with voluntary control programs. The Emergency Feed Grains bill of March 1961 had become a model for others. It came in response to an emergency situation in which corn and other feed-grain surpluses had reached around 84 million tons, with an estimated increase of 10 million tons for 1961, necessitating additional storage facilities. Lack of controls and low feed-grain prices had contributed to the problem. The Kennedy bill elevated support prices for 1961; corn, for example, went up from $1.06 to $1.20 per bushel. Freeman would have raised price supports even higher had the White House not become apprehensive about higher farm prices. The bill provided increased price supports to farmers who reduced their acreage at least 20 percent below their 1959–1960 amount. Noncooperating farmers could grow as much as they wanted, but only at the open-market price. The government would keep that price down by dumping surplus grain into the market to induce farmers to participate.

The 1961 bill retired some 26 million acres of land. However, since corn yields increased six bushels per acre, which the administration attributed to excellent growing weather and an increased use of fertilizer, the overall production level dipped about 11 percent below 1960 instead of the anticipated 16 to 18 percent. This amounted to a production drop of 13 million tons in feed grains, leading to a decrease of 280 million bushels in surplus stock, the first meaningful reduction since 1952. Most important, net farm income rose $1 billion, an eight-year high, in large part the result of the feed-grains bill. Meanwhile, retail prices remained steady. The major weakness of the bill, the administration acknowledged, was its cost. The government paid $786 million for land diversion, some of which it recovered through storage-cost reduction.

Like other Kennedy farm bills the Emergency Feed Grains Act had met considerable congressional opposition. In the House of Representatives, it cleared by a margin of seven votes, with only 4 Republicans voting for it and 161 rejecting it. Most of the forty-one negative Democratic votes came from the South. Led by the Farm Bureau, opposition centered on the anticipated costs and the unprecedented powers given to the secretary of agriculture to manipulate grain prices by dumping surpluses. In the Senate only eight Democrats voted against it, but eighteen out of twenty-nine Republicans did.

Nonetheless, the feed-grains bill proved to be popular with participants, making it more difficult to obtain mandatory controls because of the belief that they were unnecessary. Thus Congress extended the feed-grains program into 1962 with modifications. Additionally, it established a voluntary wheat-control program, which required at least a 10 percent cut in wheat acreage for participants, with land being diverted to conservation uses. In return wheat farmers received a cash or in-kind payment on the diverted acreage. The bill also provided for a stiffer penalty for growers who failed to make the 10 percent cutback. It passed Congress convincingly, but in the House 112 out of 161 Republicans opposed it; in the Senate, it carried by a voice vote.

The wheat- and feed-grains provisions for 1962 further reduced surpluses. Feed-grains inventories dropped some 500 million bushels from their 1961 peak, with wheat surpluses down 250 million bushels over the same period. By March 1963 Freeman reported a combined reduction of feed-grains and wheat holdings totaling over 1 billion bushels. The voluntary feed-grains and wheat programs also retained their popularity with farmers. Nonetheless, per capita farm income, even though rising, stood at only 60 percent of nonfarm income, and USDA commodity expenditures continued high, partly because of the costly voluntary programs. The feed-grains expenditure in 1963, for example, was over $1 billion, minus storage-cost reductions, as surpluses were brought lower. Compared to the Benson years, however, the Kennedy administration did make progress in the two major areas of commodities.

In commodities such as cotton and dairy products, the administration failed to secure necessary legislation. Freeman compared the elusive cotton problem to quicksilver. The difficulty included the statutory national allotment of 16 million acres opposed by the Farm Bureau-dominated Cotton Council, representing larger producers. The council wanted to increase the acreage in order to tap the export market more. At the same time it opposed the administration's efforts to raise cotton-farm income to ensure the survival of smaller producers, whose political support was necessary in 1964. Finally, the government-export producer-subsidy of .085 cents, to make U.S. cotton competitive in the world market, aroused the opposition of domestic cotton mills that were buying cotton at the price-support level. By 1963 the administration proposed legislation both to compensate domestic mills and to expand the national acreage allotment, enabling farmers to produce cotton for the export market at the world price. Congress, however, would not agree to a compromise bill until March 1964.

Overproduction and underconsumption continued to plague the dairy industry. By early 1963 the government held over 300 million pounds of butter in storage even with giveaway programs. Federal expenditures rose over $500 million a year despite the low parity level of 75 percent required by law. Dairy-farmer income, meanwhile, fell over $100 million annually by 1963. After failing to obtain mandatory controls the administration proposed voluntary ones to turn the situation around. Freeman subsequently blamed legislative inaction on lack of leadership in the dairy industry, hostility from the dairy group, and the pervasive influence of the Farm Bureau.

Aside from seeking to reduce commodity production, the administration also strove in other ways to achieve agricultural balance. Domestically demand could be elevated by keeping farm prices low and by promoting economic growth. Indeed no significant increases in farm prices resulted during the Kennedy years, and the economy improved. In addition, Kennedy's giveaway programs could reduce farm surpluses while fulfilling a Democratic commitment to the downtrodden, and food assistance efforts could win over urban congressmen for commodity programs.

Kennedy's first executive order directed Freeman on 21 January 1961 to increase food assistance to the needy, and the president soon announced a pilot food-stamp program embracing six areas, the first such commitment since World War II had ended the 1938 project. In 1962 the administration expanded the program to eighteen areas, feeding 240 thousand people at an annual cost of about $22 million. Kennedy also invigorated the school-lunch and milk programs begun in the Eisenhower administration, enabling seven hundred thousand more children to enjoy a hot school lunch and eighty-five thousand more schools, child-care centers, and camps to receive fresh milk.

The administration's efforts to revitalize rural America also partly reflected a desire to improve the agricultural situation. First begun in the Eisenhower period with virtually no governmental support, the Rural Areas Development (RAD) program represented in 1962 a diverse approach to strengthen rural income, stimulate new economic activity, develop outdoor resources for city people, and cut farm surpluses. It included a rural renewal component patterned after the urban model in which local rural development authorities, aided by federal assistance, would attract industry and promote the development of woodlots and recreational activities in areas as impoverished as urban ghettos. Freeman placed considerable emphasis upon recreational uses of land as a profitable way to fulfill an urban need for camping, fishing, and golf while gaining essential urban congressional support for commodity programs. Rural renewal's conservation features would also appeal to urban America. Furthermore, it would remove land from commodity production, which would supposedly require 50 million fewer acres by the 1980s.

Freeman believed that RAD land-conversion projects would also assist the family farmer and nearby townspeople in more stable areas, thereby preserving a culture that remained a part of our national heritage. This involved more than altruistic considerations. "I am confident," he wrote Kennedy, that "there is great political mileage here, particularly as it will blunt . . . criticism that smaller farms are being run out by the Democrats just as surely as they were by Benson and the Republicans."[24] At the same time Freeman understood that technology doomed the small farmer; at best government could only ease the process.

In the last year of the Kennedy presidency nothing excited Freeman more than RAD. But as a crusty USDA bureaucrat suggested, "If [Freeman] brings it off, he will find walking on water a fairly simple trick."[25] Freeman in fact faced resistance from both the White House and Congress. The former refused to recommend the necessary $300 to $400 million to launch RAD properly, probably because of its desire to reduce USDA expenditures and its belief that Congress would oppose a large outlay. In 1962 Congress indeed weakened the program by limiting land-conversion expenditures to $10 million annually and by defeating a rural-renewal proposal to enable the administration to purchase lands for recreational and related development. The 1962 Food and Agriculture Act provided only for federal loans and technical assistance to state and local governments for rural-renewal projects. The opposition came from Republicans and southern Democrats, the former balking for partisan and ideological reasons mostly. Southern Democrats opposed the USDA's bearing the expense of a supposed welfare program. Some reacted against Kennedy's growing civil rights commitments by suggesting that RAD's recreational features would force southerners "to sleep with niggers."[26]

Consequently, the RAD program represented at best a modest effort. In spring 1963 pilot activities existed only in forty-one counties in regard to cropland conversion, and rural-renewal pilot projects in six states awaited funding. On 10 May 1963 Freeman reported that "substantial public support is building for the Rural Areas Development," but "it will, of course, require appropriations and leadership." Little of either occurred during the Kennedy presidency; a paltry one hundred thousand dollars went into the rural-renewal program for the 1964 fiscal year.[27] Overall, despite Freeman's efforts rural America remained virtually unchanged during the Kennedy period.

Agriculture fared better in the international realm, where Freeman sought to use American abundance constructively. Increasing farm exports would reduce surpluses and world hunger and promote American foreign policy. Freeman frequently publicized that Soviet consumers spent 56 percent of their income on food in comparison to 20 percent in the United States. Moreover, United States agricultural efficiency enabled 8 percent of the population to produce more than enough to feed the nation, but the Soviet system required a farm population of over 50 percent and supplementary imports. Freeman used various world food conferences to propagandize the "superiority of 'free' American agriculture." In 1962 Freeman used the Soviet minister of agriculture's visit to the United States "to dramatize . . . to the rest of the world how far American agriculture is ahead of the Soviet[s]." Freeman claimed some gain for his efforts, alluding to newly emerging nations in Africa and the Middle East who were moving away from Soviet collectivism "in light of the smashing success of American agriculture and the well advertized failure of Communist agriculture."[28]

The United States could best win over have-not nations by providing economic aid, particularly food, and the Food for Peace program became the major vehicle. This commitment had originated with the passage of the Agricultural Trade Development and Assistance Act of 1954 (Public Law 480), permitting the donation, barter, and sale of governmental surpluses. The law initially focused solely upon the removal of agricultural surpluses, but by the late 1950s liberal senators, led by Hubert Humphrey, wanted to go beyond the primarily domestic objectives of PL 480. They thought in terms of a major assistance program that took into consideration the long-range needs of newly developing nations. In 1960 Humphrey recommended a "Food for Peace Administrator" who would serve as a special assistant to the president. These proposals invited the opposition of both the Eisenhower administration and the Senate Agriculture Committee.

In 1960 Kennedy embraced the idea of Food for Peace and established the White House Office of Food for Peace. He suggested that "American agricultural abundance offers a great opportunity for the United States to promote the interests of peace and to play an important role in helping to provide a more adequate diet for peoples all around the world."[29] Meanwhile, the United States would also be resolving a domestic farm problem.

Under the leadership of George McGovern, its first director, Food for Peace coordinated with the USDA and the Agency for International Development (AID). It now became more of an economic development program, as the government appreciably increased food donations to the newly emerging nations while reducing surplus sales under PL 480. Total commitments of Food for Peace remained comparable with those of the late Eisenhower presidency, with the amount rarely exceeding $2 billion annually. During the Kennedy years Congress continued to cut appropriation requests and generally opposed the expansion of the program; differences also developed between Freeman and McGovern, with the former successfully opposing McGovern's efforts to expand Food for Peace above the $2 billion annual level. Freeman instead sought to improve distribution and to protect the normal commercial relations of recipient countries. More importantly he feared that considerable expansion would provide a "convenient hook for any commodity leader to use in resisting supply management programs on the grounds that all we have to do is ship it abroad." Freeman's belief that the USDA should have operational control of Food for Peace undoubtedly intensified philosophical differences.[30] McGovern finally resigned in July 1962, winning a United States Senate seat that November.

McGovern's replacement, Richard Reuter of CARE, worked more closely with Freeman. By 1963 Food for Peace surpluses fed some 92 million a day, including 35 million school children in impoverished countries of the Third World. The food in some instances served as wages to finance economic development projects such as hospitals, schools, and road construction. Yet Kennedy himself admitted in a 2 April 1963 message to Congress that "the relative burden of our assistance programs has been steadily reduced—from some two percent of our national product at the beginning of the Marshall Plan to seven-tenths of one percent today—from 11.5 percent of the Federal Budget in 1949 to 4 percent today." When a reporter asked why the United States did not do more, Kennedy alluded to the "limitations of available funds."

Neither did American commercial exports substantially increase—at least not until fiscal 1964 after Kennedy had authorized the sale of surplus wheat to the Soviet Union, this in itself a major propaganda victory for Freeman. That year American exports rose from $3.6 billion to $4.6 billion. Otherwise Freeman struggled with the commercial foreign market, as Common Market countries sought to increase their tariffs. With Kennedy's assistance, Freeman prevented the State Department from making trade concessions at the expense of agriculture. Common Market tariffs even dropped after the passage of the Trade Expansion Act of 1962.

Despite the administration's successes, Freeman remained dissatisfied. One month before Kennedy's assassination he wrote the president: "I can't help but reflect what an oddity it is that . . . when we are able to produce more than adequate amounts of food and fiber . . . we seem unable to find the formula or provide the leadership to adequately use it either by way of trade or aid. We can only keep searching."[31]

In general the Kennedy farm program brought qualified results. Overproduction and a progressively shrinking farm population continued after the early 1960s. Even though large farm establishments weathered the hardships the small family farmer often could not, and rural poverty persisted virtually unabated. Kennedy lost heavily on the issue of mandatory controls; never again would a president advocate that approach. By 1965 the Johnson administration placed less emphasis on production controls in voluntary programs and instead focused on expanding exports as *the* way to deal with problems of farm surplus and low income. Neither did Kennedy reduce USDA expenditures. The agricultural budget increased from $5.9 billion in fiscal 1961 to $7.8 in 1964. Yet Kennedy failed to achieve full parity of income as promised in the 1960 campaign. Perhaps he did as well as possible, given the political realities.

On the plus side an expanded program of Food for Peace, the farm assistance efforts, including the food-stamp project, and the voluntary commodity programs, which elevated farm income and reduced surpluses, flourished. But again costly voluntary programs contributed to escalating USDA expenditures. Such programs were also of more benefit to the major commercial farmers, who received large diversion payments and profited most from higher farm prices. Thirty years afterward, the plight of the farmer continues. High interest rates and falling land prices have complicated the other problems, hurting those who overexpanded during the temporary prosperity of the mid-1970s. USDA expenditures have also risen dramatically in recent years. No administration and no Congress since Kennedy's has come to terms with the problems, leading one to wonder whether the assumptions originating in the 1930s about the commodity program remain viable in any way.

Events in the 1980s have also called into question earlier assumptions about the validity of government's antipoverty programs, many of which had their roots in the 1930s. President Johnson's massive War on Poverty has been the focus of this criticism, but critics have implicated Kennedy too because he had laid the foundation for those programs.

During the 1960 campaign Kennedy had embraced the Democratic tradition of social justice. At Hyde Park he vowed to extend Roosevelt's antipoverty efforts; elsewhere he deplored that 17 million Americans went to bed hungry nightly. The writings of Galbraith, the noted economist and author of *The Affluent Society* (1958), and of Michael Harrington, a socialist journalist who published his preliminary findings in a *Commentary* article in 1959, most influenced Kennedy. Both suggested that poverty remained hidden and existed next to widespread affluence. Harrington claimed that 50 million Americans lived in need.

Yet Kennedy actually focused very little on poverty during the campaign; no more than five or six references to it existed in his speeches. He talked much more about the necessity for jobs, which only touched on the problem of poverty (many in poverty did have jobs). When he did refer to it he tended to see it more in global terms. Neither did he really address the problem during the first two years of his presidency. What occurred were tangential or piecemeal actions—the minimum-wage law, the Housing Act, the Juvenile Delinquency bill, and Area Redevelopment legislation, to name a few. Congress balked on other efforts such as medicare and the youth conservation corps, a 1930s-style commitment that would have initially employed some six thousand youth. Sometimes Kennedy's own indifference became the obstacle. His sister Eunice, who had worked with juvenile delinquents in Chicago, repeatedly pressured him to consider a domestic peace corps for idealistic Americans wanting to work in deprived areas; Kennedy finally told her to call Bobby.[32] In 1963 the National Service Corps bill, the forerunner of Volunteers in Service to America (VISTA), failed to win House approval.

Perhaps the administration's most innovative program focused on juvenile delinquency, a special concern of Robert Kennedy, who had encouraged his brother to create the President's Committee on Juvenile Delinquency in 1961. Making himself chairman, he asked David Hackett, a fellow Milton Academy classmate, to serve as director. They then secured $30 million from Congress for grants to finance local projects to fight delinquency. They assumed, as contemporary studies concluded, that lack of opportunity in slum communities, not psychological abnormalities, created juvenile delinquents. Hackett and his dedicated recruits went to work encouraging pilot projects in ghetto areas, ultimately involving residents to help solve their own problems. Hence the concept of community action emerged, later an integral part of Johnson's War on Poverty. Much of the activity was prevention. Opportunities were unlocked through public service jobs for teenagers, neighborhood centers offering various welfare services, and nursery classes for preschool children. The reforming of indifferent local institutions such as police departments also became an objective. The results often failed to please the president's committee; still, the enthusiasm and idealism of Hackett's "guerrillas" bring to mind those who had served in some of Roosevelt's New Deal agencies.

These workers received the enthusiastic support of Robert Kennedy, whose compassion surfaced in confronting urban poverty. Hackett had introduced Kennedy to the ghettos of Harlem and Washington, D.C., and he often left deeply moved and disturbed. He sometimes visited ghetto schools where, an aide remembered, he mingled with schoolyard children—"smiling, rubbing their heads, squeezing their hands, reaching out to the smaller ones who could not get near him. This was not done for show—there were no reporters or photographers along."[33] Even though representing a small part of his official life at the time, all of this previews Kennedy's embracement of the rural and urban poor after his brother's death. The attachment apparently had less to do with political ambition than it did with the psychological makeup of one who believed that public service to the downtrodden was a class obligation. He seemed much more sensitive to this consideration than his brother.

In early 1963 Jack Kennedy finally asked Walter Heller, chairman of the Council of Economic Advisers (CEA), to determine whether poverty was as widespread as described in Harrington's *The Other America* (1962) and in Dwight MacDonald's lengthy essay in the *New Yorker* (January 1963) and as former Fair Deal economist Leon Keyserling's reports contended. Kennedy anticipated possible criticism that his proposed tax cut had failed to benefit the poor. He sensed as well a greater public concern because of recent studies on poverty—including a TV documentary—and a spiraling civil rights movement that exposed black deprivation. The country was obviously moving in a more liberal direction by 1963.

Heller, coming from a progressive University of Wisconsin background, brought into the study a deep belief that poverty was wrong on practical as well as on moral grounds because it spawned crime, disease, and other social problems, leading to lower productivity. He was also politically aware enough to believe that an antipoverty program would benefit Kennedy. He consequently asked Robert J. Lampman, a full-time CEA staffer and an expert on wealth and income distribution, to begin an investigation. Lampman soon determined that families with incomes of three thousand dollars or less had declined by 10 percent from 1947 to 1956 but that over the next five years the number had fallen only 2 percent. He asserted that economic growth and full employment would have the same impact on poverty as it had had from 1947 to 1956 and was reason enough to end the existing economic slump. This approach would have minimal effect on the aged, disabled, and families headed by women, however; thus he recommended additional forms of federal assistance.

Like Harrington and other students of poverty Lampman suspected a culture of poverty, whereby negative or defeatist attitudes and behavior perpetuated themselves from one generation to another, virtually guaranteeing its extension. To break the cycle Lampman and other administration economists emphasized the education of youth, retraining, and other rehabilitation programs, all requiring a considerable financial commitment. Neither he nor Heller favored income redistribution or transfers, which might invite political criticism. Above all they wanted a relatively modest, workable, and popular program. They favored one that promoted a sacrificial spirit, in which local well-to-do community members participated. Such proposals as a national service corps and a youth conservation corps would be natural components in any antipoverty program.

Yet no decision transpired by fall 1963 except that Kennedy had "tentatively decided that a major focus in the domestic legislative program in 1964 will be on a [commitment] variously described as 'Human Conservation and Development,' 'Access to Opportunity' and 'Attack on Poverty.' "[34] Heller asked the heads of departments and agencies for their assistance in shaping the framework. To Heller, on Armistice Day 1963, Kennedy said, "First we'll have your tax cut; then we'll have my expenditures program."[35] Three days before his assassination the president once again expressed an interest, provided that "we can get a good program."

As Carl Brauer makes clear in his 1982 study, preliminary plans emphasized "youth, human services rather than income transfers, experimentation, selectivity, coordination, and local administration."[36]

Whether Kennedy would have pushed hard for a concrete program in an election year when other legislative proposals were pending is uncertain. Nonetheless, he might have used congressional opposition as a major campaign issue, particularly if the Republicans nominated arch conservative Barry Goldwater. Ideological lines would then be clearly drawn, with Kennedy running on an updated New Deal platform in a more liberal environment than in 1960.

As it turned out, Lyndon Baines Johnson, in the spiritual aftermath of Kennedy's death, declared war on poverty, elevating it to a level probably unintended by his predecessor. As Johnson told Heller the day after the assassination, "If you looked at my record, you would know that I am a Roosevelt New Dealer. As a matter of fact, to tell the truth, John F. Kennedy was a little too conservative to suit my taste."[37] Yet Johnson profited from the planning and proposals on poverty and the concepts evolving from the Kennedy presidency. Many of the Kennedy people such as Sargent Shriver, Adam Yarmolinsky, Heller, and Wilbur Cohen played an integral part in the new administration's efforts to eradicate poverty.

Scholars remain divided in their assessments of Kennedy's domestic program. Those who adopt a favorable view point out that—despite a divided Congress, the conservatism of the time, and the distractions of several foreign crises—Kennedy's overall legislative record remains impressive: In 1961, thirty-three out of his fifty-three "major" recommendations passed Congress; in 1962, forty out of fifty-four; and in 1963, thirty-five out of fifty-eight. This compares favorably to the successes of Roosevelt after 1935. Aside from the enacted social legislation, Kennedy also succeeded in getting Congress to fund new initiatives abroad, including the Peace Corps and the Alliance for Progress, and to appropriate heavily for the national defense. Moreover, some of the failed major legislative proposals such as civil rights probably would have passed Congress in 1964 had Kennedy lived. The House Ways and Means Committee, a stumbling block for medicare in 1962, added two liberal Democrats in 1963, virtually assuring approval of the bill. Throughout it all, Kennedy remained on good terms with Congress, recognizing that "I have to have the Congress behind me, I can't afford to alienate them."[38]

Critics, meanwhile, observe that many of his most important bills—the heart and soul of the New Frontier—failed or were badly emasculated, including education, medicare, urban affairs, civil rights, agriculture, and tax reform. These ran into difficulty not only because of external considerations but also because of the failings of Kennedy, of O'Brien's office, or of the party leadership. Furthermore, Kennedy has not escaped the growing reaction of the Left and the Right over the validity of his programs.

In retrospect Kennedy had the misfortune of being compared to his own high expectations and lofty rhetoric and to the great achievements of Johnson's Great Society. In reality, although his presidency fell far short of both, the New Frontier did successfully embody the Roosevelt and Truman legacies. At the same time it also offered America newer approaches.

6

★ ★ ★ ★ ★

OLD IDEAS AND
NEWER APPROACHES

The Kennedy presidency sometimes employed newer approaches in dealing with the problems and challenges of the 1960s. It made its greatest inroads in the areas of economic growth and well-being, women's rights, anticrime enforcement, space exploration, and the Peace Corps. Representing matters the administration thought significant, they exemplified the direction in which Kennedy was moving. Today they are inexorably linked to the New Frontier, which encompassed the initiatives of both domestic and foreign policy. The approaches might have been new, but the ideas were not.

Few domestic concerns posed more demands than that of the economy, and nowhere else perhaps did Kennedy alter his personal views and policy more. By 1963 in fact he adopted the novel principle of proposing a massive tax cut in the face of an existing deficit and an improving economy. He strove to generate greater consumer buying in order to spark economic growth, reduce unemployment, and ultimately increase federal revenues. For him as well as for his party this endeavor represented a significant departure.

Kennedy, like most presidents, entered the White House with little background in economics. At Harvard he had taken only the basic survey course, and contrary to myth, illness had forced him to withdraw one month after he registered at the London School of Economics. It is doubtful that he had ever attended. Thus during this period he received virtually no exposure to Keynesian economics, the liberal doctrine of his times. John Maynard Keynes, the enormously influential British economist, had first preached the benefits of self-instituted deficits during the Great Depression as a way to unleash the economy. Though Keynes had focused more on deficit spending, he wrote that tax cuts could also provide economic stimulation whenever taxes were high. Such was the case in the postwar era.

Kennedy's economic education had slowly evolved in those years. Paul Samuelson, an early Kennedy economic adviser, remembered that Kennedy initially had not "thought too much about [economics]."[1] Neither had Senate aide Theodore Sorensen, who looked down on economists. Yet economist Walter Heller recalled that Kennedy had told him in 1960, "You know, I think you'll find me not only more interested in economists than my predecessor, but possibly just a little bit more competent."[2] Kennedy had impressed Heller because he asked intelligent questions and revealed an enormous capacity to learn.

Kennedy entered the presidency as a fiscal conservative. Throughout his congressional career he had remained a balanced-budget proponent, even while favoring social programs and tolerating deficits and increased expenditures during economic downturns. He came by his viewpoints honestly, for his father had never felt comfortable with New Deal economics. Moreover, his tightfisted parents, despite a seemingly lavish lifestyle, had persistently sought to keep expenditures down even when it meant paying employees low wages. Jack Kennedy shared those same values. As president he reduced the White House staff, becoming so concerned about the number of White House gardeners that he brought his own to Washington to evaluate the costs. "I'm for economy," he claimed, "after all, I'm a taxpayer myself."[3] Nothing bothered him more than to see his wife on extravagant shopping sprees, and he attempted to curb her expenditures. He insisted that the White House order groceries from reasonably priced stores. At the same time external considerations also influenced his financial conservatism. He ran for the presidency believing that liberal administrations "had been wrecked on the rocks of unsound financial policy" and determined that this would not happen to him. As a result he learned to respect the views of financiers such as Douglas Dillon and Robert Lovett.

Even so, Kennedy realized that he needed to broaden his economic viewpoints, partly for political reasons. By the late 1950s he had met periodically with liberal Harvard and MIT economists. One well-publicized meeting included John Kenneth Galbraith, Seymour Harris, and Samuelson at Hyannis Port shortly after the 1960 convention. As president Kennedy would adopt a more moderate posture on public expenditures as he outspent Eisenhower in military and social programs. Regarding the latter he once told Heller, "What I want from you are good programs by which money can be spent effectively."[4] In that way he could reconcile a liberal social and a conservative financial philosophy. Still of concern were deficits, inflation, and public perceptions.

Political considerations most dictated Kennedy's conservative financial beliefs. Despite the recession confronting him at the outset of his presidency, he feared being thought a reckless spender, a label that had hung on practically every Democratic presidential candidate since Roosevelt. The influence of financial conservatives in the Congress caused him to proceed cautiously with the economic downturn. Otherwise, "they would kick us in the balls," Kennedy commented.[5] Not only did he object to excessive expenditures but he also at first opposed a tax cut as an economic stimulus. He resisted the cut because of potentially increasing deficits and because it ran counter to his call for personal sacrifice. He told his economic task force, chaired by Samuelson and including Heller, to remove that recommendation from its draft report. Immediately following the inauguration Kennedy instead promised congressional leaders that he would seek a balanced budget. By that time a recession had already been lingering for seven months, and the economic growth rate over the last three-and-a-half years had averaged about 2.5 percent instead of the historic average of 3.5 percent. There had been no substantial economic growth for the past seven years. More alarmingly, the unemployment rate neared 7 percent by January.

Furthermore, Kennedy confronted a balance-of-payment deficit in which more dollars left the country than came in because of increasing American imports as well as rising investments and expenditures abroad, the military buildup in Europe contributing to the latter problem. Trade revenues were not enough to overturn the imbalance. The problem worsened in 1960 when foreign nations exchanged dollars for gold, causing a drain on United States gold reserves. This became a primary concern for the president, who believed that the country was only as strong as its currency.

During the campaign Kennedy had committed his administration to a 5 percent annual growth rate, a reduction of unemployment, and a reversal of the balance-of-payment deficit. As a result of the latter obligation, he could not deal with the depressed economy by imposing monetary solutions. A reduction of interest rates would fuel inflation and worsen the imbalance of payments by forcing U.S. dollars into foreign markets. Nor did he feel that he could appreciably increase the budget deficit because it would cause foreign bankers to doubt the strength of the dollar, leading to the withdrawal of more gold. Most advisers nevertheless felt that Kennedy overreacted to the balance-of-payment problem. They concerned themselves more about the domestic economy.

The president moved against the domestic economy as if he were walking on ice. In a special message to Congress on 2 February he stressed the necessity of taking strong measures but reaffirmed a commitment to balance the budget. His initial actions included increases in domestic and defense expenditures. The administration elevated Social Security payments and privileges, proposed extending state unemployment benefits for thirteen weeks, obtained a minimum-wage increase, and accelerated the apportionment of highway construction funds. Congress subsequently passed the Area Redevelopment bill, the Omnibus Housing bill, and a farm measure. The government also provided for earlier income tax refunds and issued veterans' life insurance dividends for the entire year during the first quarter.

Liberal economist Galbraith prodded Kennedy to increase expenditures for public works. Though Kennedy truly liked Galbraith, he did not often listen to him, causing Galbraith to write Kennedy on 2 February, "I am a little appalled at the eloquence of the explanations as to why things, neither radical nor reactionary but only wise, cannot be done."[6] Galbraith recommended an omnibus measure to assist families of the unemployed, to extend emergency grants and loans for towns with serious unemployment, to provide a system of grants and/or deferred-interest loans to unemployed families for the renovation of their houses, and to create a youth conservation corps to help unemployed teenagers. "Should the foregoing be unacceptable," Galbraith concluded, "there is still clean living and regular prayer."[7]

The leading newspapers echoed Galbraith's displeasure. The *New York Times* and the *Washington Post* used such expressions as "cautious" and "careful" to describe the president's actions. Heller of the CEA also labeled the Kennedy program tentative, arguing that "it is heavily dependent for its success upon what consumers and businessmen choose to make of it." One liberal economist even referred to the Kennedy presidency as the "Third Eisenhower Administration."[8] It was obvious that Keynesian economists such as Galbraith, who opted for more public expenditures, or Heller, who favored a general tax cut, had limited influence on Kennedy during this period.

Kennedy did meet frequently with Heller's CEA, however, unlike Eisenhower, who consulted only with CEA chairman Arthur Burns. The council proved to be active, unified, and persistent. All three council members—Heller, James Tobin of Yale, and Kermit Gordon of Williams College—were Keynesians, respected in the profession and among the White House staff. Their mission in 1961 was to educate the president economically; during that first year, however, their efforts were not always successful.

Kennedy listened more to Dillon, the Republican secretary of the treasury, who had close ties with the financial community. More than anyone Dillon in 1961 called into question liberal economic theories— particularly Galbraith's. Whenever Ambassador Galbraith returned from India he invariably offered Kennedy unsolicited advice on economic policy. The president would then phone or send a memo to Dillon. After one call, Dillon responded, "Fine, Mr. President, I'll think about it but I just wonder if Ken Galbraith is in town?" The president started laughing and said, "he's right here. Do you want to talk to him?"[9] Dillon favored focusing on the balance-of-payments problem, controlling expenditures, and initiating a business-investment tax credit of 7 percent to stimulate economic growth. Besides Dillon, Heller and Galbraith had to compete with William McChesney Martin, the chairman of the Federal Reserve Board, who remained wary of fiscal and monetary stimulation. In spring 1961 Galbraith urged Martin to lower the rediscount rate. "I realize that to get down rates and liberalize credit is not easy." Yet mortgage rates at excess of 6 percent retarded recovery, he warned.[10] But for the most part the financial homilies of the Eisenhower era held sway during the early Kennedy presidency.

Nevertheless, the recession suddenly ended in mid-February and a slow upswing began, thanks to Kennedy's increases in expenditures, many of which were earmarked for the military, including $3.7 billion for "urgent" national-security needs and $3.5 billion in July in response to the Berlin crisis. New domestic programs attracted $2.3 billion. The 1961 deficit, despite the economic downturn and Eisenhower's budgetary overestimation of revenue and underestimation of expenditures, hit only $3.3 billion, an indication of Kennedy's conservative financial approach.

The Berlin crisis of that summer reinforces the assessment, as Robert Kennedy proposed a 1 percent increase in income and corporation taxes to finance the rise in military expenditures and to lay the basis for a balanced budget. This also represented a way for Americans to heed Kennedy's sacrificial call. The measure had Dillon's and the president's enthusiastic approval until the CEA persuasively called it "bad economics" and warned that the tax increase might well "choke off" full recovery. The CEA also rejected the assertion that inflation threatened because of a growing deficit. Moreover, it questioned whether a tax measure would create a spirit of sacrifice since the hike was not substantial. From New Delhi Galbraith echoed that the administration must cease promising a balanced budget. "You must emphasize instead that the budget is under control," he argued. "Control you must make the *sine qua non* of fiscal responsibility, which indeed it is. If we have a deficit it is because we want it and accept the necessity. Far better to have a deficit that we expect

127

and predict than one that comes as an admission of error— especially as we will have a deficit in either case."[11] Thus the economic education of John Kennedy continued.

And so did slow economic growth. In the first quarter of 1962 the GNP inched upward only 1.1 percent from the preceding quarter. Heller called it an unusually small gain for a period of emerging growth, citing the decline of housing construction and consumer durables and stagnant business investment as problem areas. He consequently lowered the projected $570 billion annual GNP to $565 billion or lower; the economic forecast for 1962 became much less promising.

Other related problems surfaced that spring when President Kennedy sought to implement guideposts created by the CEA to keep prices and wages at a level not to exceed the productivity rate (output per worker) for any given industry. The administration was responding to wage-price spirals in key industries such as steel, automobile manufacturing, and construction, where powerful unions forced higher costs upon equally mighty corporations who then passed on the markup to consumers in the form of higher prices. Government intervention could hold inflation in check and improve the marketability of American goods abroad.

Kennedy's guideposts reflected an overall desire to work closely with big business in the common interest of an expanding economy, a theme begun in the 1960 campaign. He recognized that the anti–big business, trust-busting perception of the Democratic party must be overturned if he were to win business' confidence. Yet Kennedy had sent mixed signals. He had courted corporate executives with budget-balancing rhetoric, tax incentives, and conservative appointments such as Dillon's. At other times he had sounded like a New Dealer in presenting legislation to Congress. He also had appointed Lee Loevinger, a Minnesota antitrust attorney and judge associated with Hubert Humphrey, as head of the Department of Justice's Antitrust Division. By 1962 that division had filed ninety-two cases, the most ever, many of them in the price-fixing category.

Other "suspicious" appointments included William L. Cary, chairman of the Securities and Exchange Commission (SEC), Newton Minnow, chairman of the Federal Communications Commission, and Paul R. Dixon, chairman of the Federal Trade Commission. None antagonized big business more than the appointment of Luther Hodges as secretary of commerce. Hodges, a self-made entrepreneur from North Carolina, opposed the powerful Business Advisory Council, created in 1933 to ensure that federal agencies followed approaches acceptable to the corporate elite. He especially objected to the council's long-time role as an official advisory agency to the Commerce Department. Consequently, he sought to exert his authority by approving all corporate executives slated for membership in that organization. He also wanted to extend membership to heads of small businesses, influence the agenda of the conferences, and open meetings to the press. Thus a council delegation informed a surprised Kennedy in July 1961 that the council was disaffiliating itself from the federal government. Roger Blough of United States Steel, the new council president, headed the delegation.

Kennedy's clash with United States Steel in April 1962 compounded the overall distress. His assault on big steel preceded the collapse of the stock market in May. While corporate leaders claimed that Kennedy's actions eroded business confidence, leading to the market decline, his backers cited a Securities and Exchange Commission report that stocks had been overpriced in relation to company earnings. Actually both probably contributed. A concurring May 1962 CEA report also mentioned the problem of gold outflow and higher interest rates at commercial banks and savings and loan institutions, which lured small investors away from the market. Regardless of the cause, the stock-market collapse had a detrimental effect because it reduced capital investment necessary for economic growth.

The conflict with steel meanwhile had emerged over that bellwether industry's response to Kennedy's price-wage guideposts. Labor Secretary Arthur Goldberg, a former attorney for the United Steel Workers of America, had pressured the union to accept a contract that provided a 2.5 percent increase in benefits, well within the wage-price guidelines. The steel companies, of course, had benefited from the government's intercession and therefore were expected to hold the line on a price increase, especially since the companies had not indicated otherwise.

But on Tuesday 10 April 1962, the bespectacled, scholarly looking Blough handed President Kennedy a mimeographed press release, indicating that the company was raising prices to $6 a ton, a 3.5 percent increase that exceeded the guidepost limitations. This proved necessary, the memo explained, because of a price-cost squeeze. One day after Blough's announcement seven competitors, including Bethlehem and Republic Steel, followed with similar raises. On 10 April the press had quoted the president of Bethlehem as saying at a stockholders' meeting that "there shouldn't be any price rise. We shouldn't do anything to increase our costs if we are to survive." Had the powerful Blough engaged in collusion?

Blough, ignoring the conspiracy charge, insisted that he had often hinted at a possible increase and questioned the administration's contention that the industry could overcome the recent hike in labor costs without a substantial price rise. Steel profits, Blough claimed, were at an all-time low. He thought it unfair that no steel price increase had occurred since 1958, despite a substantial wage boost in January 1960, which Vice-President Nixon had encouraged the industry to absorb—at least until after the election.

Blough might have succeeded had he only waited a decent interval before announcing selective price increases. In that way the administration's credibility and authority would not have been so flagrantly challenged. Was Blough that insensitive? Just as puzzling, the general price hike could only make steel even less competitive with foreign producers. Europe already underpriced Americans by 30 percent. Had Kennedy not forced rescission, steel might have had to reverse its price increase on some products out of economic necessity. At the time, however, Blough apparently counted on improved domestic demand, modernization, and a stronger, lighter steel to overcome the foreign competition. One wonders, however, whether Blough also attempted to challenge a supposedly unfriendly Democratic administration that had dangerously increased federal authority over the price sector—an allegation Blough later bitterly denied. If that indeed were a motive, his effort backfired.

On this issue Kennedy responded forcefully and resolutely. After Blough informed him of the price hike, a stunned Kennedy told him that he was making a mistake. Kennedy clearly understood the impact this would have on his presidency and on the country. He quickly called Goldberg, who arrived in less than five minutes. Blough's maneuver so upset Goldberg that he tendered his resignation, insisting that he had lost credibility with labor as the result of the supposed double cross. He also expressed his anger to Blough for his alleged duplicity during the wage negotiations. "You kept silent and silence is consent. One thing you owe a President is candor." Immediately after Blough's departure, Kennedy phoned David McDonald, president of the Steelworkers Union, to say, "Dave, you've been screwed and I've been screwed."[12]

The president refused to accept Goldberg's resignation. After consulting with Sorensen, the CEA, his brother, Goldberg, Special Assistant Kenneth O'Donnell, and others, he read a statement at a press conference the day following Blough's bombshell, charging that the steel price increase "constituted a wholly unjustifiable and irresponsible defiance of the public interest." He then recited how others had heeded his call for sacrifice—including servicemen in Vietnam—before chiding the "tiny handful of steel executives whose pursuit of private power and profit exceeds their sense of public responsibility." He made it clear that he wanted the price increases rescinded.

Publicly Kennedy remained calm but determined; never before, however, had he been so critical and brusque at a press conference. Privately he expressed considerable anger. He asked Benjamin Bradlee of *Newsweek*, "Are we supposed to sit there and take a cold deliberate fucking?" He soon answered his own question by saying, "They fucked us, and we've got to try to fuck them."[13] To staffers he raged that "my father always told me that all businessmen were sons of bitches, but I never believed it till now." The politically damaging comment leaked to *Newsweek*, causing Kennedy to deny that he damned all businessmen. His father had referred only to steel men, he protested. Despite loyalists like Sorensen, who echoed the president's explanation, there is little reason to question the reporting. Joe Kennedy, after all, had expressed contempt for businessmen after the 1929 crash. Besides, in the Kennedy Library the "all businessmen" quote exists in the "doodles" file in Jacqueline Kennedy's handwriting, penned sometime in April 1962. Unlike Eisenhower, according to journalist Charles Bartlett, Kennedy never had a high opinion of most businessmen.[14]

One thing is clear: Kennedy was prepared to throw the full power of the government against steel to force a rescission. To do otherwise not only would have reflected badly on his economic policies but also on him personally. The last thing he wanted was the perception of being weak within his own party—particularly with organized labor, which had grudgingly supported his economic program. Robert Kennedy, shortly after the president's death, revealed the extent to which they were willing to go to pressure steel; it included a grand jury investigation in which steel executives were subpoenaed. "We were going for broke," he admitted:

> their expense accounts and where they'd been and what they were doing. I picked up all their records and I told the FBI to interview them all—march into their offices the next day. We weren't going to go slowly. I said to have them done all over the country. All of them were hit with meetings the next morning by agents. . . . I agree it was a tough way to operate. But under the circumstances we couldn't afford to lose.[15]

No wonder Republican opponents accused the administration of adopting Gestapo-like tactics.

The attempt to disclose price-fixing led the FBI to question journalists who had reported that the president of Bethlehem Steel had opposed a steel increase but reversed himself after Blough's announced hike. FBI agents called on reporters in the middle of the night, inviting further criticism in the press. Whether the attorney general had anything to do with this is unclear. In any case, in addition to encouraging investigations of steel by the antitrust division, the Federal Trade Commission, and congressional committees, the administration applied pressure in other ways, much of it counterproductive, ineffectual, and unnecessary, inviting criticism from the press. Certainly it did nothing to improve Kennedy's relations with congressional Republicans, who bitterly resented his forceful interference in the private sector.

Kennedy's most effective action included efforts to rally public opinion. Practically every major administration official became involved in coordinated press conferences and speeches. Some, like Heller, who had friends in the business world, made timely telephone calls. The administration also employed economic leverage effectively. Defense Secretary Robert McNamara, for example, ensured that a $5.5 million order for steel plate for Polaris submarines went to Lukens Steel, a company that did not raise prices. Such actions represented a strategy of divide and conquer, designed to prevent other companies from raising prices.

The administration had other economic weapons, including its support of tax-depreciation measures. No corporation wished to see these endangered. Consequently, three key companies—Inland Steel, Kaiser Steel, and Armco—soon decided not to raise prices. Even though the offending companies controlled about 85 percent of the market, they still became vulnerable to contract losses. Roger Blough, at a news conference, admitted the difficulty his company faced. It worsened when Bethlehem rescinded its increase, starting a chain reaction until United States Steel followed suit on 12 April. Seventy-two hours after it began, the crisis ended. Kennedy was elated. Despite some negative criticism from the press, he came out of the crisis with his popularity intact. He received only a 22 percent disapproval rating in a 20 May Gallup Poll and secured a 73 percent presidential-approval rating in another poll three days later.

Scholars have generally responded favorably to Kennedy's handling of the steel crisis. While recognizing that he might have overreacted, they acknowledge that a failure of leadership would have affected his ability to deal with the economy and other issues. Arthur Schlesinger in particular views Kennedy's actions in the progressive tradition of strong presidents since Jackson who contended against the private sector. He easily could have compared Kennedy with the two Roosevelts in their efforts to elevate the national government over big business. Other scholars such as Bruce Miroff point out that Kennedy—like earlier "progressive" presidents—sought intervention in the economy not so much to check corporate power but to stabilize and rationalize it. Even the most critical scholarly appraisal, however, has few kind things to say about Blough and his cohorts. At the same time most historians note that steel companies won a belated victory with selected price increases in April and October 1963, amounting to an overall hike of about 3 percent, which Kennedy only mildly protested.

Kennedy had realized that he needed to mend fences with the business community following the steel crisis and the May stock market crash. Corporate executives wearing buttons with "SOB club" captions and purchasing bumper stickers stating "I miss Ike—hell, I even miss Harry" flaunted their hostility. Kennedy understood that a strained atmosphere would contribute to the economic woes. Lower business profits meant reduced government revenues; the last thing he wanted was to jeopardize economic growth. In public statements he emphasized the necessity for business, labor, and government to work together, proclaiming himself no enemy of big business.

Indeed no previous Democratic administration proved as supportive of corporate interests. This approach sometimes perplexed old-line Democrats like Felix Frankfurter, the elderly and ill Supreme Court Justice whom Kennedy visited in July just prior to Frankfurter's retirement. Hardly a flaming liberal at this stage in his life, Frankfurter reminded Kennedy that Democratic presidents had a long-standing tradition of opposing the monied interests. This opposition developed from broader concerns and values that often conflicted with business interests. As a consequence Democratic presidents should expect the resistance of corporate executives and think nothing of it, Frankfurter advised.[16] Kennedy responded sympathetically, but his actions belied the lessons of the past, provided by a ghost of the New Deal.

Kennedy was already appeasing business. Sorensen, who took charge of the campaign in June, proposed that the White House and cabinet officers sponsor a series of black-tie dinners to court business leaders, a practice soon adopted. Heller had already attended the Business Council Conference at Hot Springs, Arkansas, in May, where he reached out to Blough and others to discuss national economic problems informally. Kennedy had earlier disappointed Hodges by indicating that the White House and governmental agencies' doors remained open to Business Council members. Sorensen's recommendations that the administration publicize the ways in which it was probusiness soon involved most governmental departments in a concerted effort.

Loevinger, for example, now argued that antitrust action was inherently probusiness because "its objective is to increase business freedom and maintain the free enterprise system."[17] Assistant Attorney General Nicholas Katzenbach further pointed out that antitrust litigation generally stemmed from complaints from businessmen "who have been unfairly damaged by the illegal and predatory activity of the antitrust violators."[18] In the same way, Katzenbach contended, the administration's war against organized crime also served the business community. By early 1963 the administration moved Loevinger, whom businessmen labeled a frustrated crusader, out of Justice, despite his supposed pro-business, antitrust approach. Businessmen perceived this action as yet another effort to improve the climate between the White House and the corporate boardroom. Ultimately the Kennedy administration did no better than Eisenhower in enforcing the antitrust laws.

By summer 1962 that was clearly what the administration wanted. Sorensen, in his June 1962 memorandum to Kennedy, had asked whether the president or the attorney general would meet individually with heads of regulatory agencies, including the Antitrust Division and the Food and Drug Administration. Sorensen wished this message to be conveyed: "There are times to steam ahead, to pursue, to be zealous, and there are times to be cooperative and understanding (and the latter is more appropriate now)." Sorensen wondered also whether the SEC could "tone down" its investigations or whether the Antitrust Division encouraged treble damage suits. Did the NLRB give "public emphasis to those of its decisions that favor[ed] management?"[19]

Although he valued Sorensen, Kennedy also looked outside of the administration for advice. He asked the venerable Robert Lovett how he might repair the recent economic damage, including the perception of his being antibusiness. Lovett recommended lowering taxes to encourage capital accumulation. Kennedy went ahead in July through executive action with new depreciation allowances for machinery and equipment, which amounted to a tax cut for business. Business would gain $1.5 billion in lower taxes in the first year alone. In October Congress also passed Kennedy's investment tax-credit bill, which gave business a 7 percent tax credit on new investment. First introduced in April 1961, most businessmen initially opposed it, primarily because they thought it a substitute for accelerated depreciation allowances. These actions were expected to stimulate economic growth, promote modernization, and impose trade opportunities abroad, thereby helping the payment imbalance; they would also establish Kennedy as a probusiness president. Heller emphasized the latter point in his meeting with corporate executives where he "made clear that there never *was* an administration so dedicated to the free market system, so devoted to private enterprise, profits, and investments, so determined to restrain government expenditures, so diligent in stimulating competition—as the Kennedy administration."[20] Robert Kennedy later claimed that "I think more was done for business [by the Kennedy administration] than has ever been done. . . . When the story is eventually written it will be rather impressive."[21]

The story must also include Kennedy's commitment to a general tax cut in 1962, which further served the corporate interest. He finally began to consider tax reduction in the summer following difficulties with the steel and the stock market. While the economy continued its disappointing, gradual rise during this period, several weak spots stood out, including insignificant plant expansion and declining retail sales. The CEA, fearing a recession sometime in 1962, recommended in June an immediate tax cut of between $5 and $10 billion. On the advice of Dillon, Sorensen, and others, Kennedy rejected a "quick fix" on the assumption that Congress and the American public would "piss all over" a 1962 tax-cut measure. Chairman Wilbur Mills of the House Ways and Means Committee had already indicated his opposition to a quick cut.

The Republican leadership, concerned about a rising deficit, was even more negative. The political obstacles, given the problems with Kennedy's other domestic proposals, appeared formidable. Also, as Heller admitted, 72 percent of the respondents in a recent Gallup Poll survey disapproved a tax reduction (probably out of concern for the national debt). Besides, by August the economy seemed improved. In a nationwide address on the thirteenth Kennedy told the American people that since no clear and present danger to the economy existed, he was rejecting an immediate tax cut. He intended, however, to submit a bill to reduce personal and corporate taxes the next year retroactive to January 1963. In layman's terms he explained that the current tax rate, having developed out of the World War II era, had retarded economic growth. The right kind of tax cut, he insisted, would eventually reduce deficits by increasing productivity, employment, and hence federal revenues.

Sometime in early 1962 Kennedy had become a convert to Keynesian economics. A remarkably educable president, he had grasped the logic of accepting temporarily larger deficits to achieve economic well-being. His frequent meetings with the CEA, along with Heller's superbly clear memos, had convinced him, as had his own studies on the greater growth rate of competing Western European countries.

Of course Heller and the council had also prescribed the specific remedy—a general tax cut. The losers were liberals like Galbraith and Leon Keyserling, who favored the Keynesian alternative of vastly increased federal spending in the public sector to effect stimulation through improved parks, schools, hospitals, and welfare programs—all of which were badly needed, they argued. "I am not sure," Galbraith said, "what the advantage is in having a few more dollars to spend if the air is dirty, the water is too polluted to drink, . . . the streets are filthy, and the schools so bad that the young . . . stay away." Keyserling, dismayed by Kennedy's choice of Keynesian approaches, commented that he was "as bad as Eisenhower," a statement that angered the president.[22] Keyserling and others refused to acknowledge that Congress—and big business—would resist spending programs more than a tax cut.

Yet Heller underwent some disappointments too. He had failed to obtain a quickie tax cut in 1962. To win Kennedy over for 1963 he needed the approval of Kennedy's "chief financial officer," Douglas Dillon; this necessitated concessions. Dillon, more flexible than his Republican friends had anticipated, had effected a harmonious relationship with the council and with Federal Reserve head Martin. Nevertheless, he warned that Kennedy must not pierce the deficit ceiling of the Eisenhower period or else he would not be able to sell a tax cut to Republicans. To keep the deficit down Kennedy would probably have to postpone such programs as medicare—much to Heller's chagrin. Too, Dillon convinced Kennedy to incorporate a reform provision in the tax bill to tighten loopholes and remove inequities. Tax reform could increase federal revenues by some $3 billion and win over Chairman Mills and others who deemed tax reform necessary.

Dillon also engineered the reduction of personal income rates at the upper level as well as the lowering of corporate taxes from 52 to 47 percent. This led Galbraith and others to argue that tax cuts by nature favored those who needed them the least, unlike social expenditures, which worked in behalf of the disadvantaged. Prophetically, Galbraith feared that if "we started encouraging the economy with tax cuts, it would sooner or later become an uncontrollably popular measure with conservatives. And tax cuts would be urged as a way of getting public expenditures down."[23] Galbraith's prophecy found fruition in the Reagan years of the early 1980s, at least in respect to social programs.

But in 1962 Kennedy fought an uphill battle to sell Keynesian economics to the establishment, despite its general acceptance by economists. One major effort to do so came in his widely publicized commencement address at Yale University on 11 June, written by Sorensen, Galbraith, Heller, and Schlesinger and reworked by Kennedy on the plane to New Haven. It revealed how far he had come since 1960, and clearly represented one of his most thoughtful speeches. He gave the address after receiving an honorary doctor of laws degree, enabling him to quip that now "I have the best of both worlds, a Harvard education and a Yale degree."

Many of his remarks focused on dispelling mythology. "For the great enemy of truth," Kennedy asserted, "is very often not the lie—deliberate, contrived, and dishonest—but the myth—persistent, persuasive, and unrealistic." He first addressed the myth of a growing federal government, which, he contended, had grown less rapidly over the last fifteen years than the economy as a whole. He then challenged the belief that federal deficits caused inflation and budget surpluses prevented it. He reminded the audience that budget surpluses after the war had failed to prevent inflation and that the deficits of recent years had left the price stability unaffected. He also said that deficits—and surpluses—were neither always dangerous nor beneficial. Furthermore, he strongly disputed that the national debt had grown enormously since World War II; in relation to a rising GNP, the debt had dropped considerably. In absolute terms the national debt had increased only 8 percent since 1945 at a time when private debt had risen 305 percent and that of state and local governments had jumped 378 percent. Borrowing proved also neither bad nor good, he maintained. It could lead to overextension and collapse as well as to growth and strength. He resurrected the words of Jefferson in invoking the need for new phrases and approaches to fit changing times. In this way the nation could achieve full employment, increased productivity, stable prices, and a strong dollar.

Kennedy's public profession of Keynes might have pleased liberals, but "the old Elis had listened with acute discomfort," wrote Schlesinger.[24] Coming on the heels of the steel crisis, the speech undoubtedly seemed heretical to a concerned business community, thus further explaining the administration's concerted efforts to win over business in summer 1962. The reaction also caused Kennedy to fear even more the political repercussions of exorbitant deficits, a matter that he addressed in his August TV speech. Clearly all of this drew him closer to Dillon, the architect of the proposed tax-cut measure as much as Heller.

The president's address before the Economic Club of New York on 14 December, which Galbraith called the most "Republican speech since McKinley," reflected Dillon's influence.[25] Kennedy spoke before an audience of mostly Republican businessmen whose approval he—and Dillon—thought essential. Consequently, according to one news magazine, he sounded more like an officer of the National Association of Manufacturers. After first praising the free-enterprise system, he stressed the need to keep public expenditures down while encouraging private spending through incentives. He assured corporations and upper-income individuals that they would be treated favorably. He then claimed that he had hoped originally to provide comprehensive tax reform in the atmosphere of a balanced budget but national defense expenditures mostly had prevented him from doing this. Furthermore, budget deficits, he insisted, "are not caused by wild-eyed spenders but by slow economic growth and periodic recessions, and any new recession would break all deficit records." His goals, he concluded, remained greater profits and a balanced budget, which could be achieved through a tax cut.

Kennedy's well-received Economic Club address went a long way in winning the approbation of business; he had clearly addressed the concerns of the Business Council. He had also won the endorsements of the labor organizations, despite apprehension about the nature of the cuts and the desire for spending programs. The speech's reception also contributed to his own enthusiasm for a tax cut. On 24 January 1963 he presented a special message to Congress on tax reduction and reform.

The Kennedy tax proposal included reductions at every tax level. The personal income rates would change from a range of 20 ($4,000 and under) to 91 percent ($400,000 and over) to a range of 14 to 65 percent. Corporate income taxes would drop from 52 to 47 percent, with special breaks given to small business. The total tax reduction came to $13.6 billion—$11 billion for individuals and $2.6 billion for corporations. It was adjusted to $10.2 billion after incorporating the anticipated $3.4 billion gain from tax reform. The latter tightened personal itemized deductions, capital gains, and dividend exclusion and credit allowances and also provided tax advantages for the aged and those with physical handicaps. Kennedy spread the tax cut over a three-year period to be fully effective by 1 January 1965. He balanced Heller's desire for a full cut in the first year to ignite economic growth with his own concerns that the annual deficit not exceed $12.8 billion, Eisenhower's 1958 performance level. In short he did everything he possibly could to make the measure palatable to Congress.

Yet congressional opposition came as expected from Republicans and, to a far lesser extent, from southern Democrats. They portrayed Kennedy as a spendthrift president carving out a legacy of increased expenditures, astronomical deficits, and emerging inflation. A tax cut, they argued, must accompany a promise to reduce expenditures. It did not seem to matter that Kennedy had agreed to promote economic growth mainly through private initiative. House Republicans moved to recommit the bill, with instructions to make the tax cut conditional on Kennedy's limiting expenditures to $97 billion in 1964 and $98 billion in 1965, reductions of about $4 billion annually from the president's suggested budgets for those years. Despite 173 out of 174 Republicans voting for it, recommittal failed, largely because the vast majority of southern Democrats stuck with the party leadership.

Following the recommittal fight, primary attention shifted to tax reform, with the administration caught in a crossfire between liberals and conservatives. Most of the fireworks came from the latter, representing vested interests who objected to the closing of various tax loopholes. As a result the administration abandoned most of the revenue-saving reforms, including the provisions for tightening of capital gains and personal deductions and the raising of taxes in the oil and gas industry. This invited liberal criticism that the administration showed "insufficient enthusiasm" for tax reform. Yet neither Dillon nor Kennedy wished to jeopardize the tax cut in the face of mounting opposition. With major interest-group support, the amended bill sailed through the House on 25 September 1963. It likely would have cleared the Senate in early 1964 had Kennedy lived. As it turned out President Johnson provided the final touches in January 1964. To appease the Senate economy bloc he slashed the 1964 budget to $97.9 billion and also shifted more of the tax cut into 1964. This bill then passed the following month.

The Kennedy tax bill represents one of his most innovative and enduring initiatives. No other president had dared to impose a tax cut on top of a significant deficit or to ask for deficits to avert a possible recession. That a lagging economy had marginally improved from 1962 made his action more politically difficult. Yet Kennedy understood that growth had barely kept pace with an expanding labor force—one that would require 12 million new jobs over the next ten years. He faulted an antiquated tax structure, which caused an annual loss of $30 billion of potential output. As a newly converted Keynesian, Kennedy put his faith in the multiplier effect. A $10 billion tax cut, he reasoned, would create an additional $20 billion fiscal stimulus in the GNP, as business investment increased due to consumer demand. This in turn would generate full employment, which the CEA defined as 4 percent unemployment. Kennedy risked the political repercussions of short-term, near-record deficits on the assumption that a limping economy in November 1964 would be a greater liability.

The Revenue Act of 1964 did seem to have an appreciable impact on the economy. Unemployment dropped from 5.5 percent in December 1963 to 5 percent by the end of the following year. By the close of 1965 it plummeted to 4.1 percent, close to the CEA's definition of full employment and a far cry from the 7 percent unemployment rate Kennedy had inherited. The annual growth rate rose from 2.5 percent in 1960 to over 6 percent by 1964, surpassing Kennedy's 5 percent goal of 1960. The GNP had jumped over $100 billion in that period. Profits also soared by 1964. And despite the lower tax rates, federal receipts increased in the years after the tax cut, as Kennedy had predicted. More remarkably, the inflation rate held at 1.3 percent, unlike during the Johnson presidency when the economy overheated because of a guns-and-butter policy and a failure to raise taxes as U.S. involvement in Vietnam escalated. Nor did Kennedy leave enormous budget deficits. Though his average yearly deficit exceeded that of Eisenhower's, he avoided the double-digit annual deficit that afflicted both Eisenhower ($12.8 billion in 1958) and Johnson

($25.1 billion in 1968), all of which strengthened Sorensen's 1987 assertion that Kennedy was "more [fiscally] conservative than any president we've had since."[26]

Kennedy also improved the balance-of-payments situation—especially the gold loss. The Trade Expansion Act eventually expanded exports, and the administration worked to make American goods competitive with foreign products, persuading other nations to buy more military goods from the United States. It also made headway in inducing our Allies to assume some of the foreign aid and military obligations. Moving against the so-called tourist gap, it wooed foreigners to this country and reduced the amounts that Americans could spend abroad without paying duties. The administration also nudged upward short-term interest rates to discourage the investment of capital abroad, at the same time keeping long-term interest rates on bonds and mortgages down so as not to retard domestic economic growth. It imposed a 1 percent tax on foreign securities purchased by Americans to encourage domestic investments. As a result, the crisis over gold outflow ended because of Kennedy's actions. The amount of gold leaving the country fell by more than one-third, an indication of increased confidence in United States currency by foreign countries.

Kennedy also eased some of the difficulties that women faced as wage earners. Once again he adopted new approaches in dealing with a problem that grew more serious as the number of women in the workplace increased. In 1960, for example, 34.8 percent of all women worked for wages, an increase of more than 3.5 percent since 1950, and the number of working women who had children under the age of six virtually doubled in this period. Most female employees confronted an enormous differential in wages with their male counterparts, discrimination in hiring practices, and a lack of day-care facilities for young children. Of equal concern to Kennedy, a sizable number of skilled and talented women had surrendered careers to become full-time homemakers, thereby denying cold war America needed skills in such fields as science, education, and medicine.

By 1960 women's groups had grown more impatient with injustices. This reached greater intensity with Betty Friedan's *Feminine Mystique* in 1963, laying the foundation for the National Organization for Women (NOW), which called into question women's traditional roles along with a multitude of discriminatory practices. During the 1960 campaign Kennedy had responded to such practices by endorsing the Democratic party platform of equal pay for equal work and by calling for the adoption of the Equal Rights Amendment (ERA), guaranteeing women complete legal equality with men.

But Kennedy did remarkably little in behalf of women in his early administration, partly because of the diversion of crises such as Berlin. Also, his background had provided him with little sensitivity to women or to women's issues. (Robert Kennedy even privately remarked in 1961 that "a woman's place is in the home").[27] In any case, President Kennedy made only ten Senate-confirmed appointments of women, at least five less than Truman and Eisenhower. Unlike Eisenhower, he made none at the cabinet level. Only 2.4 percent of all Kennedy's appointive positions went to women, a percentage comparable to the two previous administrations. Furthermore, Kennedy failed to consult Margaret Price, the vice-chair and director of women's activities for the Democratic National Committee, and other leading Democratic women when making appointments. Nor did he address the economic problems that working women faced. Not surprisingly, he came under fire, particularly from May Craig, a long-time White House reporter, known for her tough-minded questions at press conferences. On 9 November 1961 she asked Kennedy what he had done for women in accordance with the party platform. Recognizing a loaded question, Kennedy smilingly responded, "Well, I'm sure we haven't done enough, Mrs. Craig," amid considerable laughter.[28]

Yet May Craig had made her point as Kennedy acknowledged on 12 February 1962 when he explained why he had created the President's Commission on the Status of Women: "One [reason] is for my own self-protection: every two or three weeks Mrs. May Craig asks me what I am doing for women!" Kennedy could have mentioned the criticism he had also received from Eleanor Roosevelt and several others. Politically, a response seemed appropriate; more importantly, he recognized the problems women faced in the workplace, particularly with discrimination in wages and hiring. That same concern had motivated him to push for a stronger minimum-wage law for all workers.

Kennedy charged the commission to "review progress and make recommendations as needed for constructive action" relating virtually to every aspect of female employment. For the first time, a study of the status of women received national focus. Kennedy chose Eleanor Roosevelt as chairperson, to highlight its significance. Much of the work, however, fell to Esther Peterson, the new director of the Women's Bureau, whom Kennedy had also appointed as assistant secretary of labor. Peterson, enormously capable and well connected to organized labor, became the administration's key spokesperson on women. She had a long-time association with Kennedy, beginning with his tenure on the House Labor Committee and her service as lobbyist for the Amalgamated Clothing Workers.

Peterson reflected the viewpoint that the administration should concentrate less on appointing women to governmental offices and more on improving their economic status in society. She more than anyone else convinced Kennedy to create the twenty-six person presidential commission, undoubtedly hoping to control the direction of the women's movement through her involvement in the commission. Coming from a strong labor background, she represented traditional feminism, which feared that protective labor legislation, in existence since the Progressive era, was in jeopardy as a result of the ERA. She contended that the ERA would only benefit women in the professions and business, who least needed assistance. Although the commission contained all points of view, Peterson's followers naturally dominated it.

The commission issued its final report, "American Women," on 11 October 1963, the birthday of Eleanor Roosevelt, who had died that previous November. It emphasized that "equal opportunity for women in hiring, training, and promotion should be the governing principle in private employment." Yet the commission predictably hedged on the ERA in concluding that "a constitutional amendment need not now be sought in order to establish this principle."[29] Most commission members contended that the Fifth and Fourteenth Amendments could ensure equality of opportunity, particularly if the Supreme Court validated that assertion through appropriate test cases.

Even before the final report, the administration had responded to the commission's concerns. In May 1963 Congress approved an administration bill that guaranteed equal pay to women doing work equal to what men did. First considered in Congress in 1945, the Equal Pay Act, an amendment to the Fair Labor Standards Act of 1938, applied only to those workers covered by the Fair Labor Standards Administration (approximately 7 million women). It meant little to the many women engaged in sexually segregated occupations or in plants of fewer than twenty-five employees. Other critics asserted that the phrase "comparable" work instead of "equal" might have served women better. Despite the act's minimal practical impact, Cynthia Harrison, the leading scholar of this legislation, rightly argues that it "marks the entrance of the federal government into the field of safeguarding the right of women to hold employment on the same basis as men."[30] In that respect it represented a milestone in anti-discrimination legislation, one that other administrations, beginning with Johnson's, further extended.

In July 1962 Kennedy also directed the chairman of the Civil Service Commission to ensure that employment in the federal service be based solely on individual merit and fitness. That same year Congress acted on Kennedy's recommendation to assist states in establishing day-care facilities, in May appropriating $800,000 for that purpose, a far cry from the president's $5 million recommendation. Yet this represented the first day-care expenditure since World War II. The Kennedy administration also eliminated the quota system, which limited the number of women military officers. Following the commission report in October, Kennedy complied with its recommendation to provide for continual governmental action on behalf of women by creating the Interdepartmental Committee on the Status of Women and the Citizens' Advisory Council. These committees provided ongoing leadership.

The Kennedy administration thus took the crucial first steps in improving the economic well-being of women. By publicizing discrimination and injustice, the President's Commission contributed to the establishment of commissions on the state level. It also unwittingly spurred the women's-rights movement, which went well beyond the administration's limited goals and its view of women's primary role as mother and homemaker. Kennedy in fact wondered how women could meet their responsibilities to their children and also make a contribution to society. He assumed that most women worked to support their families. The commission furthermore argued that women workers had "special" attributes which might permit "justified" discrimination.[31] All of these assumptions would be called into question, as would traditional roles for women. In May 1963 Friedan, in her best-seller, called the American home a "comfortable concentration camp," an assessment that most likely troubled Kennedy, Peterson, and the commission members.

The administration's campaign against organized crime also set it apart from its predecessors, even though governmental activity against crime was nothing new. In 1929 President Herbert Hoover had established the Wickersham Commission to study its machinations and had leaned on the Treasury Department and other federal agencies to bring the notorious Alphonse Capone to justice. Not until the early 1950s and the Senate Special Committee to Investigate Organized Crime in Interstate Commerce did Congress involve itself in an indepth study. Chaired by Senator Estes Kefauver (D.-Tenn.), the committee shocked a national TV audience by revealing a nationwide crime syndicate or confederation—the Mafia—which had infiltrated approximately fifty areas of legitimate businesses and had engaged in political corruption to sustain its activities. The committee focused on organized crime's involvement in casino gambling, illegal slot machines and punchboards, and narcotics and on its use of unscrupulous business practices, extortion, murder, and bombing.

The committee's revelation of a national crime syndicate gained credence on 14 November 1957 when a state policeman investigating a suspicious gathering in upstate New York near Apalachin discovered that more than sixty Mafia crime-family members nationwide were in attendance, most of them soon identified. The Apalachin enclave spurred more than 133 investigations by grand juries and various law enforcement agencies. Attorney General William Rogers established a Special Group on Organized Crime to delve into Apalachin, which cooperated primarily with the Federal Narcotics Bureau, long interested in organized crime.

Robert Kennedy became tangentially linked to the anticrime activity in January 1957 as chief counsel of the Senate Select Committee on Improper Activities in the Labor or Management Field—nicknamed the McClellan committee after its chairman, Senator McClellan of Arkansas. The committee included Senator John Kennedy of Massachusetts, who chaired the Subcommittee on Labor Reform. The McClellan committee investigated labor racketeering, a pursuit that Joe Kennedy reputedly described as madness because it could only invite animosity from labor against the Kennedys. But for the next three years, largely under Robert Kennedy's relentless direction, the McClellan committee exposed the corruption and fraud—including misuse of union pension funds—of the Teamsters' Union, resulting in the conviction of its president, David Beck and the indictment of his successor, Jimmy Hoffa. Bobby, the "rich man's kid," fought a virtual war with the combative Hoffa in the committee room, the courts, and the media.

Robert Kennedy came to view Hoffa as evil, as one who not only engaged in criminality but also whose organization, because of its considerable control of transportation, represented a danger to the nation. All of this revealed an obsessive, compulsive side to Kennedy, which he had also exhibited in his anticommunism during the 1950s, soon followed by his frenetic management of the 1960 campaign, his efforts to get Castro after the Bay of Pigs and big steel after the 1962 price increase, and his eventual crusade against social injustice. He threw everything into whatever he thought important, letting it assume control of his life. Robert Kennedy was a zealot—he knew how to hate and to care with equal ferocity.

As the committee cast its net more widely by 1958, Kennedy became more aware of the extent to which organized crime controlled a part of our national life. He learned in greater detail the manner in which it had infected the political process and had seized not only unions but also legitimate businesses. Indeed, Kennedy entitled his 1960 book on the McClellan investigation *The Enemy Within*. "If we do not on a national scale attack organized criminals with weapons and techniques as effective as their own," he wrote, "they will destroy us."[32] This statement gave both criminals and civil libertarians pause as he entered the Justice Department in 1961.

He initially proclaimed organized crime and antitrust violations, not civil rights, as the two major priorities. According to one Justice Department spokesman, "Kennedy's zeal to break up the [crime] syndicates was reminiscent of a sixteenth-century Jesuit on the hunt for heresy."[33] What helped was a brother as president whose support he could say he had, even though Jack Kennedy gave the anticrime commitment no attention. In order to proceed the attorney general first had to win over the bureaucracy, the most imposing hurdle being J. Edgar Hoover, the egotistical and hoary FBI director, who had long operated independently of the Justice Department, with direct access to the president.

Robert Kennedy changed that arrangement by insisting that Hoover go through Justice. All FBI press releases and speeches passed through Kennedy's office, and he also installed a special interoffice phone, enabling the agency to have direct contact. Even though their father had been close to Hoover, both Kennedys viewed him as dangerous. Given what Hoover knew of the president's sexual escapades, the brothers were vulnerable to his extensive and incriminating files. Thus, Hoover had to be controlled, but he could not easily be fired; out of office, he could become even more menacing. Robert Kennedy therefore avoided antagonizing Hoover, often visiting him for business instead of summoning the FBI director to his office. He even arranged for the president to lunch with Hoover every couple of months.

Yet Hoover deeply resented the attorney general, and it was not entirely related to the new constraints. Like Hoffa, he viewed Robert Kennedy as a smart-aleck rich kid who arrogantly flouted decorum by working in rolled-up shirt sleeves, throwing darts at a wall target, and bringing a monstrous dog to the department. FBI tour guides undoubtedly reflected some of those antagonisms when announcing, until Kennedy put a stop to it, that "Mr. Hoover became the Director of the Bureau in 1924, the year before the Attorney General was born."[34]

Hoover also resented the direction in which the department—and hence the FBI—was moving. The slow shift into civil rights was bad enough. Yet the main thrust in 1961 came against organized crime, a peril that Hoover had denied existed. It was Robert Kennedy, then, who forced him to moderate his crusade against Communist subversives and to focus on an investigative area where Hoover professed to have inadequate legal jurisdiction. To overcome that obstacle the attorney general secured five anticrime bills directed against those who aided interstate racketeering or gambling enterprises or who transported gambling paraphernalia, gambling information by wire, or firearms (by felons) across state lines. The only legislation that Kennedy failed to achieve would have broadened the use of wiretapping by governmental officials.

As a result of the bills, Hoover dramatically increased the number of agents working on organized crime. In New York City the total eventually expanded from 10 to 115. In Chicago, according to Kennedy, the figure jumped by 1,000 percent. Kennedy also increased by 60 percent the number of attorneys who worked in Justice's Organized Crime and Racketeering Section. Kennedy brought in tough-minded, aggressive people who used their legal options to the fullest. Consequently, Robert Kennedy's concerted effort eventually involved some twenty-seven intelligence-gathering agencies, including the Internal Revenue Service (IRS), the Secret Service, and the Bureau of Narcotics.

Kennedy induced the IRS to investigate the tax returns of major racketeers—soon a top priority of IRS officials, who worked closely with the Justice Department toward prosecution. The IRS slapped an $835,000 tax lien on Carlos Marcello, the Mafia boss of New Orleans, and a $200,000 lien on Santos Trafficante, the mob leader in Tampa. Overall, roughly 60 percent of all organized crime cases ended up being revenue cases. Kennedy also used the Immigration and Naturalization Service to deport the alien Marcello to Guatemala, following his claim of a Guatemalan birth certificate, which the Justice Department knew to be a forgery. Kennedy removed Marcello with such dispatch that he had no opportunity to inform his family or even pack a suitcase. Marcello reportedly swore vengeance against the Kennedys after his illegal return to New Orleans.[35] In another instance noted racketeer Joseph Aiuppa of Chicago, through the initial efforts of the Park and Wildlife Service, faced a Justice Department conviction for violation of the Migratory Bird Act. Aiuppa had 563 frozen, dressed mourning doves in his possession, 539 over the legal bag limit.

Meanwhile, Hoover's agents employed informants, including infiltrators, to delve into criminal operations, which usually followed FBI electronic eavesdropping. Two forms of this activity existed: wiretapping—the tapping of telephone lines to record calls—and bugging—the planting of a concealed microphone in a person's room. Bugging usually involved surreptitious entry. Since 1934 an attorney general has been able legally to authorize wiretapping but only against "persons suspected of subversive activities against the United States." Unlike some in Justice, Kennedy, according to Victor Navasky, "had no moral qualms about wiretapping" in his war against crime.[36] Schlesinger claims, however, that after failing to get Congress to strengthen the wiretapping law, Kennedy authorized no wiretapping against racketeers or Teamsters, even though he approved 140 wiretaps in 1961, 198 in 1962, and 244 in 1963, supposedly for reasons of national security. Even Schlesinger concedes that Kennedy handled wiretap authorizations with "surprising casualness and inattention."[37]

Furthermore, as the House Assassinations Committee revealed in 1978, the FBI wiretapped with impunity during Kennedy's tenure. Hoover also bugged in a big way, often by trespassing, in gross violation of personal-privacy rights. This became a more frequent occurrence as the anticrime campaign heated up, undoubtedly enhancing the campaign's success. Eventually, however, it spawned considerable criticism as some of Hoover's bugging operations became public knowledge. In 1966 Hoover finally responded that he had engaged in electronic activity only with the authorization of the attorney general, an allegation that Robert Kennedy vehemently denied. While it is difficult to prove Kennedy's complicity, Joseph Dolan, a long-time Kennedy associate, confided in 1967 that "Kennedy had full knowledge of all technical devices being used by the FBI."[38] One is also reminded of Kennedy's earlier Machiavellian statement, "If we do not on a national scale attack organized criminals with weapons and techniques as effective as their own, they will destroy us."

Critics have raised other objections to Kennedy's anticrime campaign, including the disproportionate number of resources that went into that fight. "Too many brilliant young men who might have been bringing Southern sheriffs or Eastern conglomerates to justice were out chasing Hoffa," complained one Justice lawyer.[39] The department also compiled a list of twelve hundred top suspected racketeers and then investigated them for criminal violations, including tax fraud. The idea of going after people rather than investigating specific crimes bothered civil libertarians like Ramsey Clark, an assistant attorney general and future attorney general, who favored more even-handed justice.

Jimmy Hoffa in particular felt the sting of the Kennedy approach. Kennedy had organized a group of attorneys in Justice, headed by Walter Sheridan, not a lawyer but a veteran of the McClellan investigation, to complete the unfinished work on Hoffa. The Get Hoffa Squad relentlessly pursued the Teamsters' boss, with the attorney general much involved. William H. Orrick, Jr., an assistant attorney general, remembered the frequent departmental conversations about Hoffa. Robert Kennedy, he claimed, was worried that he could not snag Hoffa. In explaining how this might be possible, Orrick asked Kennedy to be Hoffa and he would be the lawyer. "State your name," Orrick asked, pretending to take a deposition. "He could hardly gag out, 'Jimmy Hoffa,' " according to Orrick.[40]

But persistence paid off. After several indictments and lengthy trials Hoffa was finally convicted of jury tampering in March and pension-fund fraud in August 1964. The Get Hoffa Squad secured the indictment of 201 Teamsters' officials and their associates, 126 of whom were convicted. Additionally, the Organized Crime and Racketeering Section's efforts produced 615 indictments in 1963 in contrast to 121 in 1961. Convictions, which lagged two to three years behind indictments, jumped from 73 in 1961 to 288 in 1963. A number of top syndicate figures were indicted, including Anthony "Tony Pro" Provenzano of New Jersey. Others such as Sam Giancana of Chicago and John Roselli of Los Angeles clearly felt threatened. No one recognized the dangerous impact of organized crime more than Robert Kennedy; to him it remained an evil conspiracy.

Academic historians have virtually ignored the extent to which Kennedy's war on crime placed both his life and the president's in danger. It has been left to others—mostly free-lance writers—such as John H. Davis, G. Robert Blakey, Richard Billings, Anthony Summers, and David E. Scheim to explore this linkage. Evidence from FBI informants and electronic surveillance, coming out of the House and Senate investigations of the 1970s and of recently opened FBI files, reveals the tremendous hatred and vows of revenge that came from Hoffa, Giancana, Marcello, and other mob figures.

After all, mobsters such as Giancana had reportedly made campaign contributions in 1960 through Joe Kennedy. Giancana's money and influence in Cook County helped swing the close Illinois election to Kennedy in 1960—at least Giancana contended it did.[41] Crooner Frank Sinatra's friendship with John Kennedy partly explains Giancana's motives. Sinatra had an unusually close relationship with Giancana, Roselli, and other mobsters. Giancana—and others—counted on Sinatra's White House influence to keep federal investigators away. That John Kennedy showed his gratitude by appointing his brother attorney general to wage a crusade against the syndicates offended Giancana and his friends. They also thought Kennedy a hypocrite for having used Sinatra to woo prospective Hollywood starlets, including Judith Campbell, a comely brunette with whom Kennedy had an affair from 1960 through spring 1962. Campbell's 1977 book, *My Story*, detailed titillating and convincing specifics of the relationship, and telephone logs exposed her frequent calls to the White House, averaging two a week, during the early Kennedy presidency. FBI reports confirmed the telephone contacts.[42]

J. Edgar Hoover informed the Kennedy brothers in early 1962 of what he knew about Campbell, including her lengthy affair with Giancana, begun in April 1960, three months after Kennedy first met her. Several questions remain unanswered: Did Giancana mistakenly believe that he had more insurance against prosecution because of that relationship? Did Campbell know exactly who Giancana was? Was the president aware of her intimacy with the Chicago mobster? Did Kennedy know that Giancana had been recruited by the CIA to assassinate Castro? It seems probable that Campbell's simultaneous relationship with both men was hardly coincidental. In any case, shortly after meeting with Hoover, Kennedy ended his associations with both Campbell and Sinatra. Nevertheless, Giancana and other underworld figures who knew of the Campbell affair and of Kennedy's other assignations, including one with Marilyn Monroe, apparently sought to blackmail the Kennedys—to no avail.[43] But the Kennedys and the mob were on a collision course by fall 1963.

Only after Kennedy's death in November did the war on organized crime subside, with the new administration soon concentrating more on street crime, which had evoked a public outcry following the rioting of the mid-1960s. Yet the Kennedy administration's efforts inspired subsequent studies on organized crime as well as the Omnibus Crime Control and Safe Streets Act of 1968 and the Organized Crime Control Act of 1970. These laws provided for the widespread use of wiretaps and witness immunity. When the federal government accelerated its anticrime campaign in the early 1980s it did so with more effective tools.

In more dramatic fashion the Kennedy administration ambitiously pledged to land a man on the moon before 1970—a significant departure from the space-exploration policy of Kennedy's predecessor. Space soon became the symbol of the New Frontier. The idea of a lunar landing had long captivated writers of the Western world, beginning with astronomer Johannes Kepler's seventeenth-century saga involving the use of supernatural techniques to propel a space vehicle to the moon. In 1960 the National Aeronautics and Space Administration (NASA) had recommended that the United States embark on such a venture by the early 1970s. NASA's Apollo program was proposed after the Soviets' launching of Sputnik into orbit in 1957, a success that had sent shock tremors nationwide when it appeared that the Soviets were winning the war in space. In the Senate Lyndon Baines Johnson insisted that the "control of space means control of the world. From space, the masters of infinity would have the power to control the earth's weather, to cause drought and flood, to change the tides and raise the levels of the sea, to divert the gulf stream and change temperate climates to frigid."[44] Johnson and others challenged the nation to overtake Soviet domination of space. The frenetic activity that followed included the creation of the Special Committee on Space and Aeronautics in the Senate, chaired by Johnson; a science adviser to the president; the implementation of the space program by NASA; and a nine-member Space Council, involving the president, the secretaries of state and defense, and the director of NASA, to establish a comprehensive policy and to select specific programs.

The Eisenhower administration never shared the concerns and enthusiasm of those committed to an energetic space program. Ike denied that the United States was competing with the Russians and played down the military and technological significance of Sputnik. Although Eisenhower unenthusiastically backed Project Mercury's objective of sending an American into space, he balked at a projected manned lunar landing by 1970. At a December 1960 White House meeting he asked why such a commitment should be made. When someone compared the venture to Columbus's voyage to America, Ike reportedly responded that he was "not about to hock [the] jewels" in order to land on the moon.[45] He soon labeled a lunar space race as nothing more than an extravagant stunt. Eisenhower further showed his ambivalence by ignoring the Space Council, but Johnson prevented a move to terminate it in 1960. That same year Eisenhower delivered his "military-industrial complex" address in which he expressed a concern about a "scientific-technological elite" endangering the nation-state.

John Kennedy sought to capitalize on Eisenhower's sluggish response, despite expressing no interest in or knowledge of space issues prior to 1960. On more than thirty occasions, however, he told campaign audiences that our failure to be number one in space had cost Americans dearly. He argued that Third World nations now viewed the Soviet Union as equal if not superior to the United States. He also alluded to the military dangers of Soviet dominance of space and suggested that the United States must win the moon race to reestablish its technological superiority.

Following the election, however, Kennedy moved cautiously, partly because Laos, Cuba, and other matters seized much of his attention, and he needed time to study a complex program beset with uncertainties. He did ask for legislation enabling the vice-president to replace the president on the Space Council, since Johnson clearly would have the time and inclination to resurrect that important instrument. Johnson in turn used his influence to engineer the appointment of the powerful Robert Kerr of Oklahoma to chair the Senate Space Committee, but the vice-president failed to secure "general supervision" over all space and national defense agencies as he had requested. In gracefully turning down Johnson's proposed executive order, Kennedy made it clear that he himself intended to make the key policy decisions.

What those decisions were to be seemed less clear, following the report he received from his eight-member task force on space, chaired by Jerome Wiesner, the pipe-smoking MIT scientist. The committee shared the opposition of the scientific community to investing significant resources in manned flights, which had little scientific value. Kennedy, feeling that he needed to know more, made the much respected Wiesner his space adviser as a counterweight to Johnson, who favored a lunar landing, and thereby encouraged dialogue. In February Kennedy, partly on Johnson's advice, appointed James Webb, an aggressive administrator, as director of NASA. Webb soon endorsed NASA's plan for a lunar landing by 1969–1970 and requested a 30 percent increase in Eisenhower's fiscal 1962 NASA budget of $1.1 billion.

The major turning point came following Yuri Gagarin's round-the-earth flight on 12 April 1961. The Soviet became the first human in space, an accomplishment Khrushchev eagerly exploited as another Communist triumph over a decaying capitalistic system. Americans were understandably dismayed. Kennedy soon faced tough questioning at press conferences on why he was ignoring his campaign pledge to energize the space program.

Kennedy realized that he could no longer temporize. In fact the events of the next three weeks pushed him closer to a lunar commitment. In an important White House meeting two days after Gagarin's flight, he impatiently questioned the experts about how the United States might overcome the Soviet advantage. "Is there any place where we can catch them? What can we do? Can we go around the moon before them? Can we put a man on the moon before them? Can we leapfrog?"[46] The disastrous consequences of the Bay of Pigs operation on 17–18 April brought on even greater concern about the erosion of America's prestige as well as his own. Sorensen, Wiesner, and Bundy all later contended that Kennedy now felt even more pressure to respond.

Then on 5 May, after several postponements, Alan Shepard soared into suborbital space before a national TV audience in Project Mercury's initial venture, making him a hero to an American public anxiously awaiting some good news. Few people knew of the near cancellation of Shepard's flight because of a fear of failure in the face of considerable hype, causing one NASA official to comment to Kennedy: "Why postpone a success?" Had Shepard met with disaster, the project would have been in jeopardy. As it turned out Shepard's achievement pumped new blood into a program that Kennedy had tentatively decided to move forward.

He had laid the groundwork for such action by asking Johnson on 20 April to convene the Space Council to determine whether the United States had the capabilities of beating the Soviets in a manned lunar enterprise and what it would cost the taxpayer. Kennedy also talked with hundreds of people about the feasibility of the project. Nine days later

Johnson, after pressing NASA, submitted recommendations to include the manned lunar landing as the major objective of the space program. Kennedy's decision became public in a 25 May speech before Congress: "This nation should commit itself to achieving the goal, before this decade is out, of landing a man on the moon and returning him safely to earth. No single project . . . will be more exciting, or more impressive to mankind, or more important for the long-range exploration of space; and none will be so expensive to accomplish."

Nothing troubled the president more than the attendant financial obligation. The anticipated cost over a ten-year period would be between $30 and $40 billion, an enormous figure given his concern about deficits. Moreover, economists had informed him that the nature of the expenditure would only minimally promote economic growth. He knew the immense challenge of developing powerful booster rockets capable of sending a manned capsule far into space. The United States seemed years behind the Soviets in this developmental area, thanks ironically to American technology, which so reduced the weight of the missiles that much less was required in rocket thrust. Just as troubling, scientists remained unconvinced that a manned lunar venture promised as much scientific gain as other space endeavors. Kennedy, Webb, and others naturally soon stressed the scientific, technological, and military values of the Apollo program as well as the continuation of other projects. Webb also cultivated Wiesner, who had close ties with the scientific community.

Kennedy finally came to believe that the lunar program's positive aspects outweighed the negatives. Despite Eisenhower's private opposition and a skeptical public (58 percent were against the $40 billion lunar project in a May Gallup Poll), powerful congressional support existed, as witnessed by the project's approval by a voice vote after little debate. Significantly, several key congressional leaders such as Democratic congressman Albert Thomas of Houston represented districts and states that stood to gain economically from the program. Kennedy undoubtedly hoped that all of this would somehow translate into greater cooperation for domestic programs.

Yet there would have been no race to the moon without the cold war; the space program became as much a part of that conflict as Cuba, Berlin, and Laos. With typical hyperbole Johnson stated that he did not "believe that this generation of Americans is willing to resign itself to going to bed each night by the light of a Communist moon."[47] Others also feared— and exploited—the military implications of Soviet dominance of space. Kennedy saw a lunar commitment as a way to restore United States prestige, particularly with Third World nations, the new battleground of the cold war. A moon launch would lessen the frustrations of Cuba,

Southeast Asia, and Berlin. Kennedy's concerns touched on personal and foreign as well as on domestic considerations. Furthermore, it fit his New Frontier theme, preaching dedication and sacrifice. According to Robert Kennedy, it reflected the president's striving for excellence and admiration of courage. Additionally, a space race would unify Americans, creating a pride heretofore lacking. In a 12 September 1962 address in Houston, Kennedy rhetorically asked, "But why, some say, the moon? Why choose this as our goal? . . . Why does Rice play Texas?" Kennedy saw the race to the moon as a fitting challenge, one that Americans could win.

This much is certain: Kennedy had grasped that the United States had the science and technology to overcome Soviet advantages. He skillfully cast the United States as an underdog as accomplishments slowly unfolded. In February 1962 John Glenn flew around the earth in his Mercury capsule *Friendship*, equaling Gagarin's feat and making Glenn another hero of his times. He had been helped by a space budget that had jumped to $1.8 billion for 1962. NASA's budget doubled one year later. In January 1963 Kennedy also announced a successful unmanned Mariner flight past Venus and, one day before his assassination, referred to the completion of the "largest booster in the world," the Saturn C-1 rocket, soon to carry the largest payload ever to be sent into space.

Kennedy had managed to weather the frustrations connected with the space program in 1963. For the first time, though, it faced criticism inside and outside of Congress because of escalating costs, which ultimately exceeded $30 billion by 1969. Housing and education programs, liberals argued, deserved more funding, and the intensification of racial discontent further heightened the need to refocus upon domestic problems as priorities. Sociologist Amitai Etzioni called Apollo a "moondoggle." Conservative Republicans clamored for a shifting of funds into military projects such as the Titan-3 missile and space stations. The House Space Committee even recommended a reduction in space appropriations.

The truth is that the race to the moon seemed less pressing by 1963. Journalists repeatedly printed stories that the Soviets were disengaging from the attempt. According to one contemporary authority, the USSR was focusing on space stations and unmanned explorations, reinforcing Khrushchev's 1961 claim at Vienna that he had no compulsion to go to the moon. The United States, he had said, was rich; it should go first. Furthermore, the Cuban missile crisis of October 1962 had shown Americans the frightening aspects of technology in a thermonuclear era, leading to improved relations between the two superpowers. Kennedy talked even more openly now about space cooperation with the Soviets, including a joint moon launch, which few experts took seriously, given the existing mutual suspicions. Still, this contributed to the congressional opposition toward the space program in 1963.

Kennedy remained solidly behind the Apollo project to the end. His comments at an April 1963 press conference expressed his beliefs: "I have seen nothing . . . that has changed my mind about the desirability of our continuing this program." Johnson continued the commitment, even managing to increase the space budget to over $5.2 billion in 1964 before facing the strains of Vietnam, mounting social tensions at home, inflation, and Apollo cutbacks. Thus on 20 July 1969 four American astronauts finally landed their module on the moon. Advocates everywhere shared in the glory of that accomplishment, and many remembered Kennedy on that special day. But what did it all mean to those who lived in 1969? Did it represent the triumph of technology, with all of its psychological and material benefits and potential dangers? Was it instead a wasteful, misguided effort, given the enormous social ills afflicting the American society of the 1960s? Or was it a "delayed consequence of the Cold War, beginning with President Kennedy's resolve to outrace the Russians?" Was it a worthwhile or a questionable legacy of the Kennedy presidency? Americans were not altogether sure. Regardless of the answers, the Apollo program, along with the Peace Corps, will always be inexorably linked to Kennedy; both reflected an innovative and activist presidency.

Even more than the space effort the Peace Corps represented Kennedy's "most affirmative and enduring legacy" and became one of his most innovative programs.[48] It enabled more than one hundred thousand Americans to serve in Third World countries over a twenty-five-year period. The prevailing popular image remains a romantic one of "idealistic, patriotic, freedom-loving" young Americans, enduring in mud huts with the "patience of Job, the forbearance of a saint, and the digestive system of an ostrich."[49] In the process they contributed much to the improvement of the American image abroad and provided useful skills to emerging nations.

The idea of the Peace Corps predated the Kennedy presidency. Various voluntary organizations had advocated or instituted service endeavors, ranging from the missionary work of young Mormons to the Operation Crossroads Africa program in the 1950s. During the 1930s the Civilian Conservation Corps and the National Youth Administration were perhaps the Roosevelt administration's domestic equivalents. The idealism of that era was not lost to those in the 1950s who envisioned that government could create comparable programs for the Third World. Truman's Point Four Program, first introduced in 1950, represented a modest, short-lived effort to do that very thing. By the late 1950s Senator Hubert Humphrey called for a Peace Corps, the first use of that specific name. In the House of Representatives Henry Reuss (D.-Wis.) proposed the idea in 1957; by 1960 the House provided ten thousand dollars for a study of a Point Four Youth Corps. Ike later labeled such a commitment a "juvenile experiment." Though Kennedy remained silent on the topic until late 1960, his understanding and acceptance of nationalism had made him an opponent of colonialism, which he felt encouraged Communist insurgency. He later told Harris Wofford he sought the presidency to develop a "new relationship" with the developing world.[50]

Yet during the 1960 campaign Kennedy said nothing about new initiatives until a 2:00 A.M. appearance at Ann Arbor, Michigan, immediately following the third debate with Nixon on 14 October. Ten thousand excited University of Michigan students—including Tom Hayden, the future founder of the Students for Democratic Society—met with Kennedy at the student union that morning. Kennedy asked how many would be prepared to give years of their lives working in Asia, Africa, and Latin America. The overwhelming response to this and other related questions reaffirmed to Kennedy an emerging idealism among college youth, causing the *Harvard Crimson* to write: "This is the first generation of students which is not going to school for purely economic reasons."[51]

Not until the last week of the campaign, however, did Kennedy propose a Peace Corps in a speech at the San Francisco Cow Palace. He spoke eloquently of talented young men and women, well trained in the languages, skills, and customs of the host country, who would serve a three-year tour as an alternative to military service. By helping impoverished nations help themselves, Kennedy asserted, volunteers could erase the image of the Ugly American and overcome the efforts of Khrushchev's "missionaries." Kennedy clearly viewed the idea of the Peace Corps as more than altruistic; he saw the Corps as another tool in the cold war. He subsequently spoke of halting Communist expansion by helping to develop the resources of the Third World. The Peace Corps also became a symbol of the nation's moral impulse and of Kennedy's own call for sacrifice and the drive for excellence. More immediately he counted on something dramatic in the last week of the campaign to overcome the impact that Eisenhower was making in Nixon's behalf. In terms of good politics, Kennedy's promotion of the Peace Corps could be compared to his campaign telephone call to Coretta Scott King. How much it affected the election results is indeterminable, but by the end of 1960 he had received more letters on the Peace Corps than on any other topic. According to one Gallup survey, 71 percent favored the idea, while only 18 percent opposed it.

The Peace Corps's phenomenal positive image, however, came about only as a result of some fortuitous circumstances. Most importantly Kennedy made his brother-in-law Sargent Shriver the director. The perfect choice, Shriver was an idealist with a world of experience in business, education, and international travel. Handsome, tireless, vibrant, and caring, he became the prototypical New Frontiersman. His charisma helped to attract a talented supporting cast, including Wofford, the twenty-six-year-old Bill Moyers, Johnson's key aide, and William Haddad, a former prize-winning journalist for the *New York Post*. The staff soon reflected the personality of Shriver in its hard-driving, idealistic ways.

The Peace Corps program emerged during Kennedy's first one hundred days. Its impetus came from a task force headed by Shriver, which proposed a large and independent agency to begin activities almost immediately. Significantly, the military service exemption was removed for political reasons. To avoid probable congressional delay, Shriver recommended that Kennedy issue an executive order to give the organization life through the first year. From the outset Sorensen and other White House staffers reacted negatively to this approach; they pondered the potential dangers of sending youthful Americans abroad as part of a hastily conceived program. They favored a smaller, low-cost, less ambitious operation tied to the overall federal assistance program.

Though Kennedy agreed to issue an executive order, he too felt that the Peace Corps should come under the newly proposed Agency for International Development (AID), along with Food for Peace, the Development Loan Fund, and the International Cooperation Administration. This made administrative and political sense, particularly since it would facilitate congressional approval. Shriver argued that under this arrangement the Peace Corps would lose its "distinctive identity and appeal." The president remained unpersuaded, at least until his vice-president reinforced Shriver's concerns. Moyers had taken the matter to Johnson, who immediately responded; under AID, the Peace Corps would become "just another box in an organizational chart, reporting to a third assistant director of personnel for the State Department." According to one contemporary, Johnson soon "collared Kennedy . . . and in the course of the conversation badgered him so much that Kennedy finally said all right."[52] The action proved truly consequential; the Peace Corps could now freely develop without the burden of restrictions.

Perhaps initially it became more independent than it wished to be, as White House staffers and the president reacted coolly toward the Peace Corps following the organizational fight. The White House almost to the end refused to fight for the bill to extend its existence after 1961. Shriver, told by Kennedy that he was on his own after failing to accept White

House advice, worked the congressional offices and corridors with such passion that he won the admiration of countless congressmen. Many in the affirmative majority probably voted more for Shriver than for the program. Shriver also soon won the approbation of Kennedy, who quipped: "I don't think it is altogether fair to say that I handed Sarge a lemon from which he made lemonade, but I do think he was handed one of the most sensitive and difficult assignments which any administration in Washington has been given in this century."[53] Kennedy eventually took great pride in the Peace Corps and often asked visitors how the "kids" were doing. He did whatever the organization asked him to do, meeting with volunteers, participating in ceremonies, and ensuring that the CIA stayed out of its activities. Yet he generally left the Peace Corps alone, knowing that it was in good hands.

The Peace Corps in the Kennedy years sent volunteers to forty-four countries requesting Americans. The thousands who served underwent intense training on college campuses before qualifying for foreign service. From 1961 to 1963, 22 percent of all trainees in fact failed to make it through the program. The objectives were threefold: to provide a needed skill to an interested country; to increase the understanding of Americans by other people; and to increase American understanding of other people. For the most part, the Corps generally met these goals despite the inevitable problems of too many volunteers lacking necessary skills, finding themselves with no definite jobs, or having too little to do. Contrary to myth, few lived in mud huts; most taught English in schools. Although Shriver and other Peace Corps administrators painted a romantic picture, the fact is that volunteer life sometimes involved frustration and failure as much as success. In rarer instances volunteers even committed public and private indiscretions that necessitated their recall.[54]

Yet stories abound of individual achievement and sacrifice. One young volunteer in Panama stayed away from the Peace Corps office in Panama City for ten months while working alone with Caribbean coastal Indians. Every couple of weeks he navigated up the river to deliver pig-meat, fish, and rice to local communities. Paul Tsongas, a future Democratic senator from Massachusetts, lived with ten students in an Ethiopian village where he not only taught mathematics and science but also constructed timber footbridges over muddy streams and ditches. One popular volunteer in the Liberian bush became so culturally immersed that the local tribe adopted him as a son. A black corpsman in Tanzania, hailed as "Negro Bwana," enraptured his community to the extent that villagers offered him a wife and a small farm to entice him to stay. In so many different settings and ways barriers broke down, encouraging Third

World peoples to cast aside their suspicions and to express genuine sorrow whenever volunteers left their communities. For this reason, Peace Corps volunteers have been called Kennedy's "Real Best and Brightest."

Recent studies further document the successes even though the Peace Corps did little to achieve national economic growth in host countries. Its person-to-person approach elevated the lives of many impoverished people. No agency showed others the idealistic side of America more clearly. Moreover, the volunteers' overseas experiences would serve them well, as many former members went into the Foreign Service and other governmental agencies, bringing an understanding of Third World cultures heretofore lacking. Other former volunteers carried that idealism and knowledge into the schools as teachers or graduate students. Many others soon found themselves involved in the civil rights and anti–Vietnam War protest movements. Most retained their overseas contacts.

The Peace Corps also served as an effective instrument in improving Third World relations. It transcended the Bay of Pigs, the missile buildup, and the other negative aspects of the Kennedy foreign policy and furthered the impression that Kennedy understood and empathized with the national aspirations and problems of Third World peoples. Yet its greatest success came as a result of its refusal to push the merits of U.S. foreign policy upon host nations. By ignoring ideology and responding to needs and problems, it won over many Third World people. Paradoxically it thus became an important element of United States foreign policy. The American people realized its significance in a 1963 Harris Poll when they rated it the third most popular act of the Kennedy administration, after "national security" and "Berlin."

Enough departures and newer approaches transpired, then, to justify the image of the New Frontier. The Alliance for Progress, Interior Secretary Stewart Udall's conservation initiatives, the Trade Expansion Act, and several other activities could be added to any list. Although Kennedy did not always assume primary leadership, he was crucial to implementation. Unlike Eisenhower, he reworked old ideas into programs and policies in his response to existing challenges. In his own way he had promised and encouraged change. Yet never did change come with as much controversy, apprehension and lasting effects as it did in the area of civil rights.

7

★ ★ ★ ★ ★

THE TRAVAIL OF CIVIL RIGHTS

No domestic struggle occupied the Kennedy presidency more over a longer duration than civil rights. This was not of course by choice. Kennedy had intended to effect racial advances gradually, smoothly, and with a minimum of conflict. However, civil rights activists, confronting considerable southern resistance, continually prodded the administration to move more forcefully against racial injustices, beginning with the Freedom Rides of 1961, followed by the desegregation effort at the University of Mississippi in September 1962, and culminating in the demonstrations in Birmingham in spring 1963. Kennedy's responses to these and other challenges disappointed many civil rights activists and latter-day scholars, but he went beyond Truman's program in helping usher in what C. Vann Woodward and others have labeled the Second Reconstruction. Never since the immediate post–Civil War era had the federal government focused as much on the removal of racial barriers. In the process Kennedy became a more vigorous advocate of black America, his support leading to the Civil Rights bill of 1963. Indeed his belated awareness of racial injustice—and civil rights contributions—paved the way for the greater successes of Lyndon Johnson.

Kennedy's background had hardly prepared him for race-related issues. Journalist and family friend Arthur Krock commented that he "never saw a Negro on level social terms with the Kennedys. And I never heard the subject mentioned." Indeed a black porter remembered the Kennedys, loaded down with luggage, always undertipping at Boston's Logan Field.[1] Jack Kennedy reflected that upbringing. Characteristically detached, he rarely thought or felt deeply about such matters. Moreover, he began his political career in a state that lacked a sizable black population, despite the black wards of Boston and other neighboring municipalities. His environment provided him with little opportunity to see that blacks had to face special problems, yet he recognized their potential political significance as he actively sought their votes.

As close friends admitted, Kennedy, as a congressman and as a senator, favored civil rights legislation "more as a matter of course than of deep concern."[2] He soon disappointed civil rights advocates because political ambition had sensitized him to southern feelings. By the mid-1950s the NAACP and other civil rights organizations viewed Kennedy with greater suspicion. His unexpected popularity with southern delegates in his unsuccessful drive for the vice-presidential nomination in 1956 seemed to bode ill, even though his remark—"I'm going to sing Dixie for the rest of my life"—remained private.[3] More disturbingly, Kennedy voted for the pro-South jury trial amendment to the Civil Rights Act of 1957.

Afterward he sought to attract black leaders without alienating the South—a prerequisite for serious Democratic presidential contenders. Knowing few blacks personally, he soon began to attend their organizational activities. He employed a black secretary in his Boston office as well as two well-connected black attorneys from Washington, D.C., as advisers. When the civil rights movement reached greater intensity by 1960 he began to focus more on racial issues. Even so he was soundly booed at a civil rights gathering.[4] After his nomination Kennedy vowed to pursue bold executive action and legislation to implement the party's liberal civil rights commitments. Discrimination in housing, he insisted, could end by a stroke of the presidential pen. He assured black Americans that a Democratic administration would move quickly on all fronts. "If there is anything that history has taught us," he claimed, "it is that the great accomplishments of Woodrow Wilson and of Franklin Roosevelt were made in the early days, months, and years of their administrations."[5] Success would come through "moral and persuasive" presidential leadership, something that Eisenhower had lacked. Through these campaign promises and an opportune telephone call to Coretta Scott King, Kennedy won over the black community in sufficient numbers to swing the election.

Yet he had also held the Democratic South, in part by criticizing Eisenhower repeatedly for using federal troops in Little Rock in 1957. He had further reaffirmed his moderation on the racial issue by choosing Johnson as his running mate. Thus Kennedy's civil rights commitments were more acceptable to southern Democratic leaders, who grudgingly comprehended political necessity. What counted more were the obstacles that civil rights legislation faced in the Congress—a fact the South and Kennedy clearly understood.

Kennedy initially neutralized the racial issue by presenting an acceptable image both to black and southern America. He promised to act against racial discrimination for political, international, and moral reasons. As a nationalist above all, Kennedy recognized that racism weakened the United States because of its wastefulness and divisiveness. It also debilitated this country internationally as the United States sought to improve relations with African nations and to capitalize on Soviet human-rights violations. At the same time he proceeded gingerly in the face of stark political realities, including the miniscule election victory, a stronger conservative coalition in Congress, and unfavorable public opinion. Opinion polls revealed that despite a budding civil rights movement the vast American majority still believed that integration should be implemented gradually rather than through immediate federal action. In one Gallup Poll, respondents listed civil rights next to last in a long list of matters that Congress should address. Besides, Kennedy also embraced the legislative strategy of wooing recalcitrant southern Democrats on behalf of his liberal legislative program. If civil rights remained part of it, reforms such as medicare and minimum-wage increases would probably fail, hurting blacks in the process.

As a result President Kennedy made it clear that he would propose no civil rights legislation in 1961, much to the chagrin of black leaders. Roy Wilkins of the NAACP viewed Kennedy's approach as a tactical error because he was informing the opposition that he was not "going to use the forward pass." He questioned Kennedy's assumption that southern gratitude could ever be won by postponing civil rights legislation. For the duration of the Kennedy presidency, Wilkins and fellow NAACP officials thought him inept as a legislative leader, no matter how they felt about him otherwise. Nor had Kennedy appeased Wilkins at a 6 January 1961 meeting at the New York Carlyle Hotel when he proposed to proceed by piecemeal executive action. The longtime black leader heard the president-elect reject his counterproposal of a sweeping executive order to address a multitude of topics, including housing. Wilkins later recalled viewing an impressionistic painting in the meeting room by a black artist—Romare Bearden—which resembled a "big blob." He wondered whether that painting symbolized the administration's policies toward blacks.

Kennedy did nothing to overcome that impression when he neglected civil rights in his inaugural address and failed to appoint a task force for civil rights, an indication that matters of race warranted no such attention and that he wished no liberal input. His appointment of Burke Marshall, an antitrust specialist from Yale, rather than Harris Wofford, a civil rights advocate, as head of the Justice Department's Civil Rights Division also caused consternation. Robert Kennedy had privately labeled Wofford "a slight madman," arguing that Wofford's advocacy would transcend the law and his brother's interests.[6]

The president at first sought to divert most civil rights activities to the Department of Justice, thereby lessening the emotional impact of the racial controversy by emphasizing the legal over the moral dimension. His brother, who commented that he did not stay "awake nights worrying about civil rights" before becoming attorney general, consequently had free rein to enforce the law vigorously against civil rights violations.[7] He delegated civil rights matters to an extremely competent, youthful staff of Ivy League law graduates after outlining the enforcement philosophy in his first public speech, delivered at the University of Georgia on 6 May 1961. He suggested that the administration would seek strict compliance with civil rights statutes and court orders through amicable negotiation. If voluntary compliance failed, then the administration would undertake legal action. He tempered his remarks by emphasizing that racial discrimination remained a national problem, stressing the need to avoid violence and incidents such as the one at Little Rock Central High.

President Kennedy made one early concession to civil rights advocates by installing a civil rights adviser on the White House staff. Harris Wofford soon organized a subcabinet body representing seventeen agencies, which periodically exchanged ideas and shared reports. Yet Wofford served merely as a buffer between Kennedy and the civil rights leadership; so much did a shield exist that Martin Luther King, Jr., had to wait until fall 1961 before he could see the president. Undoubtedly the press of international crises contributed to the delay, but Kennedy had no desire to face the black leader's moral strictures for a supposed practical and political matter. Wofford, a strong defender of King, also became an outsider to many on the White House staff, who thought of him as the civil rights community's representative to them, rather than vice versa. Kennedy often teased Wofford by asking, "Are your constituents happy?"[8]

Yet next to Eisenhower, Kennedy seemed a breath of fresh air to many blacks. Through executive action he significantly improved the lot of some black Americans, which had an important symbolic impact. Noticing an all-white Coast Guard unit at the inauguration parade, he pressured the academy to recruit blacks. By executive order he created the President's Committee on Equal Employment Opportunity (PCEEO), chaired by the vice-president, to ensure that all Americans would have equal employment within government and "with those who do business with government." Although an extension of the idea of Truman's Government Contract Compliance Committee, the PCEEO had unprecedented powers to institute investigations and to terminate contracts where discrimination existed. And no other president had provided blacks with as many federal appointments. "Kennedy was so hot on the Department heads, the cabinet officers, and agency heads that everyone was scrambling around trying to find himself a Negro in order to keep the President off his neck," wrote Wilkins.[9] The Civil Service Commission made a major effort to recruit blacks at college campuses. Kennedy also appointed some forty blacks to top administration posts, including Robert C. Weaver as administrator of the Housing and Home Finance Agency, slated for cabinet level status; Andrew Hatcher, associate White House press secretary; and Carl Rowan, deputy assistant secretary of state for public affairs. Additionally, Kennedy selected five black federal judges, including Thurgood Marshall, for the second circuit court of appeals in New York, an important symbol to black America, given his role in *Brown v. Board of Education of Topeka.*

Other symbolic gestures abounded. Despite his initial reluctance to see Dr. King, Kennedy invited more blacks to the White House than any previous president had. Not only did they attend meetings and social functions, which were well publicized in the black press, but they also became the house guests of Robert Kennedy and other New Frontiersmen. Moreover, the attorney general resigned, with attendant press coverage, from the exclusive Metropolitan Club after a six-month attempt to persuade its board of directors to admit blacks. Most significantly, the president withdrew his membership from the Cosmos Club following its rebuff of Carl Rowan. In 1961 Interior Secretary Stewart Udall also pressured the National Football League's Washington Redskins to end its ban on black players. Under the ownership of the controversial George Marshall, that team stood alone in its refusal to hire blacks. In March Udall informed Marshall that he could no longer use the federally financed D. C. Stadium (today JFK Stadium) unless he changed his policy against black players. The following year the Redskins drafted three black players and traded for future Hall of Famer Bobby Mitchell. The magazine *Ebony*, in including the desegregation of the Redskins as one of the administration's many civil rights achievements, claimed that more progress toward racial equality was made in 1961 "than any other year in the last decade."[10] On the school desegregation front, Robert Kennedy threatened to seek contempt-of-court sentences against Louisiana officials if they continued to deny state funds to the recently desegregated schools of New Orleans. By September 1961 Atlanta and Memphis followed New Orleans in successful school-desegregation efforts.

Whenever Kennedy failed to satisfy civil rights leaders, he responded with finesse and good manners. Wilkins recalled that when an NAACP delegation visited the Oval Office in 1961 to discuss civil rights, "JFK charmed the delegates, getting chairs for the women," taking the delegates on a personal tour of the White House, and "listening intently to . . . the need for legislation to supplement what the President was doing on the executive level." Kennedy claimed that he could not immediately effect legislation. "But everyone went out of there absolutely charmed by the manner in which they had been turned down."[11]

On another front the Justice Department brought suits against illegal violations of black voting rights in the South. In the Eisenhower period, the department had introduced only six suits and none in Mississippi, where only 6 percent of voting-age blacks were registered. The enormous effort required to win discouraged such actions; in each case the evidence submitted exceeded a thousand pages. Yet Kennedy's Justice Department instituted fifty-seven voting-rights suits, thirty of them in Mississippi, including one in Senator Eastland's Sunflower County, an indication that the administration did not completely acquiesce to southern political power.

But neither the White House nor the NAACP controlled the timetable of the civil rights movement in 1961. It marched to the beat of more aggressive black organizations, such as King's Southern Christian Leadership Conference (SCLC), the Congress of Racial Equality (CORE), and the Student Nonviolent Coordinating Committee (SNCC), which had first engineered the sit-ins and other nonviolent direct actions in 1960 to eradicate segregation in restaurants, hotels, and other areas of public accommodations. Kennedy's New Frontier had inspired young activists; at the same time, they felt the administration needed some nudging. James Farmer's rejuvenated CORE intended to do exactly that by forcing federal compliance with a 1960 Supreme Court decision, *Boynton v. Virginia*, which extended the court's prohibition of segregation on interstate buses to terminal facilities. Farmer sought to provoke southern authorities into arresting the Freedom Riders, thereby compelling the Justice Department to enforce the law of the land.

On 4 May seven blacks and six whites left Washington, D.C., on a Greyhound and a Trailways bus. They traveled south, where they challenged whites- and coloreds-only accommodations at terminal restaurants and restrooms. Violence first occurred at Rock Hill, South Carolina, where a black and a white Freedom Rider entered the whites-only

Greyhound waiting room. Twenty white hoodlums, wearing ducktail haircuts and leather jackets, mauled the two victims before the police intervened. This scenario recurred elsewhere with resultant rider arrests, but it did not evoke national attention until 14 May, when the Greyhound entered Anniston in eastern Alabama. An angry mob, armed with iron bars, dented the vehicle, shattering windows and slashing tires. After the arrival of lawmen, the bus departed, followed by mobsters in cars. About six miles west of Anniston, the Greyhound's tires went flat; once again the mob attacked the bus. Someone smashed the back window and hurled an incendiary bomb into the vehicle, causing passengers to flee the burning Greyhound; some were attacked in the process. Afterward the Reverend Fred Shuttlesworth, who had dispatched several cars, drove the shaken Freedom Riders to Birmingham.

The Freedom Riders on a Trailways bus pulled into Anniston one hour after the first attack; they fared no better. Hoodlums entered the bus, forcing blacks to the rear, cursing, hitting, and kicking them and their white colleagues. One retired professor suffered brain damage from a blow to the head. With the hoodlums seated in the front of the bus the driver headed north to Birmingham where a mob of forty whites greeted the passengers at the terminal. When the black riders approached the whites-only lunch counter, toughs hammered them with pipes and fists, beating one unconscious; others suffered severe lacerations. Only after the battering did police appear, despite a forewarning of trouble and the two-block proximity of the police headquarters. Immediately afterward the CORE-directed Freedom Ride ended, and the participants left Birmingham by air for New Orleans.

SNCC sponsored the next effort soon afterward. Starting out from Nashville, black and white students, many of them sit-in veterans, headed for New Orleans via Birmingham, Montgomery, and Jackson, Mississippi. Their greatest test came at Montgomery, where the bus entered the eerily quiet terminal. As students got off the Greyhound, a screaming mob of three hundred descended on them from the terminal and nearby buildings, swinging baseball bats, pipes, and sticks and shouting racial obscenities. Veteran activist John Lewis suffered a concussion. As he lay prostrate in a pool of blood, a state official handed him an injunction order prohibiting interracial travel in Alabama. Mobsters set another black afire by pouring kerosene on him. They also struck two white Freedom Riders, who begged motorists for assistance. Aid did come from John Seigenthaler, Robert Kennedy's administrative assistant and a Nashville native. Seigenthaler had gone to Montgomery as the president's special emissary to Governor John Patterson. While Seigenthaler helped victims into the car, he was knocked unconscious; for twenty-five minutes he lay on the pavement before police drove him to a hospital. Patterson blamed Seigenthaler for the mishap because he had driven an unmarked vehicle, worn informal clothes, and carried no identification. "I wouldn't have gone down there like that," Patterson intoned; "we have police for that kind of work." A shocked and angry Robert Kennedy—"he looked like he'd just been poleaxed himself"—telephoned Seigenthaler at the hospital. Kennedy's characteristic use of humor to show affection soon followed, as he thanked his assistant for helping with the black vote.[12]

In many ways the Freedom Rides represented a frustrating experience for the Kennedys. It revealed, first of all, their underestimation of the depth of the problem. Civil rights was not merely a political matter that could be easily orchestrated from the White House by pulling the right strings with business, political, educational, and judicial leaders. Kennedy, preoccupied with Khrushchev and the Berlin crisis, showed a profound ignorance when he angrily asked Wofford to tell the Freedom Riders to "call it off."[13] The attorney general reacted more emotionally. On the one hand, according to Burke Marshall, his compassion for the underdog might have made him a Freedom Rider as a private citizen. But as his brother's agent, it angered him that the rides continued, along with the participation of northern "celebrities" such as the Reverend William Sloane Coffin of Yale.[14] All of this, he thought, embarrassed the United States' image abroad on the eve of Vienna, which consequently led him to question the riders' patriotism. Yet he reacted even more strongly against the violation of the activists' constitutional rights and to the attendant violence. He also gradually became more aware of the racial militancy of the South, for which negotiations offered no easy solutions. "Despite the enlightened Southerners among us," Robert Kennedy later admitted, "we lacked a sense of Southern history."[15]

The attorney general became the administration's point man during the crisis of the Freedom Rides. His primary objective was to protect the activists rather than to engage in a civil rights crusade that would turn the Democratic South against the administration as well as exacerbate the conflict. He knew that 63 percent of the American people opposed the Freedom Rides. Former President Harry Truman helped little by railing in the national press against meddling northern "busybodies." Yet Kennedy could not permit Freedom Riders to remain at the mercy of southern police authority, nor could he be indifferent to those defending their constitutional rights, no matter how much he might have disagreed with their methods.

Kennedy's efforts at crisis management became more severely tested after he failed to win the cooperation of southern governors, particularly

Patterson, whose blatant racism transcended his earlier ties with the Kennedys. The Alabama governor refused even to return the attorney general's telephone calls. Neither could Kennedy rely on the support of Hoover, who insisted that the FBI was not a protection agency. More to the point, J. Edgar Hoover deplored the civil rights movement. He also cultivated a close relationship with southern law enforcement agencies, which assisted the bureau enormously in such crimes as auto thefts. His agents in the South, native southerners sensitive to the biases of local communities, did nothing more than take notes as they witnessed southern brutality.

The attorney general consequently resorted to the use of federal marshals—not troops—to protect the Freedom Riders, after obtaining an injunction against those interfering with interstate travel. That obligation had finally overcome his sensitivity to a federal system that placed law enforcement in the hands of local authorities. Following the hospitalization of Seigenthaler between 350 to 400 United States marshals converged on Montgomery and were soon deployed. The occasion was a mass rally organized by King and involving over twelve hundred people, who jammed into the Reverend Ralph Abernathy's First Baptist Church in support of the Freedom Rides. A white mob soon appeared, attacking those outside the church and hurling firebombs and stenchbombs through the windows. Even after marshals formed a cordon around the church, the threat of a burning was so great that those inside sang hymns to calm their fears, while King, on the telephone with Robert Kennedy, pleaded for more assistance. With pressure from Kennedy, Patterson called out the National Guard and state troopers to disperse the crowd.

Kennedy's involvement in the Alabama crisis went beyond the use of marshals. He had pressured "Mr. Greyhound," as he referred to a company executive, to provide a driver for a stranded Freedom Ride vehicle in Birmingham. He also negotiated a deal with Senator Eastland, sanctioning the arrest of Freedom Riders coming into the Magnolia State in return for a pledge of no mob violence. Because of their refusal to pay the fines, Freedom Riders went to jail in Jackson, much to the chagrin of Kennedy, who called for a "cooling-off period."

Other Freedom Rides followed that summer, involving over a thousand persons, most of them black and southern, and their continual pressure on the federal government eventually brought results. It enabled the attorney general to obtain a ruling from the Interstate Commerce Commission, decreeing that all seating in interstate buses would be without reference to race, color, or creed and that all terminals would be integrated. By fall 1961 this had been largely implemented. Overall, the Kennedy administration had handled the Freedom Ride crisis reasonably well; much of the credit belongs to Robert Kennedy, who had kept his brother out of it. He had protected the constitutional rights of interstate travelers in a way that satisfied moderates both North and South. However, this approach failed to mollify many northern liberals, who criticized him for not embracing the moral cause of the Freedom Riders; at the same time southern extremists accused him of aiding and abetting a Communist-instigated movement. Still, such opposition hurt the administration very little in 1961.

By the end of the summer the civil rights movement had entered a different phase, now centering on black voter registration in the South. Kennedy's Justice Department strongly encouraged this approach. Kennedy had told King, "you register these people to vote and Jim Eastland will change his mind . . . or there will be somebody replacing him." A voter-registration commitment seemed a suitable substitute for civil disobedience, which inflamed southern emotions. One black scholar called it Kennedy's effort to "get the niggers off the street."[16] A series of meetings between the Justice Department and black civil rights groups in summer 1961 led to the formation of the Voter Education Project, financed by private foundations, to embark on an $870,000 registration campaign from April 1962 to October 1965. SNCC, buoyed by its recent successes, played the key role, attracting hundreds of students to the project. Ironically this new venture created even more problems for the Kennedy administration.

Difficulties began when Robert Kennedy and Burke Marshall left SNCC officials with the clear impression that the department would protect those engaged in voter registration. Kennedy, arguing that the greatest registration potential existed in southern cities, probably did not anticipate that SNCC workers would concentrate on the most remote, rural counties, deep in the black belt of Mississippi and southwest Georgia where no black was registered. According to Seigenthaler, Kennedy had failed to understand the moral imperative that forced activists into those southern counties.[17] In fact, places such as McComb, Mississippi, soon experienced baptisms of fire. Aggressive SNCC workers assisted blacks in registering only to see them lose their tenancy and welfare assistance. SNCC volunteers also faced assaults from private citizens and good-old-boy sheriffs. From 1961 to 1963 SNCC recorded some sixty-two incidents of racial violence in Mississippi alone. One civil rights activist complained, "To have the FBI looking out of the courthouse windows while you were being chased down the street by brick throwers deeply offended the sensibilities. So people wept and cursed Robert Kennedy and Burke Marshall more than the FBI, whom they never had any confidence in to begin with."[18]

SNCC workers felt especially betrayed after their frantic calls and letters to the Justice Department brought only polite and sympathetic replies. The department, Justice officials explained, was powerless to act because the federal system prohibited the national government from interfering with local enforcement. Only if local authorities showed themselves wholly incapable of upholding law and order could Washington intervene. This doctrine clearly had the backing of most in Justice, including the attorney general, who later somewhat callously asserted that "Mississippi is going to work itself out. . . . Maybe it's going to take a decade and maybe a lot of people are going to be killed in the meantime. . . . But in the long run I think it's for the health of the country and the stability of the system."[19] The Justice Department condemned the violence and sought to negotiate with southern officials to end it but did little else.

Not surprisingly, civil rights attorneys questioned the assumptions of the administration's federalist approach. They argued that by using United States criminal codes (e.g., USC 18, sections 241 and 242), the Justice Department could have instituted legal action against civil rights violations and police brutality. They also challenged the department's refusal to employ marshals or to seek injunctions to protect SNCC workers because of the alleged lack of statutory authority or interstate activity. Navasky noted in *Kennedy Justice* the curious inconsistency between Robert Kennedy's overcautious approach to civil rights and his obsessive war against organized crime, where he often overreached his authority. To Navasky, federalism "was an enlightened apology for the existing order," a conclusion that several later scholars understandably share.[20]

Undoubtedly federalism partly served as a cover for the administration's other reservations about interfering with southern justice. Those included Justice's lack of resources in staff, given the unavailability of the FBI in civil rights matters and the Civil Rights Division's heavy involvement in voting-rights suits. The point is that there were too many McCombs. Furthermore, Robert Kennedy remained personally apprehensive about using force in the South. Thus it is no wonder that idealistic and defenseless SNCC and CORE workers came to view the Kennedy administration as the enemy by 1962. As white violence continued, they also called into question King's nonviolent and integrationist approaches. Partly from the crucible of the voter-registration movement, then, emerged the driving force of black power as an eventual major component of SNCC and CORE. As a result of this shift, the administration's attitude toward these organizations became more negative. In 1962 James Farmer of CORE, in meeting with the Kennedy brothers, detected a "little coldness and aloofness and perhaps suspicion even, while there was much more warmth toward . . . Whitney Young [National Urban League] and Roy Wilkins." One year later President Kennedy privately asserted that "SNCC has got an investment in violence. They're sons of bitches."[21]

The administration also found itself at odds in 1962 with the Civil Rights Commission, an independent body created by the Civil Rights Act of 1957 and liberalized through Kennedy appointments. Led by liberal members such as Father Theodore Hesburgh, president of Notre Dame University, the commission soon expressed dissatisfaction at the slowness with which the administration was moving on civil rights. White violence against civil rights workers in Mississippi particularly angered commissioners, who sought to institute hearings. Only the objections of Robert Kennedy, who alleged that the commission would be duplicating the work of the Justice Department, prevented the inquiry. In a critical interim report in March 1963, the commission nevertheless outlined the ways in which voting rights were being denied in Mississippi. The report cited beatings, shootings, and other acts of terrorism and recommended that the administration deny Mississippi federal assistance until abuses were corrected, a proposal the president rightly rejected. Even black newspapers agreed that such a withdrawal of funds would hurt Mississippi blacks.

The administration's cautious response to the Albany crisis led to further criticism in 1962. A southwestern Georgia city of over fifty thousand persons, including approximately twenty thousand blacks, Albany became the focal point of SNCC's efforts in Georgia to register blacks and to desegregate public facilities. Because of the city's determined resistance, the protest mounted, eventually involving King of SCLC and hundreds of local blacks, who created the Albany Movement. Their massive demonstrations led to several hundred arrests, including King's, as blacks sought to flood the jails to force concessions. The city fathers' continual obstinance caused King and others to seek federal assistance.

Characteristically, the Kennedy administration tried to negotiate with the two sides because it wished to avoid jeopardizing the gubernatorial candidacy of a moderate who was running against extremists in the Democratic primary. Its desire to restore order as a top priority once again frustrated black leaders. King in particular sought something more than crisis management and became more upset after a district judge appointed by Kennedy imposed a temporary injunction against the demonstrators. "We thought the Kennedy administration worked against us," King's lieutenant Andrew Young recalled.[22] This action led to demonstrations outside the Justice Department, causing the attorney general to come outside and link arms with marching picketers.

President Kennedy responded on 1 August at a news conference. For the first time he extended moral support to the Albany protesters: "I find it wholly inexplicable why the city council . . . will not sit down with the citizens of Albany, who may be Negroes, and attempt to secure them, in a peaceful way, their rights. The United States Government is involved in sitting down at Geneva with the Soviet Union. I can't understand why the government of Albany . . . cannot do the same for American citizens." Yet King achieved little from the Albany demonstrations. Even though that city reluctantly desegregated its interstate terminal facilities and permitted more blacks to register, it closed its parks, sold the swimming pool, integrated the library only after removing its seats, and refused to desegregate the schools. Other black grievances received no redress, particularly those related to criminal justice. By 1963 the police still beat demonstrators and permitted white prisoners to do the same. According to a leading authority on southern criminal justice, "the Justice Department sent FBI agents and attorneys to Albany as observers, but they did virtually nothing to halt the violence."[23]

The department's greatest legal initiative in Albany ironically came at the expense of civil rights activists. In August 1963 the government, responding to an unsympathetic local United States attorney, indicted nine leaders of the Albany Movement for conspiring to obstruct justice. Their crime was picketing a store owned by a white man who had helped acquit a sheriff accused of shooting and beating a black person. Jack Newfield, a radical reporter for the *Village Voice* who had become a Kennedy backer by 1968, loathed Robert Kennedy in 1963, partly because those nine indictments came at a time when whites who burned down black churches and attacked civil rights activists went unpunished.

The administration also received enormous criticism for not ending discrimination in housing. In 1961 Americans reminded the president of his "stroke of the presidential pen" campaign statement by inundating him with pens and instituting an "ink for Jack" drive. "Send [the pens and ink] to Wofford," an exasperated Kennedy replied. Blaming Wofford for the idea, he also teased Theodore Sorensen for incorporating it into one of his speeches, even though Sorensen claimed he had had nothing to do with it. Richard Goodwin later admitted writing the "stroke of a pen" phrase, which Kennedy had expounded in 1960 "without the slightest hint of doubt or equivocation."[24] In any case, politics constituted the major reason for the hesitancy in issuing the housing order. The administration believed that it would jeopardize congressional approval of the proposed Department of Urban Affairs bill and the planned appointment of Robert Weaver as the first black cabinet member. Kennedy's initial instincts were to issue the order anyway, but Sorensen and Lawrence O'Brien talked him out of it at a November 1961 meeting at Hyannis Port. Ironically, Kennedy failed to obtain the Urban Affairs bill.

The proposed housing order then became enmeshed in the politics of the congressional election of 1962. According to Robert Kennedy, even several northern liberal congressmen wanted no order until after the November election because it might hurt them at home. The announcement of the order belatedly came on Thanksgiving eve, 1962, sandwiched between two significant foreign policy statements; the president hardly could have lessened the impact of its publicity more. Moreover, the administration restricted Executive Order #11063 to housing facilities owned or operated by the federal government and to those obtaining federal loans, grants, or loan guarantees. The law was not retroactive nor did it apply to private bank loans covered by the Federal Deposit Insurance Corporation. The administration hesitated to go further because it doubted that it had the authority through executive action to impose restrictions on the potentially recalcitrant FDIC. As Marshall soon admitted, the housing order "has not been very meaningful."[25]

The President's Committee on Equal Employment Opportunity also proved disappointing, especially the Plans for Progress project headed by Robert Troutman of Georgia, who resigned under fire in June 1962. Herbert Hill of the NAACP called Plans for Progress "one of the great phonies of the Kennedy administration's civil rights programs." It had sought to negotiate agreements with private corporations to hire more blacks, and many companies had willingly agreed to participate. All of this had occurred in the midst of considerable fanfare, but in the process, the PCEEO had exaggerated the successes and misrepresented the statistics. A 100 percent increase in black employment meant little, the administration soon acknowledged, if the number of blacks in a major company jumped from one to two. Aside from the Plans for Progress fiasco, the PCEEO also failed to raise black employment substantially in federal agencies or in corporations doing business with the federal government. One study revealed that in Birmingham, Alabama, black employment in federal agencies amounted to .001 percent of the total work force.

The Kennedys privately blamed the PCEEO's chairman, Lyndon Johnson, for the shortcomings. According to Robert Kennedy, who came to dislike Johnson more and more, the president "almost had a fit" when he saw the uncomplimentary statistics. In blaming the vice-president President Kennedy supposedly said, "That man can't run this committee. Can you think of anything more deplorable than him trying to run the

United States?"[26] Yet he remained reluctant to make changes so as not to offend Johnson. Robert did not share such sensitivity. On one occasion, he and Marshall attended a PCEEO meeting where Kennedy expressed dissatisfaction with the lack of significant progress; when the vice-president began to defend the committee, Kennedy and Marshall walked out. They had reason to be disappointed. Despite some twenty-five thousand all-white companies under federal contract, the PCEEO never once used its authority to terminate a work agreement. Yet Johnson was only reflecting the administration's cautious style and approach; nonetheless, the PCEEO experience, with all of the attending criticism, probably contributed to the president's eventual decision to play down executive action.

In 1962, however, a limited legislative approach also proved frustrating and lacking in any real progress. Despite congressional approval of the poll tax amendment (ratified in 1964), the administration failed to obtain a literacy-test bill enabling blacks with a sixth-grade education to vote. Majority leader Mike Mansfield missed coming anywhere near the two-thirds vote required for cloture, causing him to comment privately that a Democratic administration could never pass a civil rights measure. Furthermore, the president found himself in the political position of having to accept segregationist judges in the South. He felt equally impotent to do much about school segregation.

During 1962 the limitations of Kennedy's civil rights actions seemed much more pronounced to activists; even if they considered the political constraints, they still found him lacking. King accused him of "aggressively driving toward the limited goal of token integration," and another black activist claimed that "we've gotten the best snow job in history. We lost two years because we admired him."[27] The administration faced the same strictures from the white South, epitomized in the desegregation crisis at the University of Mississippi in September, which thrust the civil rights conflict once again to the forefront. Once again the administration found itself engaged in crisis management.

The impetus for the desegregation of that university came primarily from James H. Meredith, a twenty-eight-year-old grandson of a slave. The quiet, slim, and unflappable Meredith had served in the Air Force for nine years, and following an honorable discharge he had returned home with a handful of college credits. After attending black Alcorn College, which had only one Ph.D. on its faculty, he reaffirmed his desire to attend the University of Mississippi, the promise of the early Kennedy administration having encouraged him to apply. The university's strategy of calculated delay forced him to seek the assistance of the NAACP, which obtained a circuit-court order commanding the university to enroll

Meredith. Because of the school's continued resistance, the court gave the Justice Department permission to seek compliance. For political, legal, and moral reasons the department had no alternative but to force the desegregation of the Oxford, Mississippi, campus. Its greatest concern was that it do so without the employment of federal troops, whose presence would symbolize Reconstruction.

The initial conflict pitted Robert Kennedy against Mississippi governor Ross Barnett, seemingly a kind, rags-to-riches, soft-spoken man, an appearance belying a deep-seated racism reinforced by the political considerations of his native soil. Kennedy again underestimated the emotional intensity of the issue, believing that persuasion, accommodation, and legal pressure would bring about Meredith's registration. As one contemporary wrote, "the Governor's initial courtliness sounded like accommodation."[28] As it turned out, even the intervention of the president could not move Barnett. Yet Barnett also misunderstood the resolve of Robert Kennedy; otherwise he would not have suggested so casually that Meredith go elsewhere. Kennedy's quick retort, "But Meredith likes Ole Miss," gave Barnett an inkling of what lay ahead.

The Ole Miss crisis ultimately became a learning experience for both Kennedys, as Barnett broke several arrangements relating to the registration of Meredith and the providing of police protection. Only after days of patient phone conversations and legal maneuverings did the administration succeed in obtaining a contempt charge against Barnett and then pressuring him to permit Meredith's secret arrival on campus on Sunday, 30 September, for registration the following day. The appearance of Meredith in Oxford, along with some five hundred marshals to preserve order, invited a reaction that went deeper than the enrollment of a black student. It summoned the nostalgic, bitter emotions of the "lost cause," in which Mississippians sought once again to grasp a fallen standard previously held by Jefferson Davis and his Confederate legions.

The culprit remained the intrusive federal government, led this time by a young, brash president with a "foreign" accent. Quite clearly, prior to the university crisis, southern invective against the administration had focused almost totally on the attorney general. Given the president's role in Mississippi, he could no longer be easily exempted, judging by the anti-Kennedy slogans around the university, along with the repeated playing of "Dixie" and the flying of the Stars and Bars on car aerials. The arrival of retired general Edwin Walker, a John Bircher, only fanned the flames of rebellion as he extended encouragement to the large number of angry students and armed outsiders. Adding to the chaos the highway patrol had succumbed to the whims of Mississippi politicians, alternately withdrawing and returning to campus during the course of the evening.

The Justice Department, which had general supervision of the civilian marshals, had failed to ensure that everything was in order, the suddenness of the decision to move Meredith on campus contributing to the problem. The marshals arrived without bullhorns and adequate supplies of tear gas; the bullhorns were especially needed following the decision to use gas. Because members of the highway patrol had their backs turned to the marshals as they sought to contain the mob, they failed to hear the warnings and ended up being gassed along with the students. The marshals had employed tear gas for self-preservation; by late afternoon, a bottle- and rock-throwing crowd had backed them up against the Lyceum, the main administration building, where Meredith was to register. Later that day the crowd grew even more ugly, as armed good-old-boys intermingled with students. Two persons perished by gunfire, one of them a French reporter. About one-third of the marshals sustained injuries, twenty-eight from gunshots. Having run out of tear gas, the marshals requested permission to use their firearms.

By that time both Barnett and President Kennedy had delivered separate television addresses. From Jackson, Barnett indicated that he had bowed to a superior force while maintaining his convictions, meanwhile urging Mississippians to preserve peace. He undoubtedly hoped that an angry mob would force Meredith off the campus, causing Kennedy to reassess his approach in light of dangerous circumstances. Kennedy, meanwhile, spoke to a nationwide audience at 8:00 P.M. Not yet knowing that the situation had turned brutal on campus, the president spoke loftily of the past courage, patriotism, and contributions of Mississippians. "This is the State of Lucius Lamar and many others who have placed the national good ahead of sectional interest," he recalled. "This is the State which had four Medal of Honor winners in the Korean war alone." He reminded viewers as well that "Americans are free, in short, to disagree with the law but not to disobey it." Had the police powers of the state been employed to back the court orders and had the university fulfilled its obligations as other universities had done elsewhere in the South, federal intervention would have been unnecessary, he continued. He appealed to students to uphold the "tradition of honor and courage won on the field of battle and on the gridiron as well as the university campus."

Kennedy's remarks probably had no impact on University of Mississippi students, nor did he change the avowed segregationists, who found more reason to detest him. Yet his efforts to retain moderate support from the business, academic, and professional communities proved more successful. Business in particular took to heart Kennedy's appeals that compliance, rather than rebellion, best served the state's economic interests.

Kennedy's moderation failed to satisfy the civil rights leadership, however. A despondent King was particularly bothered by Kennedy's lack of moral conviction, as the president patronizingly—and politically—cast his remarks to Mississippi war and football heroes. Others wondered too why the president neglected to praise James Meredith's cause and courage.

That moderation became severely tested later that Sunday, following the threatened marshals' request to draw their pistols. However, the president, Robert Kennedy, and others who stayed at the White House command post throughout the night remained cool and under control. The attorney general relayed President Kennedy's order that the marshals must not fire their weapons unless Meredith's life was endangered. As the situation worsened the Kennedys sometimes reverted to gallows humor. The president remarked that he hadn't "had such an interesting time since the Bay of Pigs." On another occasion aide Edwin Guthman's telephone report from campus that "it's getting like the Alamo" elicited the reply from Robert Kennedy, "Well, you know what happened to those guys, don't you?"[29]

Under the circumstances the president had no alternative but to employ federal troops. He had wisely federalized the Mississippi National Guard and ordered United States Army units to nearby Memphis. The request for forces came from Deputy Attorney General Nicholas Katzenbach, who was on campus, about one hour after the first marshal was shot. The only troops that responded quickly were the fifty-five member Oxford, Mississippi, Guard unit commanded by Capt. Murray Falkner, a cousin of author William Faulkner. Not until five hours later, at 2:12 A.M., did the first soldiers from Memphis appear. The delay angered the president, who speculated privately that Khrushchev would have gotten "those troops in fast enough. That's what worries *me* about the whole thing."[30] The attorney general, who prided himself on his organizational skills, accepted the blame for the failure, even though the "army had botched it up." Almost miraculously neither Meredith nor the marshals suffered any fatalities. The following day Meredith registered and soon attended classes, albeit with a military police escort. He graduated the following year, and other blacks eventually matriculated at Oxford without incident.

For the Kennedys the University of Mississippi fight represented yet another successful example of crisis management—one that had the approval of the American majority. More importantly it left an enduring intellectual impact on Kennedy, causing him to recast traditional beliefs about Reconstruction following the Civil War—and hence race relations during the 1960s. The way in which Mississippians reacted emotionally and distorted the marshals' actions appalled Kennedy, causing him to wonder if such distortions might have existed nearly a hundred years earlier. Robert Kennedy recalled that his brother "would never believe a book on Reconstruction again," at least not one that dwelled on the "terrible tales of the northern scalawag troops."[31] The attorney general helped expose him to the new interpretations of Reconstruction history by inviting the distinguished professor David Donald to a White House seminar. Donald more charitably interpreted the motivations of Radical Republicans such as Senator Charles Sumner and House Speaker Thaddeus Stevens and more critically assessed southern reaction to Reconstruction—an analysis that challenged Kennedy's earlier views in *Profiles in Courage*. The crisis at the University of Mississippi, more than Donald, however, had influenced the president to consider a fresh historical perspective, one that still competed with his political pragmatism as 1963 unfolded.

That year's first major civil rights activity transpired in Birmingham, Alabama, the Johannesburg of the South, where urban segregation held its strongest grip. Only the interstate transportation terminals had been integrated. Blacks faced whites-only signs at restaurants, restrooms, and water fountains and were able to procure only the most menial employment. Despite the apparent limitations of direct action in Albany in 1962, King remained determined to make it work in Birmingham. Facing the challenge of competing civil rights organizations, pressured by his own followers, and frustrated by the seeming ambivalence of the Kennedy administration, he and the SCLC decided to act in early April 1963. Aided by substantial local black support, King engineered a protest campaign that included sit-ins at downtown stores, street marches, and pray-ins. On Good Friday, 12 April, King was incarcerated for violating an injunction against demonstrations. His "Letter from the Birmingham Jail," an eloquent justification for civil disobedience and nonviolent protest, soon followed. King sought "to create a situation so crisis-packed that it will inevitably open the door to negotiation." Otherwise black frustration and injustice would lead to street violence and black nationalist ideologies— which King wished to avoid.

The Birmingham crisis escalated after King's release a week later. On 2 May for the first time he mobilized more than one thousand children in street marches, most of whom were arrested. As demonstrators filled the jails, other protesters also fell victim to "Bull" Connor, the enraged police commissioner, who used police dogs, high-pressure fire hoses, and nightsticks to punish them. Vivid images of lunging police dogs and blacks tumbling before powerful jets of water dominated the evening television news, causing the president to remark that the pictures made him "sick." Connor soon became a symbol of racial oppression, and King reemerged as the most prominent force in the movement.

The Kennedy administration was not inactive during the crisis. Once again Kennedy telephoned Coretta Scott King, and he and Robert helped to ease her husband's confinement. On 4 May the attorney general sent Marshall and Joseph F. Dolan, an assistant, to Birmingham to mediate between the two sides. A black leader recalled that Marshall, sitting with arms folded and saying nothing, looked "like a Mr. Chips coming to town"; but Andrew Young later testified that the "Justice Department did a tremendous behind-the-scenes job of pulling the Birmingham community together."[32] Kennedy meanwhile used the occasion of a press conference to goad Birmingham business leaders to meet "the justifiable needs of the Negro community," which resulted in a satisfactory agreement for both Kennedy and King. The white leadership pledged to desegregate public facilities such as lunch counters within ninety days, to promote blacks from menial positions, and to hire other blacks within sixty days. Birmingham had elevated the intensity of the movement to a much higher level, inspiring more blacks to move into the streets and spawning demonstrations in several other southern communities. It also caused "blacks en masse [to forsake] gradualism for immediacy."[33]

After Birmingham the Kennedy administration found itself further entangled in the movement. For Robert Kennedy especially, it remained a learning experience. His exploratory breakfast session on 23 May with the brilliant black writer James Baldwin led to a meeting that Kennedy had arranged at the family apartment in New York City. Baldwin and thirteen other black personalities, including Kenneth Clark, a well-known psychologist; Clarence B. Jones, representing King; famous entertainers Harry Belafonte and Lena Horne; Lorraine Hansberry, an accomplished playwright; and Jerome Smith, a CORE field worker victimized by Mississippi justice, participated. The session was a "brutal" experience for Kennedy; John Seigenthaler remembered it as the worst day of the year prior to November 22.

It began when Kennedy asked them to get involved in the civil rights movement and then proceeded to outline the administration's commitments. Jerome Smith, who stammered when upset, set the tone by professing to be nauseated from having to share the same room with the attorney general, volunteering that "I've seen what government can do to crush the spirit and lives of people in the South."[34] Vividly, he recalled waiting vainly in a Mississippi jail for the FBI or the Justice Department to respond and expressed shame for his country and an unwillingness to defend it militarily. All of this shocked Kennedy, who took it personally and turned his back on Smith. "That was a mistake," Baldwin later said, "because when he turned toward us . . . Lorraine Hansberry said, 'You've got a great many very accomplished people in the room, Mr. Attorney General. But the only man you should be listening to is that man over there.' " For three excruciating hours, then, Kennedy heard what it meant to be black in a racist society. He listened to their description of the festering problems of the northern black ghetto, not an unfamiliar topic to him. And he also heard their denunciations of the FBI and the administration in general. Kennedy at first had sought to defend himself but ended up silent and tense. According to Clark, they attempted to make the point that the Kennedys had "a tremendous amount of credit with the American people. This credit must be used by them . . . to lead the . . . people into an awareness and understanding of the nature of the problem."

Clark left the meeting convinced "that this man was an extraordinarily insensitive person, extraordinarily loyal to his brother. . . . I did not leave there feeling that he was a racist, by any means [but he did] not have empathy." Kennedy returned to Justice angry and hurt, yet soon afterward he tried to comprehend more deeply what had happened. On one level he thought that several of those at the meeting had "complexes about the fact that they've been successful, while this poor boy [Smith] had been beaten by the police."[35] But he also pondered that if he had had Smith's experience, he too might not want to fight for his country. Significantly, Kennedy eventually reestablished ties with those in attendance at that meeting. The Baldwin gathering had alerted him to the intensity of the blacks' frustration and to the need for government to do more. As a consequence no one in the administration that summer felt more strongly about pushing for civil rights legislation.

The desegregation crisis at the University of Alabama came first, however. The Kennedys had heard that spring from the university president that two blacks sought entry for the summer term. The cocky and pugnacious George Wallace, elected governor on a segregationist platform in 1962, opposed their admission and of course had considerable support, including the Ku Klux Klan, whose national headquarters virtually bordered the university's main campus in Tuscaloosa. Yet the situation in Alabama seemed less ominous than it had at Ole Miss. The university president, its faculty, and its trustees disagreed with Wallace, as did many state officials, including the attorney general. Moreover, most newspapers and business establishments turned against the governor. To activate corporate disapproval, "we wrote down . . . the names of every company with . . . more than 100 employees," Robert Kennedy recalled. "All those names were distributed at a Cabinet meeting. . . . Then, we got in touch with the heads of all the other departments and agencies in the government."[36] They made calls to company executives with whom they had associations. Corporate interests understood that any repeat of the crisis at the University of Mississippi would be detrimental to business. Wallace received fifteen to twenty calls a day from concerned businessmen.

By registration day on 11 June, Wallace clearly wanted a way to save face. He planned to stand in the "school house" door before yielding to overwhelming federal force. The Kennedy administration wisely took him seriously. Federal troops sat in helicopters at nearby Ft. Benning, Georgia, to avert repeating the military dilatoriness of the Mississippi crisis. On campus Nicholas Katzenbach went face-to-face with Wallace, who positioned himelf behind a lectern in front of the registration building. After delivering a prepared statement, Wallace refused to step aside. Katzenbach and a small number of marshals returned to their cars, where Vivian Malone and James Hood, the two black students, sat. As planned, the marshals escorted them to the dormitories. President Kennedy thereupon federalized the Alabama National Guard, signaling Wallace that he intended to enforce the court order militarily if necessary. In the afternoon the students went to registration without opposition, and Alabama became the last southern state to begin the integration of its universities. That evening Kennedy delivered a moving address on civil rights; some considered it his best speech. An overjoyed King described it as "eloquent" and "profound." Wilkins, calling it the "message I had been waiting to hear," "fell asleep that night feeling new confidence."[37] Kennedy had asked for airtime only in the event of serious problems at the University of Alabama, but persuaded by his brother, he decided to speak anyway. As it turned out, Sorensen barely managed to complete the speech in time. Kennedy had constructed his own outline while waiting for the draft, and that effort comprised the concluding portion of the address.

Eloquently, Kennedy focused on the moral dimension of civil rights for the first time. No longer was government responding solely to restore order, protect lives, or enforce court orders; it was doing so, Kennedy asserted, because it was the right thing to do. "We are confronted primarily with a moral issue," he attested.

> It is as old as the scriptures and is as clear as the American Constitution. The heart of the question is whether all Americans are to be afforded equal rights and equal opportunities, whether we are going to treat our fellow Americans as we want to be treated. If an American, because his skin is dark, cannot eat lunch in a restaurant open to the public, if he cannot send his children to the best school available, if he can not vote for

the public officials who represent him, if, in short, he cannot enjoy the full and free life which all of us want, then who among us would be content to have the color of his skin changed and stand in his place? Who among us would then be content with the counsels of patience and delay?

He asked individual Americans to examine their own consciences on this issue and urged private enterprise and municipal leaders to employ blacks and to desegregate public facilities. He pointed out that communities suffering from racial disturbances attract less capital and business. After having spent weeks encouraging business leaders and mayors to respond, he realized, however, that some were unwilling to act alone. Consequently, in the 11 June address he chose to announce a comprehensive civil rights bill to be submitted to Congress in seven days. It represented an admission that the administration needed to go beyond executive action.

The metamorphosis had begun in late 1962, a time of frustration for the administration over growing southern violence, the slowness of civil rights advances, and criticism from virtually all civil rights groups. Even some Republicans flayed the administration for a failure to push civil rights legislation. Kennedy recognized the discontent and perceived a need for action. He proposed a modest bill in February to improve black voting rights and to assist school desegregation financially.

Yet it took Birmingham in 1963 to move the civil rights movement to center stage in dramatic fashion—thanks to the leadership of King and the shocking reaction of Connor, whom Kennedy quipped did as much for civil rights as anyone. As more Americans became appalled by injustice to blacks and as their concern about increasing violence grew, Kennedy felt the need to cool tensions in the South. Otherwise further demonstrations could lead to more violence, possibly necessitating federal military intervention. Furthermore, if his administration failed to address the moral imperatives of racism, it might lose not only the black community but also the opportunity to respond forcefully to wrongs which Kennedy knew existed.

Kennedy's focus on the moral dimension was not wholly political. Given his own experience with bigotry in the 1960 campaign, he could speak movingly on 11 June that "no one has been barred on account of his race from fighting or dying for America—there are no 'white' or 'colored' signs on the foxholes or graveyards of battle." But as he and his associates admitted, he was responding primarily to the successes of Birmingham and to the changing mood of northern society. He strove to shift the activity from street demonstrations to the White House, recognizing that great leaders must seize the moment to take charge. Considering himself an activist president, he placed himself in the tradition of Lincoln one hundred years after the Emancipation Proclamation. Politically, Kennedy's move involved risks because of the likely alienation of southern Democrats and the difficulties of passing civil rights legislation.

"This is a very serious fight," Kennedy acknowledged to King in June. "We're in this up to the neck. The worst trouble of all would be to lose the fight in Congress. . . . A good many programs I care about may go down the drain as a result of this—We may all go down the drain . . . so we are putting a lot on the line. What is important is that we preserve confidence in the good faith of each other."[38] All of this explains why the president faced so much hesitation from his staff. Vice-President Johnson recommended delay until the approval of the tax cut and until the president had laid a better foundation for its passage, including winning over Everett Dirksen (Ill.), the Senate minority leader, and other Republicans; obtaining a joint declaration of support from the three former presidents, Hoover, Truman, and Eisenhower; and making civil rights more of a moral issue by speaking in southern states on the incongruity of serving in Vietnam while not being able to buy a cup of coffee in a Mississippi lunchroom.[39] His advice caused Kennedy to focus more on the moral aspects and to lobby the Congress more intently. Yet only the attorney general pushed strongly for a civil rights bill in June; he had immense influence, in large part because his instincts mirrored the president's.

The attorney general also shaped the writing of the bill. Its key feature, the public accommodations provision, would guarantee citizens equal access to hotels, restaurants, places of amusement, and retail establishments, effectively removing most of the reasons for the recent protest. The bill also further challenged the denial of black voting rights. It gave greater authority to the attorney general in matters of school desegregation and provided for technical and financial assistance to schools undergoing desegregation. It also recognized the necessity to improve economic opportunities for blacks by expanding various development and training programs and by ending racial discrimination in the workplace. It fell short of what civil rights leaders wanted by failing to provide for a Title III provision, authorizing the attorney general to institute suits on a variety of civil rights infractions, including school segregation. Nor did the bill include a strong Fair Employment Practice Commission (FEPC) provision with statutory authority to end discrimination on the part of employers and labor unions. Kennedy would only endorse the idea, which was incorporated into a separate nonadministration proposal.

For the remainder of Kennedy's life debate swirled around the nature of the bill. The problem became more acute after Congressman Emanuel Celler's (D.-N.Y.) liberal-dominated House Judiciary Subcommittee loaded it down with FEPC, Title III, a broader public-accommodations provision, and other clauses. In the process they alienated the Republican congressional leadership that initially had expressed a willingness to work with the administration. Robert Kennedy angrily referred to such liberals as obstructionist "sons of bitches," accusing them of "being in love with death."[40]

Domestically, nothing occupied the administration more that summer and fall than civil rights. The president staged several White House meetings involving White House, congressional, and civil rights leaders to work out an acceptable compromise. He consulted Eisenhower, who thought an omnibus bill a mistake but expressed a willingness to cooperate. All of this resulted in an informal agreement to work closely with the Republican leadership in modifying the bill in the House Judiciary Committee. House Minority Leader Halleck and William M. McCulloch (Ohio), ranking Republican on the judiciary committee, who, Kennedy believed, could deliver sixty house colleagues, became the key people. They both sought a reasonable bill. Halleck conceded that "a colored man has a right to find a place to eat and sleep. If he buys a pair of pants [in an establishment], he has a right to buy a sandwich there too."[41] Halleck and McCulloch also came to see merit in an FEPC.

White House tapes of those meetings reveal the president's developing relationship with Halleck and McCulloch over civil rights. The Kennedys, however, never did understand why some Republicans cooperated so willingly. President Kennedy conceded that conscience motivated McCulloch but "trying to touch Charlie is like trying to pick up a greased pig." Yet Halleck's biographer echoed Halleck's assertion that civil rights was "not a political question but a matter of what's right."[42] At any rate, Halleck's surprising support soon invited strong criticism from the Republican rank and file. Meanwhile the president had calculated that forty-four senators favored the administration's bill and forty opposed, not nearly enough for cloture. He consequently focused on twenty-five swing votes, most of them midwest Republicans, figuring that probably only Senate Minority Leader Dirksen's support could win them over. Kennedy had a close relationship with Dirksen, whom he wooed through patronage and by not strongly opposing his reelection in 1962. More than likely, he would have come over had Kennedy lived; but just as likely, this would have come at the expense of FEPC, Title III, or perhaps a broad accommodations section.[43]

As it turned out, in the House Halleck directed the bipartisan measure out of the Judiciary Committee in October. At this stage the legislative proposal remained stronger than the administration's original effort since it provided for a watered down Title III and a permanent Civil Rights Commission. It figured to clear the House Rules Committee, following the delaying tactics of Chairman Howard Smith. Kennedy expected the House to pass it in early 1964. The Senate vote on cloture would supposedly occur sometime that spring. After Kennedy's assassination the Johnson administration succeeded in getting the bill through the Senate on 10 June. What seems clear is that Kennedy's efforts, not his death, had contributed most to its passage. Had he lived there would have been a law, even though different content and time frames would have resulted.

In Kennedy's last months the administration had also become entangled in two related civil rights issues involving Martin Luther King and the March on Washington. In both instances the administration sought to impose more control over the civil rights movement. At the same time the Kennedys remained somewhat suspicious of King, having received reports from Hoover that King had been consorting with known Communists. The FBI director, believing that Communists had first infiltrated the civil rights movement in the mid-1950s and hoping to use that concern to break the movement, raised the specter of Stanley Levison, a New York lawyer and long-time King adviser and speech writer. Hoover called Levison a key figure in the Soviet intelligence apparatus in the United States. Without obtaining conclusive evidence from the bureau, the attorney general authorized the wiretapping of Levison's office telephone and King's office and home phones after King refused to break completely with his friend and adviser. Hoover also proceeded to bug King indiscriminately.

In June 1963 the president spoke to King in the White House Rose Garden about the danger of associating with Levison. Kennedy warned that the FBI had the civil rights leader under electronic surveillance, causing King to conclude that Kennedy's stroll in the garden must have reflected the president's own fears of Hoover. While extensive wiretapping failed to reveal evidence of Communist linkage regarding any civil rights activist, the taps inexcusably continued until 1965.

This episode reveals more than the Kennedys' desire to protect themselves, civil rights legislation, and King; it shows their continued belief in an internal Communist menace. Robert Kennedy thought Levison was an important Communist who had a dangerous influence on King and was particularly troubled that King laughed about such allegations.[44] Although Levison proved to be more than an innocent victim, he had long before become disenchanted with the Communist party. David

Garrow's study on the FBI and King confirms Levison's early Communist affiliations as well as his break with the movement in 1955. Garrow convincingly contends that the bureau had no first-hand evidence that Levison had resumed his ties during the Kennedy era.[45] Yet Hoover continued to probe indiscreetly into King's private life, a practice he first had begun against others during the 1930s. Meanwhile, Robert Kennedy continued to advise the president that King remained a potential problem.

Another troublesome matter was that black leaders planned a march on Washington for summer 1963. President Kennedy seemed initially as unenthusiastic about this effort as Franklin Roosevelt had been about a similarly planned march in 1941. The administration had two concerns: The march would be directed against the government for not moving faster on civil rights, and it would jeopardize the civil rights bill. "We want success in Congress," the president said to civil rights leaders on 22 June, "not just a big show at the Capitol. Some of these people are looking for an excuse to be against us. I don't want to give any of them a chance to say, 'Yes, I'm for the bill, but I'm damned if I'll vote for it at the point of a gun.' " King argued that he had "never engaged in any direct action movement which did not seem ill-timed. Some people thought Birmingham ill-timed." "Including the Attorney General," Kennedy responded.[46]

Despite the advice of several congressmen Kennedy wisely endorsed the march after ensuring that it would serve the administration's purpose. In several ways he contributed to its colossal success. He worked closely with Walter Reuther, the auto workers' union leader, to involve the labor movement, churches, and other groups, making it interracial in nature. The attorney general put one staffer on the project full time for four weeks to guarantee that toilets, food, drinks, and other essentials would be provided. The administration had also induced the movement's leaders to shift the program from the Capitol to the Lincoln Memorial. Even the speeches came under indirect scrutiny by the administration, as march organizers forced John Lewis, chairman of SNCC, to tone down his denunciation of the administration's civil rights bill. According to one account Kennedy aides stood ready "to pull the plug" on the public address system in the event that anything went awry. It is little wonder that critics charged Kennedy with co-opting the movement, and black militant Malcolm X called it "The Farce on Washington."[47]

Yet a quarter of a million people came to Washington on 28 August in an upbeat, orderly procession of interracial solidarity. They were moved by the music of Joan Baez ("We Shall Overcome"), Peter, Paul and Mary, Bob Dylan, and Mahalia Jackson and by the addresses of so many others.

Perhaps King's greatest speech stirred them most. Standing before the Lincoln Memorial, as a bright sun glistened on the reflecting pool and upon thousands of people around it, he expressed that immortal ideal:

> I have a dream that one day . . . when we let freedom ring, when we let it ring from every village and every hamlet . . . , we will be able to speed up that day when all God's children, black men and white men, Jews and Gentiles, Protestants and Catholics, will be able to join in the words of that old Negro spiritual 'Free at last! Free at last! Thank God almighty, we are free at last!'

Afterward Wilkins, Bayard Rustin, King, A. Philip Randolph, and the other march leaders visited the White House for a meeting and refreshments. Kennedy greeted them by saying, "I have a dream." Never before had the civil rights movement evoked such a positive image of good will, strengthening popular support for civil rights legislation.

The year's civil rights successes had culminated in the March on Washington. In his remaining days Kennedy had reason to take pride in those recent advances, including the desegregation of the University of Alabama, the Birmingham agreement, the Kennedys' sustained dialogue with private industry and local governments to end discriminatory practices, and the most comprehensive civil rights bill in American history, a clear indication that the president had come full circle regarding his campaign promises. These, along with the earlier gains, had grudgingly mollified many civil rights leaders. Even King probably would have endorsed Kennedy in 1964. Of course SNCC, CORE, and the Black Muslims remained another matter. John Lewis of CORE spoke for many when he called Kennedy's civil rights bill "too little, too late."[48] Years later black historian Vincent Harding more thoughtfully expressed the movement's differences with the Kennedys when he categorized them as liberals who sought reform by working with the southern power structure. Even though the Kennedys sought to avoid a "tearing of the [societal] fabric," such tearing, Harding contended, "was absolutely necessary for something real to take place."[49]

Wofford compared Kennedy to Abraham Lincoln who, unlike the abolitionists, saw black rights in the broader, conflicting context of other goals and problems. Lincoln too had come under fire for temporizing and limiting the scope of his Emancipation Proclamation. As agents of change both Lincoln and Kennedy stood well behind advancing social forces, but their restraining actions made those changes more acceptable. In Kennedy's case, he tried to nudge civil rights forward without severing ties with the white South.

Even so, Kennedy's support in Dixie eroded substantially. In a September Gallup Poll, although 89 percent of blacks approved of his presidency, 70 percent of southern whites believed that he was pushing integration too fast, compared to 50 percent nationwide who agreed. His approval rating in the South dropped from 60 percent (March) to 44 percent (September.) Moreover, southern and border Democrats in Congress now became less cooperative toward administration programs. They caused the defeat of the reauthorization of the Area Redevelopment program by five votes, despite its convincing enactment in 1961. Realistically, Kennedy could expect less support in the South in 1964. The Kennedy presidency had indeed become controversial, as Herbert Parmet has noted. Racial challenges still remained. White violence in the South persisted, underscored by the September church bombing in Birmingham, which resulted in the deaths of four black girls. The beginnings of a white backlash against the civil rights movement had emerged in the North, and continued problems in Congress caused the civil rights bill to move with painful slowness.

Yet Kennedy viewed the future with optimism, believing that racial progress now seemed inevitable. He also received a 62 percent overall approval rating in September 1963. His more recent successes in foreign policy undoubtedly contributed to his continued popularity. Foreign policy in fact dominated his thinking. To John Kennedy the 1964 race would hinge on issues of war and peace, and he intended to show that the United States commanded a stronger world position as a consequence of his presidency.

8

★ ★ ★ ★ ★

THE MISSILES OF OCTOBER

In a 1965 interview Robert Kennedy singled out Cuba as the cause of the administration's greatest difficulties, particularly the humiliating defeat at the Bay of Pigs and the missile crisis of October 1962, which elevated the specter of nuclear holocaust to its highest level. Yet the October crisis also became Jack Kennedy's greatest cold war victory, according to contemporary judgment. Most world and domestic leaders praised his courage, determination, and patience as he defused the Soviet nuclear threat in Cuba. Americans generally agreed that the president had overcome his greatest test in crisis management. As a result the Kennedy foreign policy achieved a boost, and relations with the Soviet Union had mellowed by 1963.

Few Americans at the time understood the ways in which the first Cuban crisis contributed to the second one and the extent to which government leaders helped to provoke Cuba II. Nor did anyone comprehend fully the degree to which Castro and Khrushchev feared a United States invasion of Cuba in summer 1962. Misperceptions and miscalculations abounded on both sides prior to and during that thirteen-day crisis and indeed explain why scholars and former participants from the United States and the Soviet Union have focused so much recent attention on it.[1] The inescapable conclusion is that crisis avoidance—rather than management—must be the determining consideration if superpowers are to avert nuclear catastrophe. This necessitates mutual understanding and frank exchanges, both of which were often lacking in the early 1960s.

The administration contributed to the coming of the missile crisis seven months after the Bay of Pigs when President Kennedy approved Operation Mongoose, a CIA-inspired covert plan to topple Fidel Castro. By 1962, operating largely out of Miami, the anti-Castro activity comprised about four hundred Americans, two thousand Cubans, and an annual budget of about $50 million. The CIA promoted countless sabotage activities in Cuba designed to disrupt the economy, contaminated a sugar export shipment from there, encouraged European exporters to ship defective ball-bearings into the country, sent in agents and weapons, and sought to assassinate Castro. By early October the operation increased its activities as a dissatisfied Robert Kennedy undertook administrative supervision of the "secret war." Overall, however, that effort failed in all of its objectives.

In retrospect Operation Mongoose did nothing more than provide the administration with a means to vent its frustrations over Castro. National Security Adviser McGeorge Bundy later called it "the psychological salve for inaction."[2] No one felt more frustration and anger than Robert Kennedy, whose obsession with Castro was comparable to his crusade against Hoffa. Ray Cline of the CIA remembered Kennedy as "always bugging the agency about the Cubans."[3] Both Kennedys exaggerated the Castro menace partly out of their staunch anticommunism and their vendetta against the Cuban leader and also because of the political climate at home. This in turn explains their early 1962 embargo on trade with Cuba, their successful efforts to ban Cuba from the Organization of American States (OAS), and their other attempts to isolate Castro, all of which bound Cuba closer to the USSR, making Castro an even greater menace. Equally provocative, the extensive United States maneuvers in the Caribbean that April involved marines seeking to liberate an island from a mythical dictator whose name was "Ortsac" (Castro spelled backwards).

By summer 1962 political considerations played an increasing part in stimulating further action by the administration. The Republican National Committee announced that Cuba would be "the dominant issue" in the fall congressional campaign. Republicans could scarcely forget Kennedy's 1960 criticism of GOP inaction against Castro in light of his own irresolution during the Bay of Pigs invasion, and the drive to show Kennedy as soft on communism resumed. As an alarmed Khrushchev pumped military and economic assistance into Cuba during the summer, the Republican attack grew more furious, led by Senators Homer Capehart (Ind.) and Kenneth B. Keating (N.Y.). On 31 August Keating charged that he had evidence of twelve hundred Russian troops and the beginnings of a Soviet missile base in Cuba and in the weeks ahead relentlessly hammered at the Soviet buildup. In September Capehart urged a military invasion of Cuba. That same month a Gallup Poll revealed that 71 percent of the "informed" public wanted action; the press, particularly the popular columnists, echoed similar sentiments.

Kennedy responded by instituting U-2 surveillance of Cuba, which detected on 29 August Soviet SAMs (surface-to-air missiles) but no ground-to-ground missiles or other offensive weapons. On 4 September Kennedy issued a policy statement outlining the nature of the Soviet buildup to reassure Americans and to warn Khrushchev about provoking policy changes in the Western Hemisphere. Otherwise "the gravest issues would arise." His 13 September announcement cautioned that any menacing Soviet military change in Cuba would cause the United States to do "whatever must be done to protect its own security and that of its allies." At the same time he again challenged the Republican assertion that recent Soviet shipments constituted a threat to the Western Hemisphere. In retrospect Kennedy's September statements, despite the warnings to Moscow, seem ambiguous and most likely reinforced Khrushchev's belief that the United States would not respond strongly to Soviet offensive missiles in Cuba.

That same month Kennedy also requested congressional authority to call up 150,000 reservists, probably to defuse Republican criticism. He also welcomed a congressional resolution sanctioning the use of force to protect the hemisphere against Cuban aggression or subversion. Meanwhile CIA activity in Cuba intensified, which, along with the other escalating actions and rhetoric, contributed to several Soviet warnings in late September that an American attack on Cuba would mean war. Moreover, by 15 October the United States, through U-2 reconnaissance, had confirmed that the USSR was constructing medium-range missile (MRBM) sites in western Cuba, putting American east coast cities in jeopardy.

These missiles, Khrushchev subsequently explained, served a defensive purpose; along with the ILB-28 bombers and Soviet troops, they would deter an invasion of Cuba. For years Khrushchev's explanation, expounded in his memoirs, *Khrushchev Remembers*, seemed no more than a rationalization. However, recent Soviet scholars and former missile-crisis participants have emphatically and persuasively outlined Khrushchev's anxieties—if not paranoia—about a United States move in Cuba, alluding to Mongoose and other CIA activities, the expulsion of Cuba from the OAS, the proposed call-up of reservists, and other military and diplomatic maneuverings. McNamara, for one, conceded retrospectively that although "there was no intent in the White House or in the Pentagon . . . to overthrow Castro by force . . . [,] if I were on [the Soviet side] I'd have thought otherwise."[4] For these reasons, the defense-of-

Cuba hypothesis has gained greater acceptance among American scholars.

But as Khrushchev and Soviet scholars have admitted, a Russian missile gap also motivated the missile transference to Cuba. Scholarly differences remain about whether this constituted the primary or the secondary consideration, but as one recent study concludes, "one does not need to decide which of two birds is the most important target when both can be killed with one stone."[5] The fact is that the Soviets lagged in missile development because their huge rockets were both incredibly expensive and inaccurate. Both powers knew that an overwhelming discrepancy existed between United States and Soviet nuclear warheads and intercontinental ballistic missiles (ICBMs). As it turned out, even the Kennedy administration underestimated the variance, for the Soviets had only between 20 and 44 ICBMs and no submarine-launched ballistic missiles (SLBMs) compared to 161 United States ICBMs and 144 Polaris SLBMs at the conclusion of the crisis. In terms of atomic warheads the United States had the advantage of about a seventeen-to-one ratio.[6]

Khrushchev sought to lessen the nuclear imbalance by placing some forty-eight medium- and intermediate-range missiles ninety miles away from American shores, in effect improving his ICBM capability by closing the gap "on the cheap." The missiles enhanced the Soviet's feeble first-strike capability, but they in no way altered the overwhelming strategic imbalance even though they could reach the United States sooner and more accurately, coming from Cuba. Given the strategic superiority of the United States, Khrushchev counted on the nuclear force in Cuba to stabilize the crisis in that neither side would have a decisive military incentive to attack first.

Khrushchev might have considered other advantages in this gambit though the evidence seems less certain. Missiles in Cuba could have improved his position in Germany; Rusk believed that the United States would have faced an eventual ultimatum requiring a trade of the missiles for West Berlin. Additionally, Khrushchev might have sought to outmaneuver other adversaries—the Stalinists, the generals, or the Chinese—by such a move. But, as Soviet scholars emphasize, rational aims alone did not motivate the risk-taking, emotional Khrushchev.

He first contemplated the missile deployment in spring 1962. While visiting the Balkans he became more aware of the pending American Jupiter missiles and military bases in Turkey bordering the Soviet Union and reasoned that the United States might view events differently if it too had missiles on its flank. In July he met with Defense Minister Raul Castro's Cuban delegation, which detailed Kennedy's secret war against that nation. Khrushchev soon began the commitment of military weapons, including nuclear missiles, and troops to Cuba, seeking to duplicate what the United States had done with Thor missiles in Britain and Jupiters in Italy and Turkey.

Khrushchev's "adventurism" led him into serious miscalculations. First of all he gambled that Kennedy would prove too young, weak, and intellectual to respond effectively, despite the latter's thwarting of the Soviet challenge in Berlin. Khrushchev had formed this impression as a result of Vienna and Kennedy's indecision at the Bay of Pigs, and he believed that if the missiles could be emplaced prior to American detection, Kennedy would have to acquiesce. How he thought he could have managed such a logistical operation without disclosure is inconceivable. Moreover, the Soviets failed to understand the extent to which the United States government would find this action unacceptable.

On Monday evening 15 October, two U-2 flights, soaring nearly fourteen miles above ground, finally gathered photographic evidence that the Soviets were constructing launching sites for one thousand-mile medium- and twenty-two hundred-mile intermediate-range missiles near San Cristobal in western Cuba. Subsequent flights would indicate that this represented only the tip of the iceberg. Bundy, awaiting the detailed analysis of the photographs, elected to inform the president early the next morning. He found him sitting on the edge of the bed in his bathrobe, sipping coffee, as he skimmed a half-dozen newspapers. Kennedy quickly commented, "We've just elected Capehart in Indiana, and Ken Keating will probably be the next President of the United States."[7] He immediately called for additional U-2 flights and ordered a meeting that morning, requesting the attendance of Bundy, Secretary of State Dean Rusk, Defense Secretary Robert McNamara, Robert Kennedy, Vice-President Lyndon Johnson, CIA Director John McCone, Treasury Secretary Douglas Dillon, Chief Counsel Theodore Sorensen, Undersecretary of State George Ball, Deputy Undersecretary of State Alexis Johnson, Chairman of the Joint Chiefs of Staff Maxwell Taylor, Assistant Secretary of State for Latin America Edward Martin, former Ambassador to Russia Llewellyn Thompson, Deputy Secretary of Defense Roswell Gilpatric, and Assistant Secretary of Defense Paul Nitze. Also joining the group—later known as the Executive Committee of the National Security Council (ExComm)—were UN Ambassador Adlai Stevenson, White House Appointments Secretary Kenneth O'Donnell, and former Secretary of State Dean Acheson.

ExComm reflected Kennedy's penchant for smaller ad hoc advisory groups rather than the more unwieldy National Security Council preferred by Eisenhower. In the course of the exhausting thirteen-day crisis from October sixteenth through the twenty-eighth, ExComm met secretly in three separate rooms: the cabinet room and the Oval Office of the White House and the rectangular conference room across from George Ball's State Department office. Attendance varied, with Rusk and Johnson often absent because of other obligations; others such as Acheson attended only some of the meetings. Robert Kennedy requested that the president stay away from several sessions to lessen the group-think inhibitions that had plagued the Bay of Pigs meetings. In fact a concerted effort existed to overcome the decision-making inadequacies of the earlier crisis—hence the inclusion of Kennedy's personal advisers, Robert Kennedy and Sorensen, as intellectual watchdogs. The former sometimes acted as a devil's advocate in asking penetrating questions. All hypotheses and recommendations received intense scrutiny, especially those coming from the military. To develop more critical thinking the committee sometimes divided into subgroups to formulate position papers for critique. It held informal meetings and invited conflicting views—at least during the first five days, with deputies often challenging their chiefs. It asked participants to be generalists, enabling them to speak freely outside of their areas of specialty. In the interest of fresh viewpoints, outside experts appeared. Particularly invaluable was an expert on Soviet behavior, a position Thompson skillfully filled. He insisted that participants should put themelves in Khrushchev's shoes to gain more understanding.

Robert Kennedy and McNamara emerged as leaders in the ExComm sessions. McNamara led by the sheer force of his personality, a quick and incisive mind, and articulate and logical arguments. As secretary of defense his opposition to the JCS's recommendations to undertake more forceful military action became crucial. Robert Kennedy also had considerable influence, particularly because of Rusk's reluctance to preside and McNamara's aversion to usurping the secretary of state's position. As a result the younger Kennedy sometimes served as presiding officer, but he often said little and occasionally positioned himself in a chair away from the table to lessen his presence. He surprised participants by suppressing his passion and knee-jerk reactions. Ball saw him as a "stabilizing influence," a "force for caution and good sense."[8] Undoubtedly, the president's adjutant, as one writer called him, quickly sensed the gravity of the situation and hence the need for caution and careful deliberation. Neither Robert Kennedy nor anyone else could always keep meetings on track, however. Acheson, unaccustomed to such free-wheeling during his Truman days, soon labeled the gatherings "repetitive, leaderless, and a waste of time."[9]

Psychological stress became yet another hurdle; every participant experienced it over the grueling, tension-filled thirteen days. Sorensen later wrote of his waking in the middle of the night, thinking that "no other decision in his lifetime would equal this." A raw-nerved president found himself losing his famous "cool" on at least a dozen occasions, and McNamara claimed that this crisis induced "the most intense strain I have ever operated under."[10] Even though situationally induced stress can improve task performances to a point, it has the opposite effect once individual thresholds are crossed. Furthermore, stress can manifest itself in intensified fears, anxieties, or aggressions, affecting individual personalities differently. While Rusk and McNamara adopted exaggerated fears of Armageddon (McNamara thought he had witnessed his last Saturday on 27 October), others seemed more combative. Overall, however, there is little evidence to suggest that stress had a decisive effect on anyone or on the decision-making process.

Despite occasional problems, ExComm systematically explored eight major options on how to deal with the crisis. Participants analyzed the strengths, weaknesses, and the possible repercussions of each. Eventually they narrowed the options to two before providing the president with a recommendation that he himself preferred. Unquestionably, President Kennedy ultimately guided them in the direction of that final recommendation but only after considerable open debate. Never, however, did he achieve a consensus, an indication that participants felt free to speak throughout the crisis.

As important as ExComm was, it did not have exclusive influence. Kennedy consulted with many others, including former Truman officials Charles Bohlen and Robert Lovett, both of whom urged restraint. Moreover, Kennedy deliberated more with select ExComm members, particularly his brother and Sorensen in the privacy of the Oval Office. Whatever faults the process had, it represented a marked improvement over that of the Bay of Pigs. It also revealed a more perceptive, discerning, and questioning president, one capable of keeping his own counsel. The caution that Kennedy had exhibited in the first crisis highlighted this one too but not in a way to question his resolution or courage.

That this crisis afforded Kennedy—and Khrushchev—sufficient time to evaluate courses of action proved critical. At the first ExComm meeting on 16 October, most participants initially proposed an immediate air strike; Kennedy himself had favored that sort of response. Robert Kennedy had even suggested manufacturing another "sinking of the Maine" incident to facilitate United States involvement.[11] Others spoke openly of invasion. Gilpatric remembered President Kennedy appearing "very clipped, very tense. I don't recall a time when I saw him more preoccupied and less given to any light touch."[12] The president, Rusk, and McNamara readily expressed their concern about a possible

Soviet launch from Cuba, once the missiles became operational. Most were still in shock that the missile sites were even there. Only John McCone had postulated beforehand that the SAMs were a prelude to the ground-to-ground missiles. The administration had obviously too readily accepted State Department reports that Khrushchev would never place nuclear missiles in foreign countries. Kennedy eventually blamed himself for not being more emphatic in his earlier warnings.

Administration officials could only speculate as to why Khrushchev had responded so provocatively. As Sorensen contends, "I don't know now, and I didn't know then. None of us knew."[13] Curiously, no person in the ExComm meetings even hinted that the administration's covert actions against Castro might have been a possible cause, suggesting a rather ethnocentric attitude. Instead speculation centered around Berlin, internal considerations, China, and the missile gap. Kennedy thought that the Soviets must not be "satisfied with their ICBMs." Rusk brought up the Jupiter missiles in Turkey as a possible motivating factor. In another context on the sixteenth, the president had the Jupiters in mind when he said, "It's just as if we suddenly began to put a major number of MRBMs in Turkey. Now that'd be goddam dangerous, I would think." When Bundy responded, "Well, we *did*, Mr. President," Kennedy followed with, "Yeah, but that was five years ago."[14] The same sort of conversations might have taken place in the Politburo, illustrating again the fear, narrow-mindedness, and misunderstanding that affected both sides.

The first ExComm meeting also assessed the significance of the Cuban missiles. Disagreement remained strong on this issue, in turn affecting the recommendations for their removal. On the one hand, McNamara insisted, remarkably for a secretary of defense, that "a missile is a missile." The some forty Soviet missiles in Cuba seemed of little significance to McNamara because they were no more dangerous than Soviet-based ICBMs, nor did they have an appreciable effect on the overwhelming variance existing between the two countries. McNamara's initial reaction was not to force the issue. On the other hand, Dillon, Nitze, and Acheson argued that the Cuban missiles significantly altered the nuclear balance. Nitze called it the first step toward nuclear parity—"not in numbers but in military effectiveness—because their capability in an initial strike . . . would be tremendous."[15]

The two Kennedys and Sorensen offered another viewpoint, probably the prevalent one. While believing that the strategic balance remained unaffected, they focused on the missiles' enormous political and psychological impact. Certainly this would affect United States' relations with Latin America and the NATO alliance, which would draw their own conclusions about American power. Much speculation existed too on how Castro might use his newly found force in dealings with Latin republics. More to the point, Kennedy rightly perceived that the missiles would represent an enormous blow to his—and his nation's and party's—prestige. Conversely, the Soviets naively viewed the matter as primarily an international legal question, comparable to Turkey's request for Jupiters. Khrushchev ignored the tremendous public intolerance of Soviet involvement so close to American shores. Robert Kennedy understandably suggested to his brother that "if you hadn't acted, you would have been impeached." The Soviet gambit became even more objectionable because it occurred surreptitiously and deceitfully. After informing United States leaders repeatedly that they had no intentions of placing offensive weapons in Cuba, they did that very thing. It made Kennedy appear naive for having trusted the Russians.

Khrushchev's subsequent disclaimer that ground-to-ground missiles were offensive carried little weight, even though intent constitutes a consideration in determining the offensive or defensive nature of weapons. At the same time the Kennedy administration stood on less solid ground when it claimed that its missiles in Turkey were defensive because of their being placed there in the NATO context. From a legal standpoint, then, differences between the situations in Cuba and Turkey remained less clear than administration officials suggested.

Little disagreement existed at that first ExComm meeting that the missiles must be removed from Cuba. But how? At first, most participants—including Dillon, Taylor, Bundy, and Acheson—favored either a surgical or a broader air strike, arguing that this represented the most expeditious way of removing the missiles. Some—particularly Nitze and McCone—contended that an invasion should follow a strike. This was pushed so vociferously at the 16 October evening session that Robert Kennedy slipped a note to Sorensen saying that he now knew "how Tojo felt when he was planning Pearl Harbor." The air-strike approach generated resistance because it seemed unduly provocative. Several thousand Soviet troops and technicians would be killed even in a so-called surgical operation. Llewellyn Thompson got Kennedy's attention when he argued that Soviet deaths in Cuba might induce Khrushchev to unleash the surviving missiles on the United States. More probably, there might be a Soviet move elsewhere, either against Berlin or on the Jupiter missiles in Turkey. As more discussion followed, it became clearer from a military standpoint that to mount a successful air attack against Cuba, the SAM installations and the three air fields must be hit also. Gen. Walter C.

Sweeney, commander of the Tactical Air Command, recommended an attack force of five hundred planes—a figure unlikely to win supporters to the cause.

Unlike those at the Bay of Pigs planning sessions, ExComm members did give attention to moral considerations, thus weakening the air option. On Wednesday the seventeenth Robert Kennedy first opposed that choice because a surprise attack would kill thousands of civilians, insisting that "my brother is not going to be the Tojo of the 1960s." In calling it a "Pearl Harbor in reverse," he enraged Acheson, who argued that the president's primary responsibility in this "test of wills" remained the security of the American people and the free world. Acheson lambasted Kennedy's Pearl Harbor allusion as "a thoroughly false and pejorative analogy." The attorney general's response followed on Friday. He reasoned that the traditions and history of the United States would never allow for the surprise attack of a large nation against a small one; such an act would have monumental impact on America's moral position both at home and abroad.[16] His moral suasion convinced Dillon to reverse his position on the air strike.

A naval blockade represented the most viable alternative. First proposed by McNamara on Tuesday, it had been casually discussed during the summer as a way to curtail arms shipments to Cuba on Soviet ships, yet it too posed problems. According to international law, a blockade could be considered a warlike—if not an illegal—act. Moreover, it evoked terrible memories of Berlin in 1948. To alleviate these stumbling blocks, advocates took a leaf from Franklin Roosevelt in adopting "defensive quarantine" as a substitute term while making it clear that it was a "visit and search" action solely against suspected offensive military shipments to Cuba. To strengthen this move legally and politically, OAS approval was essential, but this required a two-thirds vote, an imposing obstacle. More seriously, the blockade might hinder a quick solution, for Khrushchev could resort to delaying tactics to seize the diplomatic initiative. Furthermore, it seemed more likely to prevent missiles from entering Cuba rather than forcing their removal.

Yet the option of a blockade grew in popularity. By Thursday the eighteenth the president secretly and tentatively favored it. It won his, Sorensen's, McNamara's, Robert Kennedy's, and probably Rusk's support because it represented a limited, flexible, and bloodless response. Moreover, with OAS approval, it would have the cloak of international legality. Gilpatric later stated it best: The question was "whether the President would start out with limited or unlimited action, and he thought it should be limited action."[17] In short, an air strike or invasion remained viable options should the quarantine fail.

Those who favored the blockade became known as "doves," while air-strike advocates were labeled "hawks," the first time these terms were employed together. Doves tended to take more seriously the possibilities of an inadvertent nuclear encounter. They, like Kennedy, understood the relevance of Barbara Tuchman's recent *The Guns of August*, which depicted how European nations had stumbled into World War I. Despite the overwhelming nuclear advantage of the United States, McNamara especially worried about the possibility of a Soviet missile hitting American cities. The hawks, led by Acheson, Nitze, Taylor, and Dillon (until Friday), feared a military showdown much less. Most had participated in the tension-filled days of the early cold war when American might had forced the Soviets to back down in Berlin in 1948 and had contained the Chinese in Korea; they felt that superior power would deter the Soviets again.

Both groups, however, supported the president in rejecting a diplomatic approach to resolve the crisis—making the term "dove" somewhat of a misnomer. The administration could have presented its photographic evidence to the Soviets privately, enabling them to reverse the buildup without a confrontation. Soviet scholars have improbably insisted that Khrushchev would have withdrawn the missiles, especially if the United States had promised not to invade Cuba. Kennedy, of course, said nothing to the Russians until immediately prior to his dramatic blockade speech on Monday 22 October. Why he elected to adopt a brinkmanship policy remains unresolved among scholars. His most steadfast critics, like Bruce Miroff, contend that he might have wanted a showdown to demonstrate his toughness. Others, including Thomas Paterson, refer to his cold war views, his hostility toward Castro, his boldness of style, and his resentment toward Khrushchev for having tried to trick him. Still others focus on domestic-political considerations.

More likely, Kennedy believed that the element of surprise placed him in the most advantageous position to eliminate the missiles; otherwise, a wily Khrushchev could have used private notification to his own advantage. Kennedy painfully remembered the Soviet's manipulative skills at Vienna. The last thing he wanted was a diplomatic stalemate that would reach the UN. Nevertheless, Sorensen did try to draft a letter, as Bohlen and Stevenson persuaded him to do, but it never saw the light of day, partly because of a concern that Khrushchev might delay responding until the missiles became operational. Apprehension and mistrust, more than boldness, dictated the president's decision.

In any case, the Kennedy administration endured a horrendous week. Not only did officials attend daily ExComm meetings, some well into the night, but they also continued to perform most of the day-to-day work that usually ceases in crises, partly to preserve secrecy. The president set the pace. He flew to Connecticut on Wednesday to campaign for Abraham Ribicoff and other Democratic candidates to prevent Republican congressional gains that November. Upon returning he rushed in and out of ExComm meetings, generally keeping in touch by phone and through individual members. Following the various sessions, he sat in his rocker with a yellow legal-sized pad in his lap, scrawling page after page of notes, littering the floor with them. Secretary Evelyn Lincoln then gathered the sheets and edited and typed notes for the next day. On Thursday the eighteenth he met with Acheson, who reiterated the illogic of the attorney general's Pearl Harbor analogy. Kennedy listened politely, then walked over to the french doors facing the Rose Garden, peered outside, and turned around to say, "I guess I better earn my salary this week."

Later that afternoon he met with the stoical Andrei Gromyko, the Soviet foreign minister, who had requested the meeting. After shaking hands, Gromyko sat on one of the sofas; Kennedy occupied the nearby rocker. Gromyko remembered this meeting as "perhaps the most difficult that I have had." He recalled that Kennedy was "nervous, though he tried not to show it."[18] Quite probably Kennedy's apprehension that Gromyko might raise the missile issue initially elevated the anxiety level. With relief he heard the Soviet say that he had come primarily about Berlin, which would remain a closed issue until after the November elections; afterward, Gromyko continued, the two powers must come to an agreement. Gromyko then complained about United States hostility toward Castro and reaffirmed that the Soviet weapons there were "by no means offensive." Kennedy listened impassively, suppressing his urge to confront him with the photographic evidence. Instead he slowly read to him his 4 September statement that warned the Soviets about placing offensive weapons in Cuba. It was Gromyko's turn to listen impassively. Neither individual revealed himself fully; both sought to deceive the other. Gromyko must have wondered whether Kennedy's silence about the missiles reflected ignorance or acquiescence. Perhaps the Soviet leader thought that the U.S. had detected the missiles but had decided to remain silent until after the congressional elections to reduce the political risks.[19]

The next morning Kennedy resumed his campaign activities, this time in the Midwest. Before his departure he seemed discouraged and impatient, asking Sorensen and the attorney general to "pull the group together quickly—otherwise more discussion and delay would plague whatever decision we took."[20] He had just visited with the joint chiefs, who again urged an air strike. He undoubtedly felt that both hawks and doves had received a full hearing. Meanwhile, the Soviets were frantically moving to put the missiles into an operational state, and reporters were raising questions about troop movements toward Florida, Rusk's recent speech cancellation in Hot Springs, and other tell-tale signs.

Kennedy's campaign swing represented a welcome diversion as he enjoyed the animated crowds, the friendly ovations, and the colorful fall landscape. For a few moments he might have actually forgotten all of the troubles he had left behind. No indication in his campaigning exists that he sought to capitalize politically on Cuba. Nor was there much discussion of politics in the ExComm meetings even though he and others felt that domestic-political considerations remained a compelling reason for the expeditious removal of the missiles. Ironically, the Republican Dillon raised the political specter most blatantly in a note to Sorensen on the eighteenth: "Have you considered the very real possibility that if we allow Cuba to complete . . . readiness of missile bases, the next house of representatives is likely to have a Republican majority?"[21]

Kennedy's campaigning came to an abrupt end on Saturday morning when his brother telephoned him at his Chicago hotel that ExComm was ready to meet with him. He quickly informed the press that he had a cold, but when Vice-President Johnson canceled his campaigning in Hawaii for the same reason, a suspicious press wondered if an epidemic had broken out. Kennedy returned to the White House shortly after 1:30 P.M. and went to the pool for a swim. The attorney general undoubtedly described the discordant meetings on Friday, including Sorensen's admonition that the bickering was neither helping his ulcer nor "serving the President very well." Later on Friday the proponents of an air strike had lost further ground; Acheson had departed for his Maryland farm, believing the battle had been lost.

Kennedy convened the Saturday afternoon meeting in the Oval Office. Rusk responded with a two-page briefing, citing seven reasons for adopting the blockade. Both McNamara and Robert Kennedy concurred. When the president asked Johnson for his viewpoint, he answered, "You have the recommendation of your Secretary of State and your Secretary of Defense, and I would take it."[22] After the advocates of an air strike again presented their arguments and a straw vote resulted (eleven for a quarantine and six favoring an air strike), Kennedy expressed his opinion that the blockade was the way to begin since it best preserved his options as well as Khrushchev's. This did not rule out an air strike if the blockade failed, he said, nor had he made his final decision; he needed to ask further questions of the head of the Air Force Tactical Bombing Command. "There isn't any good solution," he reminded them; "whichever plan I choose, the ones whose plans we're not taking are the lucky ones."[23]

Kennedy then turned to possible diplomatic approaches to accompany the quarantine, which resulted in the biggest show of fireworks of an already stressful week. Stevenson, a recent arrival from New York, precipitated it. As UN ambassador he naturally focused on diplomacy instead of on coercion, believing that missile bases anywhere were negotiable. He was especially sensitive to the perceptions other nations might have of American actions. That Saturday, though he reluctantly accepted the blockade as an initial step, he proposed a trade of the Guantánamo Bay, Cuba, base and the Turkish and Italian Jupiters for the Soviet missiles in Cuba; he also suggested a United States guarantee of the territorial integrity of Cuba and a summit meeting to concentrate on related problems, including the neutralization of Cuba.

Stevenson was soundly upbraided. Dillon, Lovett, and McCone perhaps made him a scapegoat for all those favoring the blockade. By Saturday emotions and intolerance ran high, particularly on issues that had been seemingly resolved. Unfortunately, Stevenson had not attended the Friday sessions to witness the rejection of McNamara's proposed trade. Too, many New Frontiersmen saw the aging, increasingly rotund Stevenson as an embarrassing anachronism—an ideologically soft and prudish liberal from a bygone era. Robert Kennedy privately advised his brother to replace him with a stronger negotiator at the UN. The outwardly more objective president praised Stevenson for his convictions but rejected his proposal because early concessions would send Khrushchev, the NATO allies, and the American people the wrong message. Nothing could have illustrated the differences more between the two; while the pragmatic Kennedy's concern continued to be the removal of the missiles, Stevenson thought in terms of a broader settlement. One wonders whether Kennedy did not deliberately set up Stevenson on that Saturday so that the president might occupy the middle ground more firmly.

Following the Stevenson stir, the Kennedy-led ExComm settled on Monday evening for a nationwide presidential address announcing the blockade. That Saturday evening James Reston of the *New York Times* informed George Ball that he knew of the Soviet missiles; once again, as a result of Kennedy's phone call to publisher Orvil Dryfoos, the *Times* agreed to censor the story in the interest of national security. On Sunday morning Kennedy met with close advisers and General Sweeney of the Tactical Air Command, who reaffirmed that a tactical air strike would destroy 90 percent of the missile sites, leaving the possibility of a retaliatory strike. (Sweeney never informed Kennedy that it would take at least eight hours to prepare the liquid-fueled Soviet missiles, enabling the United States to hit the surviving missiles, nor did Kennedy know if the missiles were fully operational. As it turned out twenty warheads were on the island, with more on the way.)[24] The president also obtained the advice of long-time friend David Ormsby Gore, the British ambassador, who recommended a blockade. A relieved, grinning Kennedy responded, "You'll be happy to know that's what we are going to do." Finally he called Eisenhower, whom McCone had briefed earlier. Eisenhower thought a bombing mission "would . . . be detrimental to our cause" but assured Kennedy of his support whatever the decision.[25] Those who saw Kennedy that day witnessed a calmer president.

Monday, 22 October, dawned with the JCS completing the planning procedures for the blockade. That same day the armed forces went from peacetime alert to war alert. Two days later the Strategic Air Command (SAC) jumped to full-war footing for the first time ever—meaning that 550 nuclear-bomb-carrying B-52s took to the air. Kennedy, McNamara, and the chairman of the JCS did not know that Gen. Thomas Power of SAC, without authorization, had issued the order "in the clear" instead of in code, enabling the startled Soviets to intercept the message. This excessive flaunting of U.S. strategic superiority confirmed the president's and McNamara's fears that the military might precipitate a war. Additionally, on the twenty-second, five of the eight combat divisions of the Army Strategic Reserve went on readiness (one hundred thousand men), the First Armored Division moved from Texas to Georgia, the army established a command post in Florida for the possible invasion of Cuba, and seven thousand marine reinforcements reached Guantánamo Bay. This overwhelming show of force contributed to the poignancy of the president's evening message.

At 3:00 P.M. that afternoon Kennedy met with the NSC for the first time during the crisis and established a daily meeting time of 10:00 A.M. for the executive committee of the NSC. One hour later he convened the cabinet and informed them of the crisis; that meeting lasted five minutes. Then at 5:00 P.M. he, Rusk, McNamara, and McCone briefed some twenty congressional leaders, many of whom had returned to Washington, D.C., in air force jets from around the country. Kennedy probably delayed such a gathering because of a desire to reach a decision first and to maintain secrecy. Too, he suspected that most congressmen would want stronger action. Whatever the reason, he limited the scope of input and consequently faced a far from cordial group that afternoon. House Minority Leader Charles Halleck commented that while he would support the blockade, he wanted it recorded that he had been informed, not consulted. Moreover, Democratic Senators Richard Russell (Ga.) and William Fulbright (Ark.), among others, favored an air strike. Fulbright contended that a blockade might prove more provocative to the Russians. If a Soviet ship failed to turn back, the United States would have to sink it, he insisted. Kennedy never explained that ExComm had undergone similar reactions before resolving them over a five-day period; instead he left in a "smoldering rage," muttering to Sorensen that "if they want the job, they can have it—it's no great joy to me."[26]

About the same time in Paris, Acheson, Kennedy's special envoy, handed Charles de Gaulle a letter from Kennedy, along with a copy of his speech, informing him of the impending blockade. De Gaulle assured Acheson of his support. Chancellor Konrad Adenauer of West Germany and Prime Minister John Diefenbaker of Canada were also briefed. Acheson had already instructed Ambassador David Bruce in London to notify Prime Minister Harold Macmillan, who had been forewarned by Ormsby-Gore. Britain, of course, agreed to back Kennedy, as did other NATO Allies. Macmillan, however, refused Kennedy's request to mobilize English forces. He had perhaps learned one lesson from *The Guns of August* that the president had not: Mobilization of the great powers in 1914 had sparked World War I. He also questioned undue focus on Cuba at the expense of West Berlin, a possible victim of a Soviet-American trade.

Meanwhile at 6:00 P.M at the State Department, Rusk faced a smiling Anatoly Dobrynin, the Soviet ambassador. Rusk handed him a copy of Kennedy's scheduled speech, with a personal presidential message to Khrushchev: "The action we are taking is the minimum necessary to remove the threat. . . . The fact of this minimum response should not be taken as a basis . . . for any misjudgment on your part."[27] Rusk recalled that Dobrynin aged ten years.

Promptly at 7:00 P.M. from the Oval Office the president reported to a national television audience on the Soviet buildup, which he asserted violated the Rio Pact of 1947 and the UN charter. He announced the naval quarantine as a first step against ships carrying offensive military equipment into Cuba; he called for an immediate meeting of the OAS and the UN Security Council; he promised further action should the Soviets challenge the blockade. Any missiles launched from Cuba, he warned, would be viewed "as an attack by the Soviet Union on the United States, requiring full retaliatory responses upon the Soviet Union." He called for their prompt withdrawal under UN supervision, stressing that Soviet offensive missiles endangered the freedom of all New World countries, making them an international problem.

Twenty-five years later Sorensen admitted that the speech seemed overemotional and overstated, but it had to be, he contended, to overcome a probable Soviet defense. In fact, the administration needed a clear public position. Kennedy worried how others might view the symmetry between U.S. missiles bordering the Soviet Union and the Russian arsenal in Cuba. Khrushchev could argue that legally he had a right to place missiles in Cuba as long as that government consented. To negate Khrushchev's courting of world opinion, Kennedy directed Sorensen to emphasize "sudden and deceptive deployment."[28]

Kennedy's message raised the level of tension appreciably. Newspaper banners on Tuesday morning proclaimed a Kennedy-Khrushchev showdown. Ball, fitfully asleep on the couch in his office, stirred as he heard Rusk enter and announce, "George, we've won a great victory. You and I are still alive." That bit of relief did not last long. At 8:00 A.M. the Tass news agency issued the first Soviet response, charging the United States with violating international law, initiating piratical operations, and provoking nuclear war. Rusk believed a Soviet nuclear strike remained a definite possibility. At 9:00 A.M. he emphasized to OAS representatives in Washington, D.C., that Soviet military involvement in Cuba endangered all countries in the hemisphere. No one could have predicted that by the end of the day in a nineteen-to-nothing vote, delegates would approve a United States resolution calling for the removal of Soviet offensive weapons and the introduction of the blockade. This response gave the United States something of the legality it needed.

That same day in New York Stevenson brought the case for the United States before the Security Council even though a favorable resolution would prove impossible, given the certainty of a Soviet veto. To assist Stevenson, Kennedy had sent Republican John McCloy to cement national unity and to bolster—in Robert Kennedy's view—a weak negotiator. In response to Stevenson's opening indictment, Valerian Zorin, the Soviet UN ambassador, rejected the "false accusations" that the Soviets had "set up offensive armaments in Cuba." His counterresolution condemned the United States for violating the UN charter and for increasing the threat of war through criminal acts.

Americans responded patriotically and fearfully to the crisis. In independent polls 84 percent backed the blockade and only 4 percent opposed it; but 20 percent thought World War III inevitable, and 60 percent feared that "some shooting" would soon occur. From the vantage point of the Harvard classroom, Richard Neustadt reported to Sorensen that "those kids were literally scared for their lives and were astonished, somehow, that their lives would be risked by an *American* initiative. In short, what they have heard and said ad infinitum about hazards in our era suddenly came *home* to them; for the first time, apparently, awareness of the real world got transferred from their heads to their guts."[29]

Tuesday evening brought the showdown nearer, as Kennedy and ExComm gave final approval to the quarantine procedures and determined the prohibited offensive weapons, including surface-to-surface missiles and bomber aircraft. Kennedy then urged Khrushchev to support the blockade, which would go into effect the next morning at ten o'clock. He cautioned him to "show prudence and do nothing to . . . make the situation more difficult to control."[30] Later that evening Kennedy met with his brother, who recounted a disagreement he had had with Dobrynin over the definition of offensive weapons. Ormsby Gore, an eyewitness, later noted the president's tension that evening: "He talked at a tremendous pace, in machine-gun bursts. And his eyes were screwed tight as if to shut out a vision of a world in ruins."[31] By now Kennedy had reached the crest of his confrontational policy. As subsequent actions would reveal, he soon sought to give Khrushchev every opportunity to honor the quarantine and reach an accord, fearing that events might overtake reason and precipitate a nuclear encounter or a renewed conflict in Berlin. To ensure that things did not get out of hand, he assumed even more control over policy; Robert Kennedy recalled that he "supervised everything."[32]

The eye of the crisis came the next morning as 16 destroyers, 3 cruisers, an antisubmarine aircraft carrier, and more than 150 additional ships in reserve patrolled the interdiction line. The president shortened that belt east of Cuba from eight hundred to five hundred miles, at the suggestion of Ormsby Gore. This would allow Khrushchev more time for a decision, a circumstance from which Kennedy himself had benefited. McNamara, feeling the same concerns as the president, soon met with Adm. George Anderson to review stop-and-search procedures. When Anderson showed displeasure at the interference, McNamara had reprimanded him: "This was not a blockade but a means of communication between Kennedy and Khrushchev; no force would be applied without my permission; and that would not be given without discussion with the President."[33]

As twenty-five Soviet ships steamed toward Cuba, the Soviet leader warned that the USSR would defend its rights. During this crucial moment when the ships were drawing closer, Robert Kennedy experienced extraordinary signs of emotional tension as he and his brother gazed at each other across the table: "[Jack's] hand went up to his face and covered his mouth. He opened and closed his fist. His face seemed drawn, his eyes pained, almost gray." A transfixed Robert Kennedy thought of the times that his brother had almost died; of Jack's loss of a son; of the wartime death of Joe; and of the other hurts and strains. What brought him back to reality was his brother's question, "Isn't there some way we can avoid having our first exchange with a Russian submarine?"[34] Then at 10:00 A.M. a report indicated that six Russian ships on the edge of the quarantine had stopped or turned back, causing Rusk to say, "We're eyeball to eyeball and I think the other fella just blinked." Soon afterward, as other Soviet vessels neared the boundary, Kennedy issued an order that ships were only to be trailed, thus giving them every opportunity to reverse course.

Meanwhile sporadic official and unofficial communications continued between the two countries. In Moscow Khrushchev asked William Knox, president of Westinghouse International and in Russia on private business, to meet with him on Wednesday afternoon. Khrushchev looked like a man who had not slept all night, Knox remembered. The meeting lasted for three hours, with Khrushchev contending that he had missiles and attack planes in Cuba for defensive purposes. The United States, he continued, had to learn to live with the missiles in Cuba just as the USSR had learned to live with them in Turkey. He stressed the importance of negotiations and his displeasure with the blockade; if the quarantine persisted, he said, he would order his submarines to sink an American ship. Kennedy had obviously disappointed him; and he wondered whether approaching elections had influenced Kennedy's hardline posture. "How can I deal with a man who is younger than my son?" he complained. The next morning Kennedy's letter to Khrushchev reviewed the reasons for the crisis, focusing on Soviet deception. While Kennedy regretted the deterioration in relations, he remained adamant about the withdrawal of offensive weapons from Cuba.

Much more in public view that Thursday, the climactic meeting at the UN Security Council featured Stevenson's dramatic challenge to Valerian Zorin. "Do you . . . deny," Stevenson queried, "that the USSR has placed and is placing medium- and intermediate-range missiles in Cuba? Yes or no? Don't wait for the translation. Yes or no?" Zorin's reply that he was not in an American courtroom failed to deter Stevenson, who pressed harder after Zorin suggested that he would provide an answer in due course. With one eye on Zorin and the other on the White House, Stevenson melodramatically responded, "I am prepared to wait for my answer until hell freezes over." He then produced about a dozen large photographs on posters as he reviewed the physical evidence. Despite the convincing performance, Stevenson and Kennedy received little official support from the UN. U Thant, the acting secretary general, did propose the temporary suspension of arms shipments to Cuba and the quarantine to facilitate negotiations, but Kennedy rejected this because it removed the pressure from Khrushchev without requiring him to dismantle the missiles.

Thursday also brought renewed dangers from the quarantine site. Though missile-carrying ships had honored the quarantine, tankers and other vessels continued toward Cuba. The *Bucharest* passed through the blockade on Kennedy's orders, despite the urgings of ExComm hardliners that the tanker be boarded to show will and intent. However, Kennedy wished to avoid challenging a Soviet-owned ship; instead he selected the *Marucla*, an American-built, Panamanian-owned, and Lebanon-registered craft under a Soviet charter. He signaled Khrushchev his intention to enforce the quarantine but not in a way to embarrass him, giving Khrushchev sufficient time to make a responsible decision. This did not satisfy hardliners such as Nitze, who thought Kennedy a "pantywaist." Aside from halting the tankers, Nitze wanted the navy to board the missile-carrying ships to demonstrate the rockets' existence. He shared the frustration of others who questioned the blockade's worth, particularly since it failed to remove the missiles already in Cuba. Still, the question remained, would Khrushchev react responsibly?

A response came from an unexpected quarter on the twenty-sixth. Khrushchev used Aleksander Fomin, a Soviet embassy counselor and a personal friend, to contact John Scali, the diplomatic correspondent for the American Broadcasting Company. A haggard Fomin told Scali at a Pennsylvania Avenue restaurant that the "situation is very serious." Would Scali check with his high State Department sources about a possible settlement involving the removal of the missile sites under UN supervision in exchange for a United States pledge not to invade Cuba? Scali immediately went to the State Department; Rusk scrawled a receptive message and cleared it with the White House. Shortly afterward, Scali relayed the assurances to Fomin in a hotel coffee shop with the caveat that "time is very urgent."

That same evening Khrushchev sent a rambling personal letter to Kennedy. Hardly the "outcry of a frightened man," as early writers portrayed it, it nevertheless represented an emotional appeal for reason, trust, and responsibility. Calling war a "calamity" favored only by "lunatics," he assured Kennedy that being of "sound mind," he understood the situation: An attack by anyone would precipitate a world catastrophe. He informed the president once again that Soviet missiles in Cuba were placed there for defensive purposes as a consequence of the "threat of armed attack . . . [which] has constantly hung . . . over Cuba." Under no circumstances, he continued, did his action justify an illegal blockade, which the United States would never accept if circumstances were reversed.

Khrushchev recommended "statesmanlike wisdom," repeating what he had transmitted through Fomin: If the United States promised to disengage completely from military activities in Cuba, "then . . . the question of armaments would disappear." Relying on the vernacular of his rural upbringing, Khrushchev predicted that otherwise both sides would "clash, like blind moles," causing "reciprocal extermination." He concluded that they ought not to "pull on the ends of the rope in which you have tied the knot, because the more the two of us pull, the tighter that knot will be tied."

Following the Khrushchev-Fomin messages of the twenty-sixth, an optimism permeated ExComm as Kennedy asked the State Department that evening to analyze the letter and draft a response. The next day shattered the hopefulness, making it the darkest period of the crisis. The morning began with a disturbing call from FBI Director J. Edgar Hoover to Robert Kennedy, informing him that Soviet personnel in New York were preparing to destroy sensitive documents. What had precipitated this drastic action, Kennedy wondered. Then soon after the convening of the morning's ExComm meeting, a second Khrushchev letter to Kennedy, transmitted over Moscow radio, reached the White House; this message was much less discursive and personal than the first. Indications are that if Khrushchev had drafted it, others had edited it. Probably, as United States Ambassador Foy Kohler later heard, Khrushchev had sent the first letter without consultation, resulting in "long meetings and heated discussions" with the Presidium and consequently the second letter.[35] That dispatch focused on American missile bases in Europe; Khrushchev asked, "Do you believe that you have the right to demand security for your country and the removal of such weapons that you qualify as offensive, while not recognizing this right for us?" He proposed that an agreement include the mutual evacuation of analogous weapons from Cuba and Turkey, with pledges that the United States and the USSR respect the integrity of the frontiers and sovereignty of those two countries. What prompted the proposal for the missile trade is still indeterminable. Perhaps the Soviets interpreted Walter Lippmann's suggestion for a swap, contained in a *Washington Post* 25 October column, as an administration initiative.[36]

In any case, Khrushchev's letter dominated much of ExComm's morning meeting. Even Thompson seemed perplexed over the altered proposal, but a majority opposed trading the liquid-fuel Jupiter missiles, despite their primitive guidance system and vulnerability. Rusk later recalled joking about which direction they would travel after launching. (A contemporary study had reported that a 22-caliber rifle could put them out of commission.) The United States had committed fifteen MRBMs to Turkey in 1959 with the provision that that country would own the missiles and the United States, the warheads. They were installed in late 1961 and turned over to the Turks in fall 1962. Having serious doubts about them, Kennedy had wondered on 23 August 1962 "what action can be taken" for a withdrawal.[37] Never had he ordered them removed, however, despite later allegations that the bureaucracy had thwarted his will. In fact, the Turkish government had insisted on their retention. To remove them during the missile crisis would have sent the wrong message to NATO Allies, especially Turkey. Moreover, it would have aroused the hawks and invited strong Republican attacks during the congressional campaign.

Yet Kennedy repeatedly raised the trade option in the 27 October ExComm meetings, putting him closer to Stevenson by the hour. He seemed most concerned about having to institute an air attack and invading Cuba, thus setting off a cycle of escalation in which the Soviets would grab Berlin. The "bloodied" NATO Allies would then remind him that the Soviets had offered "a pretty good proposition." Hence Kennedy and others began to explore the possibilities of persuading Turkey—and NATO—that the United States sought the removal of the missiles only to prevent a Soviet attack on that Mediterranean nation.[38] To mollify the Turks, Polaris submarines could be assigned to the eastern Mediterranean.

That Saturday morning, the twenty-seventh, the crisis escalated when a Soviet SAM shot down a U-2 reconnaissance plane over Cuban air space. Maj. Rudolph Anderson, the pilot, died instantly. No one knew who had fired the missile, even though American intelligence identified the Los Angeles, Cuba, missile site as the culprit. That Khrushchev might have ordered such action aroused even more anger and anxiety. Not until 1985 did the *Washington Post* report a Soviet-Cuban military conflict in which Cubans had seized temporary control of the SAM site and fired the missile. Two years later the Soviets denied the assertion; Sergei Mikoyan—formerly personal secretary to his father, First Deputy Premier Anastas Mikoyan—confessed that a Soviet general in Cuba had violated instructions in ordering the SAM fired.[39]

The U-2 shooting heightened the resolve of the hawks to engineer an air strike and invasion. At the very least they expected Kennedy to take out the offending SAM site on the basis that ExComm had agreed to do this in the event of attack. Yet once again Kennedy exercised considerable restraint in arguing that the shooting might have been accidental. He favored waiting a day or two until the completion of other U-2 flights. Ball remembered the president as being "by far the most calm and analytical" in the room as he explained, "It isn't the first step that concerns me, but both sides escalating to the fourth and fifth step—and we don't go to the sixth because there is no one around to do so."[40] Kennedy quickly ordered the missiles in Turkey to be defused to prevent any accidental firing, shocking some military leaders, who believed that he "had cracked and folded."

In fact, Kennedy had reason to be concerned. On that same day, the twenty-seventh, a U-2 flight, apparently involved in a routine air-sampling nuclear detection mission for the Atomic Energy Commission, inadvertently flew over Soviet air space in northeastern Siberia. Russian aircraft chased it in hot pursuit as the pilot scrambled back on course. American fighter planes soon arrived to escort the U-2 to Alaska, and a confrontation was narrowly averted. Given the United States' full military-alert status, Moscow might have interpreted this incident as a prelude to a bombing attack or more likely as a crass reminder of American strategic superiority. In any case, both U-2 incidents further illustrated how little control governments have in a crisis. It is no wonder that Kennedy sought to lead ExComm to a diplomatic solution.

That same afternoon, Scali again met with Fomin to determine why Khrushchev had sent the second message. Fomin insisted that it represented nothing new in light of Lippmann's proposal in the *Post*. Scali responded that a missile deal was unacceptable but that a solution was urgent. ExComm finally settled on the "Trollope Ploy" in responding to Khrushchev, the term referring to the Victorian novelist Anthony Trollope, whose standard scene included a young man with no marital intentions but who nevertheless makes some imprudent gesture—a squeeze of the hand, perhaps—which the young lady chooses to interpret as a marriage proposal. Participants and scholars have customarily credited Robert Kennedy for the analogous proposal: The United States would seize upon the "offer" contained in Khrushchev's first letter and the Scali-Fomin exchange while ignoring the requisite stipulations for a missile trade in the second dispatch. The 1987 release of the 27 October ExComm transcript reveals, however, that others first suggested the ploy, including Thompson, Sorensen, and Edward Martin.[41] Robert Kennedy developed it more forcefully during a key moment in the discussions, enabling him and Sorensen to formulate the message.

The president's letter, transmitted to Khrushchev at 8:00 P.M. on the twenty-seventh, emphasized that the first requirement for a solution remained the dismantling of the missile sites and the removal of the offensive weapons under UN supervision; in return the United States would terminate the blockade and promise not to invade Cuba. The only reference to the second letter came in a willingness to explore "other armaments" issues once tensions eased. Following an ExComm discussion, Kennedy instructed his brother that evening to give Dobrynin a copy of the letter with a message. What the attorney general said is steeped in controversy; he, Khrushchev, and Gromyko left differing accounts of the meeting. What seems certain is that Kennedy did review the contents of the letter and suggested the urgency of a prompt acceptance. He reinforced Soviet perceptions by saying, according to the Soviet version, that "the Pentagon was exerting strong pressure on his brother" over the destruction of the U-2 and that the president was barely resisting "highly placed generals" with "stupid heads who were always eager for a fight." Kennedy urged that the bases be removed by the next day; otherwise, the United States would "remove" the missiles. "This was not an ultimatum," he insisted, but "just a statement of fact." Khrushchev's *Memoirs* described the young Kennedy as exhausted—"one could see from his eyes that he had not slept for days."[42]

Dobrynin raised the matter of a Turkish missile swap, and the attorney general seemed prepared for such an eventuality. The matter had been discussed outside of the divided ExComm in the Oval Office where the president, Robert, and four other advisers had agreed beforehand that the attorney general should notify Dobrynin of the proposed eventual withdrawal of the Jupiters. President Kennedy, of course, had earlier leaned toward a trade, provided that it came at the right stage in the negotiations and in a way that would not embarrass the administration. The attorney general explained to Dobrynin that the missiles would be removed in four or five months—a pledge that many ExComm members knew nothing about until the publication of Robert Kennedy's memoirs in 1969. That posthumous work, edited by Sorensen, actually underplayed the extent to which the Jupiters had become such an integral part of the understanding.[43] As it turned out President Kennedy had made a secret arrangement—potentially a politically embarrassing and dangerous maneuver—without the knowledge of Congress, the American people, and the NATO Allies. So anxious was the president to avert escalation that he remained willing to explore all avenues for settlement so as not to force Khrushchev into a corner.

No administration official expressed much optimism that Khrushchev would accept the proposal. Sorensen called that Saturday evening's ExComm session "rancorous." The discussion centered mostly on a proposed response to a possible Soviet rejection. The hawks, again claiming that the blockade had failed, pushed for an air strike no later than Tuesday morning, followed by a possible invasion. In a rare humorous moment, one person recommended that the attorney general become mayor of Havana afterward. Everyone felt considerable urgency, as Soviet technicians were working around the clock in an effort to make the missiles operational. Most ExComm members anticipated too that nuclear warheads had reached the island. Sorensen later admitted that the proponents for the air strike were gaining influence.

What Kennedy might have done in the event of a negative reply remains uncertain. On the one hand he faced mounting pressures to unleash the military; on the other hand the evidence suggests that he would have resisted escalation. On Saturday morning, in reference to *The Guns of August*, he stated to his brother that he would avoid "a course which will allow anyone to write a comparable book about . . . 'The Missiles of October.' "[44] An air strike would have invited escalation, jeopardized the OAS consensus in behalf of the quarantine, and created problems at the UN. Consequently, McNamara, Sorensen, Schlesinger, and Rusk maintain that Kennedy would have pursued alternative approaches. The tightening of the quarantine to include petroleum, oil, and lubricants remained a possible option. This solution, however, probably would have prolonged the crisis indefinitely, leading to greater pressure for military action. Furthermore, the longer the missiles remained in Cuba, the more difficult it would have been to remove them.

In 1987 Dean Rusk revealed another option that Kennedy had seriously considered on 27 October. The president in fact directed Rusk to ask Andrew Cordier, the former UN parliamentarian and a friend of Rusk's, to serve as a potential intermediary with U Thant. Kennedy proposed that, whenever he gave the word, Cordier would ask the UN secretary general to summon both powers to withdraw their missiles from Turkey and Cuba.[45] Kennedy assumed that if the initiative came from the UN, rather than from himself, Americans would find it more palatable. Even though the Cordier ploy never surfaced, it did indicate that Kennedy had seriously considered taking the heat on Capitol Hill instead of having the crisis run into the third week. By involving Rusk so directly, he also showed a lingering trust in his beleaguered secretary of state.

Khrushchev resolved the controversy by responding early Sunday —one of the most beautiful mornings of that fall. He announced that he accepted the Kennedy proposal of the twenty-seventh, requiring the Soviets to withdraw the missiles from Cuba. Unmentioned, of course, was the Kennedy pledge relating to the Turkish missiles, which the president removed by April 1963. Khrushchev had moved quickly, Soviet scholars later explained, because he had lacked "an *effective* alternative." Castro's alleged urging that Khrushchev unleash the missiles against the United States on the twenty-sixth might have further convinced Khrushchev that those weapons must come out.[46] Fear had become a driving force, also affecting the Kennedys and most of the others who shared in the decisions. Exceptions existed, however. When Kennedy invited the JCS to the White House to inform them of Khrushchev's letter and to thank them for their support, "there was one hell of a scene." According to McNamara, General Curtis LeMay came out saying, "We lost! We ought to just go in there today and knock them off!"[47]

Still, Khrushchev's public letter brought immeasurable relief to most participants. Even though ExComm members took to heart Kennedy's admonition not to gloat, for most there developed a sense of pride in their successful ordeal. Kennedy confirmed this feeling by giving to each a small, silver-plated, engraved calendar of October 1962, mounted on wood, with the dates from the sixteenth to the twenty-eighth heavily outlined. Privately that Sunday night, obviously thinking of Lincoln, he remarked to his brother, "Perhaps this is the night I should go to the theatre."

The crisis did fester following Khrushchev's letter, however. An embittered Castro, reacting to a perceived Soviet betrayal, adamantly resisted UN supervision of the missile withdrawal, and opposed continued American air reconnaissance of Cuba as a violation of Cuban air space. He balked especially on the removal of the other offensive weapons, particularly the IL-28 bombers, which the Soviets had also provided to Indonesia and Eygpt without fanfare. As a result, Khrushchev, seeking a face-saving accommodation, sought United States concessions on verification and the removal of other offensive weapons—e.g., the bombers and the torpedo boats—which had not provoked the missile crisis. The tedious negotiations took place mostly in New York, involving Stevenson and John McCloy and their Soviet counterparts. At the same time the quarantine continued as ExComm considered stronger action. Taylor, representing the JCS, favored bombing Cuban airfields.

Kennedy gave ground on UN inspection and verification after receiving Soviet assurances that the latter could occur through continued American air surveillance and the displaying of missiles on board departing Russian ships. This procedure led to groundless charges that the Soviets had duped the administration by storing missiles in Cuban caves. On related issues Kennedy was unyielding; he insisted on the removal of other offensive weapons as well as the Soviet forces. Thus special envoy Anastas Mikoyan spent twenty-two days in Havana before getting Castro's reluctant approval to release the Soviet bombers—the key issue. Finally on 20 November Khrushchev informed the president that the obsolete IL-28s would be removed in thirty days. On the twentieth the United States ended the quarantine. By early 1963 the Soviets had evacuated most of their troops, the remainder of which would precipitate a minicrisis in 1979 when Americans suddenly rediscovered them. Interestingly, the United States did not suspend the Mongoose covert operation until 20 October 1962, after Robert Kennedy had heard of its continuance. The United States, however, refused to confirm its pledge not to invade Cuba in light of Castro's rejection of UN verification.

In retrospect the Cuban missile crisis represented an "unwise, unwarranted, and unnecessary" showdown—words that Sorensen himself employed on its twenty-fifth anniversary.[48] It began because of the provocative behavior of both sides—including the Kennedy vendetta against Castro and Khrushchev's foolhardy attempt to place nuclear missiles ninety miles from Florida's shores. Both nations lacked sensitivity to the other's position. Although Khrushchev foolishly believed that Kennedy could be forced to accept the missiles, Kennedy seemed unaware that he might have invited the nuclear hardware through the Mongoose operation and the extensive strategic nuclear buildup. Moreover, both sides reverted to deception during the critical early days of the crisis when communication could have made all the difference. Whether Kennedy could have successfully employed private negotiations instead of a provocative coercive approach seems less certain. But would it have involved any greater national risk than raising the specter of a nuclear encounter?

Ultimately the responsible leadership of both Kennedy and Khrushchev prevented the crisis from spinning dangerously out of control. Both in effect blinked. They came to appreciate the symmetry of their circumstances as they "stare[d] down the gun barrel of nuclear war" together. Khrushchev dramatically described this as the moment when the "smell of scorching hung in the air." He and Kennedy, wrote Graham Allison, "were equally yoked with responsibility for irreparable consequences . . . ; [both] were partners in a game against nuclear disaster."[49] Consequently, they both rejected hardliners in their respective Ex-Comms. What made Kennedy's position different, however, was the fact that the comparative nuclear and moral positions rested in his favor. Even so, he proceeded cautiously, suggesting that a variance in nuclear superiority can be meaningless in a showdown. He realized that in any crisis "a little nuclear deterrence goes a long way."[50]

Few Americans at the time comprehended the extent of the United States' nuclear domination, nor were they aware of Kennedy's circumspection once the crisis intensified, leading to subsequent charges that the administration had exaggerated the dangers of a nuclear encounter. Dean Acheson spoke for many hardliners when he later recalled, "I felt we were too eager to liquidate this thing. So long as we had the thumbscrew on Khrushchev, we should have given it another turn every day."[51]

Nonetheless, Kennedy emerged from the crisis in a stronger political position. Because of his vigorous campaigning and handling of the situation, many thought him instrumental in his party's success in the mid-term elections even though all indications are that local issues and incumbency were the determining considerations. Not since his early presidency had he been as popular; in a December Gallup survey, he headed the list of most admired men. Public opinion polls registered his approval rating at around 75 percent, and journalists compared him to Wilson and Roosevelt. Virtually all newspapers—Republican ones included—praised him, the *New York Herald Tribune* typically expressing a national pride for his reestablishing the Monroe Doctrine. Journalists and scholars also extolled the valuable lessons in crisis management that Kennedy's actions would teach future presidents. Much less was said about how to avoid crises.

American-Soviet relations improved afterward, an indication that both leaders realized that they bore a responsibility to prevent subsequent crises. Cuba had generated a grudging mutual respect as both men grappled with long-standing differences. Within a year they agreed to institute a hot-line teletype link to provide private, almost instantaneous communication between the White House and the Kremlin. Khrushchev also ended pressure against West Berlin. In September 1963 both countries consented to a UN resolution banning nuclear and other weapons of mass destruction in outer space, and they also agreed to a mutually benefiting 65-million-bushel sale of American wheat. One month earlier, they had signed the limited nuclear test ban agreement.

The test ban treaty, though one of Kennedy's most satisfying achievements, represented a comparatively modest success, a hopeful symbol of future advancement in disarmament. In the past both sides had professed a strong commitment to nuclear weapons reduction but each had contributed to the lack of progress: Khrushchev by resuming atomic testing in fall 1961 and Kennedy by his early nuclear buildup and subsequent test resumption. The president's approach of "arm to parley" seemed to have failed. In pursuing a comprehensive test ban, both nations floundered over procedural and substantive matters, the most important of which remained on-site inspections, with Khrushchev favoring no more than three annually and the United States between eight and ten. While Khrushchev's hardliners thought multiple inspections a cloak for espionage, Kennedy faced the resistance of advisers unwilling to trust the Russians. Nothing better illustrated the limitations of an emerging détente.

Several factors made an agreement possible by 1963, not the least of which was the frightening impact of the Cuban missile crisis. Public opinion in this country strongly favored a ban initiative. Too, Kennedy and Khrushchev believed that China was on the verge of atomic testing; each had his own reasons for being concerned. Finally, Kennedy's willingness to permit underground testing made on-site inspection unnecessary. Kennedy discussed the importance of a test ban agreement in perhaps his most significant foreign policy speech, delivered at American University on 10 June 1963, one day before his eloquent civil rights message on national TV. The commencement address reflected the improving Soviet-American relations as well as furthered détente. Calling it "the best speech of any American president since Roosevelt," Khrushchev promoted it throughout the Soviet Union by ending the jamming of Voice of America broadcasts. The responsive chord Kennedy struck related to his desire for "genuine" peace—"not a Pax Americana enforced on the world by American weapons of war." Most important, he asked for a reexamination of American attitudes toward the cold war and the Soviet Union. He recognized what other presidents publicly had refused to—that "no nation . . . ever suffered more than the Soviet Union suffered" during World War II, which included the loss of twenty million Russian lives and the virtual destruction of the country's industrial base.

While acknowledging existing cold war realities, he called for cooperation in areas of convergent interests, particularly the armaments race, which inflicted heavy financial burdens on both nations. Kennedy promised that the United States would avoid atmospheric testing as long as other countries did likewise. He also announced the approaching meeting in Moscow involving the United States, the Soviet Union, and Great Britain to pursue a comprehensive test ban treaty, hopefully the first stage toward disarmament. Kennedy concealed his tremendous concern that by the 1970s some twenty nations might have nuclear capability, placing the world in even greater peril. Nothing bothered him more than the prospects of China becoming an atomic threat; as did most Americans, he thought the Chinese more hostile and much less reasonable than the Soviets. According to Glenn Seaborg, Kennedy's chairman of the Atomic Energy Commission, the fear of China's pending nuclear program became the president's "principal driving force" for instituting a test ban.[52] Kennedy believed that such an agreement might even aggravate the worsening Soviet-Chinese rift.

To emphasize the importance of the July Moscow meeting, Kennedy selected the venerable Averell Harriman, a long-time favorite of Soviet officials, to head the U.S. delegation. Harriman's appointment sent a signal to Moscow of Kennedy's seriousness about an accord. Still, the president remained in charge; he monitored the discussions in Moscow and cleared all messages to the American delegation. At the same time, Harriman's instructions were broadly stated, in order to take advantage of his experience and skill. Kennedy still desired a comprehensive ban; but if that proved impossible, he had authorized Harriman to pursue a test prohibition in the atmosphere, water, and space. The latter proposal indicated Kennedy's concerns about the environment and big-power cooperation.

Neither side obtained all that it wanted. Khrushchev failed to secure a nonaggression treaty between NATO and the Warsaw Pact, a previous Soviet precondition to an agreement. He relented after the United States failed to win French and West German approval. Nor did Kennedy succeed in checking China's nuclear ambitions, for China contemptuously rejected the treaty, and the Soviets refused to commit themselves to any proposed joint action to combat Chinese nuclear development. According to Gordon Chang, the Kennedy administration even considered a joint attack to destroy China's budding nuclear program.[53]

The three delegations reached a preliminary settlement on 26 July, following eleven days of intense negotiations. Afterward Kennedy maneuvered it carefully through the Senate. The "Treaty Banning Nuclear Weapons Tests in the Atmosphere, in Outer Space, and under Water" prohibited the signatory nations (125 by 1981) from conducting nuclear explosives in the enumerated environments and from abetting others in doing the same. Kennedy called it a "shaft of light in the darkness," even though underground tests and nuclear stockpiling remained a problem. Nonetheless, the treaty seemed a promising first step, and it did intensify the Soviet-Chinese rift. Like Kennedy, Khrushchev, anxious for greater expenditures on pressing domestic needs, expressed hope that the agreement would lead to the resolution of other questions. It never came during their tenure, but both the Treaty of Nonproliferation of Nuclear Weapons (NPT) of 1969 and the Strategic Arms Limitation Treaty (SALT) of 1972 represented belated legacies of their work.

Scholars and associates friendly to Kennedy have often noted how he sought to lessen cold war differences in the last year of his life. Had he lived, they contended, a détente would surely have become a significant reality. Richard Goodwin recently reiterated that point of view in assessing the dramatic impact of the missile crisis on Kennedy:

> Whatever John Kennedy felt he had to prove—determination, courage, will, the skillful use of power—he had proved it: to the world, to the country, and to himself. Like some fever that reaches its life-threatening height as the night moves toward dawn, and then begins to break, the

Cold War had mounted toward its moment of final agony, hovered for a fear-filled moment, and then had begun to recede. Never again would John Kennedy use the fierce rhetoric of the dedicated Cold Warrior.[54]

That argument exudes a certain charm, but it exaggerates both the changes in Kennedy and in East-West relations. In reality Kennedy pursued an ambiguous course to the end. Less than two weeks after his American University speech, he embarked on a European tour that took him to West Berlin. Hailed as the savior of Germany and speaking in the shadow of the Berlin Wall on 26 June, he exclaimed to an enormous and aroused crowd, "There are many people . . . who really don't understand . . . what is the great issue between the free world and the Communist world. Let them come to Berlin. There are some who say that Communism is the wave of the future. Let them come to Berlin. And there are some who say . . . we can work with the Communists. Let them come to Berlin." His comments dismayed some members of his entourage, as well as Khrushchev, who noted that Kennedy's remarks seemed to have been delivered by "quite a different person" from the one who had spoken at American University. Such contradictions seemingly reflected the hyperbole of a master politician. In speeches at home as well, he occasionally invoked the language of the cold war with expedient political effect. In one of his last prepared addresses, scheduled for delivery in Dallas on 22 November, he railed against international communism.

Kennedy's messages and actions regarding Castro also remained mixed. He indeed entertained the possibility of resuming relations with Cuba in 1963, provided that Castro end his submission to external communism and his subversive activities in other Latin American countries. And as Goodwin contends, unofficial low-level discussions transpired, even though little was expected on the eve of an election year. Four days after Christmas 1962 at the Orange Bowl in Miami, however, Kennedy had greeted the Bay of Pigs Brigade by promising that its battle flag would fly over "a free Havana." More significantly, by spring 1963, with or without the Kennedys' knowledge, the CIA reinstituted the secret war against the Castro regime. The agency also recruited a supposedly traitorous Cuban official (a possible double agent), Rolando Cubela Secades, and under the code name of AM/LASH, it again foolishly sought to assassinate Castro. On the day of Kennedy's own assassination, an agency operative claiming to be Robert Kennedy's "personal representative" promised Cubela whatever he needed.[55]

The arms race also continued into 1963. McNamara, anticipating a Soviet buildup, informed the Senate Foreign Relations Committee in August that the administration intended to increase its ICBM strength to seventeen hundred by 1966. The Soviet Union indeed embarked on its own missile program as a reaction to Kennedy's 1961 buildup and the Cuban missile crisis. The latter had caused Soviet diplomat Vasily Kuznetzov to remark to McCloy at the time of the missile evacuation from Cuba, "You Americans will never be able to do this to us again."[56] By 1970 the Soviet Union would reach rough parity with the United States.

Both countries also faced an increasingly multipolar world by 1963. China and some Eastern bloc countries were challenging Soviet authority. Khrushchev also failed to win Western approval of his nonaggression pact, which could have solidified his position in East Germany and Eastern Europe. The Soviet chairman moreover received criticism within his own government for the failed gambit in Cuba and for his unsuccessful domestic policies, leading to his deposal by 1964.

Kennedy's most serious alliance problem continued to be with de Gaulle, whose independent, nationalistic tendencies accelerated after the United States failed to confide in him during the missile crisis. Eleven weeks afterward he blocked Great Britain's entry into the Common Market. Additionally, he evaluated the United States' continued reliance on limited, conventional forces in Europe as a disinclination to share in the risks. To de Gaulle a limited war "would be limited to Europe[,] and the Americans and Russians could destroy each other's proxies without damage to themselves."[57] By 1966 de Gaulle would withdraw French forces from NATO and order NATO installations and troops removed from France; he also cultivated a kindred spirit in West Germany, which had its own policy differences with the United States.

Adenauer, never comfortable with the youthful Kennedy, remained suspicious that the American president would make his own accommodation with Khrushchev at the expense of German interests. Adenauer too questioned containing the Soviets with conventional forces, since war would most likely occur on German soil; nor were the Germans pleased with the United States' controlling NATO's nuclear arsenal. Differences even momentarily arose with Great Britain after Kennedy sought to eliminate that country's independent nuclear deterrent in favor of a multilateral NATO force dominated by the United States. Meanwhile, at home Democratic Senator Wayne Morse of Oregon led a senatorial attack on the costly NATO commitment, arguing that it had outlived its usefulness. On the eve of Kennedy's death, NATO seemed to teeter on the brink of disintegration. So too did Kennedy's "Grand Design," which strove to make Western Europe a more unified, faithful ally. In 1963 conflicts in Third World countries, particularly in the Congo and Vietnam, also worsened, causing Kennedy to concentrate more on those troubled areas.

9

★ ★ ★ ★ ★

THE THIRD WORLD

While traveling in Africa following the 1960 election, Democratic Senator Frank Church of Idaho and his entourage often heard the chanting of "Kennedy, Kennedy." Africans thought Kennedy a champion of Third World nationalism because of his well-publicized denunciations of French colonialism. Nationalists everywhere had reason to await his presidency with hopeful anticipation, for since the mid-1950s he had referred to the United States' tragic failure to respond to Afro-Asian nationalism. Indeed, Kennedy understood clearly what Harold Macmillan would soon call the "winds of change."

Kennedy's criticism centered on the Eisenhower-Dulles foreign policy, which had undergirded European colonialism and had judged Third World nations unfriendly because of their nonalignment. Especially reprehensible was the denial of foreign aid to countries that supposedly did not serve American interests. Kennedy also opposed Eisenhower's emphasis on military assistance, which ignored the developmental needs of emerging nations and contributed to the negative images of the United States in the Third World. The phenomenal popularity of William Lederer and Eugene Burdick's *The Ugly American* (1958) further confirmed his impressions.

During the 1960 campaign Kennedy referred to Africa nearly five hundred times. He concentrated on that continent because of the seventeen black nations that had won independence there in 1960, knowing that others would soon follow and believing that this would have a profound impact on voting patterns in the United Nations. Hence he called for a reorientation of policy to uphold the rising tide of African nationalism, promising substantial increases in economic assistance and a commitment to make the UN the central instrument in promoting the needs of Africa. Yet Kennedy said virtually nothing about Vietnam, a country destined to become his most frustrating Third World challenge. To him and many other knowledgeable Americans in 1960, South Vietnam seemed relatively stable and secure. He was far more sensitive to the conflict in Laos and to the economic wants of India.

In dealing with Latin America, Kennedy called for a dramatic new foreign policy—an Alliance for Progress—to meet the social and economic needs of a suppressed people on the brink of revolution. His proposed Peace Corps further revealed a concern for Latin America and other Third World areas. All of this he reaffirmed in an inaugural address that pledged to help the struggling masses everywhere. He professed that it mattered little whether new states always agreed with America; what mattered was that they supported their own freedom. Thus in Wilsonian terms he sought to make the world safe for diversity, an expression that he later used in his presidency.

Liberals such as Chester Bowles, Harris Wofford, G. Mennen Williams, and John Kenneth Galbraith anxiously awaited the long-needed changes; Bowles even anticipated the United States' favoring the entry of Communist China into the UN. These liberals understood, however, that changes in foreign policy should serve cold war objectives, including the resisting of Soviet inroads into the Third World. They rightly viewed Kennedy as an enlightened anti-Communist who comprehended the strategic importance of embracing Afro-Asian nationalism, an approach that proved invaluable in capturing the black and liberal vote in the 1960 campaign. After his election Kennedy became more conservative and cautious. He learned quickly that cold war exigencies sometimes would conflict with his desire to defend the revolutionary aspirations of emerging nations.

The New Frontier's greatest imprint came in Africa. It began with the appointment of Williams as assistant secretary for African affairs and Wayne Fredericks as his deputy and the selection of Bowles as undersecretary of state. All three believed that the United States must evaluate issues in Africa according to what was best for Africans—and overall U.S. policy. Dean Acheson and other establishmentarians considered this approach a betrayal of the United States' NATO partnership; the reassessment also precipitated a division in the State Department between the European and African desks, which Secretary of State Dean Rusk failed to resolve, due to his own ambivalence. For the most part

Kennedy defended the Africanists. When Williams faced rebuke for stating that Africa was for the Africans, Kennedy responded in a press conference that he did not "know who else Africa should be for." Unlike Eisenhower, Kennedy also went out of his way to meet with African leaders and to learn enough about their countries to respond to their concerns. In 1961 he received eleven African leaders at the White House, ten in 1962, and seven in 1963. Some valued him as a personal friend and wrote to him frequently. Although he never visited Africa, Kennedy sent his brothers, Robert and Edward, his brother-in-law Sargent Shriver, and Vice-President Lyndon Johnson there on diplomatic missions to underscore the importance of that continent.

Kennedy also approved an exceptionally capable array of ambassadors to African nations, many of them recommended by Bowles. He insisted that whenever possible ambassadors should be appointed who spoke the language of the country (French for many African nations). He permitted the bypassing of the stodgy Foreign Service, where a neocolonialist mentality prevailed. Younger people were selected, many from outside the government, who had experience in politics and empathy for the host nation and who usually shared Kennedy's impatient contempt for the slow-moving State Department. They included John S. Badeau, the former president of the American University in Cairo, who went to Eygpt; journalist William Attwood of *Look* magazine, to Guinea; Edmund Gullion, who taught Kennedy much about nationalism during the 1950s, to the Congo (now Zaire); and Philip Kaiser, a former Truman appointee, to Senegal. They and their staffs were encouraged to leave the embassy compounds and mingle with the people.

Moreover, Kennedy appreciably increased economic assistance to African nations. The Food for Peace program and the Peace Corps served significant roles; Agency for International Development (AID) loans virtually doubled over a two-year period. Yet nation-building necessitated more economic assistance and bureaucratic efficiency than the administration could manage. Wofford complained in early 1962 that in Togo the ambassador's aid proposals had not yet been acted on by AID after months of delay. Similar complaints from other countries caused Kennedy to change AID directors. More significantly, Wofford pleaded that Africa required an "enlarged, concentrated support" comparable to the Alliance for Progress commitment in Latin America. This included "a massive program of education on all levels — campaigns to end illiteracy, the construction of schools, the training of teachers, the expansion of universities."[1] Congress, however, refused to grant authority for long-term development and reacted to Kennedy's more liberal approach to foreign aid by slashing annual appropriation requests. In 1963 Congress pruned the AID budget from $4.9 billion to $3.2 billion, the lowest amount of foreign aid provided since 1958.

Troubled by crises elsewhere, President Kennedy concentrated on only the most pressing African-related issues. None plagued him more than the Congo, a country in turmoil for much of his presidency. In January 1961 he viewed that central African nation as one of his four major foreign problems. Belgium had acceded to Congolese independence in June 1960 without laying the foundation for self-rule. The Congolese Republic had only twenty college graduates at the time and no control of its prosperous mining industry in Katanga province, which remained in the hands of Belgian technicians and administrators. Without this economic source, the republic seemed doomed. Moreover, political disarray and civil disorder had broken out, including a Congolese army rebellion against Belgian officers; the pillaging of the Belgian community, resulting in the sending of Belgian paratroopers; the secession of Katanga province led by Moise Tshombe, the pro-Belgian provincial president; and a rift between Congolese President Joseph Kasavubu and Premier Patrice Lumumba.

On the eve of the Kennedy presidency, the UN had responded to the Congo's request to restore order by sending troops. This had followed Lumumba's unsuccessful appeal to the Eisenhower administration for military forces and his feeler to Khrushchev for assistance, resulting in the Soviets' sending a small quantity of equipment and technicians. Lumumba's latter action caused the Eisenhower administration to label him as an unstable Communist, despite the Third World image of Lumumba as a popular hero. At any rate, reportedly with CIA and Belgian assistance, Col. Joseph Mobutu placed Lumumba under house arrest following a coup, which forced the evacuation of most of the Soviets.

As Kennedy assumed the presidency, chaos in the Congo continued, involving three major factions: the Kasavubu-Mobutu government in Leopoldville; Stanleyville's radical Antoine Gizenga–Lumumba group; and the conservative Tshombe regime at Elisabethville. Like Eisenhower, Kennedy sought the ending of internal strife, which could only serve the Soviet interests. He was more willing, however, to have the UN play a stronger role in the Congo to impose order; the greater the UN presence, he thought, the less the superpowers would be involved. Kennedy understood that his commitment to African nationalism would be evaluated according to his response to the situation in the Congo. Consequently, in going beyond his predecessor, he called for a coalition government that included the Gizenga-Lumumba faction and the release of all political prisoners, without mentioning Lumumba by name. He questioned too the Eisenhower administration's favorable view of Katanga's separation, to Kennedy a vestige of Belgian colonialism and an obstacle to Congolese independence.

Kennedy found the problems in the Congo to be virtually unresolvable. His frustration began in February 1961 when the outside world finally heard of Lumumba's assassination on 17 January by Katanga authorities, with probable CIA involvement.[2] African nationalists damned Kennedy for having failed to demand Lumumba's immediate release. The Soviets, hoping to capitalize, called for UN Secretary General Dag Hammarskjöld's resignation and advocated a triumvirate to replace him. Moreover, the administration's efforts to induce the Congolese parliament to elect trade-unionist Cyrille Adoula as head of a presumably acceptable coalition government failed when the pro-Gizenga faction received unexpectedly large support from Lumumba sympathizers. Only after CIA agents had bribed Congolese delegates could Adoula be elected. Adoula then quickly requested UN forces to reintegrate Katanga, an operation that soon stalled because of the resistance of Tshombe's mercenary troops. Just prior to the secretary general's tragic death in September, Kennedy would also face the strictures of Hammarskjöld for not extending United States military assistance to end Katanga's secession. Memories of the Bay of Pigs and the expected opposition of Belgium's allies, particularly Britain and France, caused him to resist that course of action, especially when he needed their support during the Berlin crisis.

Internal considerations further contributed to Kennedy's difficulties as he received much conflicting advice. The State Department's European desk feared that United States involvement would upset the NATO alliance, yet the department's Africanists advocated immediate military assistance to preserve Congolese independence. Kennedy's refusal to commit caused them to assert privately that he was "as bad as Eisenhower." Making matters worse, Rusk "seemed transfixed by the [supposed pro-Communist] 'Gizenga danger' and largely ignored the menace posed by Katanga." To American conservatives, however, Katanga was hardly a threat; in fact, conservative senators, professors, and writers signed a full-page advertisement in the New York Times describing "Katanga [as] the Hungary of 1961."[3] Katanga had a particular romantic appeal to states-righters like Senator Barry Goldwater (R.-Ariz.). Even some Democrats such as Senator Thomas Dodd of Connecticut (sometimes called the senator of Katanga) thought Katanga a paragon of African capitalism and anticommunism. For understandable reasons, then, Kennedy held to a wait-and-see policy, willingly weathering the political flak of denying Tshombe a visa in early 1962. When journalist Arthur Krock chastised him, Kennedy offered to give Tshombe entry provided that Krock agree to entertain him at the Metropolitan Club.

The gradual weakening of Adoula, who in desperation looked to Moscow for possible military aid, eventually pushed Kennedy into a more active role. The president now began to listen more closely to Ambassador Gullion, UN Ambassador Adlai Stevenson, and Undersecretary of State George Ball, whom he asked to oversee Congolese policy. Ball, a Europeanist who came to fear an American-Soviet clash in the Congo, adamantly contended that the United States must extend military assistance to the UN and massive economic aid to Adoula and must also persuade Britain and Belgium to curtail assistance to Katanga. After Tshombe reneged on a negotiated settlement that Kennedy had approved, the president finally sent a military mission to the Congo in December 1962 to explore aiding UN forces; he continued to extend financial support. Still resisting direct military intervention, he seemed ready to lend the UN aircraft and other needed materiel.

In late December Belgian Foreign Minister Paul-Henri Spaak and the UN had more to do with the resolution of the crisis, however. Spaak, in close contact with Kennedy, courageously endorsed economic sanctions against Tshombe and accepted the UN's decision to crush the Katangan secession. On Christmas eve the Indian-led UN forces, using Swedish air strikes on Katangan military installations, implemented "Operation Grandslam," surprising Kennedy by their speedy successes in terminating Tshombe's independent rule. In assessing the ending of the three-year ordeal, Stevenson called it the UN's finest hour. The same can hardly be said of Kennedy, who nonetheless had exercised considerable restraint. He gambled that the UN would prevail without direct American military intervention—and won. But Kennedy's Congolese policy sent mixed signals to African nationalists. Although he courageously opposed Katanga's independence, he seemed indifferent toward the Congo's ultranationalists. Never did he utter a word of praise for the martyred Patrice Lumumba, a litmus test to militant Africans such as Kwame Nkrumah of Ghana. They understandably believed that Kennedy had embraced nationalism for the purpose of keeping newly emerging nations from succumbing to Soviet influence.

Nkrumah became yet another of Kennedy's problems. At one time the mercurial pan-Africanist believed the president a friend of African nationalism, but the execution of Lumumba swayed Nkrumah against all Americans. As Nkrumah consorted with the Soviet Union and China, Kennedy sought to win him back through the Volta Dam project, a $300 million electrification and aluminum-processing operation, requiring foreign capital. The Eisenhower administration, anxious to improve its relationship with the Third World, had made the first commitment in 1959, two years after Ghana's independence. But by late 1960 Nkrumah's anti-American and pro-Soviet rhetoric, combined with his increasingly totalitarian rule, had caused the Eisenhower administration to identify him as a Communist pawn and administration officials had refused to meet with him. Kennedy's campaign commitment to Africa and his pro-nationalist stance made him more receptive to the Volta project, yet Nkrumah's continued anti-Americanism caused some administration officials to advise against such an obligation. Kennedy nevertheless accepted the advice of Williams and Bowles to receive Nkrumah in Washington as an indication that the new administration tolerated neutralism and political independence. The March 1961 meeting resulted in Nkrumah's toning down his anti-American statements and in Kennedy's agreeing to uphold the Eisenhower promise to fund the Volta project.

Nkrumah returned to a pro-Soviet position, however, as he endorsed the troika proposal in the UN, advocated the diplomatic recognition of Communist China, and denounced United States imperialism in the Congo. At the nonaligned nations' conference at Belgrade in September, he criticized American defense spending and called for total disarmament, but he failed to condemn the Soviet Union for resuming nuclear testing, an omission that angered Kennedy. Moreover, Nkrumah soon indicated that four hundred Ghanaian troops were going to the USSR for training. As a result, the Volta project came under fire in the United States. Even the president's father asked his son, "What in the hell are you doing with that communist Nkrumah?"[4]

Nkrumah's actions also caused administration officials who had favored the loans to recommend a wait-and-see policy. Others, such as Roger Hilsman of the State Department, Treasury Secretary Douglas Dillon, and Robert Kennedy, remained strongly opposed to the assistance, the latter thinking that funding Nkrumah would send the wrong message to friendly African nations. The attorney general alluded to moderate leaders in Africa who wanted the money to be spread out among all needy countries. Additional critics contended that the United States–funded project would represent a windfall for American business interests such as Kaiser Industries, which would receive federal loan guarantees for aluminum production in Ghana. Clearly the tide had turned against the Volta project.

Even so, Kennedy reluctantly decided in its favor at a December NSC meeting, despite feeling the "hot breath" of his brother, who sat immediately behind him. He did so partly because the State Department felt that the United States was obligated in light of the president's pledge to Nkrumah and also because he was reluctant to renounce his well-known promise to the Third World to provide aid without political strings. He became convinced that Léopold Senghor, president of Senegal, represented the majority viewpoint of African nationalists. Senghor, a recent visitor, insisted that the loan arrangement symbolized whether Kennedy really embraced African neutralism. To reject African nationalists such as Senghor and Nkrumah might also result in cold war setbacks in Africa. Who could forget the repercussions of John Foster Dulles's reneging on American funding of the Aswan Dam project in Egypt in 1956? The Kennedy administration therefore extended a $37 million loan to Ghana and advanced loans of $96 million and investment guarantees of $54 million to an American business consortium.

As Thomas Noer contends, Kennedy's commitment to African neutralism came with conditions in spite of previous promises not to attach strings to economic aid. Partly out of domestic political considerations, administration officials in fact pressured Nkrumah to endorse political freedom and private enterprise and to pledge never to expropriate American investments in Ghana. They reminded Nkrumah that United States law compelled that such assistance go "only to nations which are free and nations which are friendly."[5] Only after Nkrumah complied did Kennedy release the funds; the Volta Dam controversy clearly revealed limitations regarding Kennedy's tolerance of Third World neutrality. At the same time his see-saw relationship with Nkrumah continued, resulting finally in a United States moral victory. During the Cuban missile crisis Nkrumah refused to give Soviet aircraft landing rights to refuel. In 1963 Nkrumah drew even closer after Kennedy's June civil rights speech during the University of Alabama desegregation controversy. The film of that address received a thunderous response during its many showings throughout Ghana.

Kennedy faced as great a test in Angola, a Portuguese colony in West Africa. Under the despot António Salazar, Portugal continued to ignore the nationalistic aspirations of Africans. Angola was already rebelling against Portuguese control, but Portugal still expected continued American acquiescence to Portuguese rule in the interests of Western unity. However, the new administration changed that traditional assumption, as Kennedy had promised to do. In March 1961, under the leadership of Stevenson, the United States endorsed a UN resolution calling for self-determination in Angola; other United States–supported resolutions against Portugal soon passed. The administration also attempted to restrict armaments to Portugal after determining that napalm and other materiel were being used against Angolan rebels. The CIA even extended a six-thousand dollar retainer to Holden Roberto, the leading Angolan nationalist, as the American government unsuccessfully leaned on Salazar to reassess four hundred years of policy. A botched putsch then followed, which the United States apparently encouraged.

Kennedy's Angolan policy spawned opposition at home and abroad. Acheson, the protagonist in Washington, contended in an April NSC meeting that "one cannot expect an alliance to hold together strongly when the leader of [NATO] is taking actions which members . . . think are directly hostile to their interests."[6] He directed much of his ire against Stevenson's UN office in New York, which he called the "Department of emotion." As on other African matters Kennedy found a divided State Department, with Rusk more sympathetic to NATO considerations.

Concern over the possible loss of United States military bases in the Azores Islands further called Kennedy's pro-Angolan policy into question. In 1962 the lease on the Portuguese base was to expire. Instead of yielding to self-determination in Africa, Salazar suggested that the United States would lose the Azores if it continued its opposition, causing a furor on Capitol Hill and at the Pentagon and intensifying Britain's and France's disapproval of Kennedy's new African policy. Kennedy soon began to waver. Despite Galbraith's assertion that "we are trading in our African policy for a few acres of asphalt in the Atlantic" and Bowles's reminder that Portugal, by providing bases, served NATO and not the United States alone, Africanists in the State Department faced frustration by 1962.[7] In abstaining on two resolutions involving Portugal, the United States reversed itself in the United Nations. On one occasion Kennedy told Stevenson "to sit back and let others take the lead."[8] Undoubtedly the missile crisis and the desire to win Allied support for the nuclear test ban treaty also forced Kennedy to yield. The lease agreement expired at the end of 1962, with the United States uneasily remaining in the Azores on a day-to-day basis. In 1963 the United States continued to explore diplomatic solutions with little results; once again cold war considerations had intervened to hurt the president's African policy.

Kennedy had even less success in dealing with apartheid in South Africa, where a white population of less than 20 percent brutally segregated and suppressed blacks. As had every American president since Truman, Kennedy denounced apartheid. Yet he refused to take significant action, partly because of the urgings of Rusk and others who recognized that the United States traded more with South Africa than any other African nation, depended on its valuable minerals including diamonds, gold, and manganese, and had strategic territorial arrangements with that country. Rusk also persuaded Kennedy that "excessive pressure" might lead to racial war and possible "communist infiltration."[9] Consequently, despite the recommendations of Williams and Bowles, economic sanctions were out, nor would the United States support a Security Council resolution calling for a total arms embargo or for South Africa's expulsion. Instead, by 1963, pressured by civil rights activists at home and by African nationalists, Kennedy announced a unilateral arms embargo to go into effect on 1 January 1964. The American action, however, contained an escape clause and permitted the purchase of spare military parts; as a result, Kennedy's largely symbolic gestures had no effect on South Africa's racial policies. Ironically, during Kennedy's presidency the South African government imprisoned Nelson Mandela, the head of the outlawed African National Congress, and other black leaders who had sharpened their protest activities.

The South African and Angolan experiences disclosed the disparity between Kennedy's rhetoric and his performance, yet he did more than the presidents who immediately preceded and followed him. According to Richard Mahoney, Kennedy "did succeed in identifying nationalism as the central reality of his age."[10] Whatever failures existed were rooted in the dichotomy of the cold war, which made it virtually impossible for the United States always to overturn past policies.

The president also faced difficulties in the Middle East, where he sought to channel Arab nationalism into constructive directions. The obstacles included an Arab-Israeli conflict, which had led to intermittent warfare ever since Israel's independence in 1948, the Soviet Union's own efforts to exert influence in the Middle East, and the complacent policies of pro-Western autocratic regimes such as Saudi Arabia and Jordan. At the same time, Kennedy was committed to assuring Israel's right to exist and was especially sensitive to this in light of the strong American Jewish vote he had received in the 1960 election. He also assumed the obligation of protecting American oil interests, particularly in Saudi Arabia.

Gamal Abdel Nasser became the key to Kennedy's Middle Eastern policy. In 1958 the popular Egyptian leader had created the United Arab Republic (UAR), a federation of Egypt and Syria. By then Nasser had turned against the Eisenhower administration, who thought him a Soviet puppet. As a result of the United States' decision not to fund the Nile River dam project at Aswan, Nasser had drawn closer to the Soviet bloc, which sold him arms and promised financial assistance. By Kennedy's inauguration, the independent Nasser had drifted away from the Soviet Union; in 1961 no Middle East leader was as powerful. He had captivated the nationalistic aspirations of Arabs seeking economic development and freedom from oppressive autocratic regimes and Western colonialism.

Kennedy departed from the Eisenhower policy by establishing closer relations with Nasser. He exchanged friendly notes, promised economic assistance, including a three-year surplus wheat arrangement, and vowed to follow an even-handed policy in the Middle East. He thought

Nasser neither a Castro-like ideologue nor a ruthless dictator but a pragmatist interested in the modernization of his country and in the transformation of the Arab world into an influential neutral force. Kennedy's objectives included a settlement of the Israeli-Arab conflict, the curtailment of Soviet inroads in the Middle East, and the furthering of the image that he embraced economic and political diversity. Nasser, pleased at being treated as an equal, promised to keep the Arab-Israeli conflict in the "icebox."

In summer 1962 the Nasser rapprochement faced a major challenge when the Kennedy administration backed a plan to resolve the Israeli-Arab dispute. The impetus came from Joseph E. Johnson, the American chairman of the UN's Palestine Reconciliation Commission, who proposed the relocation of Arab Palestinians in Israel in return for Arab acceptance of the Jewish state. Assuming that many Palestinians might wish to remain in Arab lands, the plan called for financial compensation for their lost property in Israel. After months of haggling, the main opposition remained Israel, who wanted to restrict appreciably the number of refugees entering the country to avert a fifth-column threat. To induce Israel to accept the plan Kennedy reluctantly consented to sell Hawk surface-to-air missiles to strengthen Israel's defense, following Nasser's own recent purchase of guided missiles from West German sources. Despite the public reaction of several Arab countries that the United States was tilting toward Israel, Nasser withheld criticism even after Israel decided to reject the Johnson plan. Kennedy's efforts to keep Nasser informed undoubtedly contributed to the Egyptian's moderation.

But by October 1962 Nasser's involvement in Yemen, a former British colony south of Saudi Arabia along the mouth of the Red Sea, proved a much greater obstacle to an accord. The Yemeni crisis began after a pro-Nasser revolution had toppled an inept royalist government. Saudi Arabia and Jordan, fearing pro-Nasser revolutions in their own countries, sent aid to the conservative Yemeni resisters, while the UAR dispatched an expeditionary force of seventy thousand to buttress the new radical government. Kennedy interpreted the social upheaval in Yemen as a reaction to that country's failure to modernize and to adopt progressive reforms. Concerned that changes evolve in a peaceful fashion in other Arab states, he encouraged conservative countries such as Saudi Arabia to alter their systems. At the same time, to sustain his rapprochement with Nasser and in an effort to end the conflict in Yemen, Kennedy recognized the new Yemeni government and also proposed that the Saudis and Egyptians withdraw from there.

In the months ahead the Yemeni crisis continued with neither party curtailing its assistance, severely straining the Kennedy administration's relationship with Saudi Arabia and the UAR. Yet Nasser felt the administration's lash more because he bombed Yemeni royalist camps inside Saudi Arabia and continued to inspire radical activity in conservative Arab countries, causing Kennedy increasingly to question Nasser. Kennedy also recognized Great Britain's concerns that the Yemeni conflict would spread to neighboring Aden, where Britain retained a protectorate. Nor could Kennedy ignore congressional criticism of Nasser's increasing anti-American rhetoric or the fact that the Saudis were starting to "squeeze" American oil firms.

By 1963 Kennedy had pragmatically turned toward the conservative Arab camp, the enormous American oil investment in Saudi Arabia probably becoming the major consideration. Neither a radical coup nor continued antagonism there would have served the United States' interests. In return for the Saudis' disengagement from the Yemeni conflict, the United States sent an air defense squadron to Saudi Arabia to deter UAR air activity. Meanwhile, pro-Nasser uprisings in Jordan caused Kennedy to position the Sixth Fleet in the eastern Mediterranean for possible deployment. Pro-Nasser coups had already occurred in Iraq and elsewhere.

With justifiable reason, then, Israel felt threatened in 1963; the danger of radical Arab encirclement caused that government to press the Kennedy administration for more assistance. Not only did Kennedy expedite the delivery of the Hawk missiles but he went beyond any president in assuring Israel's right to exist. In October he promised that the United States "would militarily assist Israel in case of attack." Ultimately, the failure of Kennedy's even-handed policy pushed Nasser closer to the Soviet Union for political and military support and led to additional American military aid to Israel during the Johnson administration. The Six Day War between Israel and its Arab neighbors followed in 1967, resulting in the establishment of the Palestine Liberation Organization, more bloodshed and turmoil, and greater anti-American antagonism in the Arab world.

Latin America posed an even greater challenge for Kennedy. Hostility against the United States had reached an all-time high, as witnessed in the rude reception Vice-President Richard Nixon received in a 1958 South American visit. Many Latinos looked upon the United States as a counterrevolutionary bully who favored right-wing dictatorships and opposed democratic revolutions directed against social and economic injustices. On the other hand, United States citizens focused on Castro, a supposed devil scheming to export communism. Kennedy's Latin American policy was both an idealistic and a practical response to hemispheric social and economic needs and to a perceived Communist danger.

It also reflected Kennedy's conscious effort politically to identify with the successful Democratic party programs of the past. Franklin Roosevelt's Good Neighbor policy was on his mind in 1960 when he talked about going beyond that relationship to a partnership with Latin America—an Alianza para el Progresso (Alliance for Progress). Former New Dealer Adolf Berle, who chaired Kennedy's Latin American task force, bridged the two eras. Berle and others had resorted to the analogy of the Marshall Plan in comparing the United States' postwar recovery and containment successes in Europe with prospective objectives south of the border. In 1960 the Eisenhower administration, in approving a $500 million grant to Latin America and in creating an Inter–American Development Bank, had further helped to lay the foundation for a new Latin American policy. Once again Kennedy would fashion a new approach from past ideas and actions, and his obsession with Castro compelled him to move quickly.

Kennedy formally presented the Alliance for Progress program to Latin American diplomats at the White House on 13 March 1961. He described it as "a vast cooperative effort, unparalleled in magnitude and nobility of purpose, to satisfy the basic needs of the American people for homes, work and land, health and schools." The Alianza had three components: economic assistance, land and tax reform, and political democratization, meaning a commitment to those elements and leaders who supported democratic principles. Reform and democratization represented an idealistic and dramatic effort to alter the political, social, and economic structure of generations; no American president had ever sought such monumental restructuring. The trend toward reform, Kennedy thought, was in his favor with the toppling of ten dictatorships from 1956 to 1960 and with the establishment of governments like Rómulo Betancourt's in Venezuela, a supposed model of progressive democracy. Kennedy envisioned an opportunity to guide change in ways that provided a viable alternative to Castroism.

The financial incentive came at the August 1961 conference at Punta del Este, Uruguay, when former banker Douglas Dillon promised Latin American delegates $1 billion during that first year. The United States government also pledged at least $10 billion of a proposed $20 billion in public and private monies over the next ten years to transform the social and economic landscape. In return recipient countries were expected to institute comprehensive plans to effect changes. Latin American advisers such as Arthur Schlesinger and Richard Goodwin, the twenty-nine-year-old speechwriter who coined the phrase Alliance for Progress, epitomized the hope and idealism that captivated New Frontiersmen, especially during the first year. At a late evening party in Uruguay,

Goodwin even visited with popular Cuban guerrilla leader Ernesto "Che" Guevara; Schlesinger exchanged ideas with Latin American intellectuals. Kennedy also helped to set the mood by visiting Latin American countries in all three years of his presidency, including a 1962 journey to Mexico City, where more than one million people greeted him and his wife.

The Alliance for Progress did improve social and economic conditions somewhat. It ensured the construction of schools, hospitals, roads, low-cost housing, and electrical power plants, yet the Alianza never achieved the comparable popularity of the Peace Corps nor did it meet most of the administration's elementary goals. In later years both Schlesinger and Goodwin blamed the Johnson administration for transforming the reform and democratization emphases to one that focused solely on economic aid. Schlesinger concluded that the alliance "was never really tried" since it only lasted for a thousand days.[11]

But as Schlesinger and Goodwin admitted in later writings, problems had existed from the beginning. First of all, unlike Marshall Plan aid, American assistance often came in the form of loans, not grants. Moreover, from 1961 to 1969 the net disbursement for the $10 billion assistance the United States provided was only $4.8 billion; funds remained in this country to defray Latin American debts. The administration also insisted that some of the money be used to purchase United States commodities at United States prices. Even more of a problem, the enormous population explosion in Latin America prevented the administration from meeting its stated annual per capita economic growth rate of 2.5 percent. Consequently, from 1961 through 1967, even though Latin America grew at a GNP pace of 4.5 percent, the per capita growth rate was less than 2 percent because of population increases. During this same period Latin American countries suffered from the collapse of coffee prices and the resulting balance-of-payment problems.

The Alliance's failings went even deeper, relating to organizational and bureaucratic differences, including the administration's decision to place the Alliance for Progress under the stifling auspices of AID instead of making it an independent agency like the Peace Corps and Food for Peace. As a result, imaginative approaches gave way to bureaucratic tidiness. At the same time, status quo–oriented State Department officials too often worked against Alliance objectives and idealistic New Frontiersmen such as Goodwin, who was forced out as deputy assistant for Inter-American Affairs by mid-1962. Goodwin's State Department departure hurt the Alliance.

To make matters worse, Teodoro Moscoso, the AID deputy for Latin America and overseer of the Alianza, lacked the skills and influence to overcome the obstacles. In 1963 Goodwin expressed to Kennedy his disappointment that a program so "sound in conception and historically right is operating at about one-half effectiveness." The most serious single problem to Goodwin was personnel. "The Alianza," he contended, "has the same troubles as the Washington [baseball] Nats—they don't have the ballplayers. There are, of course, some very good people, but there is also a tremendous amount of mediocrity in high places." Goodwin blamed the failure on the "complete lack of good recruiting effort, impossible personnel procedures, a structure which discourages individual initiative and responsibility, a careerist mentality, and inability to recognize mediocrity when it is seen."[12] He asked Kennedy to appoint Peace Corps administrator Sargent Shriver as head of the Alianza, at least until he could turn the program around. In late 1962 Bowles also recognized that the Alliance was "in urgent need of a success story." The Brazilian Ambassador Roberto Campos added that the program under Kennedy became "highly bureaucratized, extremely timid, and overly conservative. There was," he concluded, "a gap between . . . generous intention and the reticent performance of the administrative machinery."[13]

Faulty assumptions contributed to the disappointments, particularly the heady belief that the United States could will dramatic social and political changes in Latin America. Few questioned the premise that middle-class progressives introducing agrarian land and other reforms would supplant oligarchical regimes. Kennedyites initially placed far too much confidence in that leadership and in the concept of democratic revolution. They overemphasized too the strengths of constitutionalism in a period that saw military leaders topple six popularly elected presidents. Just as importantly, the administration found itself often unable to deal effectively with such problems. In Peru in July 1962 it temporarily broke diplomatic relations and suspended economic aid after a military cabal overthrew a popularly elected government, an approach that finally led to the scheduling of elections for mid-1963. But the administration imposed no such pressures on a military junta in Argentina that overthrew President Arturo Frondizi, most likely because that new government denounced Castro. In 1963 the administration quietly acquiesced in the face of other military coups; none of those new governments failed to receive United States financial assistance. As Theodore Sorensen later contended, Kennedy learned "that the military often represented more competence in administration and more sympathy with the U.S. than any other group."[14]

Not surprisingly, the Kennedy administration wavered on comprehensive social reform—at least when United States holdings were involved. According to Stephen Rabe, the administration ruled out "financing expropriations of land and actually opposed agrarian reform laws."[15] In 1962 Kennedy's response to a Honduran reform that confiscated fallow landholdings, including those of the Standard Oil and United Fruit companies, supports Rabe's assertion; for after listening to corporate complaints, Kennedy persuaded the Honduran president to change the law. In Brazil, too, he reacted adversely to a provincial governor's expropriating a small International Telephone and Telegraph Company utility subsidiary. Instead of having the matter handled in the Brazilian courts, he successfully ordered the State Department in 1962 to pressure the leftist national government to force a rescission.[16]

In the aftermath of the 1962 steel crisis, Kennedy, anxious to mend fences, seemed even more attentive to corporate concerns in Latin America and at the same time became less willing to favor popularly elected left-wing parties. In Chile, for example, the administration opposed Socialist Salvador Allende's Popular Action Front by increasing financial assistance to a conservative regime in an effort to influence the approaching Chilean election. It also came to understand better what Che Guevara referred to as the "intrinsic contradiction" of the alliance: "By encouraging the forces of change and the desire of the masses, you might set loose forces beyond your control, ending in a revolution which would be your enemy."[17] Concern about nationalization of United States corporate holdings and Communist successes indeed had its effect on policy.

Castro remained the administration's obsession in Latin America. By 1962 the United States was consorting with the notorious Duvalier dictatorship of Haiti because of Cuba. It in effect bribed Haiti to obtain the necessary two-thirds votes in the OAS to exclude Castro as well as to impose further economic sanctions against him.[18] The Castro bogey also caused the administration to increase military aid to Latin America by 50 percent and to create an Office of Public Safety in AID to train Latino police officers in mob control and counterinsurgency. Richard Walton alluded to the "terrible irony": "Castro . . . was largely responsible for the birth of the Alianza, yet the attempt to use it against him was largely responsible for its failure."[19] For the most part, the Alliance represents an ambiguous legacy largely because of the administration's unfulfilled and contradictory objectives. What survived was as much a military as an economic aid program; Kennedy had devoted too much attention to Castro and not enough time to the Alliance's lofty goals.

Kennedy's objectives and concerns varied toward Asia. Few countries captivated him more than India, which he viewed as a prospective counterweight against Communist China and as a possible ally. He had criticized Eisenhower for having favored SEATO member Pakistan over nonaligned India. Kennedy wished to strengthen India's "progressive" economic development and democratic system through increased economic assistance without alienating Pakistan, India's principal enemy. He also ambitiously sought an accord between the antagonists by proposing to mediate their differences, including a territorial conflict over Kashmir.

Kennedy nevertheless found Indian Prime Minister Jawaharlal Nehru indifferent and distant, despite more American economic aid. He later called Nehru's November 1961 American stay "a disaster . . . the worst head-of-state visit I have had."[20] Only Kennedy's wife seemed to please the remote prime minister. The situation worsened the following month when Nehru forcibly seized the Portuguese enclave of Goa in western India, inviting United States criticism that India had violated its own principles of nonviolence in international affairs. To Kennedy military force was not the way to alleviate Western colonialism.

China's short-lived attack along India's northern frontier in fall 1962 brought some improvement in United States–Indian relations. Precipitated by disputed territorial claims and other political objectives, China's incursion glaringly exposed India's vulnerability and caused a desperate Nehru to turn temporarily to the United States after the Soviets disappointed him. For the first time, Kennedy decided to send military aid to move Nehru away from nonalignment. This action of course antagonized Pakistan, who felt that Kennedy, in responding to a "minor" military affair, was turning on a loyal ally. The administration's failure to consult Pakistan caused that country to draw closer to China and to view India more suspiciously. At the same time, Kennedy's new policy failed to alter India's traditional nonalignment, despite its more amicable ties with America. All of this revealed several of the administration's misconceptions, including a belief that India could assist United States cold war policies and that America could have friendly ties with both India and Pakistan, resolve regional differences, and reshape relationships in South Asia. Apprehension about Communist China's impact in Asia also grew.

Kennedy's attitude toward China hardened during his presidency, after giving liberals such as Bowles the impression that he supported UN membership and normalization of relations. In 1961 State Department officials explored the possibilities of some sort of two-nation policy in which Communist China and the Nationalist Chinese government on Taiwan would both have UN membership. Kennedy, believing the existing policy unrealistic, thought that ultimately change would have to come, but he had enough problems without becoming involved with an issue that would have enraged most Republicans and the China lobby. Moreover, in July 1961 a congressional resolution opposing Communist

China's admission to the UN and diplomatic recognition passed without a negative vote in both houses. Eisenhower had already told Kennedy that he would consider returning to public life if Communist China were about to enter the UN. Public opinion surveys also showed the disapproval response to Communist China's UN admission steadily rising from 61 percent in 1959 to 71 percent in 1964. As a result, Kennedy would consider a two-China formula only if Nationalist China faced expulsion from the UN—a threat the United States squashed during this period.

The Chinese border war with India in 1962 made policy reevaluation even less likely. This conflict added to Kennedy's growing fear of China, something that Bowles and other liberals failed to understand. He believed that country to be in a Stalinist phase, ready to pounce on expansionist opportunities. Its supposed low regard for human life and its pursuance of nuclear power made it particularly dangerous, and Kennedy took seriously that nation's hostile anti-American rhetoric. Despite Bowles's and Averell Harriman's recommendations, he rejected the sale of 3 to 5 million tons of wheat to famine-stricken China and opposed the possibility of resuming trade. In his last press conference on 14 November 1963, he still had left the door ajar, however, by saying that "we are not wedded to . . . hostility to Red China." But China must demonstrate its desire to live in peace before American policy changes could be considered, he concluded. Given all the other obstacles, a reappraisal at the least would have to await an overwhelming reelection victory. After all was said and done, Kennedy's China policy represented no appreciable departure from Eisenhower's.

Indonesia provided Kennedy with a greater opportunity for change. In the 1950s that former Dutch colony, which had won its independence in 1949, had shown its nationalistic independence by leaning toward the Soviet Union and Communist China. So much did the Eisenhower administration detest its demagogic and vain ruler, Achmed Sukarno, that the CIA had supported an effort to overthrow him in 1958. Afterward, Sukarno's relationship with the United States further deteriorated as he turned to Moscow for military aid.

Before 1963 Indonesia occupied more of Kennedy's time than Vietnam. Aware of its valuable resources of tin, oil, and rubber, he called Indonesia the "most significant nation in Southeast Asia."[21] Losing it to communism, he thought, would have a domino effect on American efforts in Indochina. At the same time Kennedy's empathic understanding of Third World nationalism enabled him to adopt a more realistic anti-Communist approach. Unlike Eisenhower, he made an effort to woo Sukarno, in spring 1961 inviting him to the White House, where he returned again that September. Robert Kennedy honored him with a visit in February 1962. The attorney general not only got along well with Sukarno but also became a hit with Indonesian students. The Kennedy administration also sent Peace Corps volunteers, provided a $17 million development grant and other economic assistance, including $40 million in agricultural commodities, and organized the New Pacific Community to strengthen relations between East Asian developing nations and the United States.

Most importantly, the Kennedy administration played a significant role in resolving the conflict between Sukarno and the Netherlands over the control of West Irian (West New Guinea), located due east of Indonesia, a territory that had remained a relic of the Netherlands' former empire. Sukarno sought its incorporation even though its black people shared no ethnic or cultural bond with his nation. He threatened an invasion unless all of the former Netherlands East Indies were united under his control. Kennedy, not wishing to alienate a NATO ally or Sukarno, decided to depart from his passive neutrality when it became evident that no immediate solution seemed imminent except force. Harriman's appointment as assistant secretary of state for the Far East helped; he aided in reversing the State Department's pro-Dutch approach, thereby putting State into line with the president's viewpoints.

Kennedy and Harriman convinced the Dutch to accept UN mediation by stressing that West New Guinea was not worth a war. Robert Kennedy encouraged Sukarno to participate in negotiations with the Netherlands near Middleburg, Virginia, with the American diplomat Ellsworth Bunker representing the United Nations. The result led to a face-saving solution for the Dutch, sparing them the humiliation of turning over territory to Sukarno. The agreement provided for a four-and-a-half month UN interim administration before West Irian went to Indonesia and stipulated that by 1969 the people of West Irian would be permitted a supposed free choice to determine their fate. While Kennedy's efforts predictably failed to satisfy either side, he had maintained dialogue with Sukarno, who permitted American oil companies to renew contracts in Indonesia. He even looked forward to Kennedy's planned visit there sometime in 1964.

As it turned out, however, no Third World problem would leave a more enduring legacy than Vietnam. Within days of his inauguration Kennedy understood the seriousness of the situation there after reading a memo from Gen. Edward Lansdale, who had recently returned from South Vietnam. Ngo Dinh Diem, its mandarin president, was losing control of the countryside to South Vietnamese Communists (Vietcong) and peasant sympathizers. He had created most of his own problems by staging an anti-Communist purge beginning in 1955, causing the Vietcong to shift from political protest to armed resistance. He had also refused to implement promises for land and other social reforms, thereby alienating the peasant community. By 1960 his oppressive policies had antagonized even the non-Communist leaders in Saigon, and senior military officers had staged an unsuccessful coup. In September 1960 Ho Chi Minh's North Vietnamese government also had secretly pushed for the liberation of the South and the eventual reunification of the two Vietnams. Ho had begun to infiltrate the South with supplies and South Vietnamese guerrillas, who had migrated northward after the first Indochina war. By December Hanoi had established the National Liberation Front (NLF) in South Vietnam and was calling for a coalition government to include the Vietcong.

Despite Kennedy's anti-French and pronationalist posture, he had not opposed the Diem regime's decision in 1956 to reject the Geneva Accords of 1954, which provided for free elections to unite the two Vietnams. He knew that if such a vote were taken, Ho Chi Minh, Vietnam's most eminent nationalistic leader, would have easily won. Thus, in Vietnam more than anywhere else Kennedy revealed the limitations of his nationalism; anticommunism clearly had priority. Kennedy had provided no indication, then, that he objected to Eisenhower's post-Geneva Vietnam policy. In a 1956 speech before the American Friends of Vietnam he called South Vietnam the "cornerstone of the free world in Southeast Asia, the keystone of the arch, the finger in the dike. Burma, Thailand, India, Japan, the Philippines, and obviously Laos and Cambodia . . . would be threatened if the red tide of Communism overflowed in Vietnam." He labeled Vietnam not only "a proving ground for democracy in Asia" but also "a test of American responsibility and determination in Asia."[22] Even after one discounts the hyperbole of the occasion, Kennedy disclosed a staunch anticommunism, a commitment to containment, and an acceptance of the domino theory. Those popular views had hardened after his election, Khrushchev's national liberation speech, the Bay of Pigs, and Vienna.

Too, Kennedy knew that he had to draw the line in Vietnam following the April 1961 decision to neutralize Laos. A strong American stand in South Vietnam would send a signal to Moscow that the United States intended to oppose Communist aggression in remote places; any other approach might have weakened the American position elsewhere, he thought. Kennedy also remained responsive to domestic political influences. Eisenhower had already warned that Republicans would hold him responsible "for any retreat in Southeast Asia." Kennedy told Galbraith after the Bay of Pigs that "there are just so many concessions that one can make to the communists in one year and survive politically. . . . We just can't have another defeat in Vietnam."[23] Vietnam, unlike Laos, offered Kennedy a seemingly stable government with a well-equipped army as well as direct access to the sea, permitting the more effective use of air- and sea-power. Schlesinger justifiably surmised that Kennedy made a de facto deal with the national security establishment, which grudgingly accepted the neutralization of Laos for a more aggressive policy in Vietnam.

Kennedy and his advisers, however, never understood the enormous difficulties facing them in Vietnam, including the resolve and popularity of the Communist insurgents and the tremendous unpopularity and ineffectiveness of the Diem regime. In retrospect, the American commitment was doomed from the start. Yet Kennedy confidently believed that American power could reverse the deterioration without his having to employ combat forces; he understood clearly the French folly of committing some three hundred thousand troops in Indochina in the 1950s. Moreover, as he said repeatedly, the war in South Vietnam was one in which that government must win or lose. Characteristically, he chose to keep his options open as he made incremental increases in assistance to the Saigon government.

Except during spring and fall 1961, Kennedy devoted little time to Vietnam until summer 1963; few in the administration did. Compared to other crises it did not seem as pressing. Far Eastern correspondent Stanley Karnow, who thought otherwise, had visited Robert Kennedy in the Justice Department in 1961. After hearing Karnow's concerns, Kennedy had responded, "Vietnam, Vietnam . . . we have thirty Vietnams a day here."[24] Actually McNamara more than anyone else most shaped policy. Rusk thought State had enough to do with Berlin and other diplomatic problems and considered Vietnam a Defense Department matter. Thinking highly of McNamara, Kennedy apparently expressed no displeasure at Defense's assumption of leadership.

Designating Vietnam a military issue at the outset influenced how the administration would deal with it. Those who assisted McNamara in shaping early approaches and actions included Defense Undersecretary Roswell Gilpatric, who chaired Kennedy's Vietnam task force, military adviser Gen. Maxwell Taylor, Walter Rostow of Bundy's staff, and Gen. Paul Harkins, commander of the American military effort in Vietnam. Taylor, for all his involvement with the Special Group (Counterinsurgency), placed more faith in firepower than in counterinsurgency, which involved specially trained, small-unit forces engaged in political as much as in military activity. Rostow, whom Kennedy called "air marshal" for his recommendations for bombing of 1961, overemphasized infiltration from the North as the primary problem.[25] Harkins, an appointee recommended by Taylor, knew nothing about guerrilla warfare; in fact, he and his contemporaries had a distorted view of who constituted the guerrillas. Instead of seeing them as village peasants, Harkins and others viewed them exclusively as invaders from the North. Consequently, whatever counterinsurgency action was initiated in Vietnam was handicapped by insufficient attention to social and economic reforms, with the Diem government contributing materially to that failing by its lack of cooperation. Thus Schlesinger later contended that counterinsurgency was never really tried.

More was involved than the Defense Department's domination of the war. Kennedy, in choosing Frederick Nolting as ambassador to Saigon, had selected the successful political-section head of NATO; but Nolting knew virtually nothing of Asia and even less of civil war, bringing with him a European mentality of anticommunism. Largely left out of the early decision-making process were those who believed that the problem in Vietnam was related directly to Diem's leadership. They advocated internal reforms in the Saigon government, including in some cases the removal of Diem. This group included State Department officials such as Ball, Bowles, Galbraith, Harriman, and Hilsman; White House advisers such as Sorensen; and congressional leaders such as Mike Mansfield. Rusk remained ambivalent, aside from a reluctance to commit combat forces. Kennedy himself leaned more toward the political viewpoint but never in a way that challenged McNamara's leadership. Despite differences in policy, nobody in the administration prior to 1963 had advocated that the United States leave Vietnam. Bowles, who came the closest, had proposed that the United States seek to extend the neutralization scheme in Laos to South Vietnam, but after giving it some thought, Kennedy argued that that moment had not yet arrived. Rusk reacted more strongly in informing Bowles that "you're spouting the Communist line."[26] After North Vietnam violated the Laos accord late in 1962 by retaining troops in that country, the administration became even less amenable to proposals for neutralization.

It instead followed the traditional approach of containment. This meant accepting the recommendations of the Eisenhower administration and the Vietnam task force, including the financing of an increase of twenty thousand troops (soon raised to thirty thousand) in Diem's army, which already stood at two hundred fifty thousand regulars and auxiliaries against an estimated twelve thousand Vietcong. The force size, more than adequate to deal with the insurgency, confirmed that Diem had failed to make efficient use of his military. Instead of sending conventional American forces as the JCS had recommended, President Kennedy decided to enlarge the advisory force by four hundred so that the Green

Berets could work more closely with South Vietnamese (ARVN) units on counterinsurgency activities. For the first time the United States would exceed the 687 advisers allotted in the Geneva agreement of 1954. Kennedy also authorized modest covert activities in North Vietnam and the Laotian panhandle to deal with infiltration.

However, Kennedy ignored the recommendation of Elbridge Durbrow, Eisenhower's ambassador to Saigon, that the United States deny Diem increased assistance until he instituted reforms and reduced governmental corruption and oppression. Instead the president pursued a more sympathetic approach, designed to strengthen Diem's confidence and faith in the United States. He assumed that he could achieve more success by coaxing, rather than by pressuring, Diem. In May Kennedy sent Vice-President Johnson to meet with the South Vietnamese president as part of the new policy. Johnson, with characteristic hyperbole, publicly compared him with Churchill and confidentially offered American combat forces, anticipating that the independent Diem would refuse them and accept economic and advisory assistance.[27]

The increase in aid proved insufficient, however. By September Diem's military position had deteriorated in the face of widening attacks; the Vietcong virtually owned the countryside. In October Kennedy responded by sending to South Vietnam Taylor and Rostow, who reflected the military viewpoint despite their understanding of the president's aversion to major military commitments. No senior State Department member accompanied the delegation, precluding any proposal for neutralization. The report focused simplistically on the military aspects of the conflict, viewing it in the context of Khrushchev's speech on "wars of national liberation." It recommended the escalation of United States involvement, including the employment of eight to ten thousand American combat troops. Diem reluctantly accepted this, probably to prevent United States disengagement in the event the war worsened. More to Diem's liking, the United States promised to commit more advisers, money, and technical assistance, along with helicopter units. "In Knute Rockne's old phrase," Rostow chortled, "we are not saving them for the Junior Prom."[28]

At the same time, the administration's proposal of limited partnership, which meant direct American advisement from the upper reaches of the government down to the battalion level, caused Diem to remark that "Vietnam did not want to be a protectorate."[29] The situation clearly revealed the incremental way in which the United States was enmeshing itself in Vietnam and finding itself increasingly at odds with Saigon, which refused to accept the new restrictions.

No aspect of the Taylor report brought more disagreement than the recommendation of ten thousand American combatants. McNamara, believing it inadequate, called for forty thousand troops with a provision for two hundred five thousand if North Vietnam and China intervened militarily. In reflecting the JCS viewpoint, McNamara showed little of the caution he would display during the Cuban missile crisis, where nuclear weapons threatened. Both Ball and Galbraith strongly opposed a combat commitment. Ball warned Kennedy that in five years "we'll have three hundred thousand men in the paddies and jungles." With rare asperity, according to Ball, the president had retorted, "George, you're crazier than hell. That just isn't going to happen." Galbraith, whom Kennedy sent to Saigon for a second opinion, argued that the problem was political, not military. In alluding to Diem's staggering military advantage, he concluded, "If this is equality, the United States would hardly be safe against the Sioux."[30] Rusk continued to resist the use of American forces, which might invite North Vietnamese and Chinese intervention and adversely affect negotiations in Geneva over Laos. Like Galbraith, Rusk called Diem a "losing horse," wondering whether he was "prepared to give us something worth supporting."[31] Even the CIA opposed combat troops because it would provoke comparable action from North Vietnam.

Such negative reaction reinforced Kennedy's instinctive feeling to keep regular units out of Vietnam—at least for the moment. He undoubtedly inspired the joint McNamara-Rusk memorandum on 11 November, which accepted most of the recommendations in the Taylor report, including the provision for joint partnership, with the stipulation that the United States prepare to employ combat troops only in the event that it might later become necessary. McNamara clearly had reversed his position to accommodate the president. At the same time, a proposed contingency plan kept the Pentagon at bay.

With greater American involvement, the war seemed to turn in Diem's favor by late 1961. The use of helicopters for troop transport, reconnaissance, and fire support proved particularly effective. At first they frightened the Vietcong, who turned and ran. Not only did American aircraft play a key role in interdiction missions but also more advisers accompanied ARVN units in the field. Furthermore, Kennedy approved the limited use of defoliants and napalm, which did little to eradicate the ugly American image. On the political front the United States adopted a strategic-hamlet program, first successfully employed in Malaya and the Philippines one decade earlier. Its goal was to isolate the village population from Communist insurgents through its attempt to arm the villagers, provide self-government, and institute medical services, schools, and land reform. Its overall success hinged on a carefully developed network of interlocking hamlets, which one State Department official compared to an "oil blot."

What might have been a meaningful counterinsurgency measure failed, partly because Diem placed his nefarious brother, Ngo Dinh Nhu, in charge. Nhu's decision to establish hamlets in remote areas to "show the flag" and inflate statistics represented a total disregard of United States advice. Of the eighty-six hundred strategic hamlets claimed by the Diem government, only 20 percent met U.S. standards. Most would be overrun within a year, enabling the Vietcong to capture thousands of American weapons; the firearms they obtained from the South Vietnamese civil guard far exceeded what came through infiltration. Even more damning, Nhu failed to provide the necessary social, political, and economic reforms; money the United States allocated for such purposes never reached the peasants. Nhu clearly tried to use the strategic-hamlet system to extend his control over the countryside, and as a result the hamlet program heightened the peasants' hostility.

The Saigon military effort proved as disappointing, particularly after the Vietcong learned to fire on the approaching helicopters. All too often the South Vietnamese bombed a hostile territory prior to a ground attack, not for the purpose of softening the Vietcong but to warn them out of the area. As intelligence capabilities improved under American guidance, according to journalist Neil Sheehan, ARVN units deliberately invaded "safe" areas and needlessly discharged their weapons. Casualty lists were routinely falsified. And South Vietnamese commanders frustrated American advisers by refusing to press an advantage. The most glaring and publicized example occurred at Ap Bac in January 1963 when a government force entrapped a Vietcong battalion. Despite a four-to-one superiority in troops and an overwhelming advantage in firepower, the government forces refused to attack, permitting the Vietcong to slip away. The United States lost five helicopters and three pilots in what one American adviser termed a major defeat.

The fault lay not entirely with ARVN officers. Diem, believing that excessive casualties had caused the 1960 abortive coup, evaluated commanders on the basis of losses. Moreover, he organized and deployed the military in ways that best safeguarded his political security. His static warfare frustrated American leaders, as did his resistance to limited partnership. Yet Nolting and General Harkins remained convinced that the war was being won. Both continued to view it from a military perspective, citing the Vietcong casualty rate and the increase in strategic hamlets and the South Vietnamese forces as positive indicators. McNamara, who made his first visit to Vietnam in 1962, characteristically reported to Kennedy that "every quantitative measurement we have shows we are winning the war."[32] The president momentarily felt better about Vietnam as he concentrated on other problems.

A different viewpoint came from a small group of young reporters, including David Halberstam of the *New York Times* and Sheehan of United Press International, who saw the war without illusions. They conferred with American advisers, who reinforced their observations about the political and military failings of the Diem regime. Their critical stories in major newspapers across the United States pricked the optimism of the Kennedy administration and raised the level of public awareness regarding a war that the president would as soon bury. Ever concerned about image, Kennedy confronted *New York Times* publisher Arthur Sulzberger about Halberstam, asking "You don't think he's too close to the story?"[33] After Sulzberger said no, the president in vain asked him to transfer Halberstam; administration officials then called the *Times* reporter and his colleagues unpatriotic and sought other ways to discredit them.

In 1962 Kennedy also heard criticism from insiders. Galbraith, writing from India, gently chided him about replacing the French as the colonial military force in Vietnam. "Incidentally," he continued, "who is the man in your administration who decides what countries are strategic? I would like to have his name and ask him what is so important about this [Vietnamese] real estate in the space age."[34] Galbraith remained convinced that any replacement for Diem would be beneficial. He advised Kennedy to seek a political settlement leading to a neutral South Vietnam. Bowles also repeatedly called for a negotiated solution, while urging Kennedy to go beyond the domino theory in defining long-range objectives in Southeast Asia. Bowles saw the goals of the Alliance for Progress as a model to bring the United States closer to the aspirations of Asian people. Like Galbraith he wanted to avoid an escalating war and a humiliating withdrawal.

No indication exists that Kennedy did anything more than listen to such advice. The closest he came to exploring a negotiated settlement was in permitting Harriman to talk privately with the North Vietnamese delegation in Geneva in summer 1962. The meeting was a total disaster since the chief North Vietnamese delegate refused to acknowledge Hanoi's role in South Vietnam; he blamed the conflict on Diem's oppression and United States intrusion. Only after Americans withdrew their assistance, he insisted, could a settlement come. Though other peace feelers seemed more promising, the administration never really pursued them. Bowles contended that giving North Vietnam a "good stiff military lesson" remained the predominant attitude.[35]

In November 1962, following his return from South Vietnam, Senate Majority Leader Mansfield came the closest to shaking Kennedy's cautious optimism. Aboard the Kennedy yacht, with characteristic candor, Mansfield outlined his disillusionment with Diem and the war effort. He also advised that the incremental escalation of American advisers and support personnel was entrapping the president in South Vietnam's war. As Kennedy read the report his face turned red; he finally snapped, "Do you expect me to take this at face value?" After Mansfield reminded Kennedy that he had asked him to go to Vietnam, President Kennedy responded icily, "Well, I'll read it again."[36]

At a December press conference Kennedy indicated that although the military situation in Vietnam had improved, he failed to see a quick solution to the problems. The next month he sent Hilsman of the State Department and Michael V. Forrestal of the White House for an independent look. They called the strategic-hamlet program a sham and thought the Vietcong casualty reports grossly inflated; they also recommended that Ambassador Nolting be replaced by one who could handle Diem. The problems, they admitted, were "awesome," but in typical New Frontier fashion, they saw reason for hope. Later that month a JCS team reported the McNamara-Taylor-Harkins line that military "victory is now a hopeful prospect." Harkins and McNamara even proposed plans for the gradual phasing out of American advisers. But as spring of 1963 approached, Kennedy had reason to feel less certain about South Vietnam.

Tension had risen between Diem and the American government over the number of United States advisers, with Diem and Nhu both wanting the advisory element appreciably reduced. The Vietnamese leaders also resented Americans telling them how to run their country. In fact, Diem and Nhu were exploring a rapprochement with the NLF and Hanoi, providing for a neutral South Vietnam minus an American presence. Thus could Kennedy confide to journalist Charles Bartlett that "we don't have a prayer of staying in Vietnam. . . . These people hate us. They are going to throw our tails out. . . . But I can't give up a piece of territory like that to the Communists and then get the American people to reelect me."[37]

The Buddhist uprising in spring 1963 further threw Kennedy's Vietnam policy into disarray and led to the eventual ouster of Diem. The Catholic Diem precipitated the crisis by enforcing a ban on the displaying of religious flags during the celebration of Buddha's birthday at Hue, the ancient imperial capital. The ban had followed the flying of Catholic flags in celebration of the anniversary of the ordination of Diem's brother as archbishop. On 9 May ten thousand Buddhists gathered in protest. The Diem government broke up the demonstration with clubs and armed fire, killing seven. The incident led to the charge that the government was persecuting Buddhists, who represented the predominant religion of Vietnam.

Advised by his hardline brother Nhu, Diem blamed the violence on the Vietcong and refused to make key concessions. He proved to be an increasing embarrassment to the Kennedy administration, which had called him the embodiment of Vietnamese nationalism. The conflict intensified following the self-immolation of a seventy-three-year-old Buddhist priest in Saigon, photographs of which blanketed the front pages of American newspapers. Other Buddhist self-burnings caused Diem's acid-tongued sister-in-law Madame Nhu to refer flippantly to them as barbecues; she offered gasoline and matches to Halberstam and his compatriots so that they could follow the Buddhists' example.

The crisis worsened on 21 August. After a martial-law decree, Nhu's special forces and combat police units instituted a nationwide raid against Buddhist pagodas, killing resisting bonzes and destroying religious statues and holy relics. The action had transpired despite Diem's promise of reconciliation to Nolting, who had already decided to resign in the face of the summer turmoil. Yet even though Diem had disappointed his U.S. backers, most still favored his retention. They saw no Souvanna Phouma on the horizon to bind the country; better Diem, they thought, than total chaos or communism. Diem's implacable dependence on Nhu remained the major obstacle. Detractors stressed that Diem was oppressive and reactionary in his own right and had lost the support of the people, including top military leaders who bristled at his favoritism. He wanted, opponents insisted, more, not fewer, Nhus. By mid-August the stage was set for an American sanctioned coup.

Henry Cabot Lodge, the new American ambassador, would play a key role. Arriving on 22 August 1963, he was a surprise choice, despite his interest in Vietnam, a desire to return to public service, and his fluency in the French language. The Boston Brahmin had been Kennedy's Republican opponent during the 1952 Senate contest and Nixon's running mate in 1960; Lodge's Republicanism would make it more difficult for the opposition to rail against the administration's Vietnam policy. In Nolting's words, Lodge represented "a piece of Republican asbestos to keep the heat off of Kennedy."[38] Indeed Vietnam already had emerged as an issue in Congress as Republicans challenged the foreign aid bill.

Immediately taking charge, Lodge reported on Saturday 24 August that several South Vietnamese generals sought a green light to move against Nhu—and most likely Diem. This led to the worst intraadministration conflict of the Kennedy presidency. On one side, it reflected a long-standing State Department dissatisfaction with the Diem regime.

Harriman, the new undersecretary of state for political affairs, Ball, Hilsman, who had replaced Harriman as assistant secretary for Far Eastern affairs, and White House staffer Forrestal composed a telegram to Lodge that Saturday during the absence of other key administration officials. The cable stated that the United States government could no longer tolerate Nhu. If Diem failed to rid himself of Nhu and his wife, the United States must "face the possibility that Diem himself cannot be preserved."[39] It instructed Lodge to inform the South Vietnamese government that the United States would reassess its support unless immediate steps were taken.

The telegram writers had obtained the approbation of key officials by telephone. Forrestal had kept Kennedy, who was at Hyannis Port, informed throughout the drafting process. Now apparently questioning his early 1962 view that "Diem is Diem and the best we've got," the president gave his endorsement, but only after Forrestal had told him that events in Saigon could not await a Monday meeting and only after Rusk and Gilpatric of the Defense Department had approved the message.[40] In New York at the time, Rusk had telephoned his assent. As acting secretary of state, Ball actually signed the cable, following Gilpatric's and Richard Helms's clearance for Defense and the CIA, respectively. McNamara and CIA director John McCone, both on vacation, never saw the telegram, and Taylor of the JCS claimed not to have seen it until after it had been sent.

The matter was obviously handled sloppily, suggesting how little Kennedy had learned from the Bay of Pigs debacle, despite his cautious responses to other crises. It could be that Vietnam had failed to capture his full attention, with the civil rights March on Washington just four days away. In any case, at a 26 August White House NSC meeting, McNamara, Taylor, and McCone objected to the telegram, all three continuing to support Diem. This led to an angry verbal battle with the Harriman faction, which caused Kennedy to exclaim afterward to Bartlett, "My God, my government's coming apart." He privately chastised Forrestal and Hilsman for mishandling the operation, prompting Forrestal to offer his resignation. In response Kennedy had said, "You're not worth firing. You owe me something, so you stick around."[41] Kennedy was further angered because Taylor and others had apparently given their assent only to have misgivings afterward. Despite the division, everyone agreed that the administration could not retract the cable, although McNamara for one insisted that the United States must forewarn Diem to disengage from Nhu, a courtesy Lodge ignored.

Less than three months before his death, Kennedy's Vietnam policy was turning to mush. The "be nice to Diem" and the limited-partnership policies had collapsed. The administration remained divided on the South Vietnamese president, but division arose elsewhere, too. Lodge refused to communicate with Diem, and serious differences emerged between the ambassador and Harkins. If one can believe Robert Kennedy's 1964 testimony, the president verged on firing Lodge for failing to keep him informed.[42] Meanwhile, friction involving the Harriman and Taylor group intensified. The strategic-hamlet program was failing; long-range political objectives remained obscure; and the military results were mixed—despite McNamara's belief that the Vietcong would be crushed by 1965. Kennedy's advisers continued divided over whether the war constituted a military or a political conflict. Even more disconcerting, they could not agree on a military assessment. Kennedy began to suspect that the Halberstam-Sheehan clique in Saigon conveyed a more truthful picture than he was getting from his military advisers. Moreover, the administration seemed much more focused on the war effort than in concerning itself with the needs of the Vietnamese people; Kennedy admitted as much in one of his press conferences.

Despite having approved the 24 August cable, Kennedy still viewed any attempt at a coup with considerable trepidation. To ensure success, he wanted time to review the plans. His poignant message to Lodge on 29 August recalled a lesson from the Bay of Pigs: "I know from experience that failure is more destructive than the appearance of indecision. . . . When we go, we must go to win."[43] Even more hesitant were the coup leaders, many of them general officers. They not only failed to win over some key commanders but also sensed the indecision of the United States. On 31 August Gen. Duong Van "Big" Minh, the coup leader, called it off.

In the days ahead the Kennedy administration underwent an "agonizing reappraisal" of its Vietnam policy, which sparked a heated debate over Diem and the conduct and nature of the war. In the process the administration overwhelmingly rejected two extreme positions. A proposal to use U.S. combat troops in South Vietnam had elicited a brief uproar at one NSC meeting. Then Paul Kattenburg, a Foreign Service officer who had recently returned from Saigon and thought the problems in Vietnam almost insurmountable—and worsening—recommended withdrawing. Taylor, McNamara, and Rusk thereupon attacked Kattenburg's judgment. Rusk called his assessments speculative; he, McNamara, Vice-President Johnson, and others favored staying until the war was won. More difficult to dismiss was Robert Kennedy's probing analysis one week later. Kennedy had focused on Vietnam immediately after the controversy of the 24 August cable. After first expressing a concern for the people of Vietnam, he next wondered whether a Communist takeover could be resisted by any South Vietnamese government. "If not," he thought, "now was the time to get out of Vietnam entirely, rather than waiting."[44] However, if a takeover could be resisted, but not with Diem in charge, then he argued that the United States should help institute changes in Saigon.

How much Robert Kennedy reflected his brother's viewpoint is unknown. The president, however, did make two public statements on Vietnam in early September. In an interview with Walter Cronkite of CBS News on the ninth, he reaffirmed a long-standing belief: "We can help them, we can give them equipment, we can send our men . . . as advisers, but they have to win it—the people of Vietnam—against the Communists." Kennedy failed to make clear, however, what he would do if South Vietnam refused to make the necessary effort. When asked if the Diem government could regain the people's support, he responded frankly that "with changes in policy, and perhaps with personnel, I think it can." Otherwise its chances were not very good, he concluded. Kennedy sent an unmistakable signal that Diem must adopt reforms and rid himself of the Nhus. He also indicated that he did not "agree with those who say we should withdraw. That would be a great mistake."[45] In an interview with David Brinkley three days later, he once again ascribed to the domino theory, linking the struggle in Vietnam to expansionist China, which supposedly sought control of Southeast Asia.

Because of the existing differences in policy and assessment, Kennedy agreed to send Marine Gen. Victor H. Krulak, a Taylor favorite, and Joseph A. Mendenhall, a senior Foreign Service officer who had served in Saigon, to Vietnam. Ironically their reports on 10 September only exacerbated the divisions. Krulak provided a glowing account of the war's progression in the countryside. He spoke highly of Diem and indicated that the political problems in Saigon had no impact on the military effort. Mendenhall asserted, however, that South Vietnam bordered on political collapse and a religious civil war, prompting Kennedy to ask, "You two did visit the same country, didn't you?"[46] Rufus Phillips, the director of the AID rural assistance program in Vietnam, reinforced Mendenhall's trenchant assessment by admitting the failure of the hamlet program. He also questioned whether the United States was winning the war, particularly in the delta, south of Saigon. There, he asserted, it was "going to pieces." Following another heated debate, Kennedy angrily commented afterward, "This is impossible, we can't run a policy when there are such divergent views on the same set of facts."[47]

The lack of consensus led to another fact-finding mission on 23 September headed by McNamara and Taylor. One can only speculate on Kennedy's reasons for selecting subordinates with such similar optimistic

251

viewpoints. Schlesinger and Hilsman are probably correct in suggesting that they were sent to witness firsthand the deterioration of the war under Diem. Unable to admit that they had been wrong in earlier military assessments, McNamara and Taylor once again conveyed the favorable viewpoints of Harkins and his staffers. The report unsurprisingly praised the "great progress" of the military effort. As if to give substance to such claims, it promised the pull-out of the sixteen thousand United States forces by 1965, beginning with a reduction of one thousand at the end of 1963. Kennedy quickly sanctioned the announcement of the planned withdrawals on 2 October. The statement failed to mention, however, that the 1963 cutback involved a construction battalion that had completed its work and that other troops would soon take its place. Neither did it provide an explanation for the planned reductions. Taylor privately argued that South Vietnam needed to be put on notice; otherwise "they're just going to be leaning on us forever."[48] More to the point, the administration sought to heighten the pressure on Diem. Political considerations may have also influenced Kennedy, as Vietnam became more of a sensitive issue on the eve of a presidential election year.

The McNamara-Taylor report presented a much less optimistic picture of the Diem government. It pointed to the serious political tensions in Saigon and the increasing unpopularity of the oppressive Diem and recommended the suspension of various forms of assistance. The administration, in adopting positive pressures and in recalling a pro-Diem CIA station chief from Saigon, wittingly or unwittingly signaled the coup forces that Diem had lost favor. As a result, General Minh had approached American officials in Saigon to probe United States feelings regarding a coup. The White House indicated that although the United States did "not wish to stimulate a coup," it would not "thwart" one either.[49] It also revealed that it would not deny economic and military assistance to any new regime that actively pursued the war effort and worked closely with the United States. Diem obviously had not helped himself by his continued obstinance and his contact with North Vietnam.

Nevertheless, on the eve of the coup administration officials wavered. At a White House conference on 29 October, the president worried that the "odds are against a coup." Robert Kennedy injected that such an undertaking would mean placing the future of Vietnam "in the hands of one . . . not now known to us." Moreover, Diem would "not run from a fight. If the coup fails," the attorney general added, "Diem will throw us out." General Taylor agreed, arguing that even a successful putsch "would have a harmful effect on the war effort." Harriman and Rusk then reminded the others of the liabilities of continuing with Diem. No one seemed certain of what to do aside from letting events take their course in South Vietnam.[50]

On 1 November a junta comprising senior military officers toppled Diem and Nhu; three weeks before Kennedy's assassination they were executed in an armored personnel carrier. When Kennedy heard of their deaths, he rushed from the Oval Office "with a look of shock and dismay." He had sent long-time friend Torby Macdonald to Saigon as a personal emissary to warn Diem that his life was in danger.[51] In vain, Macdonald had advised Diem to seek asylum in the American embassy. Though Kennedy had consented to Diem's removal and had apparently known of the generals' desire to execute him, clearly he had wished Diem to be spared.

Diem's demise quickly exposed how poorly the military effort was progressing. It also accentuated the reversal as the Vietcong stepped up operations and North Vietnam ordered regular forces to move south. Hanoi's response followed Saigon's rejection of a proposal to resume secret negotiations. Politically, the new leadership lacked the unity and resolve to turn things around. Indeed in 1964 alone, seven different generals headed the Saigon government. Moreover, South Vietnam would also lack the will to oppose the introduction of large-scale American military involvement in 1965, which Diem probably would have resisted. Obviously the removal of Diem had not been the answer. The Kennedy administration had indirectly encouraged a coup, critics have contended, with little understanding of what was to follow. In the process the United States psychologically bound itself closer to South Vietnam. No promising solutions appeared on the horizon either except to tough it out. This Kennedy publicly vowed to do, necessitating a more substantial commitment. Kennedy probably would have done just enough to keep a political lid on the war during an election year. But what would he have done afterward when the North Vietnamese increased the pressure and when American advisers pushed for United States ground forces and the bombing of the North?

Kennedy loyalists have insisted that he would have disengaged from Vietnam had he lived. Just before his death, he reportedly told O'Donnell that after the 1964 election he intended to pull out because the war had gotten out of hand. When O'Donnell asked how he could devise such a move, he responded, "Easy, put a government in there that will ask us to leave." Kennedy conveyed a similar message to Senator Mansfield, explaining, "I can't [depart] until 1965—after I'm reelected."[52] Schlesinger also contends that the president had repeatedly resisted escalation and had begun withdrawal in 1963 by recalling one thousand troops. Only seventy-three American combatants died in Vietnam under Kennedy, Schlesinger points out. Yet Rusk insists that at no time did "Kennedy ever say or hint or suggest to me that he was planning to withdraw from Vietnam in 1965."[53] In December 1963 President Johnson thought likewise as he prepared to check the increasing Communist resistance in South Vietnam in the name of Kennedy. The attorney general, who knew the president best, said in a 1964 oral history that the administration had not considered either withdrawal or escalation. When asked what the president would have done had the South Vietnamese appeared doomed, Robert answered in a way that truthfully expressed the ad hoc nature of the Kennedy presidency: "We'd face that when we came to it."[54]

Given what we know of President Kennedy, it is difficult to conceive of his pulling out of Vietnam without a reasonably honorable settlement. At the same time, it is equally hard to imagine Kennedy carrying escalation to the extremes that Johnson did, who presided over five hundred thousand troops in Vietnam. Kennedy was too cautious, prudent, and distrusting of the military to have succumbed to that extent. Exactly where he might have drawn the line is anyone's guess. Much more clear is that Kennedy's Vietnam policy was in shambles at the time of his death. Obviously he and the "best and the brightest" never had any workable solutions or much understanding regarding Vietnam. If one is seeking examples of presidential growth in Kennedy's last year, one should look elsewhere rather than to Southeast Asia. His approach to Vietnam eventually called into question the Kennedy image of a sensitive advocate of Third World nationalism.

10

★ ★ ★ ★ ★

IMAGE AND REALITY

John Kennedy was one of the most image-conscious presidents of his century. The imagery sharpened during the presidential years. As president he could better shape favorable symbols, realizing that personal style could counter political frustration, mask ineptness, and create popularity in a media-oriented society. Much of the imagery centered on family life. That he had two attractive children, a glamorous wife, and greater sex appeal than Rock Hudson (according to a poll of female college students) made it easier. Photographers captured the Kennedys happily leaving Mass together or aboard the family boat with a vibrant president at the helm. They documented a coatless Kennedy delivering his inaugural address in frigid weather. Jack and Jacqueline were shown entertaining famous artists and intellectuals at White House black-tie galas. In the Oval Office the most persistent symbol became the rocking chair, suggesting informality and ease. Even in that august setting, children often rollicked into view. Although Kennedy's personal impact was significant, his life as president hardly resembled the Camelot that a grieving wife made it out to be immediately following his death.

President Kennedy began his workday around 7:30 A.M. when George Thomas, his black valet, awakened him and placed four newspapers on his four-poster bed: the *New York Times*, *Washington Post*, Baltimore *Sun*, and *Wall Street Journal*. A speed reader, he quickly absorbed the contents, concentrating on the columnists; he also read several other newspapers and news magazines during the day. The early reading usually inspired a barrage of phone calls to administration officials and requests for more information or action. To save time he shaved in the bathtub, which supported a board across it so that he could read memos or reports while soaking tender back muscles. Staffers received annotated material that bore the water stains of that early morning activity. He ate breakfast in his bedroom around 8:45, consuming a large glass of orange juice, toast and jelly, two eggs, broiled bacon, and coffee with cream and sugar. Even though Jackie remained asleep in an adjoining bedroom, Kennedy often had the company of long-time aide David Powers, who entertained him with his Irish wit and sports anecdotes. Others often joined them, especially the president's children—six-year-old Caroline (in 1963) and three-year-old John Kennedy, Jr. (John-John).

Around 9:30 President Kennedy left the second-floor family quarters with one or both of his children and rode an elevator to the first floor, where he walked down the corridor to the west wing. Dressed immaculately in a lightweight, well-tailored dark suit and monogrammed shirt, the first of three or four outfits he would wear that day, he had improved his apparel substantially since the 1950s. He wore no jewelry aside from a watch and a PT-109 tie clasp, a symbol of World War II heroism. He appeared older in person than on television. His glossy and abundant chestnut hair, which he pampered, showed some gray at the temples, and his tanned face was full and deeply lined, especially around the mouth; his hooded gray eyes added to his maturity. Nonetheless, he appeared athletic and handsome.

He entered the personable Evelyn Lincoln's office first, exchanged pleasantries with her, and checked the mail. Although some five thousand letters came to the White House daily, only one hundred reached secretary Lincoln's desk. Several required the attention of the president, who quickly dictated replies, but a young secretary signed most of the autograph requests. Then, inside the blue-carpeted Oval Office, he read a lengthy CIA intelligence briefing and visited with press secretary Pierre Salinger. They discussed late news developments and the administration's responses that Salinger would present at the morning press briefing.

Kennedy limited most appointments to fifteen minutes or less. If he was busy, he sometimes approached the entering individual in the middle of the Oval Office, soon moving toward the exit door as an indication that the meeting had ended. More often he either remained at his desk or escorted the guest to a couch near the fireplace and his therapeutically designed rocker. Almost everyone was struck by his informality, cheerfulness, and good manners. He never addressed an individual as "fellow," "son," or by a first name if that person was appreciably older or a casual acquaintance. He always used "Mrs." in addressing the wives of associates. George Kennan, ambassador to Yugoslavia, observed that Kennedy revealed an instinctive "Lindberghian boyish" courtesy, which he described as "Lincolnesque."[1] Others might attribute it to the polite manners of Harvard and the English aristocracy, which Kennedy had assimilated along with his Irish heritage. Kennan moreover correctly sensed a shyness and remoteness that remained beneath the well-crafted persona. Kennedy also exhibited an ability to listen intently, always resisting the temptation to "sound off" and ask too many questions. One visitor commented that in a ten-minute interview, Kennedy listened for nine-and-a-half-minutes, but in the end he "expressed himself . . . graphically . . . and absorbed . . . more than we came to talk . . . about."[2]

Kennedy opened up more to long-standing friends and associates. He enjoyed gossip about public figures, letting appointments run over to hear more—an indication that he was not a hostage to schedule. Ohio governor Michael Di Salle remembered his love of laughter and reminiscence and his great knack for describing people. Although the weight of office eventually reduced the casual banter, Kennedy never lost his buoyant spirit and wry sense of humor, which served a therapeutic purpose when back pain or governmental problems worsened. Nor did he bore visitors with the "awesome burdens" and the "terrible loneliness" of the presidency.

He seemed even more considerate in trying times. At the height of the Cuban missile crisis, he visited with an African head of state for forty-five minutes, patiently discussing the Third World, a courtesy that person long remembered. During another difficult period, he escorted a congressman's family into the Rose Garden and around the White House grounds, describing Andrew Jackson's planting of the magnolia trees. He showed particular consideration to the less significant. When his children's nanny sought a brief meeting for a ninety-year-old friend, a smiling Kennedy bounded out of his office to greet the elderly woman and posed for a photograph with his arm around her shoulders. While working late on a cold, bitter night, he opened the french doors of the Oval Office to tell the Secret Service guard outside that "I don't want you out there in this terrible cold." When the guard insisted that such was his duty, Kennedy reappeared with a fleece-lined coat and cups of hot chocolate for both of them. A coatless president sat on the icy steps, drinking hot chocolate with the guard.[3]

His fondness for children was genuine. After speaking to a youth symphony group and boys' choir about to perform on the White House lawn, he apologized for not being able to stay but promised to leave his office doors open, which he continued to do for all subsequent children's concerts. He had an understandable sensitivity for handicapped children. He patiently knelt down before one spastic child to comprehend a speech that left others confused. He then hurried to his office to obtain his old PT shipper's hat, which he placed on the boy's head. "His father was in PT boats, too," he later explained; "his father is dead." He especially enjoyed opening the doors to the Rose Garden around mid-morning and clapping two or three times to signal his daughter. Caroline and her classmates, in recess from the third-floor school, ran to him, followed by John-John and the family pets.

Unquestionably, however, Kennedy used his children to enhance the presidential image, as countless magazine stories, most of them with White House cooperation, focused on the most pursued children since Shirley Temple. At times their own actions unwittingly contributed to his human qualities. Caroline once responded to a reporter's question of "Where's your daddy?" by saying, "He's upstairs with his shoes and socks off, doing nothing." Publicity aside, Kennedy's affection for his children probably plumbed the deepest level of his emotions. A major regret was that a weak back prevented him from tossing his son in the air.

Kennedy was also capable of less pleasant feelings. Staffers who failed to carry out assignments or erred in judgment could expect to hear a bellowing "Jeezus Christ." His anger was real, but it seldom lasted long. And he often directed it against himself for his own shortcomings. What bothered him the most were bores—egotists, name-droppers, complainers—anyone telling demeaning ethnic jokes, and the long-winded. Those who knew him well recognized the tell-tale signs: the tapping of his finger(s) on his front teeth, knee, or furniture, and his excessive doodling. Sitting in his rocker, he would swing his right foot, and when he was really annoyed, according to Lincoln, "his left eye would get a little askew and sort of droop a little, as if there was an irritation behind it."[4] She often came to the rescue by telling him he had a phone call. Most of the time, however, his humor carried him through. After patiently listening to Chester Bowles's extended exposition of world problems, for example, Kennedy told Ambassador John Kenneth Galbraith, his next visitor: "Chet tells me there are six revolutions going on in the world. One is the revolution of rising expectations. I lost track of the other five."[5]

Like most presidents he had a love-hate relationship with the press. Himself once a reporter, he entered the White House enjoying a friendly association with journalists, but he thought of newspapers as his natural enemies. No president, however, had sought so much to cultivate the press as did Kennedy. During his first year the image-conscious president met individually with more than fifty White House reporters. He remained close to Philip Graham, publisher of the *Washington Post*. He carried on social relationships with Benjamin Bradlee of *Newsweek*, syndicated columnist Joseph Alsop, and long-time friend Charles Bartlett of the *Chattanooga Times*. Hugh Sidey of *Time* and a few others had a virtual open door into the Oval Office. Kennedy improved the dissemination of news. During the Eisenhower presidency, reporters had had to work through the press secretary; now they could contact staffers and department heads directly. Additionally, he invited publishers and editors from the hinterlands to White House luncheons and their wives to the Oval Office. The White House press corps received invitations to state dinners and other social functions. Kennedy also sanctioned several TV specials, including in-depth interviews with network correspondents and exclusive print publications, even books on his presidency. Not only did Kennedy provide occasional not-for-attribution background sessions, but Salinger also held two press briefings daily. No administration opened itself more to the press.

While most reporters succumbed to Kennedy's charm, they soon discovered its limitations; he was not always as friendly as he appeared. Some reporters even found him occasionally curt and rude. "Either you informed him or you amused him," Mary McGrory, a *Washington Evening Star* writer recalled. "Otherwise he turned away."[6] Kennedy also overreacted to supposed careless or biased reporting, causing critics to accuse him of "whining" about "picayune" matters. Merriman Smith, the dean of White House correspondents, marveled at how the White House could uncover an unfavorable statement in a paper with a circulation of three thousand, two thousand miles away: "They must have a thousand little gnomes reading the papers for them."[7] The president was particularly sensitive about critical material in the *New York Times*. "I've seen him leaf through that paper looking for criticism," according to one close friend; "ninety per cent will be favorable, but he tortures himself, seeking out the rest." He reacted much more strongly to negative personal references than to criticism of policy. In response to Kennedy's rebuke of *Time* magazine's alleged "inconsistent" reporting, publisher Henry Luce, a close family friend, reminded Kennedy of the 1962 story of JFK as the man of the year, which had concluded that Kennedy might become a great president—"language *Time* uses sparingly," Luce commented. He then recounted the many other favorable pieces.[8]

Luce had ignored Kennedy's sensitivity to perception and imagery, however. The president felt that *Time* had portrayed him unsuitably. He was extremely bothered by its man-of-the-year cover, which bore little resemblance to a smiling campaign poster. It reflected instead the work of Pietro Annigoni, an Italian painter whom Jacqueline had once admired. The commissioned artist had sketched a working Kennedy for three days, attempting to capture the "essential" Kennedy. The result caused a furious president to exclaim, "You sons of bitches have done it again." The published rendering revealed an unsmiling, dark figure with asymmetric pupils, a crooked necktie, and hair slightly askew. One reader described the portrait as "a jaundiced Dracula in ragpickers' clothing," while Caroline wondered, "Daddy, where did you get those spooky eyes?" Annigoni, known for his warts-and-all approach, explained that the president "didn't smile very much while I was there." When told he had made Kennedy appear cross-eyed, he insisted, "He *is* cross-eyed!"[9]

One month later, Kennedy's displeasure mounted when *Time* claimed in its "People" section that he had posed for a man's fashion magazine. (A well-tailored Kennedy had appeared on the cover of *Gentlemen's Quarterly*.) The president collared *Time* columnist Hugh Sidey in the midst of John Glenn's historic return from space and burst out, "This goddam magazine is just too much. Where did you get this ridiculous item about me? I'll be the laughing stock of the country. . . . People always remember the wrong things, they remember . . . Coolidge for wearing those hats and they'll remember me for this."[10]

"Unfriendly" reporters soon found their sources dissipating, and they no longer received invitations to social functions. Even Bradlee felt Kennedy's sting for a mildly critical observation in a 1962 *Look* magazine feature on the antagonism between Kennedy and the press. For three months the president and his wife discontinued their weekly social activities with the Bradlees. "The Kennedys," Bradlee remembered, "want 110 percent from their friends . . . and feel cheated by anything else."[11] Perhaps the most publicized reaction involved Kennedy's 1962 cancellation of twenty-two White House subscriptions to the Republican *New York Herald Tribune* for its alleged biased reporting. For the most part, however, Kennedy wisely contained his bitterness by reverting to humor. He joked at a May ninth press conference that he was "reading more and enjoying it less." He conceded that the press "was doing [its] task as . . . the [critical] fourth estate." Amid laughter he concluded that he and the press could live together for the duration.

Kennedy used press conferences as successfully as Franklin Roosevelt. Unlike earlier presidents, Kennedy appeared before live television in the cavernous State Department auditorium, making the television audience the primary focus. "We were props in a show," Peter Lisagor of the *Chicago Daily News* remembered; "we should have joined Actors Equity." George Herman of CBS News recalled Kennedy looking "right over our heads, right into the camera. . . . This was a man who was extraordinarily professional."[12] Indeed, public opinion surveys gave Kennedy a 91 percent approval rating for his performances. The keys to that success included the meticulous preparation involving Salinger and the departmental heads who anticipated the questions, did the homework, and prepped the president in briefing sessions. Salinger occasionally prompted friendly reporters to ask certain questions, hinting that President Kennedy would have something important to say in those areas.

Most significantly, Kennedy had the capacity to absorb an enormous amount of information, and he projected unbelievably well on television. James Reston of the *New York Times* remembered that he "either overwhelmed you with decimal points or disarmed you with a smile and a wisecrack."[13] His remarkable sense of timing and presence overcame his sometimes faulty syntax. One of his most memorable performances occurred on 16 October, the first day of the missile crisis. Coming to the assemblage very late and preoccupied, he quickly became his relaxed, unflappable self. When someone asked about an Eisenhower criticism of his foreign policy, he shrugged his shoulders and remarked, "It's that October feeling." He then raised his index finger to indicate that he was ready for the next question, adding, "We all get it when election time comes around."[14] The timing was perfect, and he brought down the house. Despite the positive impact, Kennedy had only sixty-four press conferences, fewer per month than Roosevelt, Truman, or Eisenhower. He realized the dangers as well as the possibilities of television. Overexposure became his major concern, particularly since an expanding news format provided more opportunities to cover the presidency.

His adept media performances added to the charges of press manipulation—or news management, as journalists termed it. Though allegations first arose during the Bay of Pigs calamity, they reached their zenith during the Cuban missile crisis when Kennedy first asked the press to practice self-censorship during crises. He proposed the formation of a board representing the media to screen potentially dangerous stories. The press should also honor governmental requests not to print certain information. During the missile crisis, the Defense Department issued detailed guidelines restricting the publication of supposed security-related material. All of this invited a strong reaction from the press of peacetime censorship, especially when Arthur Sylvester, the chief public-relations officer at the Pentagon, argued that news represented part of "the arsenal of weaponry" of the cold war—intimating that lying was acceptable in certain circumstances.

The press soon charged that the administration had misled them during the missile crisis and afterward had engaged in selective leaking. On 29 October, about one week before the congressional elections and immediately following the crisis, Kennedy did announce that the administration would continue its silence on Cuba because "we are not out of the woods yet." However, he and National Security Adviser McGeorge Bundy visited surreptitiously with selected reporters. Several favorable stories followed, including the influential piece by Charles Bartlett and Stewart Alsop in the *Saturday Evening Post*, accusing Stevenson of having sanctioned a "Munich" in proposing a trade of Cuban and Turkish missile bases. Kennedy not only had leaked information to Bartlett, but he also apparently had read the galleys. The president "was not too displeased" that the information about Stevenson was published, Bartlett later remembered.[15] The December *Post* article promoted Kennedy's tough and determined image at Stevenson's expense.

Perhaps President Kennedy's most successful attempt to manipulate the media came that same month when he agreed to meet with three leading journalists on national TV to review the first half of his term. Coming immediately after the missile crisis and the Democratic election successes, the TV special enabled him to build on his popularity, especially since the media consented to tape a long interview and then reduce it for the one-hour telecast. George Herman recalled that Kennedy deliberately gave the dullest possible answers to unfriendly questions, knowing that they would be dropped. Otherwise he projected a smooth, thoughtful image, showing himself able to handle peace and war. Herman called it "a fascinating performance of skill."[16]

The president continued to frustrate the media in his final year, leading journalist Arthur Krock to charge that Kennedy enforced a policy of news management "more cynically and boldly" than had any previous administration. Krock insisted that this management had been applied with unparalleled "subtlety and imagination."[17] Nevertheless, the majority of media people—particularly the working press—remained on friendly terms. They enjoyed matching wits with the president, sensing his own enjoyment, and they admired his humor, occasional candor, and ability to inspire. Above all, they were extremely flattered that Kennedy read and frequently commented on their work, a fact that overshadowed whatever criticism they had about him or about the administration's news policies.

Press relations comprised only one of many grueling aspects of the presidency. Kennedy learned to pace himself by seeing fewer people and by taking a two-hour break at mid-day. About 1:15 P.M. he went to the pool and swam in ninety-degree water to relieve some of the back discomfort, which varied from an ache to excruciating pain. He sometimes resorted to carefully concealed crutches to get around in the White House. His initial White House physician, Dr. Janet Travell, a specialist in the treatment of muscular disorders, employed procaine injections to relieve the back spasms, but as Kennedy's body became more tolerant of the drug, the dosage was increased with less effect.

The intense pain Kennedy felt in spring 1961 undoubtedly caused him to become more dependent on Dr. Max Jacobson, a New York City physician, who injected celebrities such as Truman Capote, Eddie Fisher, Tennessee Williams, Alan Lerner, and Congressman Claude Pepper of Florida with a concoction made up of amphetamines, steroids, calcium, enzymes, placenta, and vitamins. German born and trained, the sixty-two-year-old Jacobson, who had lacked hospital privileges since 1946, confined his practice to an office in which unlicensed assistants also gave injections. Known as "Dr. Feel Good" and "miracle Max," he made lavish use of amphetamines—speed—which, although legal at the time, involved risks, including addiction, hyperactivity, increased irritability, impaired judgment, hypertension, and even psychosis. At first, in lower concentrations, amphetamines induced an invigorating high accompanied by an apparent alertness, an absence of fatigue, increased self-confidence, and enhanced concentration.[18] As a result, Jacobson's patients returned frequently for treatments.

Charles Spalding, one of Kennedy's former Harvard classmates, had introduced him to Jacobson during the debilitating campaign of 1960 after Kennedy had complained of fatigue and stress. Jacobson injected Kennedy before the first Nixon debate. He also treated Jacqueline, who supposedly told him that she could not remember feeling better or more confident. Jacobson, wearing a PT-109 tie clasp, accompanied the presidential party to Paris and Vienna in 1961 and treated the president at the White House, Hyannis Port, Glen-Ora, Virginia, and New York City. According to Jacobson's son, Dr. Thomas Jacobson, he injected the president with ten to fifteen milligrams of amphetamines as often as twice a week. Jacobson contended that he came to Kennedy's assistance during the steel crisis, the University of Mississippi civil rights incident, and the missile crisis of 1962, enabling him to function efficiently with little sleep. He afterward claimed that Kennedy "never could have made it without me." Despite the objection of Robert Kennedy and others, Kennedy apparently relied on amphetamines until his death. He once asserted after one warning that "I don't care if it's horse piss [;] . . . it's the only thing that works." While Jacobson's injections might not have adversely affected Kennedy's performance, added risks existed since he took a steroid derivative for Addison's disease. Excessive corticosteroid dosages can result in restlessness, agitation, insomnia, and even manic behavior. When combined with amphetamines, the potential dangers are compounded.[19]

Physicians involved with Kennedy have avoided discussing Jacobson, who lost his medical license in 1975 for more than thirty-five counts of unprofessional conduct after a New York State Board of Regents inquiry. Following a five-month investigation, the *New York Times* had first exposed Jacobson in December 1972. In that exposé an anonymous New York doctor who had treated Kennedy claimed that he had told the president that if he "took another shot [of amphetamines] I'd make sure it was known. No President with his finger on the red button has any business taking stuff like that."[20] There is no conclusive evidence that he swayed Kennedy nor any indication that any doctor coordinated the amount of steroids the president received for his Addison's disease and from Jacobson.

By the end of 1961 the circumspect Dr. George C. Burkley, an admiral from the Navy Dispensary in Washington, D.C., had assumed overall responsibility for the president's health. He replaced Dr. Travell, who retained the title of president's physician after she failed to resign and Kennedy hesitated to fire her. Burkley, among others, strongly opposed the continuance of Travell's procaine injections for Kennedy's back problem. He recommended the employment of Dr. Hans Kraus, a New York orthopedic surgeon specializing in physical therapy. Under Kraus's general supervision, the president began a conditioning program in October 1961 in a gym adjacent to the swimming pool to stengthen weak abdominal and back muscles. By December he had increased his muscular development by 50 percent, but he never completely overcame his back problem. He continued to use crutches from time to time and wore a nonmetallic back brace. A shocked Robert Pierpoint of CBS News remembered President Kennedy once being lowered from the back of a plane in a wheelchair upon his arrival in Florida. Even on good days Kennedy had to limit his physical activity, despite the New Frontier image of touch football, fifty-mile hikes, the President's Council on Youth Fitness, and vigorous golf, tennis, and squash matches. Though he learned to play golf with little involvement of the back muscles, he limited it to an occasional nine holes. As late as September 1963 he still suffered from groin and back pains.

Contrary to public perception, other health nuisances also plagued him. He continued to suffer from allergies to animal hair and house dust, for which he received weekly injections of vaccine. His growing intolerance to milk also aggravated a gastric disorder exacerbated by the corticosteroids he ingested for Addison's disease. Doctors placed him on a bland diet and restricted his alcoholic intake to an occasional beer, daiquiri, or Bloody Mary. He also had acute stiffness in his shoulder and neck muscles. He needed glasses for prolonged reading, and by 1963 he required larger type script for speeches; he suffered from partial deafness in his right ear, and his hands trembled when he delivered addresses. Despite these many physical problems, he never complained and was rarely bedridden. Instead he conveyed an image of robust health by his youthful, trim appearance, his limited but publicized physical activity, and the rigorous escapades of associates—particularly brother Robert. The public admired Kennedy for his vigor, but his friends, who knew the extent to which he overcame daily pain, found him an inspiration. Remarkably, he managed to confront the physical and mental challenges of the presidency.

Following therapy, lunch, and a nap, Kennedy returned to the Oval Office sometime after 3:30 P.M. for more appointments and meetings. Later in the day an attractive young secretary in Lincoln's office came to massage his hair, which invited kidding between Kennedy and his balding staffers. He always watched the Huntley-Brinkley television news program afterward. Sometime around 7:00 or whenever the last visitor had departed, Theodore Sorensen and other staffers wandered into the office to reflect on the day's events. Subsequently, Kennedy headed for the pool, sometimes joined by his children, and then returned to the second-floor living quarters for dinner.

The Kennedys usually dined with friends at least two nights a week. The guests rarely included those with whom the president worked, for he sought amusement or entertainment to extricate him from the pressures of the day. Thus Robert Kennedy was rarely asked. He enjoyed old friends like Paul Fay, Charles Spalding, LeMoyne Billings, David Ormsby Gore, and Charles Bartlett. The Benjamin Bradlees, the Joseph Alsops, the Franklin Roosevelt, Jrs., and the Arthur Schlesinger, Jrs., were frequent guests, as was William Walton, an artist and former journalist. Kennedy, a consummate gossip, pumped them about peccadilloes of famous people and quizzed Bradlee about the goings-on at *Newsweek*. He also enjoyed poking fun at guests. Infrequently they even played parlor games. On one occasion Defense Secretary Robert McNamara and Jacqueline danced the "Twist" together, which leaked to the press, alarming Kennedy. Most often the Kennedys showed a film following dinner. A frequent movie viewer who once saw *Casablanca* four times, he enjoyed adventure films such as *The Guns of Navarone*. If the film bored him, as more of them did during his presidency, he turned to paperwork, occasionally returning to the Oval Office. Sometimes he left the White House to attend a cinema or a party with friends.

On nights when he and Jacqueline were home alone, he generally read reports and news-related articles. For light reading he turned to magazines such as *Variety*, which contained information about the motion-picture business. The table in front of his bed was always stacked with current periodicals and books. The opportunity to read for pleasure occurred more over the weekends when he occasionally turned to Ian Fleming thrillers, the historical novels of Mary Renault, and nonfiction works such as George Kennan's *Russia and the West under Lenin and Stalin*. He also retained an interest in publishing, but he left that activity to others, particularly Sorensen, who continued to turn out image-building books and articles in Kennedy's name. Three books were begun or completed during his presidency, including *A Nation of Immigrants*. Articles with his by-line appeared in *Look*, *American Heritage*, and *Sports Illustrated*.

He and Jacqueline often listened to music before retiring. He enjoyed Broadway show tunes, including the concluding hit from *Camelot*, but, contrary to popular myth, his favorite song remained the lively, unromantic "Bill Bailey, Won't You Please Come Home?" He went to bed between eleven and twelve and apparently slept without difficulty.

Rarely did the president spend weekends in Washington. By late Friday afternoon he would leave for Palm Beach during the winter months or otherwise for Hyannis Port. In 1961 he and Jacqueline also stayed at Glen-Ora, a home they had leased in the Virginia hunt country. The cancellation of that agreement led to the building of Wexford in 1963 on nearby Rattlesnake Mountain, enabling Jackie to fox hunt and ride horses. She sometimes escaped with the children to Virginia a day or two before Kennedy's arrival. In 1963 the family also spent weekends at Camp David because of its tighter security and because separate cottages existed for guests there. By far he enjoyed Hyannis Port the most, where he sailed, walked the beach, and spent time with his parents and other relatives. In December 1961, however, his father suffered a debilitating stroke, which ended their lively discussions. He subsequently spent hours at his father's side, consoling him, briefing him about contemporary issues, and trying to understand his gibberish. He seemed more relaxed around his father now.

Kennedy conducted little official business during the weekends, which lasted until Monday morning. Staffers and departmental heads meanwhile generally worked on Saturdays. Few logged more hours than Sorensen, who willingly sacrificed his health and his marriage for Kennedy. Not too far behind were Rusk, Salinger, and McNamara; they personified the image of the New Frontier, which prided itself on its activism, dedication, and hard work. For good reason, Kennedy occasionally persuaded them to take time off.

The press coverage of the Kennedys' long weekends confirmed the public image of an ideal marriage. The photographs were happy-family ones, involving gleeful children and laughing parents. The couple's relationship remained less than idyllic, however. Both were private, remote, and self-contained people. He admired her whimsical, mysterious demeanor, her knowledge of the arts, her beauty, and her growing popularity; she remained enthralled by his intelligence, charm, power, and wealth. How much more was there is conjectural. Certainly they shared a deep love for their children, but the marriage bore deep scars, not the least of which related to the Kennedys' stifling competitiveness, the president's consuming devotion to politics, and his extramarital affairs, which persisted throughout his presidency. Although Jacqueline had learned to accept her father's similar shortcomings, she was a romantic who often masked her feelings.

Kennedy's sexual conquests occurred in an era when national politicians often brazenly engaged in such extracurricular activity. A tryst in the Washington area seemed almost as common as golf at the country club. The press indirectly condoned such practices, believing dalliances unreportable since they did not affect public business. Journalists obviously ignored political scientist James MacGregor Burns's assertion that "a great politician's career sucks everything into its vortex—including his family and even his dog."[21] Not many national politicians were as sexually active as Kennedy; few women could resist his persuasive charm and youthful good looks. His affairs involved film stars such as Marilyn Monroe and Jayne Mansfield; would-be actresses like Judith Campbell; White House employees, including Jacqueline's press secretary Pamela Turnure and secretaries Priscilla Wear and Jill Cowen—better known to insiders as Fiddle and Faddle; socialites such as Florence Pritchett, a long-time Kennedy flame married to Eisenhower's ambassador to Cuba, Earl E. T. Smith, and Mary Pinchot Meyer, the artistic sister-in-law of Benjamin Bradlee and niece of conservationist Gifford Pinchot; and burlesque queens Blaze Starr and Tempest Storm. More alarming, Kennedy occasionally had affairs with casual acquaintances and virtual strangers, who surreptitiously entered the southwest service entrance of the White House as the result of the solicitations of friends and aides. As one White House employee wrote, they came during Jacqueline's frequent absences, joining the president in the pool and in the family quarters.[22] The White House press, at the time, either knew or suspected such activity but remained silent. Hugh Sidey later reported that one sexual encounter in September 1963 had caused the president to reinjure a weakened back.[23]

A rumored previous marriage in 1939 also received little press coverage, particularly after the Kennedys threatened to sue *Look* and the *New York Daily News* if they published the story. The issue first arose in August 1961 after someone uncovered the Blauvelt Family Genealogy, published in 1957, indicating that John Kennedy was once married to Durie

(Kerr) Malcolm, whom he and his brother Joe had dated. After Durie and other family members belatedly signed affidavits denying the marriage and after unrelated errors in the family genealogy were discovered, Bradlee and a *Newsweek* reporter obtained Kennedy's permission and FBI documents to publish a story refuting the "John's Other Wife" allegation.[24]

Much more serious were Kennedy's indiscretions that threatened the presidency, including his affair with Judith Campbell, who was also romantically involved with Mafia don Sam Giancana. In 1963 FBI reports alluded to Kennedy's possible implication in the Profumo affair, which involved the British war secretary, John D. Profumo, in a sex scandal with prostitute Christine Keeler. Keeler was associated with Dr. Stephen Ward, a London procurer for high-class harlots and a friend of Capt. Yevgeny M. Ivanov, the Soviet deputy naval attaché in London. Ivanov was also intimate with Keeler. An investigation failed to disclose that Profumo had divulged classified information, but he resigned his office and his seat in Parliament in disgrace.

The anti-Kennedy, Hearst-owned *New York Journal-American* first linked Kennedy to the scandal in a June 1963 article coauthored by Don Frasca and James Horan, the managing editor and a Pulitzer Prize winner. It claimed that one of the "biggest names in American politics"—one who held "a very high" elective office—had had an affair with Suzy Chang, a beautiful model and an aspiring London actress, who had connections with Stephen Ward. Within forty-eight hours, Robert Kennedy called the two writers to his office to confirm that they indeed meant the president and had evidence that Kennedy had had affairs in New York City in 1960 and 1961 with both Chang and Marie Novotny, a nineteen-year-old call girl from London and a friend of Keeler and Ward. Novotny shared a New York City apartment with TV producer Harry Towers, a suspected Soviet agent who had fled the country in 1962. In an interview with Peter Earle, a veteran British newspaperman, she had described in vivid detail her relationship with Kennedy. This included a group sex game involving herself and two other prostitutes—allegedly procured by Peter Lawford, Kennedy's brother-in-law—who were dressed as nurses, with the president-elect as the alleged patient. After the *Journal-American* reporters refused to reveal all of their sources, Robert Kennedy ended the meeting "most coolly," according to FBI observer Courtney Evans. Later the attorney general successfully threatened to institute an antitrust suit against the paper unless it dropped further stories on the scandal.[25]

The president's tangential linkage to "Bowtie," the FBI code word for the Profumo affair, made the Kennedy brothers even more beholden and vulnerable to Hoover and the FBI. The bureau had performed investigations for the attorney general regarding Keeler's 1962 visit to America, confirming that the president was not involved with her. Yet, probably unknown to Robert Kennedy, the FBI had gathered related compromising data on President Kennedy, some of which remains classified. Hoover might have even leaked the Chang and Novotny information to the *Journal-American*, a conservative paper with connections to the FBI since the Joseph McCarthy days.

National security considerations again potentially intersected with President Kennedy's sexual escapades when former Senate functionary Robert Baker introduced him to a twenty-seven-year-old East German model named Ellen Romesch, a hostess-service operator in Washington, D.C., who provided favors to politicians and lobbyists. The attorney general's investigation revealed that she had had an affair with a Soviet attaché. A suspected agent herself, she was quickly sent home.[26] Moreover, Anthony Summers discloses in his biography of Marilyn Monroe that the Kennedy brothers, both intimately linked to Monroe, discussed Cuba and other sensitive matters with her, despite her emotional instability and her friendship with suspected leftists in Mexico; thus she was under close FBI surveillance. The Monroe affair made the Kennedys more vulnerable to Hoover, Hoffa, and to mobsters; the latter two reputedly bugged the homes of Monroe and Peter Lawford for damaging evidence.[27]

The president's sexual indiscretions also created security difficulties regarding his physical protection since the Secret Service and FBI could not institute background checks on women discreetly smuggled into the White House. Long-time friend LeMoyne Billings revealed that "it never occurred to Jack that some of the women might be considered dangerous. They were never searched, never questioned in depth."[28] White House Secret Service agents felt powerless to overcome the problem.

In other ways Kennedy's active libido sometimes reached reckless proportions. One 1960 FBI report alluded to a photograph that Kennedy had kept above his Senate desk of himself and other men and women posing nude aboard a yacht. Not surprisingly, the report concluded that Kennedy's " 'extracurricular activities' were a standard joke around the Senate Office Building." Judith Campbell remembered that during the presidency "there were times and places when he wanted . . . to meet . . . that would have been so blatant I would have been embarrassed."[29] Kennedy also assented to the appearance of Monroe at his forty-fifth birthday gala at New York's Madison Square Garden on 19 May 1962, attended by some fifteen thousand Democrats in a massive fund-raising effort. Monroe, dressed in "skin and beads," according to Adlai Stevenson, sang "Happy Birthday, Mr. President" and a special version of

269

"Thanks for the Memories," causing Kennedy to respond, "I can now retire from politics after having had 'Happy Birthday' sung to me in such a sweet, wholesome way." Later in the evening the two met in his suite at the Carlyle Hotel for probably the last time. That summer Robert Kennedy reportedly visited her in California to reaffirm his brother's efforts to disengage from the relationship, following her many letters and telephone calls. He too soon found himself more intimately involved.[30]

Given his sensitivity in other areas, Kennedy's apparent disregard for public disclosure of his philandering seems incomprehensible. The inconsistency most likely came from a conviction that the press and the opposition party would continue to be discreet. Barry Goldwater, the likely Republican presidential nominee in 1964, remained an old friend and in some ways a kindred spirit. Kennedy thought "he was above it all," recalled Campbell.[31] He seemed to have an aristocratic view of public leaders and their private sexual adventures. Kennedy felt sorry for Profumo, without thinking that the same thing could happen to him.

Perhaps a deeper explanation exists for his recklessness. To Kennedy boredom was a cardinal sin. For some psychological reason, most likely related to his upbringing, he needed to act boldly and take risks. He had played football at Harvard and had volunteered for strenuous PT-boat duty despite his serious physical ailments. His brothers felt the same apparent need, which led to Joe's tragic death in 1944. Following the president's assassination, Robert compulsively scaled Mt. Kennedy, the tallest unclimbed peak in North America, and fought the dangerous rapids of the Salmon and Colorado rivers in a kayak. The Kennedys were also notoriously fast drivers. Yet even though President Kennedy showed a James Bond daring in defying sexual propriety, he paradoxically exercised caution in the realm of public policy. It was as if one compensated for the other.

Women intimate with Kennedy deceived themselves in believing that he cared deeply for them. Those more discerning sensed a coldness beneath the exterior charm that confirmed the appraisals of long-standing acquaintances. The fact is that he found it difficult to have deep and lasting relationships; one close friend referred to his "emotional blockage."[32] He saw women solely as sexual objects to be conquered and exploited.

Few probably understood this better than Jacqueline. Still, it made it no easier to accept, particularly his relationships with women of the same social class. Frustration may have fed her lavish tastes, which took her into New York City and elsewhere on shopping sprees for designer clothing, jewelry, antiques, and art work. This added to the marital tension as

Kennedy raged about the bills. Ordered to cut back, she reduced the food, liquor, and miscellaneous budgets but preserved the one for her clothing. Toys and food items that came to the White House during the holidays were now inspected for family use rather than being automatically shipped to orphanages. Even so, according to Mary Gallagher, her personal secretary, family expenses exceeded the president's one hundred thousand dollar salary, which he donated to charities, much to his wife's annoyance.

Disagreements also arose over the confinement of White House living, and she fled that environment as often as possible. In 1961 she spent almost the entire summer in Hyannis Port. She went on so many trips in 1962, including three weeks in Italy and three more in India and Pakistan, that the press rephrased Jimmy Durante's "Mrs. Calabash" television signature to "And good night, Mrs. Kennedy, wherever you are." The peering eyes of tourists, who intruded on private family activities, especially bothered Jacqueline. To help screen Caroline and John-John, she had thirty large rhododendrons planted along the southwest gate, despite her husband's concerns that she was blocking the tourists' view of the White House. More serious was the conflict between her and the president over how often the press could photograph and write about the children. Salinger found himself caught in the middle between Jacqueline, who wanted little coverage and Kennedy, who wanted photographers everywhere.

Jacqueline's unwillingness to assume the political obligations of first lady also occasionally strained the marriage. Determined to maintain her independence, she did only what she wanted to do. Initially she even rejected the title of first lady, claiming that "it sounds like a saddle horse." She insisted on being called Mrs. Kennedy, adding that her primary role was to take care of her husband and children. She told her press secretary that her press relations would be "minimum information given with maximum politeness." Her disdain for female reporters was widely known; on one occasion President Kennedy literally twisted her arm behind her back at a state dinner and marched her over to a gathering of women reporters, where he said, "Say hello to the girls, darling."[33] Nor would she meet with the Girl Scouts of America, the Muscular Dystrophy Association, the American Red Cross, and other service organizations, insisting that Mrs. Lyndon Johnson handle it. In other instances she came to official functions late or avoided those involving foreign leaders whom she thought unimportant. More embarrassingly, she sometimes canceled engagements because of illness, only to have the press report her waterskiing at Hyannis Port or active elsewhere.

271

She showed similar insensitivity about the social issues of the time. White House staffer Harris Wofford wrote of his bringing Martin Luther King, Jr., to the White House during a crisis in the civil rights movement. The elevator they were on inadvertently went down to the basement, where they ran into Jackie as she entered the elevator. She said in her whispering voice, "Oh, Dr. King, you would be so thrilled if you could just have been with me in the basement this morning. I found a chair right out of the Andrew Jackson period—a beautiful chair." King said in his slow, baritone voice, "Yes—yes—is that so?" Upon reaching the second floor, Jackie exclaimed, "I've just got to tell Jack about this chair." But then she caught herself, "You have other things to talk to him about, don't you?" Following her departure, King said, "Well, well—wasn't that something?"[34]

Still, Jacqueline Kennedy turned into a major asset for the Kennedy presidency. Opinion polls gave her high approval ratings, and she soon headed the list of "most admired women" (Mamie Eisenhower had never reached the top position). Some of this popularity might have been related to her youth, beauty, motherhood, and her tasteful impact on fashion, best described as the "Jackie look." It helped too that she followed the matronly Bess Truman and Mamie Eisenhower, neither of whom had had much public impact. Moreover, Jackie helped to create the cultural aura of the Kennedy years; she was artistic, multilingual, intelligent, and regal. Americans, without knowing much about her personal life, proudly perceived her as more than a match for European royalty. She channeled her strengths effectively, reestablishing the White House as a symbolic center of the nation's cultural life by recognizing artistic giants at black-tie social events, including Aaron Copland, Igor Stravinsky, Andrew Wyeth, and Pablo Casals. The Kennedys also devoted an evening to the honoring of American Nobel laureates.

She played a major part in creating a well-publicized ambience for official social functions. Guests were treated to peppy music on arrival, were served cocktails, and then were seated at small round tables for a candlelight dinner prepared by a French chef. Sixty-six of these occasions were state events involving foreign leaders—setting a record for such activity. All were imaginatively and meticulously planned, revealing Jackie's organizational skills and close attention to detail. The president capped those events by welcoming the guests in a relaxed, seemingly off-the-cuff manner that put everyone at ease. Senator J. William Fulbright remembered those witty talks as the most gracious that he had ever encountered in public life.

The restoration of the White House provided an even greater showcase for Jacqueline's talents and persistency. Despite the president's initial lack of enthusiasm, she resolved to restore the formal first-floor state rooms to their historical grandeur, reflecting more the French style of the Monroe era. This meant that the existing array of contemporary furniture had to go. She rummaged through the White House basement and attic before going to the Fort Washington warehouse in Maryland for historic White House furniture and furnishings. She then established a White House Fine Arts Committee, chaired by Henry Francis du Pont—a leading authority on historic furnishings—and composed of the wealthy and prominent, whom she induced to contribute antiques and money. Their influence proved invaluable in persuading others to support the project. She also organized a special committee for White House paintings in order to obtain historic masterpieces. Through her efforts, the position of a permanent White House curator was created, as was the White House Historical Association. Its major project was the publication of Jacqueline's book *The White House: An Historic Guide*, which eventually sold millions of copies at a nominal fee, helping to finance the restoration. The renewed interest led to her tour of the restored state rooms, televised by the three national networks. In this production she clearly outshone both a proud and peeved president, who belatedly appeared near the conclusion of the telecast.

Jacqueline also played a positive role abroad in furthering the New Frontier image. In 1961 she captivated de Gaulle, Khrushchev, and other foreign leaders as well as the European press. She did the same later in Italy and Mexico, not only by projecting youth, beauty, and poise but by being able to speak the language of the country. This made up for the president's linguistic shortcomings (according to a contemporary, he attempted French "with a bad Cuban accent").[35] On her extended trip to India and Pakistan in 1962, taken without her husband, she charmed Prime Minister Nehru, ordinarily a difficult person to move. He soon hung a picture of himself and Jackie strolling arm-in-arm in the garden. Her letters from India, Pakistan, and elsewhere reportedly provided Kennedy with insightful observations. At home as well, despite her disdain of politics, she proved a valuable go-between with Adlai Stevenson, Chester Bowles, and others whom Kennedy found hard to soothe. She also gave him occasional advice, favoring the Test Ban Treaty and the Russian wheat deal.

Jacqueline and John Kennedy drew momentarily closer by summer 1963 after the death of their prematurely born son, Patrick Bouvier. The president took the loss hard. Last to leave the funeral mass, he wept as he held onto the tiny casket, causing Richard Cardinal Cushing to whisper,

"Come on, Jack, let's go, God is good."[36] Soon afterward, concerned with Jacqueline's well-being, he consented to her joining her sister, Lee Radziwill, on a cruise aboard the luxurious *Christina* at the invitation of the Greek shipping magnate, Aristotle Onassis. This involved some political risk because Onassis faced a federal government suit for failure to pay taxes for using American surplus ships. An obvious concern was that some would interpret Onassis's hospitality as bribery. Moreover, Kennedy wondered about how the public would react to her going on a cruise in light of their recent tragedy. To soften possible criticism, he asked Under Secretary of Commerce Franklin Roosevelt, Jr., and his wife to chaperone. The press gave the cruise extensive play, covering the Aegean ports of call and describing the "lavish shipboard dinners" and the "dancing music." Some criticism focused on Jackie, particularly after a photographer caught her in a bikini, sunbathing on the deck of the ship. The publication of the snapshot triggered the president's telegram, asking her to come home, but she elected to complete the scheduled two-week trip, arriving in Washington in mid-October.

Scarcely one month remained of their life together. That time encompassed weekend excursions to Wexford, Hyannis Port, and Palm Beach, and other enjoyable moments. It also included Jacqueline's promise to accompany her husband on a political trip to Texas in mid-November, her first such venture during the presidency. Perhaps out of guilt for her recent vacation, she had also consented to play an active part in the 1964 presidential campaign. Even so, certain strains remained, which occasionally surfaced. On the evening prior to the departure for Texas, the press, covering a White House judiciary reception, heard an apparent domestic squabble between the two on the grand stairway just before their scheduled descent. Journalist Helen Thomas sensed that the first lady had been crying. Evelyn Lincoln later confirmed that the marriage had not improved, though Jacqueline wanted people to think otherwise. Lincoln contended that they were too incompatible to live in harmony.

In any assessment of Kennedy, imagery will always be a formidable obstacle. Even more than an attractive personality, his fascinating family, or the images that he actively cultivated, there exists the emotion-laden images of Dallas and its immediate aftermath, which threaten to supersede all else. Who can forget the attractive, smiling couple that morning of the twenty-second at Love Field, Kennedy handsomely attired in a gray suit and pin-striped shirt and his wife in a strawberry-pink wool outfit and matching pill-box hat, cradling a bouquet of red roses? Less than an hour later in the backseat of the Lincoln convertible came the loud, crackling sounds of gunfire, and his life suddenly ended. As the motorcade sped to Parkland Memorial Hospital, his disfigured head had replaced the roses in her arms. Other scenes, too, remain transfixed, seemingly forever: the swearing in of a new president on Air Force One with a dazed Jacqueline standing nearby in a blood-stained suit; a veiled, youthful widow dressed in black, head held erect, holding the hands of her two children; and the lighting of the symbolic eternal flame at Arlington National Cemetery, with family members kneeling in front of the burial site.

11

★ ★ ★ ★ ★

AFTERMATH AND ASSESSMENT

Kennedy's assassination on 22 November 1963 has invited almost as much scholarly attention as his presidency. Yet despite hundreds of publications devoted to the "crime of the century" and eight inquiries since 1963, investigators are no closer to resolving the mysteries of his death than they were a generation ago. In some ways the more one seems to know, the less certain one is about what happened. Contributing to the dilemma, many eyewitnesses and suspects are now dead, and key documentary evidence remains in the protective custody of the federal government.

Nevertheless, some aspects seem more certain than others, one being the inadequacy of the original investigation, which obscured evidence relating to what really occurred. The Johnson-appointed Warren Commission, headed by Chief Justice Earl Warren and including six other distinguished members (among them former CIA director Allen Dulles and Congressman Gerald Ford of Michigan), was too intent on quenching rumors and allaying suspicions of conspiracy. Concerned about the national psyche, it also felt pressure from President Johnson to prevent the assassination from becoming an issue in the 1964 presidential campaign. Consequently, it reaffirmed the conventional wisdom that evolved shortly after the November tragedy: Twenty-four-year-old Lee Harvey Oswald, an alleged misfit and Communist sympathizer, had alone killed the president, nightclub-owner Jack Ruby had alone murdered Oswald, and no one else had been involved. The commission accepted Ruby's explanation that he had wished to spare Jacqueline Kennedy and her family the grief of an assassination trial.

J. Edgar Hoover represented the greatest influence on the commission. He concluded in a 5 December 1963 report that Oswald was the sole assassin, despite FBI evidence that suggested other possible scenarios. Hoover pushed for a speedy acceptance of the lone-gunman theory, undoubtedly because of a concern that a comprehensive investigation might reveal the bureau's investigatory shortcomings. The FBI had failed to place Oswald on the Security Index, regardless of all that it should have known about him. It may have even once employed him as an informant. More importantly, Hoover's confidential sources would link Oswald with possible conspiracies involving Cubans or organized crime—a public revelation that would have been disastrous for the FBI. Viewing the blue-ribbon Warren Commission as an adversary, Hoover provided it only with information that reinforced a preconceived view.

In relying on the FBI and the CIA for information instead of conducting its own investigations, the commission unknowingly dealt with agencies that had little interest in uncovering truth. The CIA had its own reasons for engaging in a conspiracy of silence. Having employed Mafia elements in an attempt to assassinate Castro, the CIA had to be concerned about embarrassing disclosures relating to a Cuban-connected conspiracy to kill Kennedy. At the commission's first executive session, former CIA-head Dulles suspiciously provided fellow commissioners copies of a study claiming that political assassinations resulted from lone madmen.

Thus, the Warren Commission conducted an inquiry that validated the establishment's prejudgments. It not only overlooked leads but, although to a lesser degree than the FBI, it also occasionally altered the testimony of witnesses and concealed information to ensure that its reports conformed to certain preconceptions. Moreover, at no time did Robert Kennedy challenge the commission's thesis, despite his private suspicions of a probable plot involving either Castro or gangsters. Inconsolable and dysfunctional in the ensuing weeks, the attorney general was undoubtedly distraught because of the possibility that his actions might have led to his brother's death. He too, then, joined the conspiracy of silence.

It was only a matter of time before the public praise of the nine-hundred-page Warren Report turned to skepticism, as lawyers, freelance writers, and outside investigators probed the twenty thousand pages of commission documentation and one hundred thousand pages of FBI material. What they found produced a flood of critical books beginning in 1966 and generated additional inquiries, culminating with the

House Select Committee on Assassinations in 1978. That investigation proved to be almost as limited and faulty as the Warren inquiry, as House members and staffers found themselves hindered by time and financial constraints. As a result, some sixteen file drawers of CIA material remained unused as well as thousands of pages of belatedly-released FBI material. Not surprisingly, the committee neglected to explore promising leads. Its contradictory conclusion was that although it was in fundamental agreement with most of the Warren Report's assessments, acoustical evidence indicated the involvement of another gunman. The committee surmised that the most likely conspiracy involved Cubans associated with anti-Castro organizations in the United States. Building partly on Jack Ruby's close ties with organized crime and on FBI electronic surveillance and informant reports, it deduced that a criminal element also might have been connected with the assassination.

The enigmatic Oswald continues to be at the center of the controversy. One assassination scholar compares him to a Rubik's Cube: "No sooner does a side start to take shape than another side becomes disordered."[1] Was he a defector or a CIA agent during his stay in the Soviet Union? To what extent was he indirectly tied to New Orleans mobchieftain Carlos Marcello? Was his pro-Castro Fair-Play-for-Cuba chapter of two members a front for anti-Castro activity in New Orleans? Most importantly, did at least one person impersonate Oswald as the evidence suggests? Was he merely a patsy as he himself claimed to be just before his death? Critics have doubted whether Oswald could have successfully fired three shots in five to seven seconds, using an obsolete, bolt-action telescopic rifle, from the sixth floor of the Texas Book Depository. He reportedly struck Kennedy twice from behind and Governor John Connally of Texas once, while both were passengers in the same automobile. The Warren Commission implausibly concluded that one bullet exited from the president's throat before wounding Connally in the back, wrist, and thigh. The so-called magic bullet was later allegedly found on the governor's stretcher at Parkland Memorial Hospital. Spectrographic tests revealed that that bullet was far too pristine to have caused that much damage. Furthermore, questions still persist about its trajectory, which did not seem acute enough to have come from the sixth floor of the building.

Just as puzzling are the reports of eyewitnesses who noticed an unflustered Oswald on the second floor of the School Depository building ninety seconds after the shooting. It would have been extremely difficult—if not impossible—for him to have concealed the weapon and then descended four floors in that length of time. Additionally, eyewitnesses and photographic evidence revealed that minutes prior to the assassination more than one person was visible in the same sixth-floor area to several people outside the building.

The most significant testimony, however, came from more than fifty witnesses who testified that they had heard shots coming from the grassy-knoll area ahead of the motorcade. Others reported seeing smoke rising from above a stockade fence in that vicinity, and at least seven reported smelling the odor of gunpowder in the same area. Scholars who have analyzed the film of the assassination—taken by bystander Abraham Zapruder—have also been influenced by the fact that the president's head and body violently jerked backward and leftward, suggesting that he was also hit from the right front.[2] Yet the Warren Commission neglected to explore the possibilities of additional gunmen ahead and behind the motorcade.

Nor did the commission expose Ruby's underworld connections, originating from his Chicago days as Al Capone's runner. In the months prior to the assassination, Ruby had remained in contact with mob elements tied to Jimmy Hoffa and Mafia dons Santos Trafficante, Jr., and Meyer Lansky, both of Florida. He was in close touch with Dallas Mafia boss Joseph Civello, friend and associate of Marcello. Ruby's long-time efforts to cultivate the Dallas police force, which enabled him to gun down Oswald, are also well documented. More intriguing is the allegation of over a dozen eyewitnesses that he and Oswald knew each other before the assassination. All of this lends credence to the probability that Kennedy's and Oswald's deaths were a part of a gigantic conspiracy—one that most assassination historians and 80 percent of the American public today believe existed.

Though the available evidence favors a conspiracy, it would be difficult—if not foolhardy—to define its specific nature. What remains are several plausible theories. One involves the Cuban government, which was aware of the CIA's efforts to liquidate Castro. The Cubans allegedly sought retribution by killing Kennedy; Lyndon Johnson said as much to journalist Howard K. Smith in 1964. To others he accused Kennedy of "operating a damned Murder, Inc., in the Caribbean." In September 1963 Castro had warned U.S. leaders that "they themselves would not be safe" if they continued in their attempts to eliminate him.[3] Pro-Castro Cubans conceivably could have involved Oswald in the assassination plot. His activities in New Orleans put him in contact with various shadowy figures—many of them Cuban. A Latin American informant testified that Oswald—or a double—had visited the Cuban consulate in Mexico City on 13 September 1963 where he had received money—an allegation that a CIA-related source corroborated. In 1964 the CIA learned that a pro-Castro Cuban involved somehow in the assassination and with supposed ties with Cuban intelligence had crossed into Mexico from Texas on 23 November 1963. Four days later the Cuban flew to Havana from Mexico City on a commercial flight; he was the sole passenger.[4]

Suspicion also lingers that Cuban exiles in the United States sought Kennedy's life following his betrayal of the Cuban anti-Castro cause on the Bay of Pigs beaches. Certainly that element expressed considerable bitterness toward him afterward—with at least one actual death threat recorded in the FBI files.[5] Next to Miami, New Orleans remained a hotbed of activity for Cuban exiles into 1963. Oswald had strong associations with anti-Castro right-wing extremists there, including David Ferrie, who was involved in smuggling supplies to anti-Communist rebels in Cuba. Eyewitnesses observed Oswald and Ferrie together in late summer 1963 and testified to their anti-Kennedy outbursts. Interestingly, Ferrie had ties with the Marcello organization in New Orleans.

The underworld also had reason to assassinate the president. The Kennedys' war on crime had intensified in 1962 when the Justice Department tightened the screws on Marcello, Sam Giancana, and Hoffa; they and others faced federal action in the administration's final days. As a result, several mobsters, as FBI sources subsequently revealed, had privately vowed to kill Kennedy. Marcello, the head of the Mafia's "first family," especially has become a prime suspect among assassination scholars. According to Edward Becker, a Las Vegas private investigator who had befriended the Mafia boss, Marcello told him in summer 1962 that Jack Kennedy had to die and it would be arranged in a way not to implicate his own men. The mobster supposedly targeted the president instead of Robert Kennedy because if the latter were killed, Jack Kennedy would seek retribution against Robert Kennedy's enemies. But with the president gone, a defused attorney general could not count on support from President Johnson.[6]

The House Assassinations Committee—and subsequent assassination scholars—have documented Marcello's ties with Hoffa, Trafficante, Oswald, Ruby, Ferrie, and members of the New Orleans Cuban community. Conspiracy possibilities abounded, leading the House committee to conclude ambiguously that while it was unlikely that prominent mobsters were involved, Marcello, Trafficante, and Hoffa nevertheless "had the motive, opportunity, and means" to assassinate the president.[7] Since 1978 most assassination scholars have inconclusively argued that point with much greater force.

Regardless of the theories, Kennedy's sudden and tragic death contributed immensely to the romantic way in which Americans would remember his presidency, especially since it preceded violent social conflict, disillusionment, and the assassinations of Malcolm X, Martin Luther King, Jr., and Robert Kennedy. To many Americans, John Kennedy's death ended an age of excellence, innocence, hope, and optimism. It was as if his murder "opened some malign trap door in American culture, and the wild bats flapped out."[8] It also invoked immeasurable grief for a seemingly idealistic and gallant prince and his family. And unlike the deaths of other presidents, Kennedy's assassination left Americans with the image of youth—and the promise of greatness—frozen in time. It is difficult to think of Kennedy without linking him to that tragedy in 1963. We are reminded of it by the symbolic artifacts it produced: the commemorative coins, stamps, and "shrines" in his honor—especially the space center in Florida, the Center for Performing Arts in Washington, D.C., the School of Government at Harvard, and the many public buildings in local communities nationwide. Revealingly, Kennedy's public remembrance comes not on his birthday but on the anniversary of his death; the twentieth- and the twenty-fifth-year commemorations dominated the national media.

Not surprisingly, a *Newsweek* Gallup Poll in 1983 confirmed that Kennedy was easily America's most popular president. Two-thirds of the respondents believed that the United States would have been "much different" had he lived. Most Americans have apparently overlooked his recently revealed shortcomings, which to them reflected perhaps a humanity that aspired for greatness and goodness despite the imperfections. The 1983 poll revealed an almost messianic image of Kennedy, one committed to the downtrodden, to racial justice, to facing down the Soviets, and to infusing the nation with a new spirit. Like the martyred Lincoln, Kennedy has become the property of the whole nation and both political parties. Even Ronald Reagan and the Republicans invoked his name in the 1980s to remind Democrats that they, too, sought to move the nation again and restore national greatness. None has more identified with him than the Democratic neoliberals, the cool pragmatists of the 1980s who wanted to pursue traditional Democratic ideas without the ideological trappings of liberalism. Known as Kennedy's children, they included Paul Tsongas and Michael Dukakis of Massachusetts, Charles Robb of Virginia, Albert Gore, Jr., of Tennessee, and Gary Hart of Colorado, who most emulated Kennedy's personal style.

It is erroneous to attribute President Kennedy's elevation solely to the circumstances of his death. After all, he exhibited considerable popularity during his presidency, with an approval rating that never fell below 59 percent in the Gallup Polls. He will always be remembered for his style. His youthful and handsome appearance stood out among a generation of aging leaders such as Truman, Eisenhower, Adenauer, de Gaulle, Macmillan, Nehru, and Khrushchev. Yet more than this, he projected an almost indescribable aura that affected practically everyone who came in contact with him either personally or through television. Much of that appeal can be attributed to his good manners, vitality, wit, self-deprecating humor, and disarming casualness, which journalist Mary McGrory insisted made him the "most attractive man of his generation."[9] Kennedy gave the impression of liking and caring about people, and they in turn felt that way about him. The Byrds, a musical group of the late sixties and seventies, expressed a common sentiment when they sang, "Though I never met him, I knew him just the same. He was a friend of mine."[10]

Kennedy also succeeded in articulating a sense of hope and purpose that made a profound impression, particularly on the young and disadvantaged, causing them to connect with government in a way that they have not done again since then. He conveyed a lofty standard of excellence that became the perfect antidote to the mass conformity and mediocrity that seemed to characterize the society of the fifties. He stirred people the most through his moving speeches. As Daniel Boorstin writes, "a short life, unfulfilled in action, is commonly and disproportionally judged by the eloquent utterance."[11] Programs such as the Peace Corps and the Alliance for Progress further embodied that same idealistic spirit, making Kennedy an appealing leader even in the remotest areas of the Third World. In Guinea, for example, Sékou Touré exclaimed at the time of Kennedy's death, "I have lost my only true friend in the outside world."[12] At home many others expressed similar feelings.

Yet the Kennedy image also contains a lesser-known, unflattering side. Despite his promotion of the arts, ballet and opera bored him, and he knew little about painting; his tastes were more mundane. Less known until the 1970s were his frequent sexual indiscretions. Kennedy's obsession with image also caused a preoccupation with the press's treatment of him and his administration. At times he acted vindictively toward unfriendly journalists. There existed as well a certain underlying pettiness, which Kennedy displayed toward those whom he disliked. Adlai Stevenson fell victim to the Kennedy treatment following the Cuban missile crisis, when the president needlessly leaked unflattering information about him to the press. More than most politicians, Kennedy also masked an enormous ego and vanity. Yet, everything considered, this complex man will rightly always be remembered more for his attributes.

In the final analysis, as Kennedy himself believed, presidential success should be gauged primarily by concrete achievement. Such an evaluation must take into account Kennedy's untimely death, which curtailed his attainment as much as it enhanced his popular image and his pending programs. With this in mind, one might assess his presidency by addressing two questions: First, did he leave the country in better shape as a result of his tenure? Second, to what extent did he achieve his stated goals?

Kennedy had come into office with the future of West Berlin hanging in the balance. In Laos a Communist-based insurgency successfully waged war against an unpopular United States–backed regime. In South Vietnam the Vietcong had the autocratic Diem on the defensive. Civil war engulfed the newly independent Congo, where the Soviets hoped to capitalize, and a Communist regime in Cuba reportedly threatened to export its revolution into neighboring countries. Third World nations in general viewed the United States with suspicion if not contempt. Moreover, United States military and technological strength had seemingly diminished—causing Americans to believe that they were losing the cold war. At the same time, the Eisenhower presidency had made no progress in easing tensions or in obtaining a nuclear arms agreement with the Soviet Union.

Domestically, the challenges were nearly as formidable. The national government seemed almost oblivious to a budding civil rights movement. After several years of prosperity, the economy had stagnated, as the growth rate fell to a modest 2.5 percent and a balance-of-payments deficit drained gold reserves. Blight plagued the cities. Poverty remained an ignored problem, especially afflicting the elderly, blacks, Hispanics, and rural Americans. In spite of huge subsidies to major commercial farmers, agriculture had come out of the 1950s in the worst shape since the Great Depression. Federal efforts to bolster public education had been disappointing.

To turn the tide, Kennedy promised Americans a dynamic presidency—one that would formulate and fight for legislative enactments, provide moral and political leadership, and respond to the immense problems of war and peace. Probably no major-party presidential nominee had ever committed himself to doing as much—not even Roosevelt in 1932. Kennedy pledged to restore American military strength by increasing conventional forces and accelerating the missile program. At the same time, he intended to seek improved relations with the Communist world. No goal seemed more essential than an agreement for nuclear arms control with the Soviets. He promised to reassess United States policy on China, defend Berlin, rebuild NATO, increase economic assistance to the Third World, reconstruct relations with Latin America through an Alliance for Progress, encourage the newly developed nations of Africa, strengthen the UN—"our last best hope," rectify the payment imbalance, elevate the United States to the "uncharted areas of science and space," and honor all American commitments abroad. Notably, he promised to develop a "coherent and purposeful national strategy."

In the area of foreign policy, Kennedy accomplished several significant goals. He strengthened the United States militarily, which enabled him to deal effectively with Khrushchev in West Berlin and Cuba. Indeed by 1963 Berlin no longer seemed a major problem. Kennedy's substantial increase of ICBMS and other missiles, however, forced the Soviet Union into an extensive buildup, leading to parity in the 1970s and subsequent arms races. Not surprisingly, Kennedy's efforts to achieve nuclear arms control proved disappointing, despite the atmospheric test ban treaty of 1963. How much more was possible in light of a developing détente with the Soviets is uncertain. While Kennedy and Khrushchev had drawn closer, much suspicion still existed between their two countries. Kennedy probably would have accomplished no more than Johnson did in securing a nuclear nonproliferation treaty in 1967.

Moreover, Kennedy's success in increasing conventional forces and emphasizing counterinsurgency had a down side. The philosophy of flexible containment served to sink the United States more deeply into Vietnam, Kennedy's Achilles heel. Just as disturbing was the way in which Kennedy responded to an inherited Cuban vexation. Like Vietnam, Cuba—in spite of Kennedy's reputed missile-crisis triumph—became more of a problem as a result of his presidency. Castro afterward viewed the United States more suspiciously and found himself more dependent on the Soviet Union. Neither did American relations improve with Communist China, for Kennedy adhered to the stringent policy of the past. Efforts to improve economic relations with Eastern European countries such as Poland and Yugoslavia also failed, and Kennedy was unable to strengthen NATO. De Gaulle and Adenauer instead became increasingly independent, partly in reaction to United States policy. In fact, Kennedy never did develop a coherent and purposeful strategy and oscillated between hardline and conciliatory approaches with little apparent rationale.

Still, of the major foreign policy crises facing Kennedy in early 1961 (Laos, Berlin, the Congo, and Vietnam), only Vietnam remained virulent at Kennedy's death. Except for Cuba, no new crisis had emerged. Kennedy performed well as a crisis manager, even though he did less well in preventing them. Furthermore, he did much to improve the image of the United States in the newly emerging nations of Africa and Asia. The Peace Corps, Food for Peace, and AID programs helped to reduce the mistrust of new governments, who retained their neutrality in spite of Soviet efforts to win their allegiance. In the Congo, Kennedy wisely exercised restraint in working through the UN. Indeed no president backed that organization more. In Latin America Kennedy's lofty Alliance for Progress improved conditions only marginally, but Latinos continued to hope that Kennedy would make that endeavor work. Kennedy also emerged as the father of the space program as the United States launched its first man into orbit and made significant strides toward placing a man on the moon. Soviet technology no longer seemed as imposing, and by 1963 Americans felt justifiably proud that the tide was turning in America's favor.

Kennedy had also sought to revitalize a floundering domestic America. In the tradition of his Democratic predecessors, he pledged to alleviate economic stagnation, rising unemployment, wide-scale poverty, and urban squalor. He proposed expanded coverages and increases in Social Security benefits and the minimum wage, a housing program under a new Housing and Urban Affairs Department, urban renewal, tax incentives, federal aid to education, health care for the aged, and action against organized and juvenile crime. He also promised to end racial discrimination, combat the farm problem, and preserve America's natural resources. All of this he acknowledged would not be finished in the "first one thousand days" nor "in the life of this administration."

Kennedy indeed fell far short of accomplishing his domestic objectives. Even when considering the relative conservatism of the times, one is hard pressed to give Kennedy high marks in the legislative arena, as programs for civil rights, medical assistance for the aged; education, and poverty failed to materialize. While the tax-cut and civil rights bills probably would have passed Congress in 1964 had he lived, his other major proposals remained in limbo. More disconcerting was Kennedy's wavering leadership in advancing civil rights, following his encouragement of it in 1960. In response to intense pressure from black activists, however, he did morally commit the presidency to the movement by 1963—resulting in the unavoidable Democratic party demise in the South in the years afterward.

To his credit Kennedy promoted economic growth in spite of his fiscal conservatism. The Kennedy years for most Americans were a good time to live—inflation and interest rates were low, unemployment was reduced, wages were rising, and taxes were about to descend. Additionally, the balance-of-payment problem showed modest improvement. Kennedy provided job-training programs, updated traditional New Deal commitments such as Social Security and the minimum wage, and reduced job discrimination against women. Moreover, despite failing to obtain comprehensive agricultural legislation, he eased farm problems and extended rural assistance. He responded to the problems and needs of juvenile delinquency and mental retardation, implemented the first significant housing program since 1949, began urban renewal, and addressed the problem of organized crime. Even though several major domestic objectives remained unfulfilled, Kennedy left the country better off than he had found it in 1961. Too, partly because of Kennedy's efforts, the national mood seemed more receptive to change by 1963.

Kennedy's presidency was also remarkably free of notable scandal and incompetence. Not since the New Deal was the national government uniformly served so well. Kennedy had appointed an exceptional group of public servants—many of them attracted by his perceived idealism and style. Arthur Goldberg, Bill Moyers, Edward R. Murrow, Edwin Reischauer, Theodore Sorensen, Sargent Shriver, and Byron "Whizzer" White represent a sampling. They in turn encouraged others to enlist—some as volunteers in the Peace Corps. Kennedy remained a positive model to the end. He was charming, optimistic, positive, and fun to be around. If he exhibited undue activism at times, as even Schlesinger now admits, Kennedy also displayed judicious restraint and caution—an approach that served him better in the realm of foreign policy. And despite his mishandling of the Diem crisis of 1963, he showed growth in his last year.

In the 1982 Murray-Blessing presidential evaluation poll, some one thousand scholars have rated Kennedy as an above-average president in the ranking—ironically slightly below Eisenhower.[13] Of the nine presidents who served less than one full term, Kennedy alone is ranked higher than average. To many historians at least, the Kennedy glitter and promise and the tragedy of assassination have given way to the realities of Vietnam, excessive presidential activism, and the perceived limitations of liberalism at home—all of which were rooted in the Kennedy presidency. In any case, above average is where he belongs. And for those of us who reached adulthood in the early 1960s, John Fitzgerald Kennedy will always be remembered as a remarkable person, if not as a great president.

NOTES

In accordance with the style and aims of the American Presidency Series, this study cited sparingly. Many uncited quotations, dated in the text of the book, came from *Public Papers of the Presidents of the United States, John F. Kennedy, Containing the Public Messages, Speeches, and Statements of the President, 1961–1963*, 3 vols. (Washington, D.C.: Government Printing Office, 1961–1964). The sources that provided the bedrock for this work are of course mentioned in the Bibliographical Essay.

CHAPTER I
THE ROAD TO THE WHITE HOUSE

1. Dr. Janet Travell oral history transcript, pp. 3–8, John F. Kennedy Library, Boston, Mass. (hereafter JFKL). The Kennedy family remains uncooperative about releasing John Kennedy's medical records (Lawrence C. Horowitz, administrative assistant to Sen. Edward Kennedy, to author, 15 Sept. 1984). Kennedy's medical history is best covered in Joan Blair and Clay Blair, Jr., *The Search for JFK* (New York: Berkley Medallion Books, 1976).

2. Herbert S. Parmet, *Jack: The Struggles of John F. Kennedy* (New York: Dial Press, 1980), p. 16.

3. Rose Fitzgerald Kennedy, *Times to Remember* (Garden City, N.Y.: Doubleday, 1974), p. 202.

4. Blair and Blair, *Search for JFK*, p. 79.

5. Paul B. Fay, Jr., *The Pleasure of His Company* (New York: Harper and Row, 1966), p. 141.

6. Blair and Blair, *Search for JFK*, p. 369.

7. Parmet, *Jack,* p. 191.

8. Ibid., p. 15.

9. Doris Kearns Goodwin, *The Fitzgeralds and the Kennedys* (New York: Simon and Schuster, 1987), p. 708.

10. William O. Douglas oral history transcript, p. 9, JFKL.

11. Blair and Blair, *Search for JFK*, p. 535.

12. Parmet, *Jack*, pp. 394–97, 320–33; Jules Davids to author, 1 Aug. 1985; James MacGregor Burns oral history transcript, p. 31, JFKL.

13. Victor Lasky, *JFK, the Man and the Myth* (New York: Macmillan, 1963), pp. 214–15.

14. Peter Collier and David Horowitz, *The Kennedys: An American Drama* (New York: Warner Books, 1984), p. 234; Arthur Schlesinger, Jr., *A Thousand Days: John F. Kennedy in the White House* (Boston: Houghton Mifflin, 1965), p. 95.

15. Parmet, *Jack*, p. 412.

16. Herbert S. Parmet, *JFK: The Presidency of John F. Kennedy* (New York: Dial Press, 1983), p. 8.

17. Collier and Horowitz, *Kennedys*, pp. 237–38; Theodore H. White, *The Making of the President, 1960* (New York: Atheneum, 1961), pp. 128–29.

18. Theodore C. Sorensen, *Kennedy* (New York: Harper and Row, 1965), p. 167.

19. Ibid., pp. 151–52.

20. Allen J. Matusow, *The Unraveling of America: A History of Liberalism in the 1960s* (New York: Harper and Row, 1984), pp. 27–28.

21. Schlesinger, *Thousand Days*, p. 123.

22. Parmet, *Jack*, pp. 91–92. The transcriptions are available to researchers at the Freedom of Information Act (FOIA) Reading Room, FBI headquarters, Washington, D.C.

23. Ibid., p. 142.

24. Harris Wofford, *Of Kennedys and Kings: Making Sense of the Sixties* (New York: Farrar, Straus, Giroux, 1980), p. 97.

CHAPTER 2
ASSUMING COMMAND

1. Most of the statistics below are from the United States Bureau of the Census, *Historical Statistics of the United States, Colonial Times to 1970,* Bicentennial Edition (Washington, D.C.: Government Printing Office, 1975).

2. The conclusions about public feelings are drawn from the study of public opinion polls of the time, particularly in George H. Gallup, *The Gallup Poll: Public Opinion, Vol. 3, 1959–1971* (New York: Random House, 1972), and *Public Opinion Quarterly,* 25–28 (1961–1964).

3. See, for example, Henry Fairlie, *The Kennedy Promise* (Garden City, N.Y.: Doubleday, 1973), p. 105. Some have also described the speech's style as pompous and banal. See Patrick Anderson, *The Presidents' Men: White House Assistants of*

Franklin D. Roosevelt, Harry S. Truman, Dwight D. Eisenhower, John F. Kennedy, and Lyndon B. Johnson (Garden City, N.Y.: Doubleday, 1968), pp. 287–88.

4. Theodore C. Sorensen oral history transcript, pp. 14–15, JFKL.

5. *John F. Kennedy: A Compilation of Statements and Speeches Made during His Service in the United States Senate and House of Representatives* (Washington, D.C.: Government Printing Office, 1964), p. 1109.

6. *Freedom of Communications, Part I: The Speeches, Remarks, Press Conferences and Statements of Senator John F. Kennedy, August 1 through November 7, 1960*, 87th Cong., 1st sess. (Washington, D.C.: Government Printing Office, 1961), pp. 992–93.

7. Fairlie, *Kennedy Promise*, p. 18.

8. See, for example, Myer Feldman oral history transcript, p. 354, JFKL; Kenneth Dameron, Jr., "President Kennedy and Congress: Process and Politics" (Ph.D. diss., Harvard University, 1975), p. 165; Ralph Dungan oral history transcript, p. 3, JFKL.

9. Feldman oral history transcript, pp. 368, 359.

10. Robert Donovan to author, interview, 14 Apr. 1984.

11. Anderson, *Presidents' Men*, p. 231.

12. Ibid., p. 267.

13. Arthur Schlesinger, Jr., *A Thousand Days: John F. Kennedy in the White House* (Boston: Houghton Mifflin, 1965), p. 688.

14. Orville Freeman diary, Apr. 1961, Orville Freeman Papers, JFKL; Stewart Udall oral history transcript, pp. 63–64 JFKL.

15. Frederick Dutton oral history transcript, p. 49, JFKL.

16. Freeman diary, 28 Dec. 1961, 20 Feb. 1961.

17. Udall oral history transcript, p. 68; Anderson, *Presidents' Men*, p. 290.

18. Robert Kennedy (RFK) to JFK, 14 Mar. 1963, copy, Latin America Folder, Subject Files, 1961–1964, Theodore C. Sorensen Papers, JFKL.

19. Warren I. Cohen, *Dean Rusk* (Totowa, N.J.: Cooper Square, 1980), p. 102.

20. Lee White oral history transcript, p. 30, JFKL.

21. Dameron, "President Kennedy and Congress," p. 68.

22. Claiborne Pell oral history transcript, p. 36, JFKL; Edmund Muskie oral history transcript, pp. 99–100, JFKL.

23. Lawrence F. O'Brien, *No Final Victories: A Life in Politics—from John F. Kennedy to Watergate* (Garden City, N.Y.: Doubleday, 1974), p. 112. See also Leverett Saltonstall oral history transcript, p. 26, JFKL.

24. Schlesinger, *Thousand Days*, p. 711; Wilbur Cohen oral history transcript, p. 82, JFKL; Allen Ellender oral history transcript, p. 14, JFKL; Herbert S. Parmet, *JFK: The Presidency of John F. Kennedy* (New York: Dial Press, 1983), p. 207.

25. Bobby Baker with Larry King, *Wheeling and Dealing: Confessions of a Capitol Hill Operator* (New York: W. W. Norton, 1978), p. 136.

26. White oral history transcript, pp. 21–22.

27. Joseph Alsop oral history transcript, p. 65, JFKL; Fletcher Knebel oral history transcript, p. 22, JFKL.

28. Arthur Schlesinger, Jr., *Robert Kennedy and His Times* (Boston: Houghton

Mifflin, 1978), p. 622.

29. Doris Kearns, *Lyndon Baines Johnson and the American Dream* (New York: Signet, 1977), p. 172.

30. Jack Bell oral history transcript, p. 49, JFKL.

31. Benjamin C. Bradlee, *Conversations with Kennedy* (New York: Norton, 1975), p. 194.

32. Schlesinger, *Robert Kennedy*, p. 621.

33. RFK oral history transcript, vol. 5, p. 615, JFKL.

34. Sorensen to JFK, 29 Mar. 1962, Supreme Court Folder, President's Office Files (POF), JFK Papers, JFKL.

35. Victor S. Navasky, *Kennedy Justice* (New York: Atheneum, 1971), p. 269.

36. Schlesinger, *Robert Kennedy*, p. 376.

37. Ibid., p. 307.

38. Carl M. Brauer, *John F. Kennedy and the Second Reconstruction* (New York: Columbia University Press, 1977), p. 122.

CHAPTER 3
YEAR OF CRISES AND CONFLICT

1. Arthur Schlesinger, Jr., *Robert Kennedy and His Times* (Boston: Houghton Mifflin, 1978), p. 422.

2. John H. Davis, *The Kennedys: Dynasty and Disaster, 1848–1984* (New York: McGraw-Hill, 1984), p. 430.

3. John F. Kennedy, *The Strategy for Peace*, ed. Allan Nevins (New York: Popular Library, 1961), p. 167.

4. Arthur Schlesinger, Jr., *A Thousand Days: John F. Kennedy in the White House* (Boston: Houghton Mifflin, 1965), p. 224.

5. *Freedom of Communications, Part I: The Speeches, Remarks, Press Conferences and Statements of Senator John F. Kennedy, August 1 through November 7, 1960*, 87th Cong., 1st sess. (Washington, D.C.: Government Printing Office, 1961), p. 681.

6. Stephen E. Ambrose, *Nixon: The Education of a Politician, 1913–1962* (New York: Simon and Schuster, 1987), p. 592.

7. Ibid., p. 641.

8. Trumbull Higgins, *The Perfect Failure: Kennedy, Eisenhower, and the CIA at the Bay of Pigs* (New York: W. W. Norton, 1987), p. 57.

9. Ibid., p. 83.

10. Averell Harriman oral history transcript, p. 121, JFKL.

11. Schlesinger, *Thousand Days*, p. 240.

12. Robert Amory, Jr., oral history transcript, p. 128, JFKL.

13. Schlesinger, *Thousand Days*, p. 252.

14. John Kenneth Galbraith to JFK, 3 Apr. 1961, Special Correspondence–John Kenneth Galbraith, POF, JFK Papers, JFKL.

15. RFK oral history transcript, vol. 1, p. 61, JFKL.

16. Dean Acheson oral history transcript, pp. 13–14, JFKL.

17. Higgins, *Perfect Failure*, p. 118.

18. Jack Bell oral history transcript, p. 43, JFKL.

19. David Halberstam, *The Best and the Brightest* (Greenwich, Conn.: Fawcett Publications, 1973), p. 90.

20. RFK oral history transcript, vol. 1, pp. 58–59.

21. Schlesinger, *Thousand Days*, p. 257.

22. Walter LaFeber, *America, Russia, and the Cold War, 1945–1975* (New York: John Wiley and Sons, 1976), pp. 218–19.

23. Theodore C. Sorensen, *Kennedy* (New York: Harper and Row, 1965), p. 297.

24. Lucien S. Vandenbroucke, "The 'Confessions' of Allen Dulles: New Evidence on the Bay of Pigs," *Diplomatic History* 8 (Fall 1984): 367.

25. Higgins, *Perfect Failure*, p. 130.

26. Frederick Dutton oral history transcript, p. 58, JFKL.

27. Schlesinger, *Robert Kennedy*, p. 446.

28. The two quotations come from ibid. and from Ambrose, *Nixon*, p. 632.

29. Ambrose, *Nixon*, p. 632.

30. Herbert S. Parmet, *JFK: The Presidency of John F. Kennedy* (New York: Dial Press, 1983), pp. 176–77.

31. Roberto de Oliveira Campos oral history transcript, p. 15, JFKL.

32. Schlesinger, *Thousand Days*, p. 284.

33. Higgins, *Perfect Failure*, p. 145.

34. JFK to Nikita Khrushchev, 18 Apr. 1961, copy, USSR–Khrushchev correspondence, National Security Files (NSF), JFK Papers.

35. Ibid., Khrushchev to JFK, 22 Apr. 1961, copy.

36. *Operation Zapata: The "Ultrasensitive" Report and Testimony of the Board of Inquiry on the Bay of Pigs* (Frederick, Md.: University Publications of America, 1981), p. 39.

37. Higgins, *Perfect Failure*, p. 161.

38. W. W. Rostow, *The Diffusion of Power: An Essay in Recent History* (New York: Macmillan, 1972), p. 265.

39. Statement dictated by JFK to Evelyn Lincoln, 19 Jan. 1961. Special Correspondence–Dwight D. Eisenhower, POF, JFK Papers.

40. Ibid., Clark Clifford to JFK, memorandum, 24 Jan. 1961.

41. John Kenneth Galbraith, *A Life in Our Times: Memoirs* (Boston: Houghton Mifflin, 1981), p. 465.

42. Roger Hilsman, *To Move a Nation: The Politics of Foreign Policy in the Administration of John F. Kennedy* (Garden City, N.Y.: Doubleday, 1967), p. 91.

43. RFK oral history transcript, vol. 1, p. 75; vol. 8, p. 953.

44. Mike Mansfield oral history transcript, p. 25, JFKL.

45. JFK memorandum, 28 Apr. 1961, Special Correspondence–Douglas MacArthur, POF, JFK Papers.

46. Hervé Alphand oral history transcript, p. 3, JFKL.

47. Schlesinger, *Thousand Days*, p. 338.

48. Benjamin C. Bradlee, *Conversations with Kennedy* (New York: Norton, 1975), p. 86.

CHAPTER 4
MORE CONFLICT AND CRISES

1. George Kennan oral history transcript, pp. 43–44, JFKL.

2. The three quotations come from Arthur Schlesinger to JFK, 6 Apr. 1961, memorandum, Schlesinger folder, POF, JFK Papers, JFKL; Arthur Schlesinger, Jr., *A Thousand Days: John F. Kennedy in the White House* (Boston: Houghton Mifflin, 1965), p. 381; Arthur Schlesinger, Jr., *Robert Kennedy and His Times* (Boston: Houghton Mifflin, 1978), p. 427.

3. David Halberstam, *The Best and the Brightest* (Greenwich, Conn.: Fawcett Publications, 1973), p. 95.

4. The quotation is from Mike Mansfield. Honoré M. Catudal, *Kennedy and the Berlin Wall Crisis: A Case Study in U.S. Decision Making* (Berlin: Berlin-Verlag, 1980), p. 23.

5. Schlesinger, *Thousand Days*, p. 360. For a summary of the Vienna discussions, see also the recently declassified Memoranda of Conversations, 3–4 June 1961, Countries: USSR, Vienna Meeting Memoranda of Conversations, POF, JFK Papers.

6. Thomas J. Schoenbaum, *Waging Peace and War: Dean Rusk in the Truman, Kennedy, and Johnson Years* (New York: Simon and Schuster, 1988), p. 335.

7. Kenneth P. O'Donnell and David Powers, *"Johnny, We Hardly Knew Ye": Memories of John Fitzgerald Kennedy* (Boston: Little, Brown, 1970), p. 296.

8. Schoenbaum, *Waging Peace and War*, p. 325.

9. Schlesinger, *Thousand Days*, p. 368.

10. Gordon H, Chang, "JFK, China, and the Bomb," *Journal of American History* 74 (Mar. 1988): 1289.

11. O'Donnell and Powers, *"Johnny, We Hardly Knew Ye,"* p. 285.

12. John Bartlow Martin, *Adlai Stevenson and the World: The Life of Adlai E. Stevenson* (Garden City, N.Y.: Doubleday, 1977), pp. 653–54.

13. Schlesinger, *Thousand Days*, p. 374.

14. Kennan oral history transcript, p. 110.

15. Montague Kern, Patricia W. Levering, and Ralph B. Levering, *The Kennedy Crises: The Press, the Presidency and Foreign Policy* (Chapel Hill: University of North Carolina Press, 1983), p. 64.

16. Schoenbaum, *Waging Peace and War*, p. 336.

17. David S. McLellan and David C. Acheson, eds., *Among Friends: Personal Letters of Dean Acheson* (New York: Dodd, Mead, 1980), pp. 210–11.

18. Schlesinger, *Thousand Days*, p. 383.

19. Abram Chayes oral history transcript, p. 240, JFKL.

20. Catudal, *Kennedy and the Berlin Wall Crisis*, pp. 153–54.

21. Ibid., p. 172.

22. Jerome B. Wiesner to JFK, 27 Sept. 1961, memorandum, Jerome Wiesner folder, POF, JFK Papers; Adam Yarmolinsky oral history transcript, pp. 34–35, 38, JFKL.

23. McLellan and Acheson, *Among Friends*, p. 208.

24. Walter Isaacson and Evan Thomas, *The Wise Men: Six Friends and the World They Made* (New York: Simon and Schuster, 1986), p. 612.

25. Catudal, *Kennedy and the Berlin Wall Crisis*, p. 201.

26. Hugh Sidey, *John F. Kennedy, President* (New York: Atheneum, 1963), p. 241.

27. Schoenbaum, *Waging Peace and War*, p. 344.

28. Pierre Salinger, *With Kennedy* (Garden City, N.Y.: Doubleday, 1966), p. 193.

29. Ibid., p. 192.

30. William H. Sullivan oral history transcript, p. 27, JFKL.

31. Chester Bowles oral history transcript, p. 25, JFKL.

32. Stephen Heintz, "Frustration at Foggy Bottom: Chester Bowles as Undersecretary of State, January–November 1961," senior thesis, Yale, 1974, p. 149.

33. JFK to McGeorge Bundy, 10 July 1961, memorandum, copy, Evelyn Lincoln Notebook of Memoranda to Staff file, POF, JFK Papers; JFK to Bundy, 10 July 1961, memorandum, copy, ibid.

34. RFK oral history transcript, vol. 8, p. 941, JFKL.

35. Halberstam, *Best and Brightest*, p. 89.

36. RFK oral history transcript, vol. 1, p. 110.

37. Harris Wofford, *Of Kennedy and Kings: Making Sense of the Sixties* (New York: Farrar, Straus, Giroux, 1980), p. 341.

38. RFK oral history transcript, vol. 1., p. 111.

39. Catudal, *Kennedy and the Berlin Wall Crisis*, p. 95.

40. Dean Acheson to Louis Halle, 24 July 1961, copy, State Department and White House Adviser 1961 folder, Dean Acheson Papers, Truman Library, Independence, Mo.; Robert Baker with Larry King, *Wheeling and Dealing: Confessions of a Capitol Hill Operator* (New York: Norton, 1978), p. 144.

41. Theodore C. Sorensen, *Kennedy* (New York: Harper and Row, 1965), p. 288.

42. RFK oral history transcript, vol. 1, pp. 110–11.

43. Schlesinger, *Thousand Days*, pp. 295–96; Benjamin C. Bradlee, *Conversations with Kennedy* (New York: Norton, 1975), pp. 197–98.

44. Harris Wofford to JFK, 17 July 1961, memorandum, Chester Bowles folder, POF, JFK Papers.

45. Hugh Sidey oral history transcript, p. 34, JFKL.

46. Sorensen, *Kennedy*, p. 290.

47. Schlesinger, *Thousand Days*, pp. 446–47.

48. Edwin O. Guthman and Jeffery Shulman, eds., *Robert Kennedy: In His Own Words, the Unpublished Recollections of the Kennedy Years* (New York: Bantam Books, 1988), pp. 10, 280.

49. Sullivan oral history transcript, p. 19; Charles A. Stevenson, *The End of Nowhere: American Policy toward Laos since 1954* (Boston: Beacon Press, 1972), p. 173.

50. Isaacson and Thomas, *Wise Men*, p. 618.

51. W. W. Rostow, *The Diffusion of Power: An Essay in Recent History* (New York: Macmillan, 1972), p. 290.

CHAPTER 5
LAUNCHING THE NEW FRONTIER

1. Robert Baker with Larry King, *Wheeling and Dealing: Confessions of a Capitol Hill Operator* (New York: Norton, 1978), p. 142.

2. Orren Beaty oral history transcript, pp. 288–92, JFKL. See also Thomas O'Neill with William Novak, *Man of the House: The Life and Political Memoirs of Speaker Tip O'Neill* (New York: Random House, 1987), pp. 175–76.

3. Charles Halleck oral history transcript, p. 26, JFKL; Tom Wicker, *JFK and LBJ: The Influence of Personality upon Politics* (Baltimore: Penguin Books, 1970), p. 86; Neil MacNeil, *Dirksen, Portrait of a Public Man* (New York: World Publishing, 1970), p. 194.

4. *Freedom of Communications, Part I: The Speeches, Remarks, Press Conferences, and Statements of Senator John F. Kennedy, August 1 through November 7, 1960*, 87th Cong., 1st sess. (Washington, D.C.: Government Printing Office, 1961), p. 397.

5. Wicker, *JFK and LBJ*, p. 105.

6. Ibid., p. 125; *Congressional Quarterly Almanac*, 87th Cong., 1st sess., 1961, 17 (Washington, D.C.: Congressional Quarterly, Inc., 1961), p. 217.

7. JFK to Anthony Celebrezze, 6 May 1963, memorandum, copy, Health, Education, and Welfare, 1963 folder, POF, Kennedy Papers, JFKL.

8. Anne Hodges Morgan, *Robert S. Kerr: The Senate Years* (Norman: University of Oklahoma Press, 1977), p. 221.

9. *Congressional Quarterly Almanac*, 1961, p. 76.

10. Ibid., p. 368.

11. Ibid., 1962, p. 383.

12. Arthur Schlesinger, Jr., *A Thousand Days: John F. Kennedy in the White House* (Boston: Houghton Mifflin, 1965), p. 711; Mike Mansfield oral history transcript, p. 37, JFKL; Joseph Clark oral history transcript, p. 72, JFKL.

13. *Congressional Quarterly Almanac*, 1962, p. 68.

14. Ibid., p. 513.

15. Allen Matusow, *The Unraveling of America: A History of Liberalism in the 1960s* (New York: Harper and Row, 1984), p. 105.

16. Hugh Davis Graham, *The Uncertain Triumph: Federal Education Policy in the Kennedy and Johnson Years* (Chapel Hill: University of North Carolina Press, 1984), p. 51.

17. John Kenneth Galbraith, *A Life in Our Times: Memoirs* (Boston: Houghton Mifflin, 1981), p. 357.

18. Orville Freeman to JFK, 23 Jan. 1962, copy, Correspondence Jan. 1962 folder, Orville Freeman Papers, JFKL; "Farm Message," *Reporter*, 15 Feb. 1962, p. 14.

19. Freeman to JFK, 21 Sept. 1962, copy, Correspondence Sept. folder,

Freeman Papers; Freeman to JFK, 1 May 1962, copy, Correspondence May 1962 folder, ibid.

20. Orville Freeman diary, JFK and congressional leadership, 1963 entry, microfilm copy in Freeman Papers; Allen J. Ellender oral history transcript, pp. 13–14, JFKL.

21. "What They Say about JFK: Congressmen Tell What's on Their Minds," *U.S. News and World Report*, 30 July 1962, pp. 31–34; "Why Congress Doesn't Give JFK What He Wants," ibid., 18 Mar. 1963, pp. 38–42.

22. "Get off That Tiger," *Time*, 21 Dec. 1962, p. 21; "Wheat Vote: Against Freeman's Program," ibid., 31 May 1963, pp. 13–14.

23. Willard Cochrane to author, 4 Sept. 1985.

24. Freeman to JFK, 28 Mar. 1962, Correspondence Mar. 1962 folder, Freeman Papers.

25. "Farmers Face Their Toughest Choice," *Saturday Evening Post*, 18 May 1963, p. 75.

26. Freeman to JFK, 16 Apr. 1962, copy, Correspondence Apr. 1962 folder, Freeman Papers.

27. Freeman to JFK, 10 May 1963, copy, Correspondence May 1963 folder, ibid.

28. Freeman to JFK, 3 Aug. 1962, copy, Correspondence Aug. 1962 folder, ibid.

29. Peter A. Toma, *The Politics of Food for Peace: Executive-Legislative Interaction* (Tucson: University of Arizona Press, 1967), p. 44.

30. Freeman to JFK, 16 Jan. 1962, copy, Correspondence Jan. 1962 folder, Freeman Papers; "How American Agriculture Can Make Its Maximum Contribution to the Foreign Aid Program," Freeman Confidential Memorandum, 16 May 1961, POF, box 68A, JFK Papers.

31. Freeman to JFK, 24 Oct. 1963, Correspondence Oct. 1963 folder, Freeman Papers.

32. Eunice Kennedy Shriver oral history transcript, p. 21, JFKL.

33. Matusow, *Unraveling of America*, p. 110.

34. Carl M. Brauer, "Kennedy, Johnson, and the War on Poverty," *Journal of American History* 69 (June 1982): 113.

35. Schlesinger, *Thousand Days*, p. 1012.

36. Brauer, "Kennedy, Johnson, and the War on Poverty," p. 113.

37. Ibid., pp. 113–14.

38. Theodore C. Sorensen, *Kennedy*, (New York: Harper and Row, 1965), p. 352.

CHAPTER 6
OLD IDEAS AND NEWER APPROACHES

1. Council of Economic Advisers oral history transcript, p. 32, JFKL.

2. Ibid.

3. Ibid., p. 387.

4. Arthur Schlesinger, Jr., *A Thousand Days: John F. Kennedy in the White House* (Boston: Houghton Mifflin, 1965), p. 649.

5. Council of Economic Advisers oral history transcript, James Tobin note, appendix.

6. John Kenneth Galbraith to JFK, 2 Feb. 1961, memorandum, Galbraith folder, POF, JFK Papers.

7. Galbraith to JFK, 25 Mar. 1961, ibid.

8. Council of Economic Advisers oral history transcript, p. 231; Seymour E. Harris oral history transcript, p. 16, JFKL.

9. Kenneth W. Thompson, ed., *The Kennedy Presidency: Seventeen Intimate Perspectives of John F. Kennedy*, vol. 4 of *Portraits of American Presidents* (Lanham, Md.: University Press of America, 1985), p. 137.

10. Galbraith to William McChesney Martin, Jr., n.d., Galbraith folder, POF, JFK Papers.

11. Galbraith to C. Douglas Dillon and Walter Heller, n.d., memorandum, Galbraith folder, POF, JFK Papers.

12. Arthur Schlesinger, Jr., *Robert Kennedy and His Times* (Boston: Houghton Mifflin, 1978), p. 403; David McDonald oral history transcript, p. 15, JFKL.

13. Benjamin C. Bradlee, *Conversations with Kennedy* (New York: Norton, 1975) pp. 77–78.

14. Doodles, 1962, KP 41–KP 45 folder, JFK Personal Papers, JFKL; Charles Bartlett oral history transcript, p. 111, JFKL.

15. RFK oral history transcript, vol. 2, pp. 299–300, JFKL.

16. Felix Frankfurter oral history transcript, pp. 10–11, JFKL.

17. Lee Loevinger to James W. Symington, 18 July 1962, memorandum, White House Memoranda folder, RFK Papers, JFKL.

18. Nicholas B. Katzenbach to Sorensen, 19 July 1962, copy, White House Memoranda folder, RFK Papers.

19. Sorensen to JFK, 20 June 1962, Sorensen folder, POF, JFK Papers.

20. Heller to JFK, 21 Oct. 1963, copy, Council of Economic Advisers folder, box 31, Sorensen Papers, JFKL.

21. RFK oral history transcript, vol. 2, p. 222.

22. Schlesinger, *Thousand Days*, p. 649; Seymour E. Harris to Schlesinger, 3 May 1963, Seymour Harris folder, Arthur Schlesinger, Jr., Papers, JFKL.

23. Kim McQuaid, *Big Business and Presidential Power: From FDR to Reagan* (New York: William Morrow, 1982), p. 219.

24. Schlesinger, *Thousand Days*, p. 648.

25. Herbert S. Parmet, *JFK: The Presidency of John F. Kennedy* (New York: Dial Press, 1983), p. 245.

26. "A Legacy of Inspiration," *Newsweek*, 29 Nov. 1983, p. 72.

27. Thompson, *Kennedy Presidency*, p. 56.

28. Regarding the few appointments of women, the administration's position was that few women were recommended. Former Administrative Assistant Myer Feldman to author, 10 Mar. 1989.

29. Patricia G. Zelman, *Women, Work, and National Policy: The Kennedy-Johnson Years* (Ann Arbor, Mich.: UMI Research Press, 1982), p. 34.

30. Cynthia E. Harrison, "A 'New Frontier' for Women: The Public Policy of the Kennedy Administration," *Journal of American History* 67 (Dec. 1980): 642.

31. Ibid., p. 644.

32. Robert F. Kennedy, *The Enemy Within* (New York: Harper and Brothers, 1960), p. 265.

33. Victor S. Navasky, *Kennedy Justice* (New York: Atheneum, 1971), p. 46.

34. Ibid., p. 8.

35. John H. Davis, *Mafia Kingfish: Carlos Marcello and the Assassination of John F. Kennedy* (New York: McGraw-Hill, 1989), pp. 91–93.

36. Navasky, *Kennedy Justice*, p. 75.

37. Schlesinger, *Robert Kennedy and His Times*, p. 272.

38. Special Agent (SA) to Special Agent in charge (SAC), Washington Field Office (WFO), 17 Jan. 1967, RFK FBI file, 1751381-1923, FBI headquarters; Athan G. Theoharis and John Stuart Cox, *The Boss: J. Edgar Hoover and the Great American Inquisition* (Philadelphia: Temple University Press, 1988), pp. 376–77.

39. Navasky, *Kennedy Justice*, p. 436.

40. William H. Orrick, Jr., oral history transcript, p. 26, JFKL.

41. To Director, memorandum, 9, 11 Dec. 1961, Sam Giancana FBI file, 92-3171-527, FBI headquarters. See also Antoinette Giancana and Thomas C. Renner, *Mafia Princess: Growing Up in Sam Giancana's Family* (New York: William Morrow, 1984), pp. 247–50, and John H. Davis, *The Kennedys: Dynasty and Disaster, 1848–1984* (New York: McGraw-Hill, 1984), pp. 305-7.

42. C. A. Evans to ? Belmont, 17 Aug. 1962, memorandum, JFK FBI file, FBI headquarters.

43. Anthony Summers, *Goddess: The Secret Lives of Marilyn Monroe* (New York: New American Library, 1986), pp. 260–61, 273–74, 302; Davis, *Kennedys*, pp. 404-5.

44. Robert H. Divine, "Lyndon B. Johnson and the Politics of Space," *Johnson Years*, vol. 2 of *Foreign Policy, the Great Society, and the White House*, ed. Robert A. Divine (Lawrence: University Press of Kansas, 1987), p. 224.

45. W. W. Rostow, *The Diffusion of Power: An Essay in Recent History* (New York: Macmillan, 1972), p. 181.

46. Hugh Sidey, *John F. Kennedy, President* (New York: Atheneum, 1963), p. 122.

47. Divine, "Johnson and the Politics of Space," p. 234.

48. The quotation comes from Gerald T. Rice, *The Bold Experiment: JFK's Peace Corps* (Notre Dame, Ind.: University of Notre Dame Press, 1985), p. ix.

49. Ibid., p. 240.

50. Ibid., p. 24.

51. Ibid., p. 30.

52. Ibid., p. 65.

53. Harris Wofford, *Of Kennedys and Kings: Making Sense of the Sixties* (New York: Farrar, Straus, Giroux, 1980), p. 267.

54. Gary May, "Passing the Torch and Lighting Fires: The Peace Corps," in *Kennedy's Quest for Victory: American Foreign Policy, 1961–1963*, ed. Thomas G. Paterson (New York: Oxford University Press, 1989), pp. 284–316.

CHAPTER 7
THE TRAVAIL OF CIVIL RIGHTS

1. Arthur Krock oral history transcript, p. 18, JFKL; Anthony Holland to the author, 17 Mar. 1989.

2. Theodore C. Sorensen, *Kennedy* (New York: Harper and Row, 1965), p. 471.

3. Krock oral history transcript, p. 16.

4. Roy Wilkins with Tom Mathews, *Standing Fast: The Autobiography of Roy Wilkins* (New York: Viking Press, 1982), p. 276.

5. *Freedom of Communications, Part I: The Speeches, Remarks, Press Conferences, and Statements of Senator John F. Kennedy, August 1 through November 7, 1960,* 87th Cong., 1st sess. (Washington, D.C.: Government Printing Office, 1961), p. 576.

6. Edwin O. Guthman and Jeffrey Shulman, eds., *Robert Kennedy: In His Own Words, the Unpublished Recollections of the Kennedy Years* (New York: Bantam Books, 1988), p. 78.

7. Arthur Schlesinger, Jr., *Robert Kennedy and His Times* (Boston: Houghton Mifflin, 1978), p. 286.

8. Harris Wofford, *Of Kennedys and Kings: Making Sense of the Sixties* (New York: Farrar, Straus, Giroux, 1980), p. 166.

9. Roy Wilkins oral history transcript, p. 7, JFKL.

10. Thomas G. Smith, "Civil Rights on the Gridiron: The Kennedy Administration and the Desegregation of the Washington Redskins," *Journal of Sport History* 14 (Summer 1987): 208.

11. Wilkins oral history transcript, p. 11.

12. John Patterson oral history transcript, p. 34, JFKL; Jean Stein and George Plimpton, eds., *American Journey: The Times of Robert Kennedy* (New York: Harcourt Brace Jovanovich, 1970), p. 103; Guthman and Shulman, *Robert Kennedy: In His Own Words*, p. 87.

13. Wofford, *Of Kennedys and Kings*, p. 156.

14. Kenneth W. Thompson, ed., *The Kennedy Presidency: Seventeen Intimate Perspectives of John F. Kennedy* (Lanham, Md.: University Press of America, 1985), 4: 79–80.

15. Edwin Guthman, *We Band of Brothers* (New York: Harper and Row, 1971), p. 181.

16. Thompson, *Kennedy Presidency*, p. 121; Kenneth O'Reilly, *"Racial Matters": The FBI's Secret File on Black America, 1960–1972* (New York: Free Press, 1989), p. 66.

17. Thompson, *Kennedy Presidency*, p. 120.

18. Victor S. Navasky, *Kennedy Justice* (New York: Atheneum, 1971), p. 118.

19. Guthman and Shulman, *Robert Kennedy: In His Own Words*, p. 100.

20. Navasky, *Kennedy Justice*, p. 185.

21. James Farmer oral history transcript, p. 10, JFKL, and David J. Garrow,

Bearing the Cross: Martin Luther King, Jr., and the Southern Christian Leadership Conference (New York: William Morrow, 1986), p. 296.

22. Garrow, *Bearing the Cross*, p. 217.

23. Michael R. Belknap, *Federal Law and Southern Order: Racial Violence and Constitutional Conflict in the Post-Brown South* (Athens: University of Georgia Press, 1987), p. 108.

24. Richard N. Goodwin, *Remembering America: A Voice from the Sixties* (Boston: Little, Brown, 1988), p. 133.

25. Guthman and Shulman, *Robert Kennedy: In His Own Words*, p. 156.

26. Ibid., p. 153.

27. Henry Fairlie, *The Kennedy Promise* (Garden City, N.Y.: Doubleday, 1973), p. 250; Wofford, *Of Kennedys and Kings*, p. 170.

28. Guthman, *We Band of Brothers*, p. 207.

29. Oral tapes transcript, Integration of the University of Mississippi, JFK Papers, JFKL; Guthman, *We Band of Brothers*, p. 204.

30. Oral tapes transcript, Integration of the University of Mississippi.

31. Guthman and Shulman, *Robert Kennedy: In His Own Words*, p. 161.

32. Stein and Plimpton, *American Journey*, p. 117.

33. Harvard Sitkoff, *Struggle for Black Equality, 1954–1960* (New York: Hill and Wang, 1980), p. 145.

34. Quotations for the New York meeting are from Stein and Plimpton, *American Journey*, pp. 119–22, and Thompson, *Kennedy Presidency*, pp. 118–19.

35. Guthman and Shulman, *Robert Kennedy: In His Own Words*, p. 225.

36. RFK oral history transcript, vol. 7, p. 822, JFKL.

37. Garrow, *Bearing the Cross*, p. 269; Wilkins, *Standing Fast*, p. 289.

38. Arthur Schlesinger, Jr., *A Thousand Days: John F. Kennedy in the White House* (Boston: Houghton Mifflin, 1965), p. 971.

39. Michael P. Riccards, "Rare Counsel: Kennedy, Johnson and the Civil Rights Bill of 1963," *Presidential Studies Quarterly* 11 (Summer 1981): 397.

40. RFK oral history transcript, vol. 7, pp. 855–56.

41. White House tape of 23 Oct. 1963 meeting, reel 117.1, JFK Papers.

42. Benjamin C. Bradlee, *Conversations with Kennedy* (New York: Norton, 1975), p. 219; Henry Z. Scheele, *Charlie Halleck: A Political Biography* (New York: Exposition Press, 1966), p. 225.

43. Edward L. Schapsmeier and Frederick H. Schapsmeier, *Dirksen of Illinois: Senatorial Statesman* (Urbana: University of Illinois Press, 1985), pp. 142–45; Carl M. Brauer, *John F. Kennedy and the Second Reconstruction* (New York: Columbia University Press, 1977), p. 308.

44. Guthman and Shulman, *Robert Kennedy: In His Own Words*, pp. 141, 146.

45. David Garrow, *The FBI and Martin Luther King: From "Solo" to Memphis* (New York: W. W. Norton, 1981), p. 97. See also O'Reilly, *"Racial Matters,"* p. 135.

46. Schlesinger, *Robert Kennedy and His Times*, pp. 349–50.

47. Garrow, *Bearing the Cross*, p. 283; Wilkins, *Standing Fast*, p. 292.

48. Garrow, *Bearing the Cross*, p. 281.

49. Stein and Plimpton, *American Journey*, p. 113.

CHAPTER 8
THE MISSILES OF OCTOBER

1. For recent symposia, see James G. Blight and David A. Welch, *On the Brink: Americans and Soviets Reexamine the Cuban Missile Crisis* (New York: Hill and Wang, 1989).

2. Ibid., p. 249.

3. Taylor Branch and George Crile III, "The Kennedy Vendetta: How the CIA Waged a Silent War against Cuba," *Harper's*, Aug. 1975, p. 60.

4. Blight and Welch, *On the Brink*, p. 250. For another viewpoint, see James G. Hershberg, "Before 'The Missiles of October': Did Kennedy Plan a Military Strike against Cuba?" *Diplomatic History* 14 (Spring 1990): 163–98.

5. Blight and Welch, *On the Brink*, p. 296.

6. *New York Times*, 5 Feb. 1989, E25; Blight and Welch, *On the Brink*, pp. 31, 229. The Soviets technically had ninety-seven short-range SLMs, but they had to surface to fire.

7. Kenneth P. O'Donnell and David Powers, *"Johnny, We Hardly Knew Ye": Memories of John Fitzgerald Kennedy* (Boston: Little, Brown, 1970), p. 310.

8. George Ball, *The Past Has Another Pattern: Memoirs* (New York: Norton, 1982), p. 290.

9. Irving L. Janis, *Victims of Groupthink: A Psychological Study of Foreign-policy Decisions and Fiascoes* (Boston: Houghton Mifflin, 1972), p. 152.

10. Ibid., p. 154; Herbert S. Parmet, *JFK: The Presidency of John F. Kennedy* (New York: Dial Press, 1983), p. 277. See also Alexander George, "The Impact of Crisis-Induced Stress on Decision Making," in *The Medical Implications of Nuclear War*, ed. Fredric Solomon and Robert Q. Marston (Washington, D.C.: National Academy Press, 1986), 552–59.

11. Presidential Recordings Transcripts, 16 Oct. 1962, Cuban Missile Crisis Meetings, 6:30-7:55 P.M. session, JFK Papers, JFKL, p. 27.

12. Parmet, *JFK: Presidency*, p. 285.

13. Blight and Welch, *On the Brink*, p. 28.

14. Presidential Recording Transcripts, 16 Oct. 1962, p. 26.

15. Blight and Welch, *On the Brink*, p. 141.

16. Arthur Schlesinger, Jr., *Robert Kennedy and His Times* (Boston: Houghton Mifflin, 1978), pp. 507–8.

17. David Detzer, *The Brink: Cuban Missile Crisis* (New York: Thomas Y. Crowell, 1979), p. 154.

18. Andrei Gromyko, *Memoirs* (New York: Doubleday, 1989), pp. 178–79.

19. Herbert S. Dinnerstein, *The Making of a Missile Crisis: October 1962* (Baltimore: Johns Hopkins University Press, 1976), p. 236.

20. Theodore C. Sorensen, *Kennedy* (New York: Harper and Row, 1965), p. 692.

21. Douglas Dillon to Sorensen, 18 Oct. 1962, Cuba general folder, box 43, Sorensen Papers, JFKL.

22. Thomas J. Schoenbaum, *Waging Peace and War: Dean Rusk in the Truman, Kennedy, and Johnson Years* (New York: Simon and Schuster, 1988), p. 314.

23. Elie Abel, *The Missile Crisis* (Philadelphia: J. B. Lippincott, 1966), p. 94.

24. Blight and Welch, *On the Brink*, p. 211; *New York Times*, 29 Jan. 1989, A1.

25. Abel, *Missile Crisis*, p. 106; Stephen E. Ambrose, *Eisenhower: The President*, 2 vols. (New York: Simon and Schuster, 1984), 2: 642.

26. Sorensen, *Kennedy*, pp. 702–3.

27. Detzer, *Brink*, p. 184.

28. Blight and Welch, *On the Brink*, pp. 245–46.

29. Richard E. Neustadt to Sorensen, 27 Oct. 1962, memorandum, Neustadt memoranda folder, box 36, Sorensen Papers.

30. Kennedy to Khrushchev, 23 Oct. 1962, reprinted in *The Department of State Bulletin*, vol. 74, no. 1795, 19 Nov. 1973, p. 637. The Kennedy-Khrushchev missile-crisis correspondence is found in this publication.

31. Abel, *Missile Crisis*, p. 140.

32. Robert Kennedy, *Thirteen Days: A Memoir of the Cuban Missile Crisis* (New York: Norton, 1969), p. 86.

33. Blight and Welch, *On the Brink*, pp. 63–64.

34. Kennedy, *Thirteen Days*, pp. 69–70.

35. Parmet, *JFK: Presidency*, p. 297.

36. Blight and Welch, *On the Brink*, p. 309. Kennedy subsequently wrote Khrushchev: "It would be a great mistake to think that what appears in newspapers and magazines necessarily has anything to do with the policy and purpose of the government." Kennedy to Khrushchev, 14 Dec. 1962, copy, Khrushchev correspondence folder, National Security Files (NSF), JFK Papers.

37. Barton J. Bernstein, "The Cuban Missile Crisis: Trading the Jupiters in Turkey?" in *The Cuban Missile Crisis*, ed. Robert A. Divine (New York: Markus Wiener, 1988), p. 247.

38. Presidential Recordings Transcripts, 27 Oct. 1962, Cuban Missile Crisis Meetings, JFK Papers, pp. 19, 27, 50.

39. Seymour M. Hersh, "Was Castro out of Control in 1962?" *Washington Post*, 11 Oct. 1987, H1; Blight and Welch, *On the Brink*, pp. 311, 369 n.118.

40. Ball, *Past Has Another Pattern*, p. 306.

41. Presidential Recordings Transcripts, 27 Oct. 1962, pp. 28, 31. See also David A. Welch and James G. Blight, "The Eleventh Hour of the Cuban Missile Crisis: An Introduction to the ExComm Transcripts," *International Security* 12 (Winter 1987/88): 19.

42. R. Kennedy, *Thirteen Days*, p. 108; both McNamara and Sorensen suspect that Robert Kennedy exaggerated what he had told Dobrynin. See Blight and Welch, *On the Brink*, pp. 187, 67, 265, 264.

43. See Sorensen's admission in Bruce J. Allyn, James G. Blight and David A. Welch, "Back to the Brink: Proceedings of the Moscow Conference on the Cuban Missile Crisis, 27 Jan. 1989,"pp. 63–64 in possession of the Center for Science and International Affairs, Kennedy School of Government, Harvard University.

44. Kennedy, *Thirteen Days*, p. 127.

45. Blight and Welch, *On the Brink*, pp. 113–15.

46. Ibid., p. 277; *New York Times*, 30 Jan. 1989, A2.

47. Blight and Welch, *On the Brink*, p. 51.

48. *Miami Herald*, 1 Nov. 1987, C1.

49. Graham T. Allison, *Essence of Decision: Explaining the Cuban Missile Crisis* (Boston: Little, Brown, 1971), p. 212.

50. Blight and Welch, *On the Brink*, p. 96.

51. Abel, *Missile Crisis*, p. 182.

52. Glenn T. Seaborg and Benjamin S. Loeb, *Kennedy, Khrushchev and the Test Ban* (Berkeley: University of California Press, 1981), p. 181.

53. Gordon H. Chang, "JFK, China, and the Bomb," *Journal of American History* 74 (Mar. 1988): 1300–1301.

54. Richard N. Goodwin, *Remembering America: A Voice from the Sixties* (Boston: Little, Brown, 1988), p. 219.

55. Warren Hincle and William W. Turner, *The Fish Is Red: The Story of the Secret War against Castro* (New York: Harper and Row, 1981), pp. 192, 219.

56. Raymond L. Garthoff, *Reflections on the Cuban Missile Crisis* (Washington, D. C.: Brookings Institution, 1987), p. 87.

57. Warren I. Cohen, *Dean Rusk* (Totowa, N.J.: Cooper Square, 1980), p. 196.

CHAPTER 9

THE THIRD WORLD

1. Harris Wofford to JFK, 20 Jan. 1962, memorandum, Harris Wofford folder 1962, POF, JFK Papers, JFKL.

2. Richard D. Mahoney, *JFK: Ordeal in Africa* (New York: Oxford University Press, 1983), pp. 70–71.

3. Ibid., pp. 101, 119.

4. Thomas J. Noer, "New Frontiers and Old Priorities in Africa," in *Kennedy's Quest for Victory: American Foreign Policy, 1961–1963* ed. Thomas G. Paterson (New York: Oxford University Press, 1989), p. 281.

5. Thomas J. Noer, "The Frontier and African Neutralism: Kennedy, Nkrumah, and the Volta River Project," *Diplomatic History* 8 (Winter 1984): 76.

6. Dean Acheson oral history transcript, p. 14, JFKL.

7. Mahoney, *Ordeal in Africa*, pp. 214–15.

8. Noer, "New Frontiers and Old Priorities in Africa," p. 273.

9. Ibid., p. 276.

10. Mahoney, *Ordeal in Africa*, p. 248.

11. Arthur Schlesinger, Jr., "The Alliance for Progress: A Retrospective," in *Latin America: The Search for a New International Role*, ed. Ronald G. Hellman and H. Jan Rosenbaum (New York: John Wiley, 1975), p. 80.

12. Richard Goodwin to JFK, 10 Sept. 1963, memorandum, Richard Goodwin folder, POF, JFK Papers.

13. Chester Bowles to JFK, undated 1962, memorandum, Chester Bowles folder, POF, JFK Papers; Roberto de Oliveira Campos oral history transcript, p. 54, JFKL.

14. Stephen G. Rabe, "Controlling Revolutions: Latin America, the Alliance for Progress and Cold War Anti-Communism" in Paterson, *Kennedy's Quest for*

Victory, pp. 114–15; Theodore C. Sorensen, *Kennedy* (New York: Harper and Row, 1965), p. 535.

15. Rabe, "Controlling Revolutions," pp. 120–21.

16. Ruth Leacock, "JFK, Business and Brazil," *Hispanic American Historical Review* 59, no. 4 (1979): 644–71.

17. Schlesinger, "Alliance for Progress," p. 73.

18. Rabe, "Controlling Revolutions," p. 116; Bruce Miroff, *Pragmatic Illusions: The Presidential Politics of John F. Kennedy* (New York: McKay, 1976), p. 134.

19. Richard J. Walton, *Cold War and Counterrevolution: The Foreign Policy of John F. Kennedy* (Baltimore: Penguin Books, 1973), p. 216.

20. Arthur Schlesinger, Jr., *A Thousand Days: John F. Kennedy in the White House* (Boston: Houghton Mifflin, 1965), pp. 525–26.

21. Timothy P. Maga, "The New Frontier v. Guided Democracy: JFK, Sukarno, and Indonesia, 1961–1963," *Presidential Studies Quarterly* 20 (Winter 1990): 93.

22. George Ball, *The Past Has Another Pattern: Memoirs* (New York: Norton, 1982), p. 364.

23. George McT. Kahin, *Intervention: How America Became Involved in Vietnam* (New York: Alfred A. Knopf, 1986), pp. 127, 474n.16.

24. David Halberstam, *The Best and the Brightest* (Greenwich, Conn.: Fawcett Publications, 1973), p. 98.

25. Roger Hilsman, Jr., oral history transcript, p. 23, JFKL.

26. Halberstam, *Best and Brightest*, p. 47.

27. *The Pentagon Papers: The Defense Department History of United States Decisionmaking on Vietnam*, Senator Gravel edition, 5 vols. (Boston: Beacon Press, 1971), 2: 55–56.

28. William J. Rust, *Kennedy in Vietnam* (New York: Charles Scribner's, 1985), pp. 31–32.

29. Ellen J. Hammer, *A Death in November: America in Vietnam, 1963* (New York: E. P. Dutton, 1987), p. 37.

30. Ball, *Past Has Another Pattern*, p. 366; John Kenneth Galbraith, *A Life in Our Times: Memoirs* (Boston: Houghton Mifflin, 1981), p. 473.

31. Rust, *Kennedy in Vietnam*, p. 49.

32. Ball, *Past Has Another Pattern*, p. 369.

33. David Halberstam, *The Powers That Be* (New York: Alfred A. Knopf, 1979), p. 446.

34. John Kenneth Galbraith, *Ambassador's Journal: A Personal Account of the Kennedy Years* (Boston: Houghton Mifflin, 1969), p. 311.

35. For the Geneva meeting, see William H. Sullivan, *Obbligato, 1939–1979: Notes on a Foreign Service* (New York: W. W. Norton, 1984), pp. 176–78; Bowles to Rusk, 16 Aug. 1962, memorandum, Chester Bowles folder, box 43, Sorensen Papers, JFKL.

36. Halberstam, *Best and Brightest*, pp. 256–57; Mike Mansfield oral history transcript, p. 24, JFKL; quotation confirmed by Mike Mansfield to author, 5 Nov. 1990.

37. Charles Bartlett, "Portrait of a Friend," in *The Kennedy Presidency: Seven-*

teen Intimate Perspectives of John F. Kennedy, ed. Kenneth W. Thompson (Lanham, Md.: University Press of America, 1985), p. 16.

38. Frederick E. Nolting, "Kennedy, NATO, and Southeast Asia," ibid., p. 232.

39. *Pentagon Papers*, Gravel edition, vol. 2, pp. 234–35.

40. Benjamin C. Bradlee, *Conversations with Kennedy* (New York: Norton, 1975), p. 59.

41. Arthur Schlesinger, Jr., *Robert Kennedy and His Times* (Boston: Houghton Mifflin, 1978), p. 714; Rust, *Kennedy in Vietnam*, p. 119.

42. Edwin O. Guthman and Jeffrey Shulman, *Robert Kennedy: In His Own Words, the Unpublished Recollections of the Kennedy Years* (New York: Bantam Press, 1988), pp. 402–3.

43. Lawrence J. Bassett and Stephen E. Pelz, "The Failed Search for Victory: Vietnam and the Politics of War," in Paterson, *Kennedy's Quest for Victory*, p. 247.

44. *Pentagon Papers*, Gravel edition, vol. 2, p. 243.

45. Ibid., pp. 241–42.

46. Ibid., p. 244.

47. Bromley Smith, Memorandum of conference with the president, 10 Sept. 1963, Meetings on Vietnam folder, NSF, JFK Papers; Rust, *Kennedy in Vietnam*, p. 137.

48. The information regarding the construction battalion and the quotation are in William Sullivan oral history transcript, p. 47, JFKL.

49. *Pentagon Papers*, Gravel edition, vol. 2, p. 257.

50. Memorandum of Bromley Smith, 29 Oct. 1963, Vietnam folder, POF, JFK Papers.

51. Maxwell Taylor, *Swords and Plowshares* (New York: W. W. Norton, 1972), p. 301; Herbert S. Parmet, *JFK: The Presidency of John F. Kennedy* (New York: Dial Press, 1983), p. 335.

52. Kenneth P. O'Donnell and David Powers, *"Johnny, We Hardly Knew Ye": Memories of John Fitzgerald Kennedy* (Boston: Little, Brown, 1970), pp. 18, 16; Mike Mansfield to the author, 5 Nov. 1990.

53. Dean Rusk oral history transcript, p. 386, JFKL.

54. RFK oral history transcript, vol. 3, p. 379, JFKL.

CHAPTER 10

IMAGE AND REALITY

1. George Kennan oral history transcript, p. 49, JFKL.

2. John A. Baker oral history transcript, p. 4, JFKL.

3. Kay Halle oral history transcript, p. 25, JFKL.

4. Ralph G. Martin, *A Hero for Our Times: An Intimate Story of the Kennedy Years* (New York: Macmillan, 1983), p. 301.

5. John Kenneth Galbraith, *A Life in Our Times: Memoirs* (Boston: Houghton Mifflin, 1981), p. 373.

6. Press Panel oral history transcript, p. 40, JFKL.

7. Charles Roberts, "JFK and the Press," in *Ten Presidents and the Press*, ed. Kenneth W. Thompson (Lanham, Md.: University Press of America, 1983), p. 74.

8. William Manchester, *Portrait of a President: John F. Kennedy in Profile* (Boston: Little, Brown, 1962), p. 103; Henry R. Luce to JFK, 21 Sept. 1960, Henry R. Luce and Clare Boothe Luce folder, POF, JFK Papers, JFKL.

9. Paul R. Henggeler, "Kennedy and the News Media: The Development of President John F. Kennedy's Media Strategy Based on *Time, Newsweek*, and Television," (Master's thesis, Bowling Green University, 1985), pp. 118–23.

10. David Halberstam, *The Powers That Be* (New York: Alfred A. Knopf, 1979), p. 360.

11. Benjamin C. Bradlee, *Conversations with Kennedy* (New York: Norton, 1975), p. 22. See also Fletcher Knebel, "Kennedy vs. the Press," *Look*, 28 Aug. 1962, pp. 17–21.

12. Press Panel oral history transcript, p. 53.

13. Martin, *Hero for Our Time*, p. 308.

14. Katie Louchheim, *By the Political Sea* (Garden City, N.Y.: Doubleday, 1970), p. 146.

15. Ralph B. Levering and Montague Kern, "The News Management Issue and John F. Kennedy's Foreign Policy," in *John F. Kennedy: The Promise Revisited*, ed. Paul Harper and Joann P. Krieg (New York: Greenwood Press, 1988), pp. 148–49.

16. Press Panel oral history transcrpt, p. 66.

17. Charles Bartlett column, clipping from *Chicago Sun Times*, 28 Feb. 1963, Charles Bartlett folder, POF, JFK Papers.

18. *New York Times*, 4 Dec. 1972, 1, 34; Report of Findings, Determination and Recommendation of the Hearing Panel of the Committee on Professional Conduct of the [New York] State Board for Medicine, Exhibit "Calendar No. 1,000," in the custody of the State Education Department of New York; telephone interview, Dr. Thomas Jacobson, 23 Oct. 1990. See also Mr. Cleveland to L. H. Martin, 18 Aug. 1972, Max Jacobson FBI file 62-84930, FBI headquarters, and C. David Heymann, *A Woman Named Jackie* (New York: Lyle Stuart and Carol Communications, 1989), pp. 296–319.

19. Telephone interview, Charles Spalding, 20 Feb. 1990; telephone interview, Dr. Thomas Jacobson, 5 May 1990; interview, Ruth Jacobson, 12 June 1990; unpublished autobiography of Dr. Max Jacobson, in possession of Ruth Jacobson; *New York Times*, 4 Dec. 1972, 1, 34. The recent opening of the White House Gate Logs discloses that Jacobson visited the White House at least thirty-four times during 1961–1962, Records of the United States Secret Service (Record Group 87), Boxes 2–11, JFKL. Jacobson's name does not appear in the logs during 1963.

20. For the particulars on the revocation of Jacobson's license, see Report of Findings, Determination . . . ; see also Doris Shapiro, *We Danced All Night: My Life behind the Scenes with Alan Jay Lerner* (New York: William Morrow, 1990), pp. 130–31, 238; *New York Times*, 4 Dec. 1972, 1, 34. That unnamed physician was probably Dr. Hans Kraus. When I called Dr. Kraus on 3 Dec. 1989, he admitted

that he was the New York doctor, but after I read him the quote, he claimed that he knew nothing about it.

21. James MacGregor Burns, *Roosevelt: The Lion and the Fox* (New York: Harcourt Brace, 1956), p. ix.

22. Traphes Bryant with Frances Spatz Leighton, *Dog Days at the White House: The Outrageous Memoirs of the Presidential Kennel Keeper* (New York: Macmillan, 1975), pp. 22–24; "Jack Kennedy's Other Women," *Time*, 29 Dec. 1975, pp. 11–12; Herbert S. Parmet, *JFK: The Presidency of John F. Kennedy* (New York: Dial Press, 1983), pp. 111–12, 304–7; Phillip Nobile and Ron Rosenbaum, "The Curious Aftermath of JFK's Best and Brightest Affair," *New Times*, 7 (9 July 1976): 22–33; Hoover's Official and Confidential File on Kennedy provides additional information. Robert Pierpoint confirmed the Fiddle and Faddle association in a telephone interview, 16 Nov. 1989. Sen. George Smathers, Kennedy's long-time friend, revealed much in Kitty Kelley, *Jackie Oh!* (Secaucus, N.J.: Lyle Stuart, 1978), pp. 127–31. For the Monroe relationship, see Anthony Summers, *Goddess: The Secret Lives of Marilyn Monroe* (New York: New American Library, 1986), pp. 239–463. The White House Police Gate Logs confirm Judith Campbell's visits in 1961 and Mary Meyer's frequent evening visits during 1962–1963, Boxes 2–18, Records of the United States Secret Service, JFKL.

23. Several reporters subsequently disclosed in print what they knew. See, for example, Maxine Cheshire, *Maxine Cheshire, Reporter* (Boston: Houghton Mifflin, 1978), pp. 55–60; Nancy Dickerson, *Among Those Present: A Reporter's View of Twenty-five Years in Washington* (New York: Random House, 1976), pp. 63–67; Hugh Sidey, "Upstairs at the White House," *Time*, 18 May 1987, p. 20. Others privately indicated that they were aware of or had heard rumors of Kennedy's dalliances: Benjamin Bradlee, David Brinkley, Robert Donovan, Rowland Evans, Fletcher Knebel, Mary McGrory, Clark Mollenhoff, Chalmers Roberts, and Thomas Wicker to the author, Nov. 1989–Jan. 1991.

24. Parmet, *JFK: Presidency*, pp. 112–14; Anonymous to J. Edgar Hoover, 30 Mar. 1962, JFK FBI file, 94-37374, FBI headquarters; Fletcher Knebel to the author, 26 Jan. 1991.

25. C. A. Evans to Director, 3 July 1963, including enclosures, JFK FBI file, 94-37374; Charles W. Bates to Director, 29 June 1963, JFK FBI file, 94-37374. See also Anthony Summers and Stephen Dorril, *Honeytrap: The Secret Worlds of Stephen Ward* (London: Weidenfeld and Nickolson, 1987), pp. 67–70, 196–204. This contains the most comprehensive account of Kennedy's possible linkage to the Profumo scandal.

26. Robert Baker with Larry King, *Wheeling and Dealing: Confessions of a Capitol Hill Operator* (New York: Norton, 1978), pp. 79–80.

27. Summers, *Goddess*, pp. 432–36, 454–61.

28. Heymann, *Woman Named Jackie*, p. 371.

29. C. D. DeLoach to ? Mohr, 19 Apr. 1960, JFK FBI file 94-37374; Sally Quinn, "Judith Campbell Exner," *Washington Post*, 24 June 1977, B3.

30. Heymann, *Woman Named Jackie*, pp. 366–67. For a contemporary source on the reported use of the Carlyle suite for sexual activities involving Monroe, see

SAC, Los Angeles, to Director, 1 Aug. 1963, Peter Lawford FBI file, 62-100760, FBI headquarters. According to journalist Clark Mollenhoff, Robert Kennedy had remained faithful to his wife until the 1960 campaign. Telephone interview, Clark Mollenhoff, 30 Jan. 1990.

31. For Kennedy and Goldwater, see Larry King with Peter Occhiogrosso, *Tell It to the King* (Thorndike, Maine: Thorndike Press, 1988), pp. 133–35; Quinn, "Judith Campbell Exner," *Washington Post*, B3.

32. Joan Blair and Clay Blair, Jr., *The Search for JFK* (New York: Berkley Medallion Books, 1976), pp. 328–29.

33. The three quotations come from J. B. West with Mary Lynn Katz, *Upstairs at the White House: My Life with the First Ladies* (New York: Coward, McCann and Geoghegan, 1973), p. 268; Heymann, *Woman Named Jackie*, p. 267; Cheshire, *Maxine Cheshire*, p. 44.

34. Harris Wofford, *Of Kennedys and Kings: Making Sense of the Sixties* (New York: Farrar, Straus, Giroux, 1980), p. 128.

35. Bradlee, *Conversations with Kennedy*, p. 87.

36. Peter Collier and David Horowitz, *The Kennedys: An American Drama* (New York: Warner Books, 1984), p. 391.

CHAPTER 11
AFTERMATH AND ASSESSMENT

1. Henry Hurt, *Reasonable Doubt: An Investigation into the Assassination of John F. Kennedy* (New York: Holt, Rinehart and Winston, 1985), p. 254.

2. See, for example, Michael L. Kurtz, *Crime of the Century: The Kennedy Assassination from a Historian's Perspective* (Knoxville: University of Tennessee Press, 1982), pp. 226, 228, 231.

3. The three quotations are found in Harris Wofford, *Of Kennedys and Kings: Making Sense of the Sixties* (New York: Farrar, Straus, Giroux, 1980), p. 418 and Kurtz, *Crime of the Century*, p. 235.

4. Hurt, *Reasonable Doubt*, p. 420.

5. Ibid., pp. 325–27.

6. John H. Davis, *Mafia Kingfish: Carlos Marcello and the Assassination of John F. Kennedy* (New York: McGraw-Hill, 1989), p. 109.

7. Select Committee on Assassinations of the U.S. House of Representatives, *Investigation of the Assassination of President John F. Kennedy: Appendix to Hearings before the Select Committee on Assassinations, and Investigation of the Assassination of President John F. Kennedy*, p. 61.

8. Lance Morrow, "JFK: After Twenty Years, the Question: How Good a President?" *Time*, 14 Nov. 1983, p. 63.

9. Press Panel oral history transcript, p. 57, JFKL.

10. The Byrds' song on Kennedy was entitled, "He Was a Friend of Mine," a 1966 release, Columbia Records, CBS Inc..

11. Daniel Boorstin, "JFK: His Vision Then and Now," *U.S. News and World Report*, 24 Oct. 1988, p. 30.

12. Arthur Schlesinger, Jr., *A Thousand Days: John F. Kennedy in the White House* (Boston: Houghton Mifflin, 1965), p. 1029.

13. Robert K. Murray and Tim H. Blessing, *Greatness in the White House: Rating the Presidents, Washington through Carter* (University Park: Pennsylvania State University Press, 1988), p. 16.

BIBLIOGRAPHICAL ESSAY

Serious scholars of the Kennedy presidency must sooner or later make the trek to the John F. Kennedy Library, a modern building of white concrete and black glass overlooking Dorchester Bay on Columbia Point just south of downtown Boston. It is here that material on Kennedy and other related source materials are located, including papers of associates close to the president and his brothers. The library holdings of manuscripts, oral histories, audiovisuals, and printed material are compiled in the *Historical Materials in the John F. Kennedy Library* (Columbia Point, Boston, Mass.: John F. Kennedy Library, 1990). The documentary evidence at the library is voluminous, but 30 to 40 percent of the crucial manuscript material remains closed because of security classification, insufficient staffing, or deed-of-gift considerations.

The security restrictions have tightened since the Reagan era, as few State, NSC, CIA, or other government documents on the Kennedy presidency have been declassified during the 1980s. Other collections such as the White House social files are also still unavailable because an overloaded staff cannot devote sufficient time to process them. Even more disconcerting are the deed-of-gift restrictions imposed by the Kennedy family and other donors that prevent researchers from seeing the most pertinent material. The Kennedys have excluded all items related to the personal, family, and business affairs of John Kennedy and his relations. This means that scholars will learn little about the president's medical history or personal affairs from researching at the library. The Kennedy Papers contain virtually no personal presidential correspondence, raising a suspicion that that material remains in the custody of the family. Kennedy donors have also specified that sources that might "injure, embarrass, or harass" any person be restricted. The term "embarrass" is particularly unfortunate because it permits a cautious archivist to deny documents to researchers for the flimsiest of reasons.

Furthermore, the Kennedys have used their donor policies to provide privileged access to scholars such as Arthur Schlesinger, Jr., who has been the only researcher given access to Robert Kennedy's personal papers for the attorney general years, and Doris Kearns Goodwin, who alone has been permitted to use the Kennedy family papers for her book on the Kennedys and the Fitzgeralds. Others have also had privileged entry into supposedly closed materials.

Aside from personal and public papers, the Kennedy Library also houses more than eleven hundred oral histories of individuals who were involved with the Kennedys. This is an invaluable collection of primary material that supplements the manuscript collections. Yet even here some serious limitations exist. For example, many oral histories were conducted shortly after John Kennedy's assassination, which made the interviewer reluctant to raise tough-minded questions. Some of the early oral histories are so laudatory and amateurishly done that they are useless to researchers. It is not too late for the library to redo those early interviews, as many former participants are still alive.

Some of the transcribed oral histories have been partly restricted because of "embarrassing" material. Too, about three hundred interviews are unavailable to scholars as a consequence of deed-of-gift stipulations or because of the failure of the interviewee to complete the paper work following the interview. The currently unavailable oral histories include those of Jacqueline Kennedy Onassis, McGeorge Bundy (except to Arthur Schlesinger, Jr.), Robert McNamara, Kenneth O'Donnell, Eunice Kennedy Shriver, and Barry Goldwater. Only recently has the library consented to releasing a list of unprocessed oral histories, enabling scholars to contact the interviewee directly.

Primary materials on Jack Kennedy also exist in published form. Indispensable are the *Public Papers of the Presidents of the United States, John F. Kennedy, Containing the Public Messages, Speeches, and Statements of the President, 1961–1963*, 3 vols. (Washington, D.C.: Government Printing Office, 1962–1964); *John Fitzgerald Kennedy: A Compilation of Statements and Speeches Made during His Service in the United States Senate and House of Representatives* (Washington, D.C.: Government Printing Office, 1964); and *Freedom of Communications, Part I: The Speeches, Remarks, Press Conferences, and Statements of Senator John F. Kennedy, August 1 through November 7, 1960* (Washington, D.C.: Government Printing Office, 1961). Kennedy's publications include *Why England Slept* (New York: Wilfred Funk, 1940); *As We Remember Joe* (privately printed, 1945); *Profiles in Courage* (New York: Harper and Row, 1956); and *A Nation of Immigrants* (New York: Harper and Row, 1964).

There are several useful books on John Kennedy's parents and ancestors, including Richard J. Whalen, *The Founding Father: The Story of Joseph P. Kennedy* (New York: New American Library, 1964); David S. Koskoff, *Joseph P. Kennedy: A Life and Times* (Englewood Cliffs, N.J.: Prentice Hall, 1974); and Doris Kearns Goodwin's superior *The Fitzgeralds and the Kennedys* (New York: Simon and Schuster, 1987). See also Gail Cameron, *Rose: A Biography of Rose Fitzgerald Kennedy* (New York: Putnam, 1971) and Rose Kennedy, *Times to Remember* (Garden City, N.Y.: Doubleday, 1974). For other immediate family members, see Hank Searls, *The Lost Prince: Young Joe, the Forgotten Kennedy* (New York: World Publishing, 1969); Lynne McTaggart, *Kathleen Kennedy: Her Life and Times* (New York: Holt, Rinehart and Winston, 1983); James MacGregor Burns, *Edward Kennedy and the Kennedy Legacy* (New York: W. W. Norton, 1976); Arthur Schlesinger, Jr., *Robert Kennedy and His Times* (Boston: Houghton Mifflin, 1978); Edwin O. Guthman and Jeffrey Shulman, eds., *Robert Kennedy: In His Own Words, the Unpublished Recollections of the Kennedy Years* (New York: Bantam Books, 1988), a study based on Robert Kennedy's revealing reminiscences shortly after his brother's death; and Jean Stein and George Plimpton, eds., *American Journey: The Times of Robert Kennedy* (New York: Harcourt Brace Jovanovich, 1970), which contains invaluable recollections of contemporaries who had contacts with Robert during the Kennedy presidency. Beginning in the 1970s, revisionist works on the Kennedys have also emerged. These include Nancy Gager Clinch, *The Kennedy Neurosis* (New York: Grossett and Dunlap, 1973), an often criticized family psychobiography; John H. Davis, *The Kennedys: Dynasty and Disaster, 1848–1984* (New York: McGraw-Hill, 1984), an insightfully critical account by Jacqueline Kennedy Onassis's cousin; and Peter Collier and David Horowitz, *The Kennedys: An American Drama* (New York: Warner Books, 1984).

By far the best biography on John Kennedy is the balanced two-volume work by Herbert S. Parmet, *Jack: The Struggles of John F. Kennedy* (New York: Dial Press, 1980) and *JFK: The Presidency of John F. Kennedy* (New York: Dial Press, 1983). For Kennedy's early life, see Joan Blair and Clay Blair, Jr., *The Search for JFK* (New York: Berkley Medallion Books, 1976). The Blairs were relentless in tracking down information on Kennedy prior to 1950; much of what we know of Kennedy's medical history and early personal life came from their efforts. For a model campaign biography, based on Kennedy's papers, see James MacGregor Burns, *John Kennedy: A Political Profile* (New York: Harcourt Brace Jovanovich, 1960). David Burner's *John F. Kennedy and a New Generation* (Glenview, Ill.: Scott Foresman, 1988) is a useful brief biography. Also useful are Laura Bergquist and Stanley Tretick, *A Very Special President* (New York: McGraw Hill, 1965) and William E. Leuchtenburg's perceptive biographical essay in his *In the Shadow of FDR: From Harry Truman to Ronald Reagan* (Ithaca, N.Y.: Cornell University Press, 1983). Much less satisfactory is Victor Lasky's *JFK, the Man and the Myth: A Critical Portrait* (New York: Macmillan, 1963), a cutting, right-wing account. For a popular biography based on extensive interviews, see Ralph G. Martin, *A Hero for Our Times: An Intimate Story of the Kennedy Years* (New York: Macmillan, 1983). For an excellent historiographical essay, see Thomas Brown, *JFK: History of an Image* (Bloomington: Indiana University Press, 1988). See also Thomas C. Reeves, *A Question of Character: A Life of John F. Kennedy* (New York: Macmillan, 1991), for a recent critical assessment.

Several books on Jacqueline Kennedy also exist, including Mary Barelli Gallagher, *My Life with Jacqueline Kennedy* (New York: David McKay, 1969); Kitty Kelley, *Jackie Oh!* (Secaucus, N.J.: Lyle Stuart, 1978); and C. David Heymann, *A Woman Named Jackie* (New York: Lyle Stuart and Carol Communications, 1989). The Heymann book, which contains extensive personal information on the president, must be used carefully because of its occasional unreliability.

Any assessment of the Kennedy presidency must begin with Arthur

Schlesinger, Jr.'s, impressive *A Thousand Days: John F. Kennedy in the White House* (Boston: Houghton Mifflin, 1965) and Theodore C. Sorensen's gracefully written *Kennedy* (New York: Harper and Row, 1965). Both books, written by Kennedy associates, superbly placed the president in a favorable light and thus furthered the Kennedy adulation immediately following his assassination. Other early laudatory books written by Kennedy staffers include Pierre Salinger, *With Kennedy* (Garden City, N.Y.: Doubleday, 1966); Kenneth P. O'Donnell and David F. Powers with Joe McCarthy, *"Johnny, We Hardly Knew Ye": Memories of John Fitzgerald Kennedy* (Boston: Little, Brown, 1970); Evelyn Lincoln, *My Twelve Years with John F. Kennedy* (David McKay, 1965); and Lawrence F. O'Brien, *No Final Victories: A Life in Politics—from John F. Kennedy to Watergate* (Garden City, N.Y.: Doubleday, 1974). Former speech writer Richard Goodwin later perpetuated the same tradition in *Remembering America: A Voice from the Sixties* (Boston: Little, Brown, 1988). Less favorable than these is Benjamin C. Bradlee's *Conversations with Kennedy* (New York: W. W. Norton, 1975), written by another Kennedy intimate.

The 1970s ushered in a number of critical revisionist studies, which continued into the next decade. Among them are Henry Fairlie, *The Kennedy Promise: The Politics of Expectation* (Garden City, N.Y.: Doubleday, 1973); Bruce Miroff, *Pragmatic Illusions: The Presidential Politics of John F. Kennedy* (New York: McKay, 1976); Louis J. Paper, *The Promise and the Performance: The Leadership of John F. Kennedy* (New York: Crown, 1975); Richard J. Walton, *Cold War and Counterrevolution: The Foreign Policy of John F. Kennedy* (Baltimore: Penguin Books, 1972); and Garry Wills, *The Kennedy Imprisonment: A Meditation on Power* (Boston: Little, Brown, 1982).

For additional favorable assessments, see Irving Bernstein, *Promises Kept: John F. Kennedy's New Frontier* (New York: Oxford University Press, 1991); James David Barber, *The Presidential Character: Predicting Performance in the White House* (Englewood Cliffs, N.J.: Prentice-Hall, 1972); and Kenneth W. Thompson, ed., *The Kennedy Presidency: Seventeen Intimate Perspectives of John F. Kennedy*, vol. 4, *Portraits of American Presidents*, 4 vols. (Lanham, Md.: University Press of America, 1985). For provocative overviews of liberalism during the Kennedy period, see Allen J. Matusow, *The Unraveling of America: A History of Liberalism in the 1960s* (New York: Harper and Row, 1984), and Harris Wofford, *Of Kennedys and Kings: Making Sense of the Sixties* (New York: Farrar, Straus, Giroux, 1980).

Specialized works on the administrative operation of the Kennedy White House are few. Especially pertinent are Patrick Anderson, *The Presidents' Men: White House Assistants of Franklin D. Roosevelt, Harry S. Truman, Dwight D. Eisenhower, John F. Kennedy, and Lyndon B. Johnson* (Garden City, N.Y.: Doubleday, 1968); Margaret Ellen Flannelly, "An Analysis of the Role of the White House Staff in the Administrations of President Dwight D. Eisenhower and President John F. Kennedy" (Ph.D. diss., University of Notre Dame, 1969); Phillip G. Henderson, *Managing the Presidency: The Eisenhower Legacy from Kennedy to Reagan* (Boulder, Colo.: Westview, 1988); Richard T. Johnson, *Managing the White House: An Intimate Study of Three Presidents* (New York: Harper and Row, 1974).

Books on and by other Kennedy administration officials include George Ball, *The Past Has Another Pattern: Memoirs* (New York: W. W. Norton, 1982); Charles E. Bohlen, *Witness to History, 1929–1969* (New York: W. W. Norton, 1973); Chester Bowles, *Promises to Keep: My Years in Public Life, 1941–1969* (New York: Harper and Row, 1971); McGeorge Bundy, *Danger and Survival: Choices about the Bomb in the First Fifty Years* (New York: Random House, 1988); Harlan Cleveland, *The Obligations of Power: American Diplomacy in the Search for Peace* (New York: Harper and Row, 1966); Edward Day, *My Appointed Round: 929 Days as Postmaster General* (New York: Holt, Rinehart and Winston, 1965); Paul B. Fay, Jr., *The Pleasure of His Company* (New York: Harper and Row, 1966); John Kenneth Galbraith, *Ambassador's Journal: A Personal Account of the Kennedy Years* (Boston: Houghton Mifflin, 1969); John Kenneth Galbraith, *A Life in Our Times; Memoirs* (Boston: Houghton Mifflin, 1981); Dorothy Goldberg, *A Private View of a Public Life* (New York: Charterhouse, 1975); Thomas Powers, *The Man Who Kept the Secrets: Richard Helms and the CIA* (New York: Alfred A. Knopf, 1979); Roger Hilsman, *To Move a Nation: The Politics of Foreign Policy in the Administration of John F. Kennedy* (Garden City, N.Y.: Doubleday, 1967); Doris Kearns, *Lyndon Baines Johnson and the American Dream* (New York: Harper and Row, 1976); George Kennan, *Memoirs, 1950–1963* (Boston: Little, Brown, 1972); David Meyers, *George Kennan and the Dilemmas of U.S. Foreign Policy* (New York: Oxford University Press, 1978); Henry Cabot Lodge, *The Storm Has Many Eyes: A Personal Narrative* (New York: W. W. Norton, 1973); Robert S. McNamara, *The Essence of Security: Reflections in Office* (New York: Harper and Row, 1968); Henry Trewhitt, *McNamara: His Ordeal at the Pentagon* (New York: Harper and Row, 1971); Paul Nitze with Steven L. Rearden, *From Hiroshima to Glasnost: At the Center of Decision* (New York: Weidenfeld and Nicolson, 1989); David Callahan, *Dangerous Capabilities: Paul Nitze and the Cold War* (New York: Harper Collins, 1990); James Reston, Jr., *The Lone Star: The Life of John Connally* (New York: Harper and Row, 1989); Walt W. Rostow, *The Diffusion of Power: An Essay in Recent History* (New York: Macmillan, 1972); Dean Rusk, *As I Saw It* (New York: W. W. Norton, 1990); Warren I. Cohen, *Dean Rusk* (Totowa, N.J.: Cooper Square, 1980); Thomas J. Schoenbaum, *Waging Peace and War: Dean Rusk in the Truman, Kennedy, and Johnson Years* (New York: Simon and Schuster, 1988); Tazewell Shepard, Jr., *John F. Kennedy: Man of the Sea* (New York: Morrow, 1965); John Bartlow Martin, *Adlai Stevenson and the World: The Life of Adlai E. Stevenson* (Garden City, N. Y.: Doubleday, 1977); Maxwell Taylor, *Swords and Plowshares* (New York: W. W. Norton, 1972); John M. Taylor, *General Maxwell Taylor* (Garden City, N.Y.: Doubleday, 1989); Janet Travell, *Office Hours: Day and Night, the Autobiography of Janet Travell* (New York: World Publishers, 1968). Still lacking are biographies of such prominent people as McGeorge Bundy, Douglas Dillon, Arthur Goldberg, and Theodore Sorensen.

Among the books on and by members of Congress for the Kennedy period are Richard Bolling, *Power in the House: A History of the Leadership of the House of Representatives* (New York: E. P. Dutton, 1968); Edward L. Schapsmeier and Frederick H. Schapsmeier, *Dirksen of Illinois: Senatorial Statesman* (Urbana: University of Illinois Press, 1985); Paul H. Douglas, *In the Fullness of Time: The Memoirs of Paul H. Douglas* (New York: Harcourt Brace Jovanovich, 1971); William C. Berman, *William Fulbright and the Vietnam War: The Dissent of a Political Realist* (Kent, Ohio: Kent State University Press, 1988); Henry Z. Scheele, *Charlie Halleck: A Political Biography* (New York: Exposition Press, 1966); Vance Hartke and John M. Redding, *Inside the New Frontier* (New York: McFadden-Bartell, 1962); Hubert H. Humphrey, *The Education of a Public Man: My Life in Politics* (Garden City, N.Y.: Doubleday, 1976); Carl Solberg, *Hubert Humphrey: A Biography* (New York: W. W. Norton, 1984); Charles L. Fontenay, *Estes Kefauver: A Biography* (Knoxville: University of Tennessee Press, 1980); Anne Hodges Morgan, *Robert S. Kerr: The Senate Years* (Norman: University of Oklahoma Press, 1977); Joseph W. Martin, Jr., *My First Fifty Years in Politics* (New York: McGraw Hill, 1960); Thomas P. O'Neill with William Novak, *Man of the House: The Life and Political Memoirs of Speaker Tip O'Neill* (New York: Random House, 1987); D. B. Hardeman and Donald C. Bacon, *Rayburn: A Biography* (Austin, Tex.: Monthly Press, 1987); Bruce J. Dierenfield, *Keeper of the Rules: Congressman Howard W. Smith of Virginia* (Charlottesville: University of Virginia Press, 1987).

Kennedy and Congress are also covered in Tom Wicker, *JFK and LBJ: The Influence of Personality upon Politics* (Baltimore: Penguin Books, 1970); Alan Shank, *Presidential Policy Leadership: Kennedy and Social Welfare* (Lanham, Md.: University Press of America, 1980); Abraham Holtzman, *Legislative Liaison: Executive Leadership in Congress* (Chicago: Rand McNally, 1970); Kenneth Dameron, Jr., "President Kennedy and Congress: Process and Politics" (Ph.D. diss., Harvard University, 1975); and Robert Baker with Larry King, *Wheeling and Dealing: Confessions of a Capitol Hill Operator* (New York: W. W. Norton, 1978).

Economic matters for the period are amply covered. Among the most pertinent works are Walter W. Heller, *New Dimensions of Political Economy* (Cambridge, Mass.: Harvard University Press, 1966); Seymour Harris, *Economics of the Kennedy Years and a Look Ahead* (New York: Harper and Row, 1964); Edward S. Flash, Jr., *Economic Advice and Presidential Leadership* (New York: Columbia University Press, 1965); Herbert Rowen, *The Free Enterprisers: Kennedy, Johnson, and the Business Establishment* (New York: Putnam, 1964); Jim Heath, *John F. Kennedy and the Business Community* (Chicago: University of Chicago Press, 1969); Kim McQuaid, *Big Business and Presidential Power: From FDR to Reagan* (New York: William Morrow, 1982); Amy Elisabeth Davis, "Politics of Prosperity: The Kennedy Presidency and Economic Policy" (Ph.D. diss., Columbia University, 1988); and the relevant essays in Paul Harper and Joann P. Krieg, eds., *John F. Kennedy: The Promise Revisited* (New York: Greenwood Press, 1988), and Earl Latham, ed., *J. F. Kennedy and Presidential Power* (Lexington, Mass.: D. C. Heath, 1972). See also Lee Loevinger, "Antitrust in 1961 and 1962," *The Antitrust Bulletin* 8 (May–June 1963): 349–379.

Of the domestic issues facing the president and Congress, none has received more scholarly attention than civil rights. Works on this subject include the comprehensive and favorable Carl M. Brauer, *John F. Kennedy and the Second Reconstruction* (New York: Columbia University Press, 1977). For a contrasting critical view, see the relevant chapters in Victor S. Navasky, *Kennedy Justice* (New York: Atheneum, 1971), and Howard Sitkoff, *Struggle for Black Equality, 1954–1980* (New York: Hill and Wang, 1981). Much less satisfactory are Harry Golden, *Mr. Kennedy and the Negroes* (Cleveland and New York: World Publishing, 1964), and James C. Harvey, *Civil Rights during the Kennedy Administration* (Hattiesburg: University and College Press of Mississippi, 1971). For more specialized studies, see Michael R. Belknap, *Federal Law and Southern Order: Racial Violence and Constitutional Conflict in the Post-Brown South* (Athens: University of Georgia Press, 1987); Hugh Davis Graham, *The Civil Rights Era: Race, Gender, and National Policy, 1960–1972* (New York: Oxford University Press, 1990); Clayborne Carson, *In Struggle: SNCC and the Black Awakening of the 1960s* (Cambridge, Mass.: Harvard University Press, 1981); James Peck, *Freedom Ride* (New York: Simon and Schuster, 1962); Walter Lord, *The Past That Would Not Die* (New York: Harper and Row, 1965); Kenneth O'Reilly, *"Racial Matters": The FBI's Secret File on Black America, 1960–1972* (New York: Free Press, 1989); and Roy Wilkins with Tom Mathews, *Standing Fast: The Autobiography of Roy Wilkins* (New York: Viking Press, 1982). For Kennedy and Martin Luther King, Jr., see David J. Garrow, *Bearing the Cross: Martin Luther King, Jr., and the Southern Christian Leadership Conference* (New York: William Morrow, 1986); David Garrow, *The FBI and Martin Luther King: From "Solo" to Memphis* (New York: W. W. Norton, 1981); Stephen Oates, *Let the Trumpet Sound: The Life of Martin Luther King, Jr.* (New York: Harper and Row, 1982); and Taylor Branch, *Parting the Waters: America in the King Years, 1954–1963* (New York: Simon and Schuster, 1988).

Works on other domestic matters deserving attention include Cynthia Harrison, *On Account of Sex: The Politics of Women's Issues, 1945–1968* (Berkeley: University of California Press, 1988); Patricia G. Zelman, *Women, Work, and National Policy: The Kennedy-Johnson Years* (Ann Arbor, Mich.: UMI Research Press, 1982); Don F. Hadwiger and Ross B. Talbot, *Pressures and Protests: The Kennedy Farm Program and the Wheat Referendum of 1963* (San Francisco: Chandler Publishing, 1965); Peter A. Toma, *The Politics of Food for Peace: Executive-Legislative Interaction* (Tucson: University of Arizona Press, 1967); Hugh Davis Graham, *The Uncertain Triumph: Federal Education Policy in the Kennedy and Johnson Years* (Chapel Hill: University of North Carolina Press, 1984); Carl M. Brauer, "Kennedy, Johnson, and the War on Poverty," *Journal of American History* 69 (June 1982): 98–119; John M. Logsdon, *The Decision to Go to the Moon: Project Apollo and the National Interest* (Cambridge, Mass.: MIT Press, 1970); Walter A. McDougall, *The Heavens and the Earth: A Political History of the Space Age* (New York: Basic Books, 1985); Athan G. Theoharis and John Stuart Cox, *The Boss: J. Edgar Hoover and the Great American Inquisition* (Philadelphia: Temple University Press, 1988); Howard Chase, *Federal Judges: The Appointing Process* (Minneapolis: University of Minnesota Press, 1972); Leon Friedman, comp., *Justices of the United States Supreme Court, 1789–1969* (New York: Chelsea House, 1969).

The most useful works on the media are Joseph P. Berry, Jr., *John F. Kennedy and the Media: The First Television President* (Lanham, Md.: University Press of America, 1987); Montague Kern, Patricia W. Levering, and Ralph B. Levering, *The*

Kennedy Crises: The Press, the Presidency, and Foreign Policy (Chapel Hill: University of North Carolina Press, 1983); Kenneth W. Thompson, ed., *Ten Presidents and the Press* (Lanham, Md.: University Press of America, 1983); Elizabeth Anne Keyes, "President Kennedy's Press Conferences as 'Shapers of the News' " (Ph.D diss., University of Iowa, 1968); Paul R. Henggeler, "Kennedy and the News Media: The Development of President John F. Kennedy's Media Strategy Based on *Time, Newsweek,* and Television" (Master's thesis, Bowling Green University, 1985); David Halberstam, *The Powers That Be* (New York: Alfred A. Knopf, 1979); Hugh Sidey, *John F. Kennedy, President* (New York: Atheneum, 1963); Marquis Childs, *Witness to Power* (New York: McGraw-Hill, 1975); Helen Thomas, *Dateline: White House* (New York: Macmillan, 1975); Chalmers M. Roberts, *First Rough Draft: A Journalist's Journal of Our Times* (New York: Praeger, 1973); and Arthur Krock, *Memoirs: Sixty Years on the Firing Line* (New York: Funk and Wagnalls, 1968).

The personal side of the Kennedy presidency is covered in several of the aforementioned books. See also William Manchester, *Portrait of a President: John F. Kennedy in Profile* (Boston: Little, Brown, 1962); Jim Bishop, *A Day in the Life of President Kennedy* (New York: Random House, 1964); Rita Dallas and Jeanira Ratcliff, *The Kennedy Case* (New York: G. P. Putnam's Sons, 1973); and Letitia Baldrige, *Of Diamonds and Diplomats* (Boston: Houghton Mifflin, 1968). Information on Kennedy's other women is found in Judith (Campbell) Exner, as told to Ovid Demaris, *My Story* (New York: Grove Press, 1977); Anthony Summers, *Goddess: The Secret Lives of Marilyn Monroe* (New York: New American Library, 1986); Anthony Summers and Stephen Dorril, *Honeytrap: The Secret Worlds of Stephen Ward* (London: Weidenfeld and Nickolson, 1987); Traphes Bryant with Frances Spatz Leighton, *Dog Days at the White House: The Outrageous Memoirs of the Presidential Kennel Keeper* (New York: Macmillan, 1975); Igor Cassini with Jeanne Molli, *I'd Do It All Over Again* (New York: G. P. Putnam's Sons, 1977); Maxine Cheshire, *Maxine Cheshire, Reporter* (Boston: Houghton Mifflin, 1978); Nancy Dickerson, *Among Those Present: A Reporter's View of Twenty-five Years in Washington* (New York: Random House, 1976). Kennedy's dalliances are also documented in his FBI file, which is available in the Federal Bureau of Investigation reading room, Washington, D.C.

No area of policy received Kennedy's attention more than foreign relations. An excellent comprehensive introduction is Thomas G. Paterson, ed., *Kennedy's Quest for Victory: American Foreign Policy, 1961–1963* (New York: Oxford University Press, 1989). Still very useful is David Halberstam, *The Best and the Brightest* (New York: Random House, 1969). For broader perspectives, see John Spanier, *American Foreign Policy since World War II* (New York: Praeger, 1973); Walter LaFeber, *America, Russia, and the Cold War, 1945–1984* (New York: John Wiley and Sons, 1985); and Walter Isaacson and Evan Thomas, *The Wise Men: Six Friends and the World They Made* (New York: Simon and Schuster, 1986).

For the economic dimension, see John W. Evans, *The Kennedy Round in American Trade Policy: The Twilight of the GATT?* (Cambridge, Mass.: Harvard University Press, 1971), and Allen J. Matusow, "Kennedy, the World Economy, and the Decline of America," in *John F. Kennedy: Person, Policy, Presidency,* edited by J. Richard Snyder (Wilmington, Del.: Scholarly Resources, 1988). For provocative insights, see Irving L. Janis, *Victims of Groupthink: A Psychological Study of Foreign-policy Decisions and Fiascoes* (Boston: Houghton Mifflin, 1972). Covert operations are well treated in Warren Hincle and William W. Turner, *The Fish Is Red: The Story of the Secret War against Castro* (New York: Harper and Row, 1981), and Lyman B. Kirkpatrick, Jr., *The Real CIA* (New York: Macmillan, 1968).

Military, nuclear, and defense considerations are dealt with in Robert J. Art, *The TFX Decision: McNamara and the Military* (Boston: Little, Brown, 1968); Bernard J. Firestone, *The Quest for Nuclear Stability: John F. Kennedy and the Soviet Union* (Westport, Conn.: Greenwood Press, 1982); Glenn T. Seaborg and Benjamin S. Loeb, *Kennedy, Khrushchev, and the Test Ban* (Berkeley: University of California Press, 1981); and Jeffrey Graham Barlow, "President John F. Kennedy and His Joint Chiefs of Staff" (Ph.D. diss., University of South Carolina, 1981).

Focusing on the Berlin crisis are Honoré M. Catudal, *Kennedy and the Berlin Wall Crisis: A Case Study in U.S. Decision Making* (Berlin: Berlin-Verlag, 1980); Jack M. Schick, *The Berlin Crisis, 1958–1962* (Philadelphia: University of Pennsylvania Press, 1971); Robert M. Slusser, *The Berlin Crisis of 1961: Soviet-American Relations and the Struggle in the Kremlin, June–November 1961* (Baltimore: Johns Hopkins University Press, 1973); Curtis Cate, *The Ides of August: The Berlin Crisis, 1961* (New York: M. Evans, 1978); and Peter Wyden, *Wall: The Inside Story of Divided Berlin* (New York: Simon and Schuster, 1989). See also Frank Costigliola, "The Failed Design: Kennedy, de Gaulle, and the Struggle for Europe," *Diplomatic History* 8 (Summer 1984): 227–51.

The published material on Cuba is voluminous. For the Bay of Pigs, examine Trumbull Higgins, *The Perfect Failure: Kennedy, Eisenhower, and the CIA at the Bay of Pigs* (New York: W. W. Norton, 1987); Peter Wyden, *Bay of Pigs: The Untold Story* (New York: Simon and Schuster, 1979); and *Operation Zapata: The "Ultrasensitive" Report and Testimony of the Board of Inquiry on the Bay of Pigs* (Frederick, Md.: University Publications of America, 1981). The best books on the Cuban missile crisis are Elie Abel, *The Missile Crisis* (Philadelphia: J. B. Lippincott, 1966); Robert Kennedy, *Thirteen Days: A Memoir of the Cuban Missile Crisis* (New York: W. W. Norton, 1969); Graham T. Allison, *Essence of Decision: Explaining the Cuban Missile Crisis* (Boston: Little, Brown, 1971); Abram Chayes, *The Cuban Missile Crisis: International Crises and the Role of Law* (New York: Oxford University Press, 1974); Herbert S. Dinnerstein, *The Making of a Missile Crisis: October 1962* (Baltimore: Johns Hopkins University Press, 1976); David Detzer, *The Brink: Cuban Missile Crisis* (New York: Thomas Y. Crowell, 1979); Raymond L. Garthoff, *Reflections on the Cuban Missile Crisis* (Washington, D.C.: Brookings Institution, 1987); and James G. Blight and David A. Welch, *On the Brink: Americans and Soviets Reexamine the Cuban Missile Crisis* (New York: Hill and Wang, 1989). See also Richard Ned Lebow, "The Cuban Missile Crisis: Reading the Lessons Correctly," *Political Science Quarterly* 98 (Fall 1983): 431–58, and Philip Brenner, "Cuba and the Missile Crisis," *Journal of Latin American Studies* 22 (Feb. 1990): 115–42. Several excellent articles on the missile crisis have also been published since 1987 in the journals *International Security* and *Diplomatic History*.

A number of pertinent publications exist on Latin American policy and the

Alliance for Progress, including Jerome Levinson and Juan de Onis, *The Alliance That Lost the Way* (Chicago: Quandrangle, 1970); Cole Blazier, *The Hovering Giant: U.S. Responses to Revolutionary Changes in Latin America* (Pittsburgh: University of Pittsburgh Press, 1976); Arthur Schlesinger, Jr., "The Alliance for Progress: A Retrospective," in *Latin America: The Search for a New International Role*, edited by Ronald G. Hellman and H. Jan Rosenbaum (New York: John Wiley, 1975); and Ruth Leacock, "JFK, Business and Brazil," *Hispanic American Historical Review* 59, no. 4 (1979): 636–73.

For the Kennedy policy toward Africa, Asia, and the Middle East, see Richard D. Mahoney, *JFK: Ordeal in Africa* (New York: Oxford University Press, 1983); G. Mennen Williams, *Africa for the Africans* (Grand Rapids, Mich.: Eerdmans, 1969); Madeline G. Kalb, *The Congo Cables: The Cold War in Africa—From Eisenhower to Kennedy* (New York: Macmillan, 1982); Charles A. Stevenson, *The End of Nowhere: American Policy toward Laos since 1954* (Boston: Beacon Press, 1972); Timothy P. Maga, *John F. Kennedy and the New Pacific Community, 1961–63* (New York: St. Martin's, 1990); Gordon H. Chang, "JFK, China, and the Bomb," *Journal of American History* 74 (March 1988): 1287–1310; and David Little, "The New Frontier on the Nile: JFK, Nasser, and Arab Nationalism," *Journal of American History* 75 (Sept. 1988): 501–27.

There are a growing number of studies on the Peace Corps, including Gerald T. Rice, *The Bold Experiment: JFK's Peace Corps* (Notre Dame, Ind.: University of Notre Dame Press, 1985); Brent Ashabranner, *A Moment in History: The First Ten Years of the Peace Corps* (New York: Doubleday, 1974); Kevin Lowther and C. Payne Lucas, *Keeping Kennedy's Promise: The Peace Corps, Unmet Hope of the New Frontier* (Boulder, Colo.: Westview, 1978); Coates Redmon, *Come As You Are: The Peace Corps Story* (San Diego, Calif.: Harcourt Brace Jovanovich, 1986).

Of all the topics related to the Third World, none is more significant than Vietnam. The most insightful studies on that conflict are William J. Rust, *Kennedy in Vietnam* (New York: Charles Scribner's Sons, 1985); George McT. Kahin, *Intervention: How America Became Involved in Vietnam* (New York: Alfred A. Knopf, 1986); Ellen J. Hammer, *A Death in November: America in Vietnam, 1963* (New York: E. P. Dutton, 1987); Leslie H. Gelb with Richard K. Betts, *The Irony of Vietnam: The System Worked* (Washington, D.C.: The Brookings Institution, 1979); George C. Herring, *America's Longest War: The United States and Vietnam, 1950–1975* (New York: John Wiley, 1979); David Halberstam, *The Making of a Quagmire: America and Vietnam during the Kennedy Era*, rev. ed. (New York: Alfred A. Knopf, 1984); and Neil Sheehan, *A Bright Shining Lie: John Paul Vann and America in Vietnam* (New York: Random House, 1988). For two indispensable primary sources, see *The Pentagon Papers: The Defense Department History of United States Decisionmaking on Vietnam*, Senator Gravel edition, vol. 2 (Boston: Beacon Press, 1971) 5 vols., and *Foreign Relations of the United States, 1961–1963*, vol. 1, *Vietnam 1961* (Washington, D.C.: Government Printing Office, 1988). See also Stephen Pelz, "John F. Kennedy's 1961 War Decisions," *Journal of Strategic Studies* 4 (Dec. 1981): 356–85; King C. Chen, "Hanoi's Three Decisions and the Escalation of the Vietnam War," *Political Science Quarterly* 90 (Summer 1975): 243–59; and George Herring, "The

War in Vietnam," in the *Johnson Years*, vol. 1, *Foreign Policy, the Great Society, and the White House*, edited by Robert A. Divine (Lawrence: University Press of Kansas, 1987).

Works by foreign statesmen of the time include Willy Brandt, *Willy Brandt: People and Politics, The Years 1960–1975* (Boston: Little, Brown, 1976); Charles de Gaulle, *Memoirs of Hope: Renewal and Endeavor* (New York: Simon and Schuster, 1971); Andrei Gromyko, *Through Russian Eyes: President Kennedy's 1036 Days* (Washington, D.C.: International Library, 1973); Harold Macmillan, *At the End of the Day, 1961–1963* (New York: Harper and Row, 1973); Strobe Talbott, ed., *Khrushchev Remembers: The Last Testament* (Boston: Little, Brown, 1974); and Sergei Khrushchev, *Khrushchev on Khrushchev: An Inside Account of the Man and His Era* (Boston: Little, Brown, 1990).

More books have been published on Kennedy's assassination than on any other aspect of his presidency. See Michael L. Kurtz, *Crime of the Century: The Kennedy Assassination from a Historian's Perspective* (Knoxville: University of Tennessee Press, 1982); Henry Hurt, *Reasonable Doubt: An Investigation into the Assassination of John F. Kennedy* (New York: Holt, Rinehart and Winston, 1985); Anthony Summers, *Conspiracy* (New York: Paragon House, 1989); David E. Scheim, *Contract on America: The Mafia Murder of President John F. Kennedy* (New York: Shapolsky Publishers, 1988); and John H. Davis, *Mafia Kingfish: Carlos Marcello and the Assassination of John F. Kennedy* (New York: McGraw-Hill, 1989). Examine Jean Davison's, *Oswald's Game* (New York: W. W. Norton, 1983) for a recent anti-conspiracy viewpoint.

Since this book was first printed, the following significant works have appeared: Paul R. Henggeler, *In His Steps: Lyndon Johnson and the Kennedy Mystique* (Chicago: Ivan R. Dee, 1991); Michael Beschloss, *The Crisis Years: Kennedy and Khrushchev, 1960–1963* (New York: Harper and Collins, 1991); and Dino A. Brugioni, *Eyeball to Eyeball: The Inside Story of the Cuban Missile Crisis*, edited by Robert F. McCort (New York: Random House, 1991).

INDEX